D1298109

COMIC-BOOK SUPERSTARS

Edited by
Don and Maggie Thompson

Published by

krause
publications

700 E. State Street • Iola, WI 54990-0001
Telephone: 715/445-2214

Library of Congress Catalog Number: 93-77544
ISBN: 0-87341-256-7
Printed in the United States of America

Acknowledgements

Many, many, many people made this work possible, and we thank them *all*, both those we name and those we don't. Obviously, all the comics creators who took the time to fill out and send in forms and/or illustrations are intrinsic to *Comic-Book Superstars*. We thank them. Some creators requested additional credits on the illustration they provided. Those are as follows: Den Beauvais, © 1993 Photo Features Ltd.; Fred Burke, Illustration © 1993 Mike Dringenberg. Used with permission.; Howard Cruse, © 1989 Tim J. Luddy; Harlan Ellison, Photo: Christer Akerberg/Sweden; Todd Klein, Photo: Ellen Smiga Klein; Barry Kraus, Photo: Phin Dali; Batton Lash, Photo: Jackie Estrada; Jay Lynch, Photo: Steve Shay; Don Martin, © 1993 N. Martin; Roger May, © 1992 Pete Poplaski; Ken Meyer Jr., © 1992 Ken Meyer Jr.; Rick Norwood, Photo and costume: Mary Norwood; Stan Sakai, Photo: Greg Preston; Julius Schwartz, Photo: Beth Gwin; Barbara Slate, Photo: Bert Stern; Bill Spangler, Photo: Steven P. Shumski; Andrew Vachss, Photo © Joyce Ravid; Tom Veitch, Photo: John Ridgway; Len Wein, Photo © M.C. Valada; Al Weisner, Photo: Scott Pitchon; Skip Williamson, Photo: Harriett Hiland; Marv Wolfman, © 1990 M.C. Valada.

Thanks to Eclipse for permission to use images from two of its cards, as requested by the professionals who asked that they be used: Dick Ayers and Don Rosa. © 1992 Eclipse Enterprises, Inc.

Some photos come from the files of *Comics Buyer's Guide*: Larry Mishkar took the pictures of Brian Douglas Ahern, Peter David, and Jim Shooter; Ross Hubbard took the photo of Brandon Peterson; and many pictures were taken by Don or Maggie Thompson. Valerie Thompson photographed Carl Potts.

Special thanks to Frank Miller, for the superstar silhouette seen on the cover and elsewhere in this volume.

Thanks, too, to Allen West (who put everything together into a cover design), to Brent Frankenhoff (who typed until he no longer had fingerprints), and to Judy Floistad (who noticed the little things we'd missed, as she pasted the whole thing into its final form).

We could go on (Greg Loescher, Mary Sieber, Pat Klug) — but it's time to get on to the next project, right?

Don and Maggie Thompson, Iola, Wisconsin, July 6, 1993

Introduction

Those included in this volume are creators (writers, pencillers, inkers, painters, letterers, colorists) who returned our information form and whose work has appeared in what we could determine were comic books which received wide potential distribution throughout the comic book direct market. (The direct market is the network of comics specialty shops which provides circulation to the bulk of comic books published today.)

Not included were many excellent writers whose talents have so far been directed only to writing about comics. And creators whose output — while often vastly entertaining — has thus far been devoted to circulation primarily by mail, comics conventions, and such informal networks as amateur publishing associations.

Not included were gag entries.

Not included were creators who have work under consideration at publishers but who gave no published credits as yet.

Not included either were creators (some stellar) who did not return the forms.

A word about the forms:

Participants were asked to fill in the blanks as follows:

• Name

• Current address, office address, agent's name and address — and which address was preferred [Some elected to be accessible via the Editorial Department of *Comics Buyer's Guide* (which will forward mail to those included — and many others).]

   • Birthdate and birthplace

   • College or other advanced training

   • Comics-related education

   • Biggest creative influences on their work

   • 1993 comics projects on which they are working

   • Past comics titles and related projects on which they have worked

   • Favorite comics on which they don't work

The form ended with the question, "If you could do your dream comic-book project, what would it be?"

We also asked for accompanying photographs we had permission to reproduce in this volume.

One pro remarked, when asked, that he hates filling out forms and doing his income taxes — and, therefore, he had thrown out the form as a matter of routine, when it arrived. (He did provide an entry after wheedling.)

But that's the sort of thing that keeps projects like this one from an instant expansion into total unmanageability. It's also the kind of thing that leaves editors feeling wistful and muttering, "Just wait till the next edition."

We distributed the forms as widely as possible but we are still getting entries as this is being written. We also know there are many who simply never got them.

We managed to expand the illustrations by going through the files of *Comics Buyer's Guide* for photos we have taken — and that provided a combination of elation and frustration. In many cases, we *know* that there are in our offices absolutely wonderful photos of some of those with entries here — but they couldn't be located in the window of opportunity we had available. (There comes a time when the production department says, "We have to have the paste-ups *now*.")

But we are delighted with what we received — and fascinated by the responses. (Some of the dream projects, for example, deserve prompt attention.)

Among the participants is Fred Schwab, a professional who had work in *The Comics Magazine* #1 (dated May 1936, more than two years before the first issue of *Action Comics*) — and who is still working. And there are others whose body of work in the field is so enormous they listed only general categories for their credits.

Rounding out this volume is a birthday guide of comics professionals; it is not limited to the creators listed in this volume — or even to creators, *per se*.

Had we the time, we'd have compiled a couple of lists from what is published here: a list of the most widely cited influences and a list of favorite comics of comics creators. Some rainy weekend . . .

Finally: In circulating this material, we amassed a huge list of addresses for comics professionals — including many who did not return their forms. If you want to contact them, we will do our best to forward letters. Address letters, with correct postage, to the professional c/o *Comics Buyer's Guide* Editorial Department, 700 East State Street, Iola, Wisconsin 54990. If we don't have an address, we'll return the letter to you; if we do have the address, we'll send it on.

Professionals: You needn't wait until the next volume to provide us with the information listed here — in fact, please don't wait. Just send us the information we've outlined here, and we'll enter it preparatory to the next edition.

Don and Maggie Thompson, Iola, Wisconsin, July 6, 1993

✳ **Dan Abnett.** c/o *CBG* Editorial Department, 700 East State Street, Iola, Wisconsin 54990.

Born: October 12, 1965, in Rochester, England.

College or other education: B.A. hons (English language and literature), St. Edmund Hall, Oxford University, England.

Comics-related education: On-staff training editorially at Marvel in London, working up from trainee to editor.

1993 projects as writer: *Death's Head II* ongoing series, *Dark Guard* ongoing series, *Loose Cannons* limited series, *MyS-TECH Wars* limited series (all Marvel UK), *Black Ops* limited series, *Uther Pendragon* graphic novel (Tundra/Atomeka).

1993 projects as co-writer: story arcs for *Punisher* and *Punisher War Zone*, *Scarlet Witch* limited series (Marvel US), *Battletide* (Death's Head vs. Killpower) series, *Gunrunner* limited series, *Technomancer* limited series (Marvel UK), *Pale Horses* limited series, *Lords of Misrule* ongoing series (Tundra/Atomeka).

Past titles: *Death's Head II, Punisher*, etc. *Knights of Pendragon, Mutatis* (Epic), *Doctor Who, G.I. Joe, Dinosaurs — a Celebration* (Epic), *Legends of the Dark Knight* (DC), plus a stack of junior titles like *Ghostbusters, Duckula, Rupert, James Bond Junior, Transformers, Thundercats*, etc., etc.

Influences, fave comics, and dreams: I wouldn't know where to start.

✳ **Jerry Acerno.** c/o *CBG* Editorial Department, 700 East State Street, Iola, Wisconsin 54990.

Born: January 13, 1961, in Corona, Queens, New York.

College or other education: A.A.S. degree in Graphic Arts from New York City Technical College.

Comics-related education: Assistant to Dave Simons, inking backgrounds on the original *Ghost Rider* series. Assisted Andy Mushynsky on *Power Man and Iron Fist*. Also assisted John Romita and Joe Orlando.

Biggest creative influences: Alex Raymond, Lou Fine, Matt Baker, Dick Giordano, Wally

Jerry Acerno

Wood, Joseph Clement Cole, J.C. Leyendecker, Andrew Loomis, and Howard Chandler Christy.

1993 projects: *The Dark*, published by Continüm Comics, mostly inking and some pencilling/inking, too.

Past comics titles and related projects: Inking: *Power Man and Iron Fist* #110-124, *Secret Origins* #9 (Golden Age Flash), #20 (Dr. Midnite), *All Star Squadron* #48 and 54, *Detective Comics* #595 (Batman Bonus Book), Flash Bonus Book. Various special projects for DC including art restoration on *Superman, Batman*, and *All Star Archives*. Inking on covers and interiors of various DC/TSR comics (*Spelljammer, Forgotten Realms*, and *Avatar*). Inking on *The Dark* #3 and 4. Currently working on issue #5, with some pencilling as well. Assisting on storyboards for *The X-Men* cartoon.

Favorite comics not worked on: *Xenozoic Tales, Rocketeer, Omaha*, and *1963*.

Dream comic-book project: *The Vamp of Zovia*, my magnum opus graphic novel that I've been developing for years.

✳ **Greg Adams.** c/o *CBG* Editorial Department, 700 East State Street, Iola, Wisconsin 54990.

Born: June 6, 1958, in Houston, Texas.

Comics-related education: Freelance commercial artist, instructed/advised by Kerry Gammil.

Biggest creative influences: Neal Adams, John Buscema, Tom Palmer, and Dick Giordano.

1993 projects: Regular inker on *Nomad* and *Deathlok*. *Nick Fury* bookshelf issue.

Past comics titles and related projects: *Nomad* #10 and 14-18. *Deathlok* #21, 24, 25, and 27. *Captain America Battles Drugs* #2. *Morbius Revisited* #2, cover. *Daredevil* #318. *Marvel Comics Presents* #133. *Avengers* #366, pin-up. *Deathlok* #28-30, covers. *Nick Fury* bookshelf issue.

Favorite comics not worked on: *X-Men, X-Force, Spider-Man 2099, Ravage 2099, Hulk, Avengers,* and *Daredevil.*

Dream comic-book project: To ink John Buscema on *Conan* or Neal Adams on *Batman.*

Dan Adkins

✱ **Danny Lee Adkins.** 810 North 2nd Street, Reading, Pennsylvania 19601.

Born: March 15, 1937, in Midkiff, West Virginia.

Comics-related education: Assistant to Wally Wood (16 months).

Biggest creative influences: Wally Wood and John Buscema.

Past comics titles and related projects: *Superman, Ka-Zar, Dr. Strange, Sub-Mariner, X-Men, Creepy, Eerie, T.H.U.N.D.E.R. Agents, Dynamo, Conan, The Cougar, Vampirella, Batman, Nick Fury, Jonny Quest, Green Lantern, Newstralia, Code Name: Danger, Boris the Bear, Avalon, Warlord, Whisper, Batman and the Outsiders, House of Mystery, Action Comics, Superman and The Flash, Vigilante, Batman and Blackhawk, Daredevil, Speedball, Captain America, Silver Surfer, Iron Fist, Spider-Man and The Thing, Captain Marvel, Warlock, Giant-Size Defenders, Master of Kung Fu, The Astonishing Ant-Man, The Avengers, Marvel Comics Presents, Brother Voodoo, Electric Warrior, Green Arrow, The Hulk, War of the Worlds, Killraven, The Living Mummy, The Invisible Man, Excalibur, The Thing and The Scarecrow, The Thing and Ka-Zar, Worlds Unknown, Frankenstein Monster, Masters of Terror, Blazing Combat, Adventure Comics, Superman vs. Wonder Woman, Legends of Nascar, New Gods, Detective Comics, Secrets of Haunted House, Shazam!, Nightmare, Psycho, Tower of Shadows, Ghosts, Weird War, Superman Family, Chamber of Chills,* etc.

Favorite comics not worked on: Anything by Jim Lee and Mike Mignola.

Dream comic-book project: Sub-Mariner or Dr. Strange.

✱ **Charlie Adlard.** 2 Willow Cottages, Belle Vue, Shrewsbury, Shropshire, England S43 7QL.

Agent: Star✱Reach (Sharon Cho).

Born: August 4, 1966, in Shrewsbury, England.

College or other education: Maidstone, Kent: Maidstone College of Art, B.A. in film and video.

Comics-related education: None.

Biggest creative influences: Will Eisner, Bill Sienkiewicz, Kent Williams, John Romita Jr., Marc Silvestri, Moebius, and many more!

1993 projects: *Dances with Daemons* (four-part limited series, Marvel), *Warheads: Black Dawn* (two-part limited series, Marvel), various covers.

Past comics titles and related projects: Judge Armitage nine-part, full-color strip called *Influential Circles,* two Armitage black-and-white strips (three parts each), Judge Dredd "The Hand of Fate" (one-off full-color strip), two covers — all for the *Judge Dredd Megazine* from Fleetway Publications. Two back-up *Warheads* strips

Charlie Adlard

for Marvel UK — appearing in the anthology *Overkill* (in UK) and *Warheads* (in US).

Favorite comics not worked on: *The Heckler, Next Men, Hellblazer, Animal Man.*

Dream comic-book project: An ongoing *Dr. Doom* comic book set in the present — in full Gothic splendor!

✸ **Brian Douglas Ahern.** c/o *CBG* Editorial Department,*Comics Buyer's Guide,* 700 East State Street, Iola, Wisconsin 54990.

Born: February 21, 1967, in Owosso, Michigan.

College or other education: 1991 BFA with honors Kendall College of Art and Design in Grand Rapids, Michigan (major: graphic design). Comics-related education: While a senior at Kendall, I created an independent study course, Comic-Book Scripting, under Dr. Suzanne Eberle, Ph.D., and fully scripted a six-issue series.

Biggest creative influences: Bill Mantlo, Sal Buscema, Don Newton, Albert Dorne, George Bridgman.

Brian Douglas Ahern

1993 projects: Preparing my regular *CBG* cartoon *Bumpkin Buzz* for national syndication as a daily newspaper strip (while daily practicing/polishing anatomy and perspective in preparation for comic-book freelancing).

Past comics titles and related projects: Ongoing weekly cartoon *Adventures of Bumpkin Buzz* in *Comics Buyer's Guide* since September 1991, ongoing monthly cartoon *Bleekbrook's Comic Emporium* in *Comics Retailer* since May 1992, ongoing bi-monthly cartoon *Bleekbrook's Comic Emporium* in *CBG Price Guide* since May 1993, and other strips and panels for the publications on request.

Favorite comics not worked on: Alan Davis' *Excalibur*, Mike Baron and Steve Rude's *Nexus*, Dave Sim's *Cerebus*.

Dream comic-book project: To reintroduce Marvel's *Spider-Woman* as a high-quality, ongoing series, realizing its market potential as a top seller (from both story *and* art).

✸ **Andrea Albert.** 500 Manda Lane, #406, Wheeling, Illinois 60090.

Born: November 29, 1967, in Milwaukee, Wisconsin.

Andrea Albert

College or other education: B.A. in Fine Arts.

Biggest creative influences: My dad.

1993 projects: Letterer or color artist on: *Green Hornet, Mr. T and the T Force*, and *Married with Children*.

Past comics titles and related projects: Letterer or color artist on: *Twilight Zone, Ghostbusters, Sting of the Green Hornet, Tales of the Green Hornet*, and *Kato II*.

Jeff Albrecht

✳ **Jeff Albrecht.** 429 Walnut Blvd., Rochester, Michigan 48307.

Born: October 21, 1957, in Detroit, Michigan.

College or other education: B.S.F.A.

Biggest creative influences: Dick Giordano, Jerry Ordway, and Joe Rubinstein.

1993 inking projects: *Namor* (Marvel), *Justice League Task Force* (DC), and *Mad Dog* (Marvel).

Past comics titles and related projects: *Namor, Soviet Super Soldiers, RoboCop: Prime Suspect, New Warriors, Barbie, Iron Fist*, and *Daffy Duck*.

Favorite character not worked on: Batman.

Dream comic-book project: Superman vs. X-Men.

✳ **Doug Allen.** P.O. Box 613, Bangall, New York 12506.

Born: February 22, 1956, in New Rochelle, New York.

College or other education: B.F.A., Rhode Island School of Design, 1978.

Biggest creative influences: Underground comics of the '60s and '70s (*Zap*, etc.).

1993 projects: *Steven* weeklies and compilations (for Kitchen Sink Press). *Duplex Planet Illustrated, Snake Eyes, Real Stuff, Blab!*, and *Idiotland*.

Past comics titles and related projects: *Weirdo, Snarf, Pictopia, Buzzard, Brutarian, Blab!, Snake Eyes, Idiotland, Steven, National Lampoon*, and *New Yorker* magazine.

Favorite comics not worked on: *Raw*, anything by Crumb, and *Eightball* (Clowes).

Dream comic-book project: One that makes money.

✳ **Tim Allen.** Dynamic Publishing, 1274 Sunnymeade, #6, Rochelle, Illinois 61068.

Born: June 30, in Fort Atkinson, Wisconsin.

College or other education: B.B.A., Accounting, CPA.

Biggest creative influences: Wally Wood and John Buscema.

1993 projects: *Galaxy Girl, Creatures of the Night: Love Bites, Miss Americana Portfolio, Candy's Camera*, and various licensed properties.

Past comics titles and related projects: *Galaxy Girl, Time Jumper, Aquanauts*, and *Team Lancer*.

Favorite comics not worked on: *Xenozoic Tales*.

Dream comic-book project: Undisclosed, it is currently in development.

✳ **Bob Almond.** c/o *CBG* Editorial Department, 700 East State Street, Iola, Wisconsin 54990.

Born: January 4, 1967, in Seoul, Korea.

College or other education: B.A. in Fine Arts Southeastern Massachusetts University (now UMass. Dartmouth).

Biggest creative influences: Bernie Wrightson, George Perez, Terry Austin, Jim Starlin, and John Byrne.

1993 projects: *Warlock and the Infinity Watch* (inks).

Past comics titles and related projects: *Warlock and the Infinity Watch* and *Guardians of the Galaxy Annual #2.*

Favorite comics not worked on: *Incredible Hulk*, anything by John Byrne (*She-Hulk, Next Men*), *Sandman*.

Dream comic-book project: Inking George Pérez on *The Avengers*.

✳ **Jeff Anderson.** 3 Bathgate Terrace, Elwick Road, Hartlepool, Cleveland, United Kingdom TS24 7QW.

Born: January 3, 1957, in Hartlepool, Cleveland, United Kingdom.

College or other education: B.A. (Honors), Leeds.

Biggest creative influences: Too many to say.

1993 projects: *Gunrunners.*

Past comics titles and related projects: *Judge Dredd, Transformers, Thundercats, Action Force, MyS-TECH Wars, Knights of Pendragon, William Tell, Zoids, Future Shocks* (2000 AD), and *Shadows Edge* Volumes 1 and 2.

Dream comic-book project: One that would keep me busy for the next 10 years.

✳ **Mike Anderson.** 56 Heatherside Drive, Agincourt, Ontario, Canada M1W 1T7.

Born: May 1, 1971, in Toronto, Ontario, Canada.

Mike Anderson

College or other education: Graduate of the Ontario College of Art, Communication, and Design Department.

Comics-related education: Winner of the 1992 Klaus Schoenefeld Comic Art Award.

Biggest creative influences: Public Enemy, Harvey Pekar, Spike Lee, Kyle Baker, Russ Meyer, and Dave McKean.

1993 projects: Illustrating a story for writer Joseph Nanni ("Little Grace") which will be published in a prestigious alternative comix anthology magazine (the name of which to be withheld until the time is right).

Past comics titles and related projects: "Red Necks In Blue" and "Revolting Communists Hooked on Lambada" printed in *Comix Compendium Premiere* by Mangajin Books, "From Art-Roc 2 Disc-Jok: A Comparison Between Old Scarborough and New Scarborough" to be published in the upcoming *Log* by Mangajin Books.

Favorite comics not worked on: *Peep Show, Raw, Yummy Fur, American Splendor, Why I Hate Saturn,* and *Love and Rockets.*

Dream comic-book project: A 200-page-plus book documenting the complete history of rap music and hip hop culture.

✳ **Murphy Anderson.** P.O. Box 263, Somerset, N.J. 08875.

Born: July 9, 1926, in Asheville, North Carolina.

College or other education: Two quarters at University of North Carolina at Chapel Hill,

North Carolina. (Dropped out due to World War II.)

Comics-related education: Only art school — two months of evening sketch classes at Art Student's League, New York City.

Biggest creative influences: Foster, Raymond, Fine, and Eisner.

1993 projects: Occasional freelance work when it fits with business commitments.

Past comics titles and related projects: Fiction House — *Planet Comics* (*Star Pirate* — *Life on Other Worlds*). Ziff Davis — Science fiction pulps and comics (*Lars of Mars*). DC Comics — Captain Comet, Atomic Knights, Hawkman, Flash, Green Lantern, Atom, Batman, Superman, etc. Buck Rogers.

Dream comic-book project: How can I answer such a question?

Brian Apthorp

✳ **Brian Apthorp.** c/o Sharon Cho and Mike Friedrich, 2991 Shattuck Ave., Suite 202, Berkeley, California 94702.

Born: November 28, 1955, in Hollywood, California.

College or other education: B.A. in Two-Dimensional Art from California State University at Northridge.

Comics-related education: Three extension courses through UCLA and CSUN in comic book art, taught by Don Rico. Three years at Continuity Video, Burbank, California.

Biggest creative influences: Alex Raymond, Mac Raboy, Jack Kirby, P. Craig Russell, and Neal Adams.

1993 projects: *Ms. Mystic* in "Deathwatch 2000" for Continuity, "Titan" in the "Catalyst" series for Dark Horse's *Comics' Greatest World*.

Past comics titles and related projects: *Captain Power*, *Bucky O'Hare*, five or so issues of *Armor*, *3-D Rocketeer* movie adaptation book, cover for *Cheval Noir* #33, and cover and beginnings of *Little Women* for First's *Classics Illustrated* before they folded.

Favorite comics not worked on: *Concrete*. Most anything by P. Craig Russell, Mike Mignola, Kaluta, Scott Hampton, and Moebius.

Dream comic-book project: My own story of dreams, "I of the Mind"; an adaptation of *Peter Pan* or *The Phantom Toll Booth*; a revival of Captain Marvel Jr. If all else fails, *The Encyclopedia of Teenage Sex Fantasies, Deluxe*.

Sergio Aragonés

✳ **Sergio Aragonés.** P.O. Box 696, Ojai, California 93023.

Born: September 6, 1937, in Castellon, Spain.

1993 projects: *The Mighty Magnor* for Malibu, *Groo the Wanderer* for Marvel/Epic, *Mad Marginals* and other features for *Mad* magazine.

Past comics titles and related projects: *Mad Marginals* and many other features in *Mad* magazine. *Groo the Wanderer* (began at Pacific, moved to Marvel/Epic). *Plop!* (DC Comics). Animated bumpers for *TV's Bloopers and Practical Jokes* (NBC).

✳ **Mark Askwith.** c/o TV Ontario, 2180 Yonge St., Toronto, Ontario, Canada M4T 2T1.

Born: April 6, 1956, in Toronto, Ontario, Canada.

College or other education: B.A. in English from Trinity College, University of Toronto.

Comics-related education: Managed Silver Snail from 1983-87.

Biggest creative influences: Marshall McLuhan, Will Eisner, and John Le Carré.

1993 projects: Preparing a fifth season of *Prisoner of Gravity*.

Past comics titles and related projects: Creator, producer, co-writer of *Prisoner of Gravity*, a weekly show on comics and science fiction. Interviewed over 300 creators and produced over 100 shows. Consultant for *Comic Book Confidential*. Writer of *Silencer*, co-writer of *The Prisoner*, written for *Taboo, Street Music,* and *True North*.

Favorite comics not worked on: Too many to list. Current favorites include *Yummy Fur, Cages, Sandman,* and *Sin City*.

Dream comic-book project: To translate my favorite comics to cyber books.

✳ **Robin Ator.** c/o *CBG* Editorial Department, 700 East State Street, Iola, Wisconsin 54990.

Born: August 13, 1954, in Los Angeles, California.

College or other education: B.A. in Printmaking. M.F.A. in Painting.

Comics-related education: APA5.

Biggest creative influences: Everything I've ever seen.

1993 projects: Nothing to report; currently busy with animation.

Past comics titles and related projects: *Kyra* for Elsewhere Productions; eight-page shorts for Byron Preiss Inc., and *Terminator* for Now Comics.

Favorite comics not worked on: *What The--?!.*

Dream comic-book project: Really good kids' comics, well written.

Dick Ayers

✳ **Dick Ayers.** 64 Beech Street, White Plains, New York 10604.

Born: April 28, 1924, in Ossining, New York.

College or other education: Art Career School, New York City. Cartoonists and Illustrators School, New York City.

Comics-related education: Penciller — Joe Shuster, *Funnyman*. Inker — Jack Kirby, *Sky Masters +*.

Biggest creative influences: Milton Caniff and Roy Crane.

1993 projects: Marvel's *Phantom Rider* and AC's *Femforce*.

Past comics titles and related projects: *Ghost Rider* — Magazine Enterprises, pencil, ink, and letter. *Sgt. Fury* — Marvel, pencil. *Fantastic Four* — Marvel, ink. *Human Torch* — Marvel, pencil and ink. *Bobby Benson* — Magazine Enterprises, pencil, ink, and letter. *Jonah Hex* — DC, pencil breakdowns. *Original Shield* — Archie, pencil. Also: *Jimmy Durante Comic Book, Bobby Benson, The Avengers, The Rawhide Kid, The Two-Gun Kid, Wyatt Earp, Eh! Dig This Crazy Comic,*

Captain Savage, Kamandi, Freedom Fighters, Unknown Soldier, Scalphunter, Gravedigger, Mighty Crusaders, Mantech Warriors, The Whiz Kids, Cauldron of Horror, Sunset Carson, Bombast, Fantastic Four, Thor, Hulk, Sub-Mariner, Captain America, Giant Man, and *Kid Colt.*

Favorite comics not worked on: *Conan* and *Punisher* for Marvel.

Dream comic-book project: *Ghost Rider* (Western version) graphic novel.

✳ **Chris Bachalo.** c/o *CBG* Editorial Department, 700 East State Street, Iola, Wisconsin 54990.

Born: August 23, 1965, in Portage La Prairie, Manitoba, Canada.

College or other education: B.F.A. in Illustration from California State University at Long Beach.

Biggest creative influences: Michael Golden, Bill Sienkiewicz. Made comics interesting for me.

1993 projects: *Death: The High Cost of Living, Shade, the Changing Man, X-Men Unlimited* #1, *Ghost Rider Annual* #1, and various covers and pin-ups, etc.

Past comics titles and related projects: *Sandman* #12, *Shade, the Changing Man* #1-37, *Death: The High Cost of Living* #1-3, *The Incredible Hulk* #400, numerous pin-ups, etc., and a *Batman: Legends of the Dark Knight* story yet to be published.

✳ **Mark Badger.** 429 Euclid, Apartment B, Oakland, California 94610.

Born: October 16, 1958, in Syracuse, New York.

College or other education: Parsons School of Design, B.F.A. in Sculpture.

Biggest creative influences: Learning how to draw from life and my Macintosh with Painter and Photoshop.

1993 projects: *Cambodia USA. Activists* with Joyce Brabner and A. Legends. *Instant Piano.*

Past comics titles and related projects: *Gargoyle, Greenberg the Vampire, Martian Manhunter, The Masque, The Score,* and *Batman: Run, Riddler, Run.*

Favorite comics not worked on: *Rubber Blanket.*

Dream comic-book project: I'm doing it, *Instant Piano.*

✳ **Mike Bannon.** 4804 Edgefield Road, Bethesda, Maryland 20814.

Born: June 14, 1963, in Dubuque, Iowa.

Biggest creative influences: *Cerebus,* Dave Sim, and any Gilbert Shelton material.

1993 projects: *Old Paper (Comics Buyer's Guide), Oombah, Jungle Moon Man* (Strawberry Jam Comics).

Past comics titles and related projects: *To Be Announced* (Strawberry Jam Comics), *Giant-Size Mini-Comics* (Eclipse), *Splat!* (Mad Dog Graphics), *Rip Off Comix* (Rip Off), *Oombah, Jungle Moon Man* (Strawberry Jam Comics).

Favorite comics not worked on: *Megaton Man* and *Mr. Monster.*

✳ **Whitney Barber.** Trinity Visuals, c/o Vinson Watson, P.O. Box 16582, Chicago, Illinois 60616-0582.

Born: February 9, 1975, in Chicago, Illinois.

College or other education: Gallery 37 participant. (Had art works pictured in a gallery for a few months.)

Comics-related education: Art and Graphic Design at New Expressions, drawing for Trinity Visuals.

Biggest creative influences: God, my brother, Destro, Frank Miller, and Brian Bolland.

1993 projects: *Sweet Childe* prints for New Moon Studios.

Favorite comics not worked on: *Dark Knight, Killing Joke, Batman: Year One,* and *Digital Justice.*

Dream comic-book project: My own character's book.

✳ **David Barbour.** Rebel Studios, 4716 Judy Ct., Sacramento, California 95841.

Born: August 18, 1961, in Sacramento, California.

College or other education: Film-making, cinematography, and directing short subjects.

Comics-related education: Self-taught.

Biggest creative influences: Doug Moench's *Master of Kung Fu*, Marv Wolfman's *Tomb of Dracula*, and Alan Moore's *Killing Joke* and *Swamp Thing*.

1993 projects: *Spring-Heel Jack: Revenge of the Ripper, Gothic Nights, Gunfighters in Hell*, and *Cold Shock*.

Past comics titles and related projects: *Spring Heel Jack: A Mystery of Mysteries* and *Zero Tolerance*.

Favorite comics not worked on: Peter Milligan's *Enigma*.

Dream comic-book project: *Kolchak: The Night Stalker* for my dad.

✳ **Tim Barela.** c/o *CBG* Editorial Department, 700 East State Street, Iola, Wisconsin 54990.

1993 projects: A more definitive collection of my more recent work — hopefully, it will happen. Other than that, just my regularly published comic strip.

Past comics titles and related projects: My early work appeared between 1976 and 1983 in various motorcycle-oriented periodicals: *Cycle News, Biker, Cycle World, Choppers, FTW News*, and *Biker Lifestyle*. My comic strip, *Leonard and Larry*, made its first appearance in *Gay Comics* in 1984 and was published occasionally in that series thereafter. It also appeared regularly in *The Advocate* between 1988 and 1991. It has since been published in each bi-monthly issue of *Frontiers Magazine*. *Gay Comics Special* #1 was the first collection of my *Leonard and Larry* magazine installments.

Favorite comics not worked on: Sorry, nothing comes to mind. Since I do not collaborate with anyone on any project, I could not honestly address this.

✳ **Gary Barker.** 401 West Howard, Muncie, Indiana 47305.

Born: July 31, 1957, in Indianapolis, Indiana.

College or other education: B.A. degree with Art major from University of Indianapolis.

Biggest creative influences: Curt Swan, Murphy Anderson, John Byrne, Jack Kirby, John Buscema, and Gene Colan.

1993 projects: My full-time position is as assistant cartoonist to Jim Davis on the comic strip *Garfield*; my duties are primarily pencilling the *Garfield* comic strip. I started Nov. 15, 1983.

Past comics titles and related projects: *Incredible Hulk* #389 (pencils, cover and interior), 10-page story in *Incredible Hulk Annual* #18 (pencils), three 10-page chapters for *Showcase '93* #6-8 (pencils), cover for *The Adventures of the Thing* #4 (pencils), cover for *Morbius Revisited* #1 (pencils), Morbius pin-up for *1993 Marvel Swimsuit* issue, various other work for Dark Horse and Innovation Comics.

Favorite comics not worked on: All Superman titles, *Bone, Sandman Mystery Theatre*, and *Legionnaires*.

Dream comic-book project: An issue of *Superman* or any of the Golden Age characters.

Eleanor J. Barnes

✳ **Eleanor J. Barnes.** 24 Kent Street, Quincy, Massachusetts 02169-6446.

Born: August 12, 1958, in New York City.

College or other education: A.B., Harvard, Chemistry.

Comics-related education: California College of Arts and Crafts (Illustration, 1982); School at the Museum of Fine Arts, Boston (1992-present).

Biggest creative influences: Jack Davis, Basil Wolverton, Peter Bagge, Francisco Goya, and Eliphas Lévi.

1993 projects: *The Curse* and *2976 Vienna Sausages*.

Past comics titles and related projects: "More Heat Than Light" (with Wayne R. Smith) in *Gauntlet: Exploring the Limits of Free Expression #3*, 1992. *1993 Women's Glib Cartoon Calendar*.

Favorite comics not worked on: Terry Pratchett's *The Light Fantastic*; Hunt Emerson's adaptation of *Lady Chatterley's Lover*; and *Archer & Armstrong*.

Dream comic-book project: *Seven Pillars of Wisdom*: Lawrence's account of his adventures in Arabia (a graphic adaptation).

✱ **Mike Baron.** c/o *CBG* Editorial Department, 700 East State Street, Iola, Wisconsin 54990.

Born: July 1, 1949, in Madison, Wisconsin.

College or other education: B.A. from University of Wisconsin-Madison in 1971.

Biggest creative influences: Carl Barks, Philip José Farmer, John D. MacDonald, and any and all pop culture.

1993 projects: *Nexus, Badger, Feud, Spyke, Cat People, Bruce Lee,* and *Archer & Armstrong*.

Past comics titles and related projects: *Punisher, Flash, Ginger Fox, Nexus,* and *Badger*.

Favorite comics not worked on: *American Splendor, The 'Nam, Sandman,* and Malibu's *Tarzan*.

Dream comic-book project: *Nexus* and *Badger*.

✱ **Donna Barr.** 1318 N. Montgomery, Bremerton, Washington 98312.

Born: August 13, 1952, in Everett, Washington.

College or other education: B.A. in German Language and Literature (1978, Ohio State University).

Comics-related education: Self-taught.

Biggest creative influences: Japanese "Floating World" artists, folk art, antique arts (Oriental, South American, Neolithic, etc.), Holling C. Holling, Albrecht Dürer, and 19th Century woodblocks.

1993 projects: Minor stories in various publications in the United States and United King-

dom and *The Desert Peach*. (And editing the musical so's I can offer it to a couple of interested producers/agents — Agg!! I wanted to *file* the thing.)

Past comics titles and related projects: *Stinz, The Desert Peach, The Dreamery, Albedo, Hader and the Colonel* (unfinished), *Comics Journal* "editorials," and lots of piddly stuff you do just to get some $.

Favorite comics not worked on: *Little Nemo in Slumberland*, anything by Ralf König, Brösel's *Werner*, Marc Hempel's *Gregory*, and anything by Roberta Gregory or Colin Upton.

Dream comic-book project: Finish and publish my *Musswolf* (graphic novel) and finish the full-length graphic novel of *Hader and the Colonel*. (These are lies. I would actually like to buy a farm.)

✱ **Mike W. Barr.** c/o *CBG* Editorial Department, 700 East State Street, Iola, Wisconsin 54990.

Born: May 30, 1952, in Akron, Ohio.

College or other education: B.A. from the University of Akron.

Biggest creative influences: Gardner Fox and Ellery Queen.

1993 projects: *The Outsiders* (DC), *Mantra* (Malibu Ultraverse), *The Good Guys* (Defiant), and *Star Trek: Deep Space Nine* (Malibu).

Past comics titles and related projects: *Camelot 3000* (DC), *Batman: Son of the Demon* (DC), *Star Trek* (DC and Marvel), *The Maze Agency* (various publishers), and *Detective Comics* (DC).

Favorite comics not worked on: *Mystery in Space* (1959-1964).

Dream comic-book project: *The Maze Agency*.

✱ **Mike Barreiro.** 840 Ohio Avenue, Apartment #1, Glassport, Pennsylvania 15045.

Born: April 2, 1955, in Pittsburgh, Pennsylvania.

College or other education: Graduate of the Art Institute of Pittsburgh, 1980.

Comics-related education: Graduate of the Joe Kubert School, 1992.

Biggest creative influences: Jack Kirby, Neal Adams, Rich Corben, and John Totleben.

1993 projects: *Kamandi: At Earth's End* (DC Elseworlds), *Scarab* (DC Vertigo), and *Tales of the Jedi* (Dark Horse).

Past comics titles and related projects: *Hellblazer* and *Superman: The Man of Steel Annual.*

Favorite comics not worked on: *Sandman.*

Dream comic-book project: My own concept; written, drawn, lettered, and colored by me.

Terry Beatty

✳ **Terry Beatty.** P.O. Box 1007, Muscatine, Iowa 52761.

Born: January 11, 1958, in Muscatine, Iowa.

Biggest creative influences: Classic newspaper strips, Silver Age Marvel and DC comics, EC, and Eisner.

1993 projects: *Guy Gardner* (inks) for DC, *Johnny Dynamite: Underworld* mini-series (art) for Dark Horse, *Elfquest: New Blood* (script) for Warp Graphics. Also painted covers for *Scary Monsters* magazine.

Past comics titles and related projects: *Ms. Tree, Mike Mist, Wild Dog, Phony Pages, Secret Origins,* DC's *Who's Who, Justice League Quarterly, Mr. Monster* (*Dark Horse Presents*), and more.

Favorite comics not worked on: Anything drawn by Dan Clowes, Mike Cherkas, Charles Burns, or Mitch O'Connell. *Lone Wolf and Cub.*

Dream comic-book project: I'd love to work on a super-hero book, done in the tradition of Kirby and Ditko's Silver Age work — big, bold, and colorful. I also have this nifty idea for a Captain America graphic novel or mini-series.

Den Beauvais

✳ **Den Beauvais.** 61 Chablis Street, Aylmer, P.Q., Canada J9H 5P9.

Born: June 14, 1962, in Ottawa, Ontario, Canada.

College or other education: Self-taught.

Biggest creative influences: V. Segrelle, Frank Miller, and Bill Sienkiewicz.

1993 projects: *Frankenstein* (Dark Horse).

Past comics titles and related projects: *Warlock 5* #1-13, *Aliens Vol. 2* (color, four issues), *Frankenstein* (graphic novel).

Dream comic-book project: My own project, *Firepower.*

✳ **Howard Bender.** 515 Buxton Road, Toms River, New Jersey 08755.

Born: September 25, 1951, in Cleveland — Pittsburgh.

College or other education: Associates

Howard Bender

Degree in Art and Design from Ivy School of Professional Art, Pittsburgh, Pennsylvania, (1974), Figure Drawing at Art Students League, New York City (1975-84), Layout Design at School of Visual Arts, New York City (one semester in 1984), Figure Drawing at Ocean County College, New Jersey (1989-91), and Layout Design at Artist Guild/84 (1989 to present).

Comics-related education: Production Artist at Warren Publishing in New York City (1974-75), Production Artist at Marvel Comics (1974-78), and Assistant to Cover Production Manager/Production Artist at DC Comics (1982-88).

1993 projects: *Mr. Fixitt* — created by myself and Craig Boldman. *Flare.*

Past comics titles and related projects: *Spider-Man Look and Find* for Publications International Ltd. and Marvel, Superman for *Action Comics*, Archie Comics, *Richie Rich*, Harvey, *JSA, Robotech, Honeymooners*, both *Ghostbusters, Slimer, Marvel Universe*, DC's *Who's Who, Blood of Dracula, Silverhawks, Kickersing, Young All-Stars, Dial "H" for Hero, Micronauts, Mr. Enzyme, Flare*, and *Billy and Pop* for *CBG*.

Favorite comics not worked on: *Green Lantern* and *Dr. Radium*.

Dream comic-book project: A line of Mr. Fixitt comics and cartoons, Green Lantern Hal Jordan, Star Hawkins, Davy Crockett, and Zorro.

Brian Michael Bendis

✳ **Brian Michael Bendis.** c/o Steve Donnelly, 106 S.B. Street, San Mateo, California 94401.

Agent: Steve Donnelly.

Born: August 18, 1967, in Cleveland, Ohio.

College or other education: Five years at the Cleveland Institute of Art.

Biggest creative influences: The works of stylized filmmakers (Kubrick, Scorsese, and Stone).

1993 projects: *The Realm* (Caliber, ongoing), *Fire* (Caliber, mini-series), *Total Quivers* (Caliber, one-shot).

Past comics titles and related projects: *Synergy* (Caliber), Milestone Trading Card (Milestone), *Spunky Todd* (Caliber), *Quivers* (Caliber), *Parts of a Hole* (Caliber).

Favorite comics not worked on: I find myself drawn to the ongoing work of certain creators rather than to an actual title.

Dream comic-book project: A prestige format graphic adaptation of the epic *Buckaroo Banzai*.

✳ **Dale W. Berry.** c/o *CBG* Editorial Department, 700 East State Street, Iola, Wisconsin 54990.

Born: April 20, 1960, in Taft, California.

College or other education: Bakersfield College: Scenic Design, Theater Stagecraft.

Comics-related education: Commercial Layout and Design, Computer Graphics, Airbrush:

Dale W. Berry

University of California-Santa Barbara, pursuant to certificate in Commercial Art.

Biggest creative influences: Jademan, Japanese manga, Neal Adams, Jim Steranko, Paul Gulacy, Frank Frazetta, *Ukiyo-E*, and Chinese landscapes.

1993 projects: *Dragonhead* with Eric Dinehart for Majestic Comics.

Past comics titles and related projects: *Ninja Funnies* #1 (mini, artist/writer with Ken Sperry). *Ninja Funnies* #1-5, artist/writer (for Eternity Pub.), also cover art. *Moonlight Cutter, The Duel, Sword Spirit* (written with Mysti Rubert), *White Lotus, White Lotus: Armor* (all for *Tales of the Kung Fu Warriors*, CFW Pub.) writer/artist (pencils, inks).

Favorite comics not worked on: Chinese language *Blood Sword Dynasty* (aka *Chinese Heroes*), *The Shadow*, and *Sandman*.

Dream comic-book project: To revamp *Iron Fist* and the entire Marvel Comics martial arts "world." It's mired in the '70s "kung fu" craze, has no spirituality, and is way too "white."

✹ **Kyle J. Bertelsen.** N6251 Cole Court, Onalaska, Wisconsin.

Born: May 25, 1970, in La Crosse, Wisconsin.

Comics-related education: Workshops led by Dennis Jensen.

Biggest creative influences: Dennis Jensen, Paul M. Smith, P. Craig Russell, Bill Watterson, Yoshihisha Tagami, Bernie Wrightson, and Neil Gaiman.

1993 projects: Projects currently in development.

Past comics titles and related projects: Pin-ups and back cover for *Troubleshooters* #2 from Star Warp Concepts — pencils and inks. *World of Monkey* trading cards Series 1 — pencils and inks. Assistant inks for Dennis Jensen. *Primordial Soup* comic strip — 1991 — pencils and inks.

Favorite comics not worked on: *Sandman, Hellblazer, Cerebus, Baker Street,* and *Madman.*

Dream comic-book project: A complete story with meaningful and personal themes and direction.

Al Bigley

✹ **Al Bigley.** 5003 Morning Dew Lane, Monroe, North Carolina 28110.

Born: May 20, 1965, in Camden, New Jersey.

College or other education: Ringling School of Art and Design. Completed three year course. Awarded several scholarships/awards.

Biggest creative influences: Neal Adams, Nick Cardy, Norman Rockwell, Ross Andru, Alex Toth, Irv Novick, Jack Davis, and John Romita Sr.

1993 projects: Various "special projects" for DC, featuring *Batman: The Animated Series*.

Past comics titles and related projects: Marvel: *Darkhawk* #26, 27, and *Annual* #1, *Avengers West Coast Annual* #7, *Darkhold* #5 and 6, and various *Iron Man* pin-ups. DC: *The Fly* #9, 14, several DC Special Projects: *Batman Golden Books*, T-shirt art, and game art. For *Batman: The Animated Series*: Book and cassette sets, activity books, Topps cards, etc. First Comics: *Sable* #22-24 and *Badger* #49. Quality Comics: Various covers for *Strontium Dog* and *2000 AD Showcase*. Brave New Words: *Polis* #1-3. Also worked on jobs for Gladstone and for the Children's Television Workshop.

Favorite comics not worked on: *Swamp Thing*, the Superman titles, Will Eisner's *Spirit*, *Concrete*, etc.

Dream comic-book project: Any project featuring a well-done, solid plot with good characterization.

✳ **Jerry Bingham.** c/o *CBG* Editorial Department, 700 East State Street, Iola, Wisconsin 54990.

Born: June 25, 1953, in Chicago, Illinois.

College or other education: Advanced training in all areas, then exhaustive and extensive self-imposed studies.

1993 projects: *Midnight Sons Unlimited, Spectacular Spider-Man Annual, In Darkest Knight, Reign of the Demon*, and art and designs for Malibu's Ultraverse.

Past comics titles and related projects: Comics: *House of Mystery* and *House of Secrets* (DC); *Black Panther, Iron Man, Captain America, Ka-Zar, Marvel Team-Up, Marvel Two-in-One*, etc. (Marvel); *Warp* (First); TSR; *Heavy Metal Magazine, Beowulf* graphic novel (First); *Batman: Son of the Demon* graphic novel (DC); *Onyx Overlord* (Starwatcher and Epic); *Spectacular Spider-Man* (Marvel); and dozens of covers for Marvel, DC, First, Malibu, Epic, TSR, and others.

Dream comic-book project: *The Collision and Destruction of the Entire Comic Book Universe and its Rebirth*.

✳ **Bill Black.** AC Comics, P.O. 1216, Longwood, Florida 32752.

Born: September 14, 1943, in Tarenum, Pennsylvania.

College or other education: B.A., Advertising Design, Florida State University.

Biggest creative influences: Roger Corman.

1993 projects: *Femforce, Femforce up Close, Jungle Girls*, and *Good Girl Art Quarterly*, all from AC Comics.

Past comics titles and related projects: Various stories for Warren Publications for *Creepy* and *Eerie*. Numerous stories for Marvel's *What If?* and *Invaders*. *Nightshade* and Western covers for Charlton. Tarzan. 1982-present, Editor and Publisher AC Comics: Created *Femforce, Nightveil, She-Cat, Ms. Victory, Tara, Synn* (all of which appeared in their own books). Various B-Western comics, *Roy Rogers Western Classics* and *Latigo Kid*.

Favorite comics not worked on: *Justice Society of America*.

Dream comic-book project: Doing it now, AC Comics' *Femforce*.

Barry Lawrence Blair

✳ **Barry Lawrence Blair.** Night Wynd Enterprises, P.O. Box 612 (Murray Hill Station), New York, New York 10156-0600.

Born: September 7, 1954, in Ottawa, Ontario, Canada.

College or other education: Carleton University.

Biggest creative influences: Wally Wood, Maxfield Parrish, Trina Shart-Hyman, Barrie Gustafson, and Janet and Anne Grahame Johnstone.

1993 projects: *Elflord: Dragon's Eye, Elfheim: Dragon's Dreams, Elflore: High Seas, Samurai: Demon Sword, Dragonfire*, and *War* storyline in *Elfquest: New Blood*.

Past comics titles and related projects: Writer and/or artist on: *Elflord, Samurai, Dragonring, Elflore, Elfheim, Dragonforce, Born to Kill, China Sea, Dragonfire, Demon Hunter, Dragons in the Moon, Greenhaven, Greenlock, Gun Fury, Hardkorr, Icarus, Jake Thrash, Kiku San, Leather and Lace, Logan's Run, Nocturne, Pendragon, Sapphire, Team Nippon, Vampire's Kiss, Underground, Warlock 5, Warlocks, Kimura, Serpentyne, Foxfire, Children of the Night, Stratonaut, Blitz, Blood 'n' Guts, Windblade, Gun Fury Returns, Logan's World*, and *Maelstrom*, to name but a few.

Favorite comics not worked on: *Arion, Challengers of the Unknown*, and *T.H.U.N.D.E.R. Agents*.

Dream comic-book project: A full-color, 400-page *Elflord* special once a year.

Larry Blake

✳ **Larry Blake.** 69306 St. Rt. 124, Reedsville, Ohio 45772.

Born: October 18, 1952, in Greenfield, Ohio.

College or other education: Completed one year vocational commercial art course in high school.

Comics-related education: Twenty years in small-press. Freelanced logos, covers, etc., for rock bands. Cartoons, etc., in many small independent comics. Art for rock fan clubs.

Biggest creative influences: Wayne Boring, Wally Wood, The Beatles, Kiss, movies, classical painters, Bob Burden, and 30 years of comics fandom.

1993 projects: *Agents of Oracle* for Blind Bat Press in Canada. *Mr. Faith*, a science-fiction comic for Reality Press in California. Lettering, pencils, and inks on both titles.

Past comics titles and related projects: *Johnny* #1 from New Voice, *Trial Run* (Kiss comic) for Miller Publications, *Nightstar* strips for Cat's Paw, cartoons for *CBG* and *Amazing Heroes*, text and art in *Comics Feature* magazine, *Nightstar* comic for New Voice, Kiss comic for British fan club, cartoons in national SCA magazine (*Tournaments Illuminated*), dozens of small-press publications and amateur rock 'n' roll magazines, record and tape covers (comics style) for area bands, strip in *Czar Chasm* mag, *Afterworld* (early independent comic) from Darkstar Comics, *Amazing Heroes Swimsuit Specials* (two years).

Favorite comics not worked on: *Little Lulu, Flaming Carrot, Uncle Scrooge, Batman Adventures*, and *Howard the Duck*.

Dream comic-book project: Write and draw my *Nightstar* (super-hero) for an independent. Write and draw rock 'n' roll-related comics.

✳ **Mark Bloodworth.** 3242 Coolidge, Royal Oak, Michigan 48073.

Born: February 5, 1963, in Detroit, Michigan.

College or other education: One semester of community college.

Comics-related education: None, except the comic books I've worked on.

Biggest creative influences: Ross Andru, Jack Kirby, Bernie Wrightson, Harlan Ellison, and James Whale.

1993 projects: Nothing definite yet, but something in the early stages with DC.

Past comics titles and related projects: *Nightstreets* for Arrow Comics; *Cheerleaders from Hell, Deadworld* and *Nightstreets* Books I and II for Caliber Press, *Caliber Presents; Hellraiser* for Epic Comics.

Favorite comics not worked on: *Love and Rockets* and *Madman Adventures*.

Dream comic-book project: "The Death of Aunt May" if it hasn't been done already.

Mark V. Bodé

✳ **Mark V. Bodé.** c/o Bodé Productions P.O. Box 10143, North Berkeley, California 94709.

Born: February 18, 1963, in Utica, New York.

College or other education: Fine Arts Major, School of Visual Arts; Etching and Painting, College of Marin; Animation, San Francisco State.

Biggest creative influences: Vaughn Bodé, Wally Wood, and Moebius.

1993 projects: "Cobalt 60" story for *Heavy Metal*; *Dust Devil*; "Chaboocheck" story for *Heavy Metal*; and a comics slide show tour.

Past comics titles and related projects: *Zooks, Yellow Hat, Adventures of Cheech Wizard, Cobalt 60, Zara Tungi, Miami Mice, Teenage Mutant Ninja Turtles* #18 and 32, and *Times Pipeline*.

Dream comic-book project: Iron Man vogues as a cross-dresser, all new issues.

✳ **Jacques Boivin.** c/o *CBG* Editorial Department, 700 East State Street, Iola, Wisconsin 54990.

Born: April 7, 1952, in Montreal, Quebec, Canada.

College or other education: B.A. (honors) in Visual Arts, University of Ottawa (1974).

Biggest creative influences: Hergé, Carl Barks, and R. Crumb.

1993 projects: *Melody* (Kitchen Sink Press).

Past comics titles and related projects: *Love Fantasy* (Renegade); *The Complete Fluffhead* (Phantasy Press); *Dinosaurs Comics, Aliens,* and *Land of Consciousness* (mini-comics for Phantasy Press); *Beastie and the Boo* (self-published); *Jacques* (self-published). Also: *True North II, Images of Omaha* #2, *Northguard, Amazing Heroes Swimsuit Specials, Crazy,* etc.

Favorite comics not worked on: EC reprints, *Hup, Dirty Plotte, Herbie,* Barks reprints, Don Rosa duck stories, *Stickboy, Omaha,* etc.

Dream comic-book project: The one I'm working on now.

✳ **Bruce H. Bolinger.** Freehold Studio, HCR 61, Box 148, Nicktown, Pennsylvania 15762.

Born: April 12, 1943, in Johnstown, Pennsylvania.

College or other education: B.A. from Art Center College of Design, Pasadena, California.

Biggest creative influences: Doing Don Martin's final art (inking) for his *Cracked* material (three years).

1993 projects: Four pages in each issue of *Cracked* magazine. Attempting to get published my fourth issue of *Stranger in a Strange Land*, my first comic venture with Rip Off Press.

Past comics titles and related projects: Produced three issues of *Stranger in a Strange Land*, contributed to *Rip Off Press Quarterly* for several issues, and contributed to *Warped* magazine until it folded.

Dream comic-book project: Any project that would pay on a scale equal to the effort given.

✳ **Chuck Bordell.** 2345 Dearborn, #3, Missoula, Montana 59801.

Born: March 23, 1968, in Sharon, Pennsylvania.

College or other education: B.A. in Anthropology/Archaeology from the University of Montana.

Biggest creative influences: Frank Miller, Will Eisner, Virgil Finlay, and Alphonse Mucha.

1993 projects: Inker on the *20th Anniversary E-Man* mini from Alpha Productions, inking *The Steel Mosquito Special* and *Bloodthirst* one-shot for Alpha, and inking *Sirens* and *Silverstorm II* for Gauntlet Comics.

Past comics titles and related projects: Alpha Productions: *Totem #3*, *Totem Special #2*, and *Bloodthirst: The Terminus Option*. Figment Press: Writer and illustrator of *The Crown of Kings* (1990-91).

Favorite comics not worked on: *Concrete, Excalibur, Wonder Woman*, and *Protectors*.

Dream comic-book project: Illustrating a script written by Frank Miller.

✳ **Robert Bostick.** 1820 Wooten Park, #211, Austin, Texas 78757.

Born: May 19, 1968, in Killeen, Texas.

College or other education: Central Texas College, Austin Community College.

Comics-related education: Interned at Blackbird, assisted Martin Thomas.

Biggest creative influences: Carlos Kastro, Kyle Baker, George Pratt, Bill Sienkiewicz, Jamie Hernandez, John Nordland II, Bernie Wrightson, Picasso, and Lou Reed.

1993 projects: *Living behind the Moon, Comic Ball 6,* and *Wings: Learning to Fly.*

Past comics titles and related projects: *Ninja High School* (backgrounds). *Wings: Learning to Fly* (illustration and lettering). *Grimjack* (assisted coloring). Illustrations for Brad Foster's *Stuff.* Lettering on *Heroes #2-4. Winding Road* (story and art in *Jab* #1 and 2). Inking on *Split Phaze* in *Jab* #3.

Favorite comics not worked on: *Love and Rockets, Heroes, Cerebus, Flaming Carrot*, and *Omaha.*

Dream comic-book project: Collaboration with Dave Sim.

✳ **(Dr.) Malcolm Bourne.** 2+4 Bye Road, Shuttlesworth, Ramsbottom, Bury, Lancs, BW 0HH, United Kingdom.

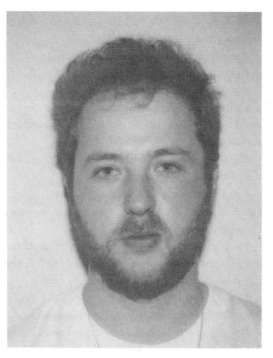

(Dr.) Malcolm Bourne

Born: May 17, 1962, in Manchester, England.

College or other education: B.A. (hons.) Oxford University, 1983, in Neuroscience; M.B., B.S. (general medical qualification, equivalent of M.D.), London, 1986; M.Sc. in Psychiatry (current-1993).

Biggest creative influences: John Irving and Tom Wolfe.

1993 projects: Definitely scheduled: *Loving Couples* with Martin Wagner (Double Diamond); *Negative Burn* (Mad Hatter Anthology), Caliber Press. Proposals in pipeline: *Looking for Nanny Katie* with Jeff Lang and Steve Veber; *House of Mirrors* with Jeff Lang and Jill Thompson; and *Pandora's Box* with Joe Pruett and Will Simpson.

Past comics titles and related projects: *Tales of Ordinary Madness #1-4*, Dark Horse, 1992, with Mike Allred and John Bolton. Text piece in *Faust #4*, Rebel Studios, 1993. Text pieces in UK DC reprints. Co-editor/publisher, *Comics Critics Cavalcade* (ongoing fanzine, current) with Mark Lucas.

Favorite comics not worked on: *Cerebus, Sandman, Hepcats, Nexus, Grendel*, and *Zot!*

Dream comic-book project: Difficult question. A series of creator-owned stories, unbound by the artificial limits imposed by genre.

✳ **Glenn Boyd.** 925 West Locust Street, Scranton, Pennsylvania 18504.

Agent: Stan Cohen, Creative Licensing.

Born: May 31, 1960, in Fort Knox, Kentucky.

College or other education: Art Institute of Pittsburgh, Associate Degree in Specialized Technology.

Biggest creative influences: Leonardo da Vinci, Frank Frazetta, and Syd Mead.

1993 projects: *Interplanetary Lizards of the Texas Plains* #7-10. *Interplanetary Lizards* video game by Christmas 1993.

Past comics titles and related projects: *Interplanetary Lizards of the Texas Plains* #1-6 and *The Book of Lost Souls* #1.

Favorite comics not worked on: *John Byrne's Next Men, Clash,* and *Aliens.*

Dream comic-book project: *Interplanetary Lizards of the Texas Plains — The Movie.*

Joyce Brabner (for picture, see Harvey Pekar)

✳ **Joyce Brabner.** P.O. Box 18471, Cleveland Heights, Ohio 44118.

College or other education: I have a B.A. in Dramatic Arts.

Comics-related education: I co-owned a comic-book store.

Biggest creative influences: My husband, Harvey Pekar. I read his stuff, wrote to him, married him, and ended up a character in his series *American Splendor.*

1993 projects: *Activists!* with Wayne Vansant and *Our Cancer Year* with Harvey.

Past comics titles and related projects: *AARGH!, American Splendor, Brought to Light, Real War Stories, Strip AIDS,* and *Twisted Sisters.*

Favorite comics not worked on: Whatever people send us in response to something *we've* published. We've made some good friends that way.

Dream comic-book project: All my stuff is done on behalf of non-profit organizations. That probably means I'm already dreaming.

✳ **Timothy Bradstreet.** c/o *CBG* Editorial Department, 700 East State Street, Iola, Wisconsin 54990.

Timothy Bradstreet

Agent: Mike Friedrich.

Born: February 16, 1967, in Cheverly, Maryland.

Biggest creative influences: Tim Truman, Paul Gulacy, Al Williamson, P. Craig Russell, Gene Day, and Frank Miller.

1993 projects: *Hawkworld* (DC), *Aliens: Music of the Spears* (Dark Horse), Clive Barker's *Age of Desire* (Eclipse), *Stations of the Cross* with Andrew Vachss and *Hard Looks* (Dark Horse). Also, secret projects for Dark Horse and an untitled Henry Rollins project.

Past comics titles and related projects: Andrew Vachss' *Hard Looks* (Dark Horse), *Dragon Chiang* with Tim Truman (Eclipse), *Hawkworld* with Tim Truman (DC), *Who's Who in the DC Universe* (DC), and covers for Dark Horse, DC Comics, and Eclipse. *Vampire: The Masquerade* for White Wolf Publishing, as well as other vampire-related projects for White Wolf. *Shadowrun RPG* from FASA Corp.

Favorite comics not worked on: *Metropol, Metropol A.D., A1, Heavy Metal, Batman: Legends of the Dark Knight, Grateful Dead Comix, Baker Street,* and *Black Cross.*

Dream comic-book project: Adaptations of lyrics and poems by Henry Rollins (currently in the works).

✳ **Shelley Braga.** 13 Huttleston Avenue, Fairhaven, Massachusetts 02719.

Born: August 11, 1969, in New Bedford, Massachusetts.

College or other education: University of Massachusetts, Dartmouth, B.F.A. in Photography, two years of Calligraphy and Typography.

Comics-related education: Adult Education Teacher — Calligraphy. Assistant teacher at University of Massachusetts, Dartmouth, in Calligraphy.

Biggest creative influences: Calligraphers: Arthur Baker, Howard Glasser, Norman Zapf, Donald Jackson (calligrapher to the Queen), and Marvel letterers.

1993 projects: *P.R.I.M.E.* by Cutting Edge Comics.

Favorite comics not worked on: *Spider-Man, Faust, Thor,* and *Warlock.*

Dream comic-book project: A project using multiple typefaces, with mega sound effects and drawn letterforms.

Mark Braun

✳ **Mark Braun.** 4028 North Osceola, Norridge, Illinois 60634.

Born: August 9, 1954, in Chicago, Illinois.

College or other education: School of the Art Institute of Chicago (no degree). Ray Vogue College of Design (nothin' there, either).

Comics-related education: 10 year member: Society of Typographic Arts/American Center for Design (1981-1991). Member: Chicago Comics and Cartooning Professionals (*really* non-formal group). Big-shot Art Director with expense account 1981-1991.

Biggest creative influences: Eisner, Stan Lynde, Carl Barks, Russ Heath (who spent several days "showing me the ropes" in 1973), Kirby, Ditko, Ayers, Toth, Corben, and Staton (hello, Joe!).

1993 projects: *B.O.N.E.S., RIP, Johnny Blood* (all self-publishing for 1994), and anything else that I can squeeze in . . .

Past comics titles and related projects: Now: *The Real Ghostbusters, Slimer! and the Real Ghostbusters* #10-on, *Married with Children* (Volume 1, #4), *Married with Children: Kelly Bundy Special* #4 (1993). Malibu: *Space Patrol* #1-3 (covers), *Read My Lips: The Unofficial Biography of George Bush* (inks). DC: *Looney Tunes* magazine, *Bugs Bunny* magazine (various pages). *Balloonaticks*: comic art for issue #1 and model sheets. Single-panel gags, spots, and illustrations for numerous publications.

Favorite comics not worked on: *Sandman, Eightball,* and *Omaha.*

Dream comic-book project: A revival of DC's old *Fox and Crow.*

✳ **Daniel Brereton.** c/o *CBG* Editorial Department, 700 East State Street, Iola, Wisconsin 54990.

Agent: Harris Miller.

Born: November 22, 1965, in Walnut Creek, California.

College or other education: Four years of art school: California College of Arts and Crafts in Oakland, California, and Academy of Art College, San Francisco, California.

Comics-related education: Twenty years of "fan-boying-it."

Biggest creative influences: N.C. Wyeth, Dean Cornwell, Frank Frazetta, Barron Storey, Jack Kirby, John Buscema, Gene Colan, Frank

Robbins, Waterhouse, and Gustav Klimt.

1993 projects: *World's Finest* (scripted by Walt Simonson), *Cable and the Six-Pack* with Fabian Nicieza (for Marvel).

Past comics titles and related projects: 1989-90: *Black Terror* for Eclipse (three-issue mini-series). 1991: *The Psycho* (three issues, DC), *Interface* #9 (25 pages). 1992: *Clive Barker's Dread* for Eclipse (64-page graphic novel). Cover work includes: *Creepy, Eerie, Badger, L.E.G.I.O.N. '9-, Lobo, Hellraiser, Nightbreed, Ray Bradbury Chronicles, Cheval Noir, Spectre, Batman: Legends of the Dark Knight, The Question, ESPers,* and *Punisher.*

Favorite comics not worked on: *Shade, the Changing Man, Eightball, Hate, Sin City, John Byrne's Next Men, Sam and Max, Watchmen, Batman: The Dark Knight Returns,* and *Batman: Year One.*

Norman Kieth Breyfogle

✳ **Norman Kieth Breyfogle.** c/o *CBG* Editorial Department, 700 East State Street, Iola, Wisconsin 54990.

Agent: Star*Reach (Mike Friedrich).

Born: February 27, 1960, in Iowa City, Iowa.

College or other education: Four years art at Northern Michigan University.

Biggest creative influences: Neal Adams, Frank Frazetta, *American Artist* magazine, impressionists, and expressionists.

1993 projects: *Prime* for Malibu (first Ultraverse title).

Past comics titles and related projects: *Tech Team* (Michigan Technical University), *Miracleman* (Eclipse), *Metaphysique* (Eclipse), *Tales of Terror* (Eclipse), *American Flagg!* (First), *Whisper* (First), *Marvel Fanfare* (Marvel), *New Talent Showcase* (DC), *Open Space* (Marvel), *Detective Comics* (DC), *Batman* (DC), *Batman: Birth of the Demon* (graphic novel, fully painted, DC), *Batman: Holy Terror* (DC), and *Batman: Shadow of the Bat* (DC). Painted covers and line-drawn covers for Now Comics and posters for DC.

Dream comic-book project: An anthology of short stories and epics written and drawn by me.

✳ **Kevin Paul Shaw Broden.** 1011 Arroyo Drive, Fullerton, California 92633.

Born: June 11, 1967, in Fullerton, California.

College or other education: Associate in Arts from Fullerton Community College (1985-89), Bachelor of Arts from California State University at Fullerton (1987-93).

Comics-related education: At Fullerton College, I took courses in basic drawing and illustration and in cartooning. I also took classes in journalism (including three years on the Fullerton College *Hornet* newspaper, where I was a cartoonist, reporter, feature page editor, and essayist for the editorial/opinion pages, having fiction published in both the *Hornet* and the school magazine, *The Torch*), and creative writing. At Cal State-Fullerton I took several courses in figurative drawing. My professor in most of the courses was Don Lagerberg, who specializes in figurative drawing and painting. The classes included basic life drawing to more detailed anatomical drawing and construction, courses on head and hands and portraiture, along with Special Study courses in narrative figure illustration which included comic books and storyboarding for movies, television, and animation, all of which have become a firm foundation for my career in comics. I have been an assistant background illustrator and colorist for Brian Murray from March 1992 to the present.

Biggest creative influences: Ray Bradbury and Neil Gaiman for creative thinking in storytelling. Jerry Ordway, Adam Hughes, and Brian Murray in art.

1993 projects: Color in *Brigade* mini-series and #1 of the ongoing series *Bloodstrike* #1 and *Supreme* for Image Comics.

Past comics titles and related projects: Over the past year I have assisted Brian Murray with background illustrations in issues #1 and 2 of *Supreme* (received first printed credits in *Supreme* #1) and color work in issues #2, 3, and 0 of *Youngblood* and *Brigade* #1-3. Color work in the *Infiniti* back-up stories and the two *Splitting Image!* issues. I have also done illustrations for an educational film entitled *HIV: The Modern Day Pirate*, and have done cel painting for an upcoming animated film called *The Tummies*.

Favorite comics not worked on: *Sandman* and the four Superman titles.

Dream comic-book project: I have many ideas of my own that I would like to someday publish, but my real dream is to work with Mike Carlin on the Superman books (in any capacity to begin with, then to write and pencil).

✳ George J. Broderick Jr. c/o *CBG* Editorial Department, 700 East State Street, Iola, Wisconsin 54990.

Born: November 15, 1957, in Pittsburgh, Pennsylvania.

College or other education: B.S. in Graphic Design from La Roche College, Pittsburgh, Pennsylvania.

Comics-related education: Internship with Dardnell Publications (1978-79) doing editorial cartoons for suburban newspapers.

Biggest creative influences: Howie Post's Harvey stuff, Jack Cole, E.C. Segar, Chuck Jones, Curt Swan, and Carmine Infantino.

1993 projects: *Lost in Space: Year Two* (editing and kibitzing), *Quantum Leap* comic (editing and scripting). What's out there? Who's hiring?

Past comics titles and related projects: Self-published *Legion of Super-Heroes* parody (1982); small press comic — story and art, *Critter Corps* (1985); *DC Bonus Book* #2 (Dr. Light Spotlight) story (1987); *Hero Alliance Spotlight* #1 and 2 — stories; *Hero Alliance* #15, three pages art; *Walt Kelly's Santa Claus Adventures* and *Bozo the Clown*,

covers; *Biff Thundersaur* — script; *Overture* #1 and 2 and *Cap'n Oatmeal* #1 — script and art; *Lost in Space* and *Quantum Leap* — scripts and editing (various).

Favorite comics not worked on: *Bone, Animal Man, Groo, Nexus, Mr. Monster, Miracleman, Sandman,* and *Justice League America*.

Dream comic-book project: Popeye! Oh, God, yes! I love that sailor man! Uh huh! Yep!

✳ Steve Brooks. c/o *CBG* Editorial Department, 700 East State Street, Iola, Wisconsin 54990.

Born: March 14, 1966, in Columbus, Georgia.

Comics-related education: I took a comic-book class at the University of Georgia.

Biggest creative influences: Early Marvel comics (1960s), Jack Kirby, Steve Ditko, Walt Simonson, Howard Chaykin, and Gil Kane.

1993 projects: I am currently doing pencil work for Allied Comics. I've done a few stories for their title *Tales from the Balcony*.

Past comics titles and related projects: The work for Allied is the first that I have done in the past few years. I did a lot of fandom work in the early 1980s but stopped drawing when I graduated high school. It's only been in the past year and a half that I have returned to drawing. I am currently trying to do as much work as possible.

Favorite comics not worked on: *Spawn* and *WildC.A.T.S.*

Dream comic-book project: I would really love to do some issues of *Doctor Strange*.

✳ Roger A. Brown. Excel Studio, P.O. Box 7122, North Augusta, South Carolina 29841.

Born: April 5, 1957, in Munchweiler, Germany.

Biggest creative influences: Tom Lyle, Rurik Tyler, Roger Stern, and Chuck Dixon.

1993 projects: Marvel's *What The--?!,* Spoof Comics line, Parody Press humor line.

Past comics titles and related projects: Marvel's *What The--?!,* DC's *Tiny Toons* and *Looney Tunes* magazines, Spoof's *Green Lanterns*, Parody Press' *Infinity Charade*, Marvel Universe

Roger A. Brown (left)

parody poster, Spoof's *Tootsie the Dinosaur Hunter*, and *Comics Interview* #93 (interview with Tom Lyle).

Favorite comics not worked on: *Spider-Man, Ghost Rider, H.A.R.D. Corps, Darkstar, Wild-C.A.T.S, Predator, Star Trek,* and *Star Trek: The Next Generation.*

Dream comic-book project: My own two creations, *Epitath* and *Cyberlords.*

Richard Bruning

✻ **Richard Bruning.** Brainstorm Unlimited, 166 Lexington Avenue, New York, New York 10016.

Born: February 7, 1953, in Middletown, New York.

College or other education: Not much.

Comics-related education: 1971-1979, fanzines (art and cartoons mostly). 1979-1980, Eclipse Art Director. 1980-1984, Capital Comics Editor/Art Director. 1985-1990, DC Design Director. 1990-present, Brainstorm (freelance design, art, and writing).

Biggest creative influences: Lee and Kirby, Eisner, R. Crumb, Frank Miller, Alan Moore, and Dave Sim.

1993 projects: Vertigo design: *Sandman Mystery Theatre* covers (monthly), *Skin Graft* covers (four issues), *Psycho Pirate/Vertigo Visions* one-shot (writing), and secret projects that I'm not at liberty to reveal.

Past comics titles and related projects: *Eclipse Monthly* #1-3. Capital Comics (*Nexus, Badger,* and *Whisper*). DC: *Year One, Dark Knight, Watchmen, Killing Joke,* science-fiction graphic novels, collected book editions (design), *Deadman, Prisoner* (editing), *Adam Strange* (writing and design), numerous other DC projects design or art direction in various prestige format, graphic novels, and limited series. Cover editor on regular books 1985-1986. Piranha Press Art Director 1988-1991, designer of *Beautiful Stories for Ugly Children* covers and interiors 1990-1991, Vertigo line designer (logo and publication format), including *Books of Magic* collected edition. Designer on Will Eisner's *Invisible People* series.

Favorite comics not worked on: *Cerebus, Love and Rockets, Akira, Sandman,* and *Maximortal.*

Dream comic-book project: I'll have to think about that . . .

✻ **Ken Bruzenak.** 11 Pennsylvania Avenue, Reading, Pennsylvania 19605.

Born: August 30, 1952, in Pittsburgh, Pennsylvania.

Comics-related education: Assistant/editor for Jim Steranko at Supergraphics, 1970-84.

Biggest creative influences: Doc Savage, Jim Steranko, Jack Kirby, and Howard Chaykin.

1993 projects: *Silver Surfer, Showcase '93, Atom Special,* and *Offcastes.*

Past comics titles and related projects: *American Flagg!, Mr. Monster, Time², The Shadow, Blackhawk, Ms. Mystic, The Punisher, Twilight, Hulk, Black Kiss, Rocket Raccoon, She-Hulk* graphic novel, *Batman: Birth of the Demon, Trekker, Nascar Comics*, Continuity Comics, and Eclipse Comics.

Favorite comics not worked on: *The 'Nam* and *Tor*.

Dream comic-book project: Captain America and Wonder Woman vs. Red Skull and Cheetah.

✳ **Rick J. Bryant.** 18 West 37 Street, #301, New York, New York 10018.

Born: July 4, 1952, in Clintwood, Virginia.

Comics-related education: Continuity (Neal Adams), Joe Rubinstein, and Bob Wiacek.

Biggest creative influences: J.C. Coll, Frank Frazetta, Jeff Jones, Bernie Wrightson, Kaluta, and Roy G. Krenkel.

1993 projects: *Predator: Race War* (inker) Dark Horse. *Shade, the Changing Man* (inker), DC. Dinosaur prints (inker), unpublished as of yet.

Past comics titles and related projects: *World of Krypton* (DC) #1 and 2. *Treasure of Tranicos*, black-and-white *Conan* (Marvel), co-inker. *Oracle* (a portfolio), inker. *Midknight Silk* (a portfolio), inker. *Windreams* portfolio (Continuity). *Rick Bryant Portfolio* (Shanes and Shanes). *Rick Bryant Sketchbook* (Tundra). *Peter Pan* (inker), unpublished (Tundra). *The Dark* (inker), Continüm Comics. *Flare* (inker).

Favorite comics not worked on: *Batman*.

✳ **Richard Buckler.** c/o *CBG* Editorial Department, 700 East State Street, Iola, Wisconsin 54990.

Born: February 6, 1949, in Detroit, Michigan.

Comics-related education: Assistant (one year) to Dan Barry (*Flash Gordon*). Assistant (two years) to Seymour Barry (*The Phantom*). Assistant to Al Williamson.

Biggest creative influences: Jack Kirby, Neal Adams, John Buscema, Harvey Kurtzman, Al Williamson, Frank Frazetta, George Bridgeman, Burne Hogarth, cinema, Renaissance painters, rock music, and Bruce Lee.

1993 projects: *Last Action Hero* (Topps), a three-issue mini-series. *Protectors* (Malibu). *Cyber-Deth* (new project for Visage Studios, currently under development).

Past comics titles and related projects: *Deathlok* (created, wrote, and illustrated) in *Astonishing Tales, Fantastic Four, Avengers, Thor, Conan, Epic* magazine, *Nova, Black Panther* (*Jungle Action*), *Star Wars, Incredible Hulk, Dracula, X-Factor, Spectacular Spider-Man, Sub-Mariner, Human Torch, Superman, World's Finest, All-Star Squadron, Justice League, Lois Lane* (*Rose and Thorn*), *Captain Marvel, Batman, Star Hunters, Warlord, Flash, Black Lightning, Teen Titans, Creepy* and *Eerie* magazines, *Galaxia* magazine (my own publication), Solson comics (creator/editor/artist of *Reagan's Raiders, How to Draw Teenage Mutant Ninja Turtles, Rich Buckler's Secrets of Drawing Comics*, and numerous other titles for Solson.). Managing Editor at Archie Comics (Red Circle Comics), artist/writer *Mighty Crusaders*, artist on numerous covers for Red Circle. Author of *How to Become a Comic Book Artist* and *How to Draw Super-Heroes* (trade paperbacks, Solson Publications). *Hybrids* (Continuity Comics).

Favorite comics not worked on: All Image titles and Milestone.

Dream comic-book project: Deathlok as he was originally conceived, as a man who battles against technology, while at the same time he is a product of that same technology — utilizing experimental narrative techniques and cinematic storytelling.

*David C*J Bunn*

✳ **David C*J Bunn.** P.O. Box 2452, Vernon, Connecticut 06066.

Born: December 9, 1953, in Hartford, Connecticut.

College or other education: Asnuntuck Community College.

Comics-related education: Worked on many publications for fun and experience.

Biggest creative influences: Bill Gaines, Jack Davis, Bob Kane, and Todd McFarlane.

1993 projects: *Midnite's Quickies* #1, *The Philistine* #1-6 (mini-series), *The Captain's Jolting Tales* #4 parts A and B, *The One Shot Press Sample Book* #1.

Past comics titles and related projects: *The Captain's Jolting Tales* #1-3. *The Cool Cat in the Hat.* Editorial cartoonist and strips for *The Asnuntuck News* with an editorial cartoon "Reagan Hood" being reprinted in *Overthrow*. Staff artist for *All About*, an arts newspaper. Also did monthly strip *Stanely*. Writer and Editor for *People's Press*, an alternative newspaper.

Favorite comics not worked on: *She-Hulk, Lobo, Spider-Man*, EC Comics, *Tales from the Crypt, Vault of Horror*, and *Haunt of Fear, Teenage Mutant Ninja Turtles, Spawn*, and *Savage Dragon*.

Dream comic-book project: The comic adaptation of *The Return of the Revenge of the Curse of the Ghost of the Evil of the Son of Frankenstein. Nocturnal Films*, available from One Shot Press.

✳ **Butch Burcham (F. Newton Burcham).** 2330 Edison Avenue, Granite City, Illinois 62040.

Agent: Terry Tidwell.

Born: April 3, 1952, in Madison, Illinois.

College or other education: Southern Illinois University-Edwardsville, Fine Arts major (no degree). Midwest School of Lettering and Design (Associates degree).

Comics-related education: A couple of private lessons under Dr. John A. Richardson (SIUE). Assistant to Tony DeZuniga.

Biggest creative influences: Frank Frazetta, N.C. Wyeth, Roy Krenkel, Wally Wood, Al Williamson, Jack Kirby, Steranko, J. Buscema, Robert E. Howard, Bernie Wrightson, Kaluta, and Jones.

1993 projects: I am currently in the process of illustrating and writing a graphic novel, *Apocalyp-*

tic Tribesmen, about New Age Indians.

Past comics titles and related projects: I have worked on *Savage Sword of Conan* and *Jonah Hex* as assistant inker to Tony DeZuniga, inked various issues of *Twilight Avenger, Miracle Squad, Seadragon, Green Hornet, Power Team, Liberator*, etc. Pencilled and inked *Fana the Jungle Girl, Star Rovers, Dark Wolf, Fist of God, Amazons, Erotic Orbits*, etc. Illustrated *Queen of the Black Coast* and *Conan World Book* for Steve Jackson Games.

Favorite comics not worked on: Anything illustrated by Bernie Wrightson, Kaluta, J. Jones, D. Stevens, or Mark Schultz.

Dream comic-book project: A book depicting the nobility of the native American illustrated in the modern classical style of Frank Frazetta.

Anthony Burcher

✳ **Anthony Burcher.** c/o *CBG* Editorial Department, 700 East State Street, Iola, Wisconsin 54990.

Born: November 4, 1959, in Yorktown, Virginia.

College or other education: B.A. in History from Christopher Newport University.

Biggest creative influences: Will Eisner.

1993 projects: Assistant Editor on *Who's Who of American Comic Books* and "Rubberstamp Parodies."

Past comics titles and related projects: *Rip Off Comix* #27, "Chiffon Manor," writer. *Barf*

#3, Revolutionary Comics, cartoons. An occasional cartoon for *CBG*.

Favorite comics not worked on: *Sandman* and *Cerebus*.

Dream comic-book project: 100 issues of *Chiffon Manor*.

✹ **Tim Burgard.** c/o *CBG* Editorial Department, 700 East State Street, Iola, Wisconsin 54990.

Born: October 5, 1957, in Long Beach, California.

College or other education: B.F.A. from Art Center College of Design, Pasadena, California.

Comics-related education: Work.

Biggest creative influences: Russ Manning, Frank Frazetta, Wally Wood, and Neal Adams.

1993 projects: I just signed a contract to ink four issues of *The Strangers* for Malibu's Ultraverse. Maybe my Tarzan two-parter will find a new publisher. Many other irons in the fire. Doing finishes over Mark Beachum for *Rose* mini-series from Heroic Publishing.

Past comics titles and related projects: Pacific Comics anthology stories, *Huntress* and *Sandman* back-ups for DC, Conan back-ups in *Savage Sword of Conan*, a fill-in *Infinity Inc.* issue between Don Newton and Todd McFarlane, wrote a science-fiction anthology story for Eclipse, first issue of *Whisper* for First, inked Rick Hoberg on *Eternity Smith*, and did a fill-in issue and back-up stories (writing and art), created "Indigo" for Heroic, redesigned Flare and drew first two issues and many covers (and some features). Part one of the two-part Tarzan series that's in limbo, along with an un-inked *Secret Origins* story at DC.

Favorite comics not worked on: *Sandman*.

Dream comic-book project: *Tarzan*. I just hope I get to finish it and you get to see it.

✹ **Fred Burke.** c/o *CBG* Editorial Department, 700 East State Street, Iola, Wisconsin 54990.

Born: January 9, 1965, in Austin, Texas.

College or other education: Bachelor of Journalism, University of Texas at Austin, 1986.

Fred Burke

Comics-related education: Eclipse Comics intern, 1985.

Biggest creative influences: Marv Wolfman, Chuck Dixon, Alan Moore, and Neil Gaiman in comics. Cat Yronwode and Louis Black in prose.

1993 projects: *Miracleman Triumphant, Aviator X, Hyperkind, Great and Secret Show, The Thief of Always, The Life of Death*, and *Morningstar*.

Past comics titles and related projects: *Phaze.* Eclipse editor — too many Eclipse titles to count, *Total Eclipse, Black Terror, Masked Man.* Viz manga co-translator — tons, including *2001 Nights, Xenon, Battle Angel Alita.* Adapter — *Tapping the Vein*, graphic albums. Author — *Clive Barker Illustrator* and upcoming sequel.

Favorite comics not worked on: *Sandman* and *The New Titans*.

Dream comic-book project: I'm lucky to be doing them now — and I look forward to more dreams in the future.

✹ **Kent Marshall Burles.** 2315 Bromsgrove Road, #93, Mississauga, Ontario, Canada L5J 4A6.

Kent Marshall Burles

Born: March 18, 1955, in Saskatoon, Saskatchewan, Canada.

College or other education: Diploma in Illustration (Sheridan College, Brampton, Ontario); Degree in Art History (McGill University, Montreal, Quebec).

Biggest creative influences: Started as a kid with Kirby and Ditko, then ran the gamut from Virgil Finlay to S. Clay Wilson, Hal Foster to Joe Coleman.

1993 projects: A short story for Heroic Publishing. Trying to land a novel adaptation with Dark Horse (*Far-Seer* by Rody J. Sawyer).

Past comics titles and related projects: Started in the black-and-white explosion working for Adventure Publications on *The Adventurers*, then moved with that title to Malibu, where I also worked on *Badaxe* (three issues) and *Planet of the Apes* (11 issues). In all, with *The Adventurers*, I did about 27 issues. At the same time, I worked on a six-part back-up feature in *Nexus* ("Judah the Hammer") and did some horror work for TSR. My latest project was the two-issue *Dr. Giggles* movie adaptation for Dark Horse, and I have just recently done some inking on some comics for the Toronto Blue Jays. (I have also done a couple of short stories for Heroic Publishing.)

Favorite comics not worked on: *Mr. Monster, New Two-Fisted Tales, Nexus*, and *The Spectre*.

Dream comic-book project: Bram Stoker's *Dracula*.

Nick Burns

✳ **Nick Burns.** P.O. Box 238, Rankin Inlet, NWT, Canada X0C 0G0.

Born: May 11, 1957, in Birmingham, England.

College or other education: Diploma in Fine Arts from the University of Manitoba.

Biggest creative influences: George Freeman and Joost Swarte.

1993 projects: *Safer Sex* comic for The Eastern Arctic and a graphic novel on animal rights.

Past comics titles and related projects: *Captain Canuck, Jack of Hearts, Charlton Bullseye, Arctic Comics, True North, Death Rattle*, and *Marvel Fanfare*.

Favorite comics not worked on: *Snake Eyes, Drawn and Quarterly, Rubber Blanket, Raw, Franka*, and *Eightball*.

Dream comic-book project: Detective graphic novel or autobiography or tabloid size comic.

✳ **John Buscema.** c/o *CBG* Editorial Department, 700 East State Street, Iola, Wisconsin 54990.

Born: December 11, 1927, in New York City, New York.

Biggest creative influences: Almost every artist around, past and present.

1993 projects: *Punisher.*

Past comics titles and related projects: *Conan, Thor, Fantastic Four, Spider-Man, Wolverine, Daredevil, Hulk, Avengers,* and others I can't remember.

Favorite comics not worked on: *Conan.*

Dream comic-book project: *Conan.*

Kurt Busiek

✳ **Kurt Busiek.** c/o *CBG* Editorial Department, 700 East State Street, Iola, Wisconsin 54990.

Agent: Mike Friedrich represents me on certain projects only.

Born: September 16, 1960, in Boston, Massachusetts.

College or other education: B.A. in English Literature from Syracuse University, Syracuse, New York.

Biggest creative influences: Milton Caniff, Jack Kirby, Steve Englehart, Leonard Starr, Walter Tevis, William Goldman, Edward Eager, and Archie Goodwin.

1993 projects: *Darkman, Marvels, Strange Tales, Teenagents, Elvira, What If?, Army of Darkness,* and some other stuff.

Past comics titles and related projects: *Green Lantern, Power Man and Iron Fist, Comics Feature, LoC, Justice League of America, Red Tornado, Marvel Age Magazine, Legend of Wonder*

Woman, Wonder Woman, World's Finest, Zot!, Liberty Project, Merchants of Death, Avengers Annual, Marvel Super Heroes, Open Space, Spectacular Spider-Man, Web of Spider-Man, What If?, Wonder Man Annual, Young Indiana Jones, Jell-O Man, Mickey Mouse, Miracleman: Apocrypha, Marvel Year in Review, Vampirella, and *Creepy.*

Favorite comics not worked on: Of all time: Caniff's *Terry and the Pirates,* Starr's *On Stage,* Lee and Kirby's *X-Men,* and Lee and Heck's *Iron Man.* More-or-less contemporary: *Crossfire, Zot!, Nexus, Ms. Tree,* and *Batman and The Outsiders.* Right now: *Sandman, Bone, Sin City,* and *Martian Manhunter: American Secrets.*

Dream comic-book project: Something I could create, co-own, and work on with talented collaborators. Or something with Hawkeye in it.

✳ **Jeffrey Butler.** c/o *CBG* Editorial Department, 700 East State Street, Iola, Wisconsin 54990.

Agent: Star*Reach Productions (Mike Friedrich).

Born: February 26, 1958, in Madison, Wisconsin.

College or other education: University of Wisconsin.

Biggest creative influences: Too many to list.

1993 projects: *Sting of the Green Hornet, Green Hornet: Dark Tomorrow* (covers for both series).

Past comics titles and related projects: *The Badger, The Green Hornet,* and *Marvel Super-Heroes Role-Playing Game.*

✳ **Nate Butler.** The Nate Butler Studio Inc., P.O. Box 27470, Albuquerque, New Mexico 87125-7470.

Born: February 1, 1954, in Meridien, Connecticut.

College or other education: On-the-job training in Graphic Design (received Master Printers of America Certificate of Craftmanship as a layout designer in 1979).

Comics-related education: One year of Famous Artists Correspondence Course back in 1973 or 1974.

Nate Butler

Biggest creative influences: Chester Gould, Steve Ditko, Walt Kelly, Jack Kirby, and Paul Murry.

1993 projects: Writer/editor/packager of the new Aida-Zee comics: *Aida-Zee* #2, *Behold 3-D* #1, and *Paro-Dee* #1.

Past comics titles and related projects: *Jughead, Hot Dog,* and other titles (Archie Comics) — writer/penciller/(and/or) inker. *Heathcliff, Muppet Babies* (Marvel/Star Comics) — writer/penciller. *Who's Who in the Legion* (DC Comics) — penciller. *Looney Tunes* and *Tiny Toons* magazines (DC Comics) — penciller/inker. *Mighty Mouse* (Spotlight Comics) — inker/cover artist. *Jetsons, Rocky and Bullwinkle,* and *Air Raiders* (Marvel Comics) — penciller/inker. Superman, Batman, Spider-Man, X-Men, Captain America (PCA Apparel) designer and/or artist.

Dream comic-book project: To co-write, ink, and color a *Dick Tracy* comic, plotted and pencilled by Steve Ditko.

✻ **Jack Butterworth.** 63 New Ocean Street, Swampscott, Massachusetts 01907.

Born: November 12, 1941, in Boston, Massachusetts.

College or other education: B.A. degree in English from Colgate University.

Biggest creative influences: Will Eisner and Al Feldstein.

1993 projects: *Taboo.*

Past comics titles and related projects: Warren Comics 1972-75, Eclipse's *Tales of Terror* and *Alien Encounters, Taboo* #1 and 7.

Favorite comics not worked on: Tom Sniegoski's *Vampirella* and anything by Alan Moore.

Dream comic-book project: A funny, realistic, cynical, violent super-hero graphic novel.

✻ **Sarah E. Byam.** 5140 A. Ballard Avenue NW, Suite A, Seattle, Washington 98107.

Born: February 9, 1962, in Indianapolis, Indiana.

College or other education: B.A. from Northern Michigan University, one year Fine Art at Center for Creative Studies, Wayne State University.

Comics-related education: Assistant to Mike Grell.

Biggest creative influences: Woody Allen, Spike Lee, Alice Walker, Maya Angelou, Louisa May Alcott, Mary Wolstonecraft Shelley, Frank Miller, DeMatteis, Alan Moore, and Los Bros. Hernandez.

1993 projects: *Elfquest: Hidden Years, Black Canary,* various Milestone books, *Colors in Black* (Dark Horse), and *Elfquest: New Blood* (Warp).

Past comics titles and related projects: *Billi 99* (Dark Horse), *Black Canary: New Wings* (DC), *Miracleman* (Eclipse), *Mists of Avalon* (Eclipse), *Aliens — DHC* (Dark Horse), *Little Women* (First), *Ponytailers* (Disney), *Captain Atom* (DC), and *Green Arrow Annual* #2 (DC).

Favorite comics not worked on: *Grendel, Rubber Blanket, Why I Hate Saturn, Moonshadow,* and *Electra.*

Dream comic-book project: *Elfquest, Daredevil,* and *Frankenstein.*

✻ **Reggie Byers.** J.Q. Productions, 1606 South Street, Philadelphia, Pennsylvania 19146.

Born: May 19, 1963, in Charlotte, North Carolina.

College or other education: Hussian School of Art, 1300 Arch Street, Philadelphia, Pennsylvania.

Biggest creative influences: Japanese manga and hip-hop graphitti art.

1993 projects: *Jam Quacky the Hip-Hop Duck, Hot 'n Tot,* and *Kidz of the King.*

Past comics titles and related projects: *Shuriken, Blade of Shuriken, Robotech: Macross, Robotech: Masters,* and *Robotech: New Generation.*

Favorite comics not worked on: *Bone, X-Men,* and *Spider-Man 2099.*

Dream comic-book project: *Spider-Man 2099.*

John Lindley Byrne

✳ **John Lindley Byrne.** Suite 103-917 Post Road, Fairfield, Connecticut 06430.

Born: July 6, 1950, in Walsall, England (but I was only born there: my residence in England was West Bromwich, Staffordshire).

College or other education: Alberta College

of Art (2½ years of 4). Degrees: 98.6 (Fahrenheit).

Comics-related education: On-the-job training.

Biggest creative influences: In roughly chronological order, remembering that there were no credits in the early days: Frank Hampson, Frank Bellamy, Bruce Harley and Don Cornwall, Carl Giles, "Bob Kane" (Dick Sprang), The Guy Who Draws Superman (Wayne Boring), The Other Guy Who Draws Superman (Curt Swan), Joe Kubert, Gil Kane, Jack Kirby, Steve Ditko, Neal Adams, John Buscema, Frank Miller, Serpieri, oh . . . *everybody*!!!

1993 projects: *John Byrne's Next Men,* writer, artist, letterer. *Aliens: Earth Angel,* writer, artist, letterer. *Mike Mignola's Hellboy,* scripter, letterer. *Penny Dredful,* writer, artist, letterer. *Elfquest,* co-plotter, inker.

Past comics titles and related projects: Charlton: *Wheelie and the Chopper Bunch, Doomsday + 1, Space: 1999,* and *Emergency!* Marvel: *Marvel Premiere: Iron Fist, The Champions, Marvel Team-Up, Marvel Chillers: Tigra, Uncanny X-Men, Fantastic Four, Incredible Hulk, Amazing Spider-Man, Spectacular Spider-Man, Avengers, West Coast Avengers, Starbrand, Sensational She-Hulk, Namor, Wolverine, Further Adventures of Indiana Jones, Marvel Spotlight, Ant-Man, Iron Man, Starlord, Superboxers* graphic novel, and about two hundred covers. DC: *Superman, Adventures of Superman, Action Comics, Green Lantern: Ganthet's Tale, OMAC, Legends, Power of the Atom, Batman,* and *Batman 3-D.* Dark Horse: *John Byrne's Next Men, Critical Error,* and *Mike Mignola's Hellboy.* Others: *Aliens: Earth Angel* and *Judge Dredd.*

Favorite comics not worked on: *Doctor Strange* and *Thor* are about the only titles I haven't done in which I have any interest.

Dream comic-book project: Someday I *will* finish the adaptation of Edmond Hamilton's *City at World's End.* Other than that — maybe She-Hulk skipping rope in the nude *without* the speed-lines.

✳ **William Byrne.** Graphic Image, P.O. Box 962, Station C, Kitchener, Ontario, Canada N2G 4E3.

William Byrne

David Campiti

Born: October 1, 1962, in Cambridge, Ontario, Canada.

Comics-related education: Took a four-week cartoon class at the YMCA and took a two-year art class at Open Door.

Biggest creative influences: Kevin Eastman, Richard Comely, Dave Sim, Steve Ditko, and George Pérez.

1993 projects: *Max Burger P.I.* #4-6, *The Mad 2992* (three-part mini-series), *H.E.L.P. International.*

Past comics titles and related projects: *Max Burger P.I.*

Favorite comics not worked on: *Cerebus, New Titans, Hulk, Spider-Man 2099, Yummy Fur,* and *Teenage Mutant Ninja Turtles.*

Dream comic-book project: My dream comic-book project would be a team-up with the Turtles and Max Burger.

✳ **David Campiti.** Glass House Graphics, 55 Joan Street, Suite 4, Wheeling, West Virginia 26003.

Born: May 9, 1958, in Pittsburgh, Pennsylvania.

College or other education: B.S., Communications, West Liberty State College.

Comics-related education: Editorial work at Sirius, Amazing, WonderColor, and Innovation, plus various management seminars.

Biggest creative influences: Stan Lee, Will Eisner, Alan Moore, Ray Bradbury, Robert A. Heinlein, Harlan Ellison, John Willie, and David Gerrold.

1993 projects: *Beauty and the Beast, Dark Shadows, The Prisoner, Lost in Space: Project Robinson,* and a "secret" super-hero project. Plus *Zamindar,* a movie we're co-developing.

Past comics titles and related projects: *Superman* for Julius Schwartz, *Greylore* for Sirius Comics, stories in *Vanguard Illustrated* and *Vanity* for Pacific Comics, *Ex-Mutants* for Eternity/Amazing/Malibu, as well as inventory stuff for Marvel, some ghost-written work at a couple of publishers, and such diverse Innovation projects as *Hero Alliance, Legends of the Stargrazers, Piers Anthony's On a Pale Horse, The Vampire Companion, Forbidden Planet,* and *Lost in Space.* Plus, a whole bunch of stuff for little companies, long since forgotten. I'm now working on a series of *Dark Shadows* novels, as well.

Favorite comics not worked on: *Rocketeer, Concrete, Uncle Scrooge* (by Barks or by Don Rosa), *Xenozoic Tales, The Spirit,* and anything by Adam Hughes.

Dream comic-book project: The original Captain Marvel.

✴ **Mark H. Campos.** P.O. Box 95234, Seattle, Washington 98145-2234.

Born: October 24, 1962, in Reno, Nevada.

Biggest creative influences: Don Martin, Dan O'Neill, Steve Willis, and Chester Carlson (inventor of the Xerox machine).

1993 projects: *Tümz: June One* (on sale mid-March); *Places That Are Gone* (working title); plus various short pieces.

Past comics titles and related projects: With Leonard Rifas: *AIDS News* (1988). Self-published: *El Mago Szabo!* (1990), *Bombast* (1992). Plus short pieces in *Itchy Planet, Gay Comix, Backlash, Cerebus Bi-Weekly, Hyena,* and *The Stranger.*

Favorite comics not worked on: Undergrounds, "new waves," and mini-comics.

If you could do your dream comic-book project, what would it be?: Financially plausible.

✴ **Gary Carlson.** 22 N. Union Street, Elgin, Illinois 60123.

Born: June 21, 1957, in Iron Mountain, Michigan.

College or other education: B.A. from Columbia College, Chicago, Illinois.

Comics-related education: John Fischetti Scholarship at Columbia — worked toward a Masters in Political Cartooning.

Biggest creative influences: Jim Shooter's 1960s DC work, Erik Larsen, and Alan Moore.

1993 projects: *Vanguard* for Image Comics; *Berzerker* for Caliber Press; *Big Bang Comics* and *Knight Watchman* for Caliber.

Past comics titles and related projects: I wrote and published *Megaton* #1-8 between 1983 and 1987 (Megaton). Published *Ramm* # 1 and 2 and *Wildman* #1 and 2 (all Megaton). Wrote for *Battle-Axe Magazine* #1 in 1989.

Favorite comics not worked on: *Savage Dragon* and *Legion of Super-Heroes.*

Dream comic-book project: Kirby's *New Gods* or Guardian.

✴ **Randy Carpenter.** Not Available Comics, 3867 Briston, Detroit, Michigan 48212.

Born: April 24, 1965, in Ada, Oklahoma.

Biggest creative influences: Dr. Seuss, Jean Bethell and Ruth Wood, Jerry West, Walter R. Brooks, John Irving, and Kurt Vonnegut.

1993 projects: *Tales of Desolation.*

✴ **Sandy Carruthers.** 123 Kensington Road, Parkdale, Prince Edward Island, Canada C1A 5J6.

Born: May 11, 1962, in Halifax, Nova Scotia, Canada.

College or other education: Two years, Design — Holland College, Prince Edward Island. One year, Illustration — Sheridan College, Ontario.

Biggest creative influences: Joe Kubert, John Byrne, Allan Davis, and Paul Neary.

1993 projects: "Eterna-Teens" for *Aida-Zee Comics* (Nate Butler Studios). Currently looking for new stuff.

Past comics titles and related projects: *Alien Nation: Public Enemy, Men in Black* #1-6, and *Invaders from Mars* #1-6 (all Malibu); "Sam Sundae — Peculiar Investigator" in *Paro-Dee* (Nate Butler Studios); *Solo Ex-Mutants* (one-shot), *Monster Frat House,* and *Headless Horseman* (two issues) (all for Eternity). *Shattered Earth* series.

Favorite comics not worked on: *Excaliber, Spider-Man, Batman,* and *Daredevil.*

Dream comic-book project: A Wolverine series — his Canadian days.

✴ **Paul Castiglia.** Cartoon Guise, P.O. Box 165, Pompton Plains, New Jersey 07444-1680 or Archie Comic Publications Inc., 325 Fayette Avenue, Mamaroneck, New York 10543.

Born: February 7, 1966, in Passaic, New Jersey.

College or other education: School of Visual Arts — Bachelor of Fine Arts. Major: Media: Animation/Cartooning.

Comics-related education: See above. Also, Saturday and night classes at Joe Kubert School.

Biggest creative influences: Jack Cole, Tex Avery, and Jay Ward.

1993 projects: *Conservation Corps, Teenage Mutant Ninja Turtles.*

Past comics titles and related projects: *Cracked, Looney Tunes, Archie, Archie 3000, Little Archie.*

Favorite comics not worked on: Jack Cole's original *Plastic Man* stories, *Concrete,* and *Bone.*

Dream comic-book project: *Plastic Man*; original graphic novel concept: *Liberace Smile*™.

✳ Mort Castle. c/o *CBG* Editorial Department, 700 East State Street, Iola, Wisconsin 54990.

Agent: Matt Jorgensen/Action-Dystel-Leone & Jaffee Agency.

Born: July 8, 1946, in Chicago, Illinois.

College or other education: B.S.E., 1968, at Illinois State University.

Biggest creative influences: Poets Bill Wantling and Lucien Stryk.

1993 projects: Only spec for now.

Past comics titles and related projects: Editor: *Horror; Illustrated Book of Fears, Rex Miller's Chaingang,* both Northstar; *J.N. Williamson's Masques,* Innovation. Writer: *Night City* with Mark Nelson; *Buzz Mason* with Gary Anaro; *Leatherface* with Kirk Jarvinen and Guy Burwell; *Monolith* with Mitch Byrd; *Masques*; and a story in *The Further Adventures of Batman* Vol. III.

Favorite comics not worked on: *Kings in Disguise* and *Omaha, the Cat Dancer.*

Dream comic-book project: To have *Masques* in the hands of a company that knew how to sell it.

✳ Sandra Chang. 2245 East Colorado Boulevard, #104, Pasadena, California 91107.

Agent: Dan Cominsky.

Born: July 10, 1964, in Kingston, New York.

College or other education: B.A. at Columbia College, New York. Major: Computer Science.

Biggest creative influences: Mark Beachum, Frank Frazetta, Bruce Lee, Jimi Hendrix, James Dean, and Michael Jackson.

1993 projects: *Achilles Storm* series.

Past comics titles and related projects: Aja Blue's *Achilles Storm/Razmataz* #1-4; Kardia

Sandra Chang

Comics' *Ho Sung Pak* #1; pin-ups for Marvel's *Hellraiser*; DC's *Impact Winter Special* (pencils, seven pages); Now Comics' *Twilight Zone* #4 (pencils); covers for *Kato* #3 and 4, *Twilight Zone* #11, *Twilight Zone 3-D Special* #1, *Twilight Zone Sci-Fi Special* #1, *Green Hornet* #12 and 18 (pencils for cover); cover for Martyr Press' *Temptress* #1, and a portfolio for Annubis Press.

Favorite comics not worked on: Simon Bisley's *Lobo,* anything by Mark Beachum or Frank Frazetta, Jim O'Barr's *Crow, Crying Freeman,* and Chinese kung fu comics.

Dream comic-book project: To do a comic book with Michael Jackson using his likeness as the protagonist.

✳ Howard Chaykin. c/o *CBG* Editorial Department, 700 East State Street, Iola, Wisconsin 54990.

Agent: Harris Miller.

Born: October 7, 1950, in Newark, New Jersey.

College or other education: Precious little.

Comics-related education: Assisted Gil Kane, Wallace Wood, Gray Morrow, and Neal Adams.

Biggest creative influences: Alex Toth,

Wallace Wood, Gil Kane, Harvey Kurtzman, and Bernard Krigstein.

1993 projects: *Midnight Men* (Marvel), *Power and Glory* (Malibu), and *Deco Batman*.

Past comics titles and related projects: *American Flagg!, Time², Blackhawk, Shadow, Black Kiss*, etc.

✳ **Michael Cherkas.** 108 Greenlaw Avenue, Toronto, Ontario, Canada M6H 3V5.

Born: December 17, 1954, in Oshawa, Ontario, Canada.

College or other education: Ontario College of Art (1975-79), four-year diploma (A.O.C.A.).

Biggest creative influences: Curt Swan, Harvey Kurtzman, Joseph Stalin, Senator Joseph McCarthy, The Cold War, and Philip K. Dick.

1993 projects: A new *New Frontier* mini-series planned for release in late '94 or early '95 and a super-hero series with D. Larry Hancock that should be out during '93.

Past comics titles and related projects: Co-creator/artist on: *The New Frontier* — three issue mini-series published by Dark Horse in late 1992 (originally published in *Heavy Metal*). *Suburban Nightmares* — four-issue mini-series published by Renegade Press in the summer of 1988 — collected into a graphic album by NBM. *The Silent Invasion* — 12-issue series published by Renegade Press from 1986-88. Later collected into four graphic albums by NBM.

Favorite comics not worked on: Too many to mention, so I don't know where to begin.

✳ **D.G. Chichester.** c/o *CBG* Editorial Department, 700 East State Street, Iola, Wisconsin 54990.

Born: August 22, 1964, in Stamford, Connecticut.

College or other education: New York University, Tisch School of the Arts, B.A. in Film and TV.

Comics-related education: Collected comics until age of 13. Marvel Editorial Assistant (read: gofer), Epic Assistant Editor.

Biggest creative influences: Rod Serling, Stephen King, Joseph Campbell, and Wile E. Coyote.

D.G. Chichester

1993 projects: *Daredevil* "Fall from Grace" storyline, "Pinhead" *Hellraiser* comic, and *Mars Attacks*.

Past comics titles and related projects: Editor: *Groo, Marshal Law, Stray Toasters, Blood, Nightbreed, Hellraiser*. Writer: *Dr. Zero, Powerline, St. George, Blood and Glory* (co-written with Margaret Clark), *Hellraiser, Nightbreed, Jihad, Punisher/Black Widow: Spinning Doomsday's Web, Wolverine: Inner Fury, S.H.I.E.L.D., Terror Inc., Nightstalkers, Primal, An American Tail: Fievel Goes West*, and *Daredevil*.

Favorite comics not worked on: *Sandman* and *Ghost Rider*.

Dream comic-book project: A revisionist look at vampirism.

✳ **Don Chin.** 2253 Ohio Street, Eureka, California 95501.

Born: October 19, 1963, in Eureka, California.

College or other education: B.A. in Journalism from Humboldt State University.

Comics-related education: Editorial cartoonist.

Biggest creative influences: Jack Kirby, John Byrne, Frank Miller, Michael Golden, Jim

Starlin, Bernie Wrightson, *Mad* magazine, and Jesus Christ.

1993 projects: *Death of Stupidman, Bloodyhot, Wildsteer, X-O-X: Man O'Romance, Zen Intergalactic Ninja, Enchanter, Rank and Stinky, Deathdate #1, Stygmata #0, Enchanter: Prelude to Apocalypse, Young Zen* mini-series, *Paro-Dee,* and editing/publishing many Parody Press comics.

Past comics titles and related projects: *X-Farce, Adolescent Radioactive Black Belt Hamsters, Meadow Lark, Pummeler, Cable TV, Yawn, Oldblood, The Sewage Dragoon, Spinelessman: $2099, Arrowman, Yawn, Stupidman, Target: Airboy, Bloodyhot, Oldblood, Overload, Freak-Out on Infant Earths, Megaton, Laffin' Gas, Enchanter* (Eclipse), *Cracked, Petworks vs. WildK.A.T.S. #1,* and miscellaneous spoof comic books by Parody Press.

Favorite comics not worked on: *Sam and Max, The Ren & Stimpy Show, Nexus, The Badger, Teenage Mutant Ninja Turtles, X-O Manowar, Calvin and Hobbes,* and anything by Mike Baron.

Dream comic-book project: An elaborate crossover with popular humorous comic-book characters like *Secret Wars.*

Bruce Chrislip

✳ **Bruce Chrislip.** 8057 13th Avenue, NW, Seattle, Washington 98117.

Born: November 10, 1954, in Youngstown, Ohio.

College or other education: Youngstown State University, Bachelor of Fine Arts, 1978.

Comics-related education: Took one car-

tooning class at Xavier University — taught the class the following quarter.

Biggest creative influences: Jay Ward, Milt Gross, *Mad,* Steve Willis, Kirby monster comics circa 1961, and Bob Clampett.

1993 projects: *Paper Tales* (solo comic book), collaborations with Steve Willis and Mark Campos, looking into anthology comics project, and writing for Bob Vojtko.

Past comics titles and related projects: Aardvark-Vanaheim: *Cerebus Bi-Weekly #12, Cerebus High Society #8, #16, Cerebus Church and State #11, 21, 29.* Eclipse: *Giant-Size Mini Comics #4.* Kitchen Sink: *Images of Omaha #1.* Starhead Comics: co-publisher and editor 1986-87. Gag cartoons in national magazines and newspapers 1986 to present.

Favorite comics not worked on: *Unsupervised Existence, Big Mouth,* comics by Steve Willis and Mark Campos.

Dream comic-book project: Just a well-written humor comic because they're so rare.

✳ **Kirk Chritton.** 601 Clinkscales, Columbia, Missouri 65203.

Born: August 20, 1964, in Mountain View, Missouri.

College or other education: Central Missouri State University, Warrensburg, Missouri.

Biggest creative influences: Stan Lee, Jack Kirby, Steve Ditko, Steve Englehart, Gene Day, and Dave Sim.

1993 projects: Two untitled projects.

Past comics titles and related projects: *Velvet* (writer) Adventure Comics, *Dai Kamikaze!* (writer) Now Comics, *Comics Career Newsletter* (editor-publisher).

Favorite comics not worked on: *Sandman, Cerebus,* and *Zot!*

Dream comic-book project: If I only knew.

✳ **Randy Clark.** c/o Steve Donnelly, Creative Interests Agency, 106 South B Street, San Mateo, California 94401.

Born: November 13, 1963, in Albuquerque, New Mexico.

College or other education: Had a community college course in Graphic Design. (Does that count?)

Comics-related education: Assistant animator at Bandelier Films Inc. (inbetweens), painted and inked a lot of cels. Nate Butler's assistant.

Biggest creative influences: Dave Stevens, Steve Rude, Marc Davis, Nate Butler, and Bernie Wrightson.

1993 projects: Majestic's *1993 Future Stars* trading cards and even more Muppet coloring books.

Past comics titles and related projects: As inker: *Nexus, Badger, Dreadstar* for First; *Parts Unknown* for Eclipse; tons of inks for *Muppet Babies* coloring books. Various pencils/inks and odds and ends for Last Gasp and Fantagraphics. Also spent a lot of hard time in the ad biz.

Favorite comics not worked on: *Reid Fleming, Love and Rockets*, and the usual long-john stuff.

Dream comic-book project: A Wonder Woman graphic novel.

✳ **Mickey Allen Clausen.** 2478 Nielsen, El Cajon, California 92020.

Born: July 8, 1955, in Jamaica, New York.

College or other education: Platt College (Computer Graphic Design).

Comics-related education: An airbrush class, self-taught.

Biggest creative influences: Byrne, Art Adams, John Romita Jr., Marc Silvestri, and Whilce Portacio.

1993 projects: Lettering and art retouching on *Raika, High School Agent*, and *Ragnarok Guy* for Sun Comics. Cover art for *Ripley's Believe It or Not Comics*.

Past comics titles and related projects: Cover colorist for Blackthorne Publishing: *G.I. Joe 3-D, Bravestarr 3-D, BattleBeasts 3-D, Transformers 3-D*, etc. Cover colorist for Greater Mercury Comics: *Grips, Edge, Legion X,* and *Legion X II*. Inker for Personality Comics: *Patrick Ewing*.

Favorite comics not worked on: *Captain America* and *Darkstars*.

Dream comic-book project: To work on *Captain America*.

✳ **Brian Clopper.** 10055 Vista Court, Myersville, Maryland 21773.

Brian Clopper

Born: September 6, 1967, in Hagerstown, Maryland.

College or other education: University of Maryland, Bachelor of Science in Advertising Design.

Biggest creative influences: Mark Wheatley, Marc Hempel, Michael Golden, Evan Dorkin, and Steve Purcell.

1993 projects: *Wingnut and Fidget: Intergalactic Bounty Hunters* (one-shot).

Past comics titles and related projects: *Partners in Pandemonium* — three issues — Caliber Press. *The Crow's Nest* — *Comics Buyer's Guide*. Pin-ups in the 1992 and 1993 *Amazing Heroes Swimsuit Issues*. Double-page spread in Marvel's *Look and Find Spider-Man*.

Favorite comics not worked on: *Sandman, Milk & Cheese, Sam and Max, Bone,* and *Xenozoic Tales*.

Dream comic-book project: A bi-monthly humor comic featuring a variety of my characters.

✳ **John R. Cochran.** P.O. Box 242, Planetarium Station, New York, New York 10024-0242.

Born: March 15, 1943, in New York City.

College or other education: Villanova University, Masters in Theatre.

Biggest creative influences: Chester Gould,

Lee Falk, Wilson McCoy, Bill Finger, C.C. Beck, and Bob Kane.

1993 projects: None at present.

Past comics titles and related projects: Editorial Director, *Creepy, Eerie,* and *Vampirella. Grave Tales,* Gladstone. *Comics Journal, Inside Comics.*

Dream comic-book project: *The Shazam! Archives.*

Michael Cohen

✳ **Michael Cohen.** 2130 Williams, #3, Bellingham, Washington 98225.

Born: August 31, 1954, in New York, New York.

College or other education: Western Washington University, B.A. in Computer/Art.

Comics-related education: Cartooning course at Western Washington University.

Biggest creative influences: Jaime Hernandez, Barry Windsor-Smith, Matt Wagner, Al Williamson, and Mark Schultz.

1993 projects: *Strange Attractors* #2, "Tolsalia," short story with Michael O'Connel. Writer on *Necromancer.* Poison Elves short story for inclusion in *Poison Elves Annual.*

Past comics titles and related projects: *Strange Attractors* #1 — self-published in collaboration with Mark Sherman.

Favorite comics not worked on: *Madman, Xenozoic Tales, Love and Rockets, Sandman,* and *Eightball.*

✳ **Eugene Colan.** c/o *CBG* Editorial Department, 700 East State Street, Iola, Wisconsin 54990.

Born: September 1, 1926, in New York City.

College or other education: Art Students League.

Comics-related education: My "education" came from fanatically practicing my craft as well as working at Timely Press, Marvel, DC, and Warren Publications.

Biggest creative influences: Milton Caniff, Harold Foster, Will Eisner, Syd Shores, film/ movies, and music.

1993 projects: *Harrowers* by Clive Barker for Marvel.

Past comics titles and related projects: *Daredevil, Iron Man, Doctor Strange, Dracula, Captain Marvel, Captain America,* and on and on.

Dream comic-book project: Written and drawn by me, but I never have the time.

✳ **Max Allan Collins.** M.A.C. Productions, 301 Fairview Avenue, Muscatine, Iowa 52701.

Agent: Dominick Abel.

Born: March 3, 1948, in Muscatine, Iowa.

College or other education: Muscatine Community College, A. of A., 1968; University of Iowa, B.A. (1970), M.F.A. (1973).

Biggest creative influences: Mickey Spillane, Dashiell Hammett, Raymond Chandler, Will Eisner, Johnny Craig, Al Capp, Chester Gould, and Jack Webb.

1993 projects: *Johnny Dynamite* mini-series for Dark Horse and *Ms. Tree* ongoing projects at DC.

Past comics titles and related projects: All as writer: *Dick Tracy* comic strip 1977-1993, TMS. DC: *Batman* comic book and syndicated strip, *Wild Dog* mini-series, and others. *Ms. Tree* comic book since 1981, various publishers. *Mike Mist* feature, various publishers.

Favorite comics not worked on: Only classics: *Lone Wolf and Cub*, *Li'l Abner*, Segar *Popeye*, etc.

Dream comic-book project: Adapting Mickey Spillane's *Mike Hammer*.

Steve Collins

✳ **Steve Collins.** c/o *CBG* Editorial Department, 700 East State Street, Iola, Wisconsin 54990.

Agent: Angie Glasby.

Born: October 26, 1954, in Tawas City, Michigan.

Comics-related education: Coursework in commercial art.

Biggest creative influences: Dick Sprang, my mentor.

1993 projects: Inking for DC comics on Warner Bros. *Looney Tunes* and *Tiny Toons*. In process of beginning to work on Disney characters for Gladstone Publications.

Past comics titles and related projects: Inking only: *Charles Barkley* — Personality Comics; *Tiny Toon Adventures* and *Looney Tunes* — DC Comics.

Favorite comics not worked on: *Batman* and *Spider-Man*.

Dream comic-book project: A long-term, never-ending, successful comic book.

✳ **Terry Collins.** 1449 Edgewood Drive, Mount Airy, North Carolina 27030.

Born: June 11, 1967, in Mount Airy, North Carolina.

Terry Collins

College or other education: B.A. in English/ Writing and Media Communications from High Point University, High Point, North Carolina. Graduated Cum Laude with honors.

Biggest creative influences: Sylvia Plath, Warner Bros. cartoons, Harlan Ellison, 1960s television, Lee, Kirby, Ditko, *Mystery Science Theater 3000, Doonesbury*, John D. MacDonald, pulp magazines, 1979-85 New Wave bands, and Ray Bradbury.

1993 projects: *Elfquest: New Blood, Tiny Toon Adventures, Looney Tunes*, Anne Rice's *The Witching Hour, The Man from U.N.C.L.E.*, and Larry Niven's *Lucifer's Hammer*.

Past comics titles and related projects: *Doc Savage, Jughead, Lost in Space*, H.P. Lovecraft's *Cthulhu, Quantum Leap*, and *What The--?!*.

Favorite comics not worked on: *Doom Patrol, Zot!, Milk & Cheese, Cerebus, Concrete, Miracleman*, and *Sam and Max: Freelance Police*.

Dream comic-book project: Created by me, it would be *Necromancer: Season of the Witch*. This is the mini-series that got me started in the business but for reasons beyond my control never was published. As for a licensed book, I'd love to do *Twin Peaks* and wrap up all the loose ends.

✳ **Tim Conrad.** 709 W. Vandeveer, Taylorville, Illinois 62568.

Agent: Star*Reach (Sharon Cho).

Born: February 3, 1951, in Springfield, Illinois.

College or other education: B.A. English.

Comics-related education: Self-taught.

Biggest creative influences: Hal Foster, Alex Raymond, Hogarth, B. Smith, Wrightson, Kaluta, Adams, Steranko, Michelangelo, Dali, etc.

1993 projects: *Savage Sword of Conan* (covers).

Past comics titles and related projects: *Almuric, Conan, Toadswart, Epic Illustrated, etc.* (the mini-series), Clive Barker adaptations, and *Hunchback of Notre Dame* (unfinished).

Dream comic-book project: An adaptation of *The Cabinet of Dr. Caligari.*

Anna-Maria B. Cool

✳ **Anna-Maria B. Cool.** 5813 Riley, Overland Park, Kansas 66202.

Born: August 22, 1956, in Harrisburg, Pennsylvania.

College or other education: Attended Moore College of Art, Philadelphia, Pennsylvania.

Comics-related education: Joe Kubert School graduate.

Biggest creative influences: Gene Colan, Marie Severin, Frank Brunner, Byrne/Austin, Frank Thorne, Japanese animation, and Kate Bush.

1993 projects: Pencilling *Barbie* and *Barbie Fashion* for Marvel and a possible mini-series for an independent publisher.

Past comics titles and related projects: Pencils on: one of the Marvel Star Comics (two issues), *Hook* (12 pages), and *Barbie* and *Barbie Fashion* since 1990.

Favorite comics not worked on: *Doctor Strange, Sandman,* and *Sensational She-Hulk.*

Dream comic-book project: A horror/fantasy/myth/romance with a dark anti-hero or heroine.

✳ **Matthew Costello.** 15 Cottage Place, Katonah, New York 10536.

Agent: Star*Reach.

Born: September 19, 1948, in Brooklyn, New York.

College or other education: B.S. R.P.I., graduate work, Columbia.

Comics-related education: Bought five 10¢ comics a week circa 1961.

Biggest creative influences: Ellison, Bradbury, Lovecraft, and Kurtzman.

1993 projects: Multimedia (CD-ROM) for Marvel licensee.

Past comics titles and related projects: *Baron Munchausen* (Now), *Fright Night* (Now), *Open Space* (Marvel), *Hollywood Kids* (Disney), *Child's Play* (novels # 2 and 3), *FTL News* for Sci-Fi Channel, and *7th Guest* (Virgin Software, script).

Favorite comics not worked on: *The Thing.*

Dream comic-book project: A good time-travel series.

✳ **Randy H. Crawford.** Nice Day Comix, 911 Park Street SW, Grand Rapids, Michigan 49504-6241.

Randy H. Crawford

Born: January 16, 1953, in Grand Rapids, Michigan.

College or other education: Life drawing and painting classes at Grand Rapids Junior College.

Comics-related education: Self-taught (from age 7).

Biggest creative influences: "I decided to create the kind of comics I would enjoy reading myself." — Stan Lee.

1993 projects: *Three Pals* (digest), *I Love Cat-Girls III* (mini-comic), *Whatever Happened to The Vindicators?* (novel), *Between the Covers* (comics shop newsletter).

Past comics titles and related projects: *XXXenophile* #3 (three pages inks) Palliard Press, *Goodies* #84 (eight-page story, script and pencils) Jabberwocky Graphics, *Goodies* #70, 71, 75, and 79 (single-page drawings) Jabberwocky Graphics, *Olivia* #4 (16 pages, pencils, inks, and lettering) Five Star Comics, *Amazing Heroes Swimsuit Issue* 1991 and 1992 (four cartoons in each) Fantagraphics, and "Off the Rack" (comic-book review column in *Music Revue* 1989-90).

Favorite comics not worked on: *Omaha, Ms. Tree, Concrete, Hellblazer, Barbarienne, Naughty Bits*, and *Flaming Carrot*.

Dream comic-book project: My self-published *Nice Day Mini-Comix* allows me total freedom to write and draw anything I want. I can't imagine a better deal (short of making it profitable). I still have a nagging childhood wish to do something for Marvel sometime. Currently, any paying job would be great.

Steven S. Crompton

✳ **Steven S. Crompton.** P.O. Box 30747, Phoenix, Arizona 85046.

Born: July 17, 1962, in Kingston, Ontario, Canada.

Biggest creative influences: 1950s *Mad* magazines, Gustave Doré engravings, and 1960s DC comics.

1993 projects: Eric Clapton bio for Revolutionary Comics, *Dark Destiny* (48 pages) for Alpha Productions, *Demi the Demoness* #1 and 2 for Rip Off Press, and *Heavy Metal Monsters 3-D* for Ray Zone.

Past comics titles and related projects: *Elves of Lejentia* #1-3 and *Traps Lite/Grimtooth Comic* both for Flying Buffalo . Ross Perot biography, *Psychoman* #1, *Starjam* #6: Luke Perry, 1st edition *Demi the Demoness* (all for Revolutionary Comics).

Favorite comics not worked on: Batman (any title), *Doctor Strange, The Spectre, Metal Men,* and *Metamorpho*.

Dream comic-book project: I would love to be the inker when DC brings back The Inferior Five.

✳ **Howard Cruse.** P.O. Box 8223, Junction Boulevard Station, Flushing, New York 11372-9997.

© 1989 Tim J. Luddy

Howard Cruse

Agent: Mike Friedrich/Star*Reach Productions.

Born: May 2, 1944, in Birmingham, Alabama.

College or other education: B.A., Birmingham-Southern College (graduated 1968). One term graduate school, Penn State University.

Comics-related education: Famous Artists Cartooning Course, 1960-63.

Biggest creative influences: Al Capp, Milton Caniff, Crockett Johnson, Walt Kelly, John Stanley, Robert Crumb, Aline Kominsky, and lots of others.

1993 projects: Graphic novel for Piranha Press (1994 publication date).

Past comics titles and related projects: *Commies from Mars, Snarf, Bizarre Sex, Dope Comix, Comix Book, Gay Comix, Anything Goes,* and *Barefootz Funnies.* Book collections: *Wendel, Dancin' Nekkid with the Angels, Wendel on the Rebound,* and

Early Barefootz. Comic strips for publication: *Barefootz, Wendel, Count Fangor,* and *Doctor Duck.* Various special strips for *The Village Voice, Heavy Metal, Artforum International,* and *Starlog.*

Favorite comics not worked on: *Little Lulu* in the Fifties and *Naughty Bits* today.

Dream comic-book project: Books such as the one I'm doing now, plus most of my past projects — except for bigger audiences and better pay.

Paul Curtis

✴ **Paul Curtis.** Marvel Entertainment Group Inc., 387 Park Avenue South, New York, New York 10016.

Born: May 15, 1958, in Meadville, Pennsylvania.

College or other education: B.A. in English, Allegheny College, Meadville, Pennsylvania.

Comics-related education: Self-publisher.

Biggest creative influences: Carl Barks, Archie Goodwin, Stan Lee, and Bill Gaines.

1993 projects: *WAM Newsline* (ongoing), Punisher story — not sure where it will appear.

Past comics titles and related projects: *Micro-Comics:* publisher, artist, writer. *SPG 3-D:* publisher/artist of 3-D minicomic. *Mr. Doom:* creator/scripter. Mike Baron's *Group Larue #2:* script. *What The--?! #24:* script.

Favorite comics not worked on: *Groo, Yummy Fur, Sandman, The Spirit, Omaha, Zot!, Uncle Scrooge,* and *Little Lulu.*

Dream comic-book project: *Spider-Man.*

✳ **Dan Danko.** Malibu Comics, 5321 Sterling Center Drive, Westlake, California 91361.

Born: September 30, 1966, in Los Angeles, California.

College or other education: B.A. in Creative Writing.

Comics-related education: Senior Editor of Malibu Comics.

Biggest creative influences: Jack Kirby, Dave Sim, Howard Chaykin, and Grant Morrison.

1993 projects: *Warstrike* (for Ultraverse) and *Man of War*.

Past comics titles and related projects: Co-creator of the Ultraverse and a ton of other stuff from Malibu over the last five years.

Favorite comics not worked on: *Cerebus*.

Dream comic-book project: Anything with the previously mentioned influences.

✳ **David Darrigo.** 25½ Chatham Street, Brantford, Ontario, Canada N3T 2N7.

Born: November 1, 1954, in Toronto, Ontario, Canada.

Comics-related education: Retailer (manager) of comics shop for 10 years. Assistant editor for Dragon Lady Press.

Biggest creative influences: Jim Steranko, Stan Lee, Hergé, Will Eisner, William Messner-Loebs, Gilbert Hernandez, and pulp and mystery authors.

Past comics titles and related projects: *Wordsmith* (Renegade Press, collected by Caliber Press), *Tony Bravado* (Renegade/Special Studio). Special Studio: *Piranha Is Loose* and *Black Scorpion*. *Green Hornet* (Now Comics), *Amazing Heroes* (Fantagraphics), and *The Detectives* (Alpha Productions).

Favorite comics not worked on: *Xenozoic Tales, Shadow Strikes!, 1963, Vietnam Journal,* and *Sandman Mystery Theatre*.

Dream comic-book project: A graphic novel series about a Mountie, done *Prince Valiant* style.

✳ **Debbie David.** St. Eve Productions, P.O. Box 1609, Madison Square Station, New York, New York 10159-1609.

Born: May 2, 1959, in New Orleans, Louisiana.

College or other education: Two years Cal Arts Disney Character Animation Program (one year Disney Fellowship, one year Disney Scholarship); one year New York University Advanced Animation and one year New York University Cinema History.

Comics-related education: High School of Art and Design, New York City; Cal Arts (see above). Training included: figure drawing and anatomy, design, composition, and character design.

Biggest creative influences: Brian Bolland, Gene Colan, Milo Minara, Steve Ditko, Go Nagai, Ishinomori Shotaro, John Romita Sr., and James Flagg.

1993 projects: *Heart and Soul* one-shot in *Bevson Funraiser* #2 and *Captain Zircon*, both for Bevson Enterprises. Pin-up and assistant inker for *Billy Joe Van Helsing* (Alpha). Art on *Ramen Rider* for Antarctic Press. I've been doing freelance color work for Defiant since April. Projects include *Splatterball*, a 12-page comic-book insert to be included with *Plasm* #0 binders.

Past comics titles and related projects: *Odd* series published in *Panorama* #1 and 2 in 1991. *Ramen Rider* solo one-shot (art only) in *Ninja High School Yearbook 1991*.

Favorite comics not worked on: *Sandman, Cages, Flaming Carrot, Archer & Armstrong, Incredible Hulk, Wolverine, Concrete,* and *Madman*.

Dream comic-book project: To draw a full-color *Doctor Strange* graphic novel written by a hot writer and to ink Gene Colan on *Odd* series.

✳ **Peter David.** To Be Continued . . . Inc., P.O. Box 239, Bayport, New York 11705.

Born: September 23, 1956, in Fort Meade, Maryland.

College or other education: New York University, B.A. in Journalism.

Comics-related education: Assistant Direct Sales Manager; Sales Manager.

Biggest creative influences: Edgar Rice Burroughs, Harlan Ellison, Myra David, Stan Lee, Stephen King, Chuck Jones, and Alfred Hitchcock.

Peter David

1993 projects: *Incredible Hulk, Spider-Man 2099, Aquaman, Soulsearchers and Company, Sachs and Violens, Tales to Astonish, Atlantis Chronicles* trade paperback, and a *Lost in Space* one-shot.

Past comics titles and related projects: All three good Spider-Man titles, *Marc Hazzard: Merc, Justice, Star Trek, Dreadstar, The Phantom, X-Factor, Rahne of Terra, Wolverine, Action Comics Weekly, Marvel Comics Presents, Little Mermaid, Sebastian, Roger Rabbit, Blasters, Creepy,* and *Classics Illustrated.*

Favorite comics not worked on: *Sandman, Cerebus, Groo,* and *Barbie.*

Dream comic-book project: Comics adaptation of Oscar-winning film I wrote.

✱ **Dan Davis.** 212 Jon Street, Mendon, Ohio 45862.

Born: September 18, 1957, in Celina, Ohio.

College or other education: B.S. in Visual Communications from Bowling Green State University.

Comics-related education: Assistant to Dan Adkins, 1974-75.

Biggest creative influences: V.T. Hamlin, Hergé, and Jim Steranko.

1993 projects: Inks on: *Green Lantern Annual* #2 (DC), *Barb Wire* and *The Thing from Another World* (both Dark Horse).

Past comics titles and related projects: Inks on: *Flash Annual* #5, *Showcase '93* #1-6, and *X* in *Dark Horse Comics* #7-9.

✱ **Gary Davis.** c/o *CBG* Editorial Department, 700 East State Street, Iola, Wisconsin 54990.

Biggest creative influences: EC Comics of the Fifties, Hal Foster, Albrecht Dürer (16th Century German artist), and others.

1993 projects: Currently working on *Paleolove* for *Dark Horse Presents* (Dark Horse Comics), script, art, etc. Two other *Paleolove* stories have been done to date for *DHP.*

Past comics titles and related projects: (*Nil-Gish* in *Heavy Metal,* 1981); (*Paleolove, Twilight of Langdarro, Delia and Celia,* and *Spacehawk* (with J. Prosser), all for Dark Horse); (*The Starvoyager Collection* (two issues) self-published); (*Bad Badgers,* published as *Warworld,* one-shot, Dark Horse); and (*Sharrin — Wavemakers* # 2, Blind Bat Press, Canada).

Dream comic-book project: *The Iliad,* Homer, *The Gospels* (Life of Christ), and a number of original science-fiction themes I've developed myself of the epic variety.

✱ **Michael Davis.** Milestone Media, 119 West 23rd Street, Suite 409, New York, New York 10011.

Born: April 29, 1958, in Queens, New York.

College or other education: High School of Art and Design, Pratt Institute B.F.A.

Biggest creative influences: Bob Dacey, Bart Forbes, Kenneth Francis Dewey.

1993 projects: Milestone mini-series, *Elementals* graphic novel, big project with Walt Simonson (can't talk about it yet). *Freedom Project.* (Tundra?/Kitchen Sink?/Who the hell knows who's going to publish this?)

Past comics titles and related projects: *Shado* (DC), *etc.* (Piranha), owns Milestone Media.

Favorite comics not worked on: Anything by Milo Manara, *Icon,* Kirby's Fourth World — anything Kirby.

Dream comic-book project: I'm actually doing my dream comic-book project with Walt Simonson — the one I can't talk about. It used to be a *Captain Marvel* (*Shazam!*) graphic novel, but this is even better.

✳ **Rob Davis.** 5200 Mt. Zion Church Road, Hallsville, Missouri 65255.

Born: August 13, 1954, in Springfield, Missouri.

College or other education: Three years at Southwest Missouri State University. Famous Artists School graduate.

Biggest creative influences: Jack Kirby and Curt Swan.

1993 projects: H.P. Lovecraft's *Picture in the House* for Caliber. Fill-in work on *Star Trek: Deep Space Nine* for Malibu. Other projects in discussion stage.

Past comics titles and related projects: *Syphons, Rust,* and *Dai Kamikaze!* (all for Now Comics). *Scimidar* and *Merlin* (Malibu Graphics). *Maze Agency, Straw Men,* and *Quantum Leap* (Innovation). *Pirates of Dark Water* (Marvel). *Star Trek* and *Star Trek: The Next Generation* (DC).

Favorite comics not worked on: *Nexus, Concrete, Grimjack,* and *Batman.*

Dream comic-book project: Right now — full-time penciller on a *Star Trek*-related comic book.

Suzanne Dechnik

✳ **Suzanne Dechnik.** 1521 West Wellington Avenue, Chicago, Illinois 60657.

Born: February 14, in Chicago, Illinois.

College or other education: Associates

degree from Chicago Academy of Fine Art/ School of the Art Institute/University of Illinois.

Comics-related education: On-the-job experience at Now, freelancing for Comico, Malibu, and Calabash Animation.

Biggest creative influences: Graham Ingels, Gustave Moreau, Ivan Albright, the French Symbolists and Decadents, Paul Klee, Rick Griffin, and psychedelic art.

1993 projects: Coloring: *Mr. T and the T-Force, Green Hornet: Dark Tomorrow, Married with Children 2099,* and the usual run o' stuff.

Past comics titles and related projects: Colored: *Terminator, Real Ghostbusters, Slimer, Green Hornet, Racer-X, Alias, Speed Racer, Bats, Cats, and Cadillacs, Twilight Zone, Fright Night, Tales of the Green Hornet, Ralph Snart, Elementals,* and *Leatherface.* Commercial animation work: Raisin Nut Bran, Illinois Lotto "Mouse Meeting," shorts for Playboy Channel, Kroger, and Tiny Toons McDonald's commercial.

Favorite comics not worked on: *Elfquest* (all titles), *Interview with the Vampire,* Gilbert Shelton's, Robert Crumb's, and Roberta Gregory's works.

Dream comic-book project: A religio-mystical, gory, revenge-from-the-grave story about women.

Jerry DeFuccio

✳ **Jerry DeFuccio.** 12 Duncan Avenue, Jersey City, New Jersey 07304.

Born: July 3, 1925, in Jersey City, New Jersey.

College or other education: St. Peter's College, Fordham University.

Comics-related education: EC Publications,

Harvey Kurtzman, *Cartoonist PROfiles* (since inception).

Biggest creative influences: Harvey Kurtzman, Will Eisner, Bill Woolfolk (best Blackhawks), Klaus Nordling, and John Severin (cousin).

1993 projects: Currently researching art career of Jimmy Thompson, syndicated artist, comic books — *Red Men, Robotman, Human Torch, Angel*, and *Mary Marvel*, for *Cartoonist PROfiles*.

Past comics titles and related projects: *Two-Fisted Tales, Frontline Combat, Mad, Cracked, Prize Western*. Syndicated attempts: *Bucky Ruckus* with Wallace Wood, *Mirk and Monty* with Jack Rickard, and *Skool Yardley, Our Man on the Corner* with Alexander Toth. Sold gags for Bud Blake's *Tiger* syndicated strip.

Favorite comics not worked on: Contemporary topics by Mike Ricigliano, now developing in *Cracked*. Best since Aragonés.

Dream comic-book project: Back to the variety comic book: super-hero, Western, soldier-of-fortune, kids, detective, and military.

✳ **Robert de Jesus.** 7272 Wurzbach, Suite #204, San Antonio, Texas 78240.

Born: December 31, 1967, in Gary, Indiana.

Biggest creative influences: Japanese manga and anime.

1993 projects: *The Solutioners* and *Cannibal Gal*.

Past comics titles and related projects: Several covers to anthology books, fanzines, and prozines. Worked as an inker on a couple of *Ninja High School* books, two short creator-owned stories in *Mangazine*, and two spin-off books titled *Small Bodied Ninja High School*.

Favorite comics not worked on: *Dirty Pair, Appleseed, Akira, Gunsmith Cats, Dragonball*, and *Hate*.

Dream comic-book project: To write and draw a story for the Japanese comic zines.

✳ **Jose Delbo.** c/o *CBG* Editorial Department, 700 East State Street, Iola, Wisconsin 54990.

Born: December 9, 1933, in Buenos Aires, Argentina.

Jose Delbo

College or other education: University of Buenos Aires Law School, National School of Arts.

Comics-related education: Assistant of Carlos Clemen, an Argentinian cartoonist.

Biggest creative influences: Carlos Clemen, Alex Raymond, and M. Caniff.

1993 projects: *Science Spider-Man*, DC Special Projects Department, *Ravage*.

Past comics titles and related projects: *Billy the Kid, The Monkees, The Yellow Submarine, The Lone Ranger, Turok, Wonder Woman, Superman* the strip, *World's Finest, Transformers, Thundercats, Superpro, Boris Karloff, Grimm's House of Mystery, The Witching Hour, Captain Planet, Shadowman, X-O Manowar*, etc.

Favorite comics not worked on: *Batman*.

Dream comic-book project: A Western story.

✳ **Michael Anthony Delepine.** 67-24 161st Street, #2L, Flushing, New York 11365-3180.

Agent: Steve Donnelly/Creative Interests Agency (C.I.A.).

Born: April 10, 1964, in New York City.

College or other education: School of Visual Arts, New York City; B.A. in Cartooning, 1988.

Comics-related education: Production Department, DC Comics, January-September 1988.

Biggest creative influences: John Workman, Ken Bruzenak, Todd Klein, and Alex Jay.

1993 projects: Regular letterer on *Protectors* and *Robotech*, Malibu Graphics; *True Crime Stories* #1, *Parts Unknown* #4, and *Blood Is the Harvest* #4, Eclipse Comics.

Past comics titles and related projects: *Debbie Does Dallas, Robotech: Cyberpirates, Sherlock Holmes: Return of the Devil, Alien Nation: The First-comers*, and *The Defenseless Dead*, all from Malibu Graphics.

Favorite comics not worked on: *Star Trek* and *Star Trek: The Next Generation*, DC Comics.

Dream comic-book project: *Legionnaires*, DC Comics.

✳ **Kim DeMulder.** Rural Route 1, Box 1069, Dingmans Ferry, Pennsylvania 18328.

Born: April 16, 1955, in Bethesda, Maryland.

College or other education: University of Maryland and Joe Kubert School.

Biggest creative influences: Al Williamson, Tom Palmer, Virgil Finlay, Franklin Booth, and Joseph Clement Cole.

1993 projects: *Swamp Thing* — inks. Teaching at Joe Kubert School.

Past comics titles and related projects: *Defenders, Airboy, She-Hulk* graphic novel, *Nick Fury* (limited series and monthly title), *RoboCop, Punisher, Superboy, The 'Nam*, and *Hellblazer* (all inks). Full art on: *Fatal Beauties Portfolios* I and II and the *Sirens of Seduction* portfolio.

Favorite comics not worked on: *Groo, Sandman*, and *The Spectre*.

Dream comic-book project: Inking Frank Frazetta pencilling *Swamp Thing*.

✳ **John Dennis.** 78 Surrey Lane, Pontiac, Michigan 48340.

Agent: Star*Reach.

Born: October 21, 1950-something, in Iowa.

College or other education: Center for Creative Studies, Detroit, Michigan.

Biggest creative influences: Infantino, Ditko, Windsor-Smith, J. Buscema, Win Mortimer, Curt Swan, and Wally Wood.

1993 projects: *Badge* for Gauntlet and *Savage Sword of Conan* for Marvel.

John Dennis

Past comics titles and related projects: *The Others* #1 — Cormac Publishing. *The Realm* #16-21 and *The Caliber Realm Christmas Story* — Caliber. *Caliber Presents* #4, 6, 8, and 10 — Caliber. *The Comet* #11 — DC. *West Coast Avengers Annual 1992* — Marvel. *Wonder Woman Annual 1992* — DC. *Tarzan* — Semic/Malibu. *Chandler* — Byron Preiss. *Sinergy* — Caliber. *Book of the Tarot*.

Favorite comics not worked on: *Doctor Strange, Legion of Super-Heroes, Adam Strange, Cerebus, Spawn*, and *Love and Rockets*.

Dream comic-book project: A Metal Men or Creeper mini-series, a Shazam graphic novel, or the *Silver Surfer* or *Fantastic Four* series.

✳ **Scott Deschaine.** c/o *CBG* Editorial Department, 700 East State Street, Iola, Wisconsin 54990.

Born: May 12, 1957, in Washington, D.C.

College or other education: Pennsylvania State University, B.A., Manchester (U.K.) University.

Comics-related education: Internship — Birmingham (U.K.) Arts Lab.

Biggest creative influences: Too numerous to list.

1993 projects: *Popcorn!, Monster Love, Blue Block, Screaming Eagle, Bird Meets Fish, Krak-A-Boom!*, etc.

Past comics titles and related projects: *Vortex, Street Music, Anything Goes, Mr. Monster, Knockabout*, many educational comics, *Mythos*, and *Free Laughs*.

David M. DeVries

✸ **David M. DeVries.** 67 Benson Drive, Wayne, New Jersey 07470.

Born: January 16, 1966, in Ridgewood, New Jersey.

College or other education: B.F.A. in Illustration, Syracuse University, graduated 1988.

Comics-related education: Internship — Marvel Comics, summer 1987.

Biggest creative influences: Bill Sienkiewicz, Simon Bisley, Dave McKean, Kent Williams, and Mike Mignola.

1993 projects: *Zenith* — Fleetway Quality Comics (12-cover run). *Elfquest: New Blood.* — Warp Graphics (one cover). These are painted/3-D covers.

Past comics titles and related projects: *Aquaman* mini-series, 1989, cover painting (DC). Hardcover edition, *Greatest Team-Up Stories Ever Told*, painting over Carmine Infantino's pencils (DC). *Dragonlance Graphic Novel #4*, painted cover (DC). *Doctor Fate #25*, painted cover (DC). *Nexus Legends #20, 21*, and *23*,

painted covers. *Elfquest: New Blood Summer Special #1* and *2*, painted covers (four interior paintings in #1).

Favorite comics not worked on: *Hellblazer, Doom Patrol* (both DC Vertigo), and *White Trash* (Tundra).

✸ **Eric Dinehart.** 1031 South Stewart Street, #1145, Mesa, Arizona 85202-8849.

Agent: Stephen Donnelly.

Born: May 14, 1952, in Grayling, Michigan.

College or other education: B.S. in Psychology, Paralegal.

Comics-related education: Clarion Writer's Conference, M.S.U., 1983; First reader for *Amazing Science Fiction Magazine*, 1981.

Biggest creative influences: Harlan Ellison, Philip K. Dick, and Alan Moore.

1993 projects: *Reiki Warriors, Klown Shock* (in *Splatter*), *Elementals, Heavy Metal Monsters, The Pelli-People Winter Fun Book, Fright Gallery*, and *Asylum*.

Past comics titles and related projects: *Alien Encounters, Tales of Terror, Drawn to Extremes, Grave Tales, Splatter, Dark Horse Presents* (story with Steven Grant and The Group), *The Libertine* (as Damon Eddy), and *Stimulator* (as Damon Eddy).

Favorite comics not worked on: The Vertigo titles.

Dream comic-book project: My own line of comics.

✸ **Chuck Dixon.** c/o *CBG* Editorial Department, 700 East State Street, Iola, Wisconsin 54990.

Born: April 14, 1954, in Philadelphia, Pennsylvania.

Biggest creative influences: My earliest influences were Archie Goodwin (the first comics writer I became *aware* of) and Stan Lee. After that I'd list Harvey Kurtzman, Milton Caniff, and Larry Hama.

1993 projects: *Detective Comics*; *Lawdog*, an ongoing Epic title I created with Flint Henry; *Guy Gardner*; *Punisher: War Journal*; *Robin*, finally in an ongoing monthly; several *Alien Legion* projects; and several *Punisher* projects.

Past comics titles and related projects: *Air-boy, Evangeline, Savage Sword of Conan, Strike!, Winterworld, Skywolf, Valkyrie, Seven Block, Robin, Batman, Detective Comics, Alien Legion, Green Hornet* (second Now series), *Racer X, The 'Nam, Alias, Mad Dogs, Punisher, Punisher: War Journal, Punisher: War Zone, Moon Knight* (third series), *Invasion '55, Time Jump War, Car Warriors,* and *The Hobbit* (an adaptation for Eclipse).

Favorite comics not worked on: *Wolverine* by Larry Hama, *Hate* by Peter Bagge, and anything by Marc Hansen.

Dream comic-book project: An updating of *The Jetsons.* Rather than setting them in a Fifties or Sixties vision of the future, I'd love to do them set in a Nineties vision of the future: a dark post-apocalyptic world full of hidden dangers and science gone terribly wrong. Only George would remain unchanged.

✳ Douglas W. Dlin. Antarctic Press, 7272 Wurzbach, Suite #204, San Antonio, Texas 78240.

Born: October 10, 1967, in San Francisco, California.

College or other education: Bachelor's in Liberal Arts (Japanese) from University of Texas-Austin.

Comics-related education: Working at Antarctic Press since January 1991, plus a lot of outside reading.

1993 projects: *Fantastic Panic, Mighty Bombshells,* ongoing issues of *Mangazine* and *Dojinshi.*

Past comics titles and related projects: *Star Trekker, Star Trekker II, Mangazine* (since #10), and *Dojinshi.*

Favorite comics not worked on: *Ninja High School* (but I'm biased), *Nausicaä, Flaming Carrot,* and various manga too numerous to list.

Dream comic-book project: I'd love to translate some of my favorite manga, such as *Prefectural Earth Defense Force,* for U.S. publication.

✳ Colleen Doran. Aria Press, 12638-28 Jefferson Avenue, Suite 173, Newport News, Virginia 23602.

Born: July 24, 1963, in Cincinnati, Ohio (a

Colleen Doran

Yankee by accident only, otherwise a true Southerner).

College or other education: Christopher Newport University, Business Management with a concentration in International Commerce.

Biggest creative influences: Hal Foster's *Prince Valiant,* Howard Pyle, and Kelly Freas.

1993 projects: *A Distant Soil, Nestrobber, Legionnaires, Guardians of the Galaxy Annual, Eclipso, Aria, A Distant Soil Sketchbook,* and *Elvira, Mistress of the Dark.*

Past comics titles and related projects: *X-Factor, Excalibur, Marvel Fanfare, Sandman, Shade, Wonder Woman, Amazing Spider-Man, Legion of Super-Heroes, Teen Titans, Teen Titans Spotlight, Captain America and The Falcon, Battle Aids, Swords of the Swashbucklers, Fallen Angels,* Clive Barker's *Hellraiser,* Clive Barker's *Nightbreed,* Walt Disney's *Beauty and the Beast,* Anne Rice's *The Master of Rampling Gate, Grimjack, Amethyst, Wonder Woman Annual, Captain America and The New Warriors Battle Drugs, Christmas with the DC Super-Heroes, Captain Atom, Secret Origins of the DC Super-Heroes, Marvel Universe, Who's Who in the DC Universe, Cerebus, Creepy, Vampirella, Warp Annual,*

Strip AIDS U.S.A., For Better or for Worse limited prints, *Robotech Art II*, and *Fortune's Friends*.

Favorite comics not worked on: *Batman* and *Desert Peach*.

Dream comic-book project: *Batman* or *Aquaman* or any of the numerous dramas and romances in my file cabinet I've never submitted for publication.

Evan Dorkin

✳ **Evan Dorkin.** c/o *CBG* Editorial Department, 700 East State Street, Iola, Wisconsin 54990.

Born: April 20, 1965, in Brooklyn, New York.

College or other education: B.F.A. in Film/Television from New York University.

Biggest creative influences: Caffeine, alcohol, insomnia, paranoia, the economy, my landlord, etc., ad nauseum.

1993 projects: *Milk & Cheese* #4 (Slave Labor), *Pirate Corp$!* #6 (Slave Labor), *Fight Man One Shot* (Marvel), *Mad Dog* (Marvel, writer), *Predator: Bad Blood* (Dark Horse), *Dork* #1 (Slave Labor), *Vroom Socko* (in *Deadline*, to be reprinted by Slave Labor), *Urban Legends* #1 (Dark Horse, contributor), *Pirate Corp$/Hectic*

Planet, Vroom Socko, Dick Wad #1, *Pirate Corp$! The Blunder Years* #½ (Slave Labor), *Instant Piano* (Dark Horse, contributor), and *Deadline* magazine (contributor).

Past comics titles and related projects: *Bill & Ted's Excellent Comic* (Marvel), *Epic Lite* (Epic), *Munden's Bar* #2 (First), *Deadline U.S.A.* contributor (Dark Horse), *Deadline* contributor (U.K.-Deadline), *Predator: Big Game* (Dark Horse), *Flaming Carrot* #20 (Dark Horse), *Cerebus Bi-Weekly* #20 (back-up), *Born to Be Wild* benefit book (Eclipse), *Pirate Corp$!* (Eternity/Slave Labor), *Wild Knights* (Eternity), *Teenage Mutant Ninja Turtles* — storyboard work for several episodes, several science-fiction book adaptations for Byron Preiss, *One Fisted Tales* (Slave Labor), *Slave Labor Stories* (Slave Labor), *Greed, Centrifugal Bumblepuppy* (Fantagraphics). Contributed comics to *The Comics Journal, Penthouse Hot Talk, X-magazine, San Diego Con Comic* (Dark Horse), *Amazing Heroes Swimsuit Issues, Official Handbook of the Marvel Universe, Born to Be Wild* (Eclipse benefit book), and various LP and CD covers featuring comic characters. Blah, blah, blah.

Favorite comics not worked on: *Eightball, Hate, Love and Rockets, Yahoo, Blab!, Big Mouth, Real Life, Way Out Strips, It's Science, Tales from the Heart, Optic Nerve, Rubber Blanket*, and *Sin*.

Dream comic-book project: To get "enough" money per issue of my own work to devote all my time to it.

✳ **Dave Dorman.** Rolling Thunder Graphics, P.O. Box 203, Mary Esther, Florida 32569.

Born: October 1, 1958, in Bay City, Michigan.

College or other education: One year at St. Mary's College, Maryland.

Comics-related education: One year at the Joe Kubert School.

Biggest creative influences: Frazetta and Bama.

1993 projects: Batman graphic novel and a variety of comic, paperback, and game covers.

Past comics titles and related projects: *Aliens: Tribes*, illustrated story album. Cover art: *Indiana Jones: Fate of Atlantis, Star Wars: Dark*

Empire, Predator: Race War, and *The Greatest Bat-man Stories Ever Told. Hellraiser.*

✳ **Susan E. Dorne.** 551 Park Avenue, Windsor, Connecticut 06095.

Born: August 6, 1958, in Manchester, Connecticut.

College or other education: Two years at the University of Connecticut.

Comics-related education: Self-taught.

Biggest creative influences: Observation of others more experienced.

1993 projects: Lettering: *. . . absolute power . . . for* Alpha Productions, *Nightvision* for Rebel Studios and Atomeka Press, *Ex-Mutants* for Malibu Comics, *Mortar Man* for Marshall Comics, *The Philistine* for One-Shot Press, and *Ratman* mini-series for Comico.

Past comics titles and related projects: Lettered: numerous biographical titles for Revolutionary Comics, *Green Hornet* and *Married with Children* titles for Now Comics, numerous Tome Press comics for Caliber Press, numerous titles for Comico, including *Monolith, Klownshock, Slash and Splatter, Volcanic Nights*, and *Incubus* for Palliard Press, *Mighty Mouse* and related titles for Spotlight Comics.

Favorite comics not worked on: *Sandman, Cerebus, Omaha, Melody, Peep Show, Cartoon History of the Universe, Xenozoic Tales*, and *Spawn.*

Dream comic-book project: To work with any (or all) of my favorite creators: Dave Sim, Neil Gaiman, Mike Grell, P. Craig Russell, Mark Schultz, Waller and Worley, Scott Hampton, etc.

✳ **Les Dorscheid.** 1415 Andaman Street, Sun Prairie, Wisconsin 53590.

Born: February 15, 1959, in Madison, Wisconsin.

College or other education: Madison Area Technical College, Associates Degree in Commercial Art. Art Center College of Design, Pasadena, California, four years, Bachelor of Arts.

Comics-related education: On-the-job.

Biggest creative influences: Frank McCarthy, Paul Callé, Bill Owen, Michael Whelan, Kieth Parkinson, the Hildebrandt brothers, John

Les Dorscheid

Asard, Darrell Sweet, San Julian, Alex Raymond, and Chuck Ren.

1993 projects: Batman hardcover with Kelly Jones, one new book whose title I'm not sure of, and a sequel to *Red Rain*. Publishing my own limited-edition prints. Covers for Fasa Games, GDW Games, and TSR Hobbies.

Past comics titles and related projects: *Nexus* for 75 or so issues, *Next Nexus, Hammer of God. Classics Illustrated: Count of Monte Cristo* and *A Christmas Carol. Ginger Fox* graphic novel, two *Agent 13* graphic novels. Most recently, *Aliens: Hive, Deadman: Love after Death* and *Deadman: Exorcism*, and *Batman/Dracula: Red Rain.*

Favorite comics not worked on: I've always wanted to paint a *Batman* cover.

Dream comic-book project: An assistant to Alex Raymond on *Flash Gordon.*

✳ **John Drury.** 116 S. Allen Street, Albany, New York 12208.

Born: April 9, 1967, in Newark, New York.

College or other education: Two years completed toward B.F.A.

Comics-related education: "Learn as you go."

Biggest creative influences: Byrne, Canniff, and Eisner.

1993 projects: *Sirens* with Sidney Williams for Caliber Press (pencils).

Past comics titles and related projects: Inks: *Cat and Mouse* #6, Aircel Comics. Full rendering: Title story, *Never Forgotten*, Caliber. Plot, script, pencils: *Pendulum*, Malibu Comics (Adventure).

Favorite comics not worked on: *Milk &*

Cheese, Baker Street, and *Grendel*.

Dream comic-book project: A horror series with a philosophical agenda.

Jo Duffy

✳ **Jo Duffy.** Blue Sky Blue, P.O. Box 415, Long Beach, New York 11561.

Born: February 9, 1954, in New York, New York.

College or other education: Wellesley College.

Comics-related education: School of hard knocks.

Biggest creative influences: Comics, novels, plays, movies, animation, TV, comic strips, everything else I read, and real life.

1993 projects: *Nestrobber, Catwoman, Elvira, Akira*, maybe *The Punisher*.

Past comics titles and related projects: As writer: *Power Man and Iron Fist, Moon Knight, Star Wars, Wolverine, Punisher, Back down the Line, Fallen Angels, A Distant Soil, Crystar, Batman, Detective Comics, Conan, P. Craig Russell's Night Music, Wolverine, Amazing Spider-Man, X-Factor,*

Daredevil, The Defenders, Epic Illustrated, Willow, Marvel Two-in-One, Teenage Tokyo, Marvel Comics Presents, Marvel Spotlight, Chuck Norris, Wonder Woman and the Star Riders, Starriors, St. Francis, X-Men Classics, Marvel Fanfare, X-Men: Heroes for Hope, What If?, Creepy, and too many editing jobs to list.

Favorite comics not worked on: *Sin City, John Byrne's Next Men, Ranma ½, Banana Fish*, almost anything written by Chris Claremont, either Simonson, or Roger Stern.

Dream comic-book project: *Nestrobber* selling well enough to publish more often.

✳ **Pat Duke.** Antarctic Press, 7272 Wurzbach, Suite #204, San Antonio, Texas 78240.

Born: July 15, 1969, in Japan.

College or other education: M.F.A., University of Texas at San Antonio.

Biggest creative influences: Masamune Shirow, G. Harpam, Wendy and Richard Pini, and M. Wagner.

1993 projects: *ESPolice*. Production Manager on all Antarctic Press titles.

Past comics titles and related projects: *Mighty Tiny Mouse Marines, Captain Harlock, Mangazine*, and *Ninja High School*.

Favorite comics not worked on: *Elfquest, Appleseed*, and *Battle Angel Alita*.

Dream comic-book project: A comprehensive study of the comics medium in relation to cognitive theory of learning and communication.

✳ **Ben Dunn.** 7272 Wurzbach, Suite #204, San Antonio, Texas 78240.

Born: April 17, 1964, in Ping-Tung, Taiwan.

College or other education: Five years at St. Mary's University.

Biggest creative influences: 1960s manga superhero comics and *Richie Rich*.

1993 projects: *Ninja High School, Project: A-KO*, and *Speed Racer/Ninja High School* crossover.

Past comics titles and related projects: *Tiger-X, Mighty Tiny, Scout, Airboy, Dynamo Joe, Popeye, Zetraman, Ninja High School, Captain Harlock*, and *Queen Emereldas*.

Favorite comics not worked on: *Nausicaä,*

Flaming Carrot, Cud, Hate, Dr. Slump, and *Tazunuto*.

Dream comic-book project: *The Fantastic Four* (my first super-hero comic).

Robert Durham

✷ **Robert Durham.** 207 E. 13th Street, Chester, Pennsylvania 19013.

Born: April 10, 1963, in Chester, Pennsylvania.

College or other education: Art Institute of Philadelphia, Associates Degree in Commercial Art.

Biggest creative influences: Warren and Marvel publications of the 1970s, Frank Frazetta, and Norman Rockwell.

1993 projects: *Tales from the Balcony* for Allied Comics.

Past comics titles and related projects: *Shrike* and *Torture* for Catwild Inc. Comics, *Blade of Shuriken* for Eternity Comics, *Phase One, Komodo and the Defiants*, and *Shuriken* for Victory.

Favorite comics not worked on: *Cerebus, Lobo, WildC.A.T.S*, and *Deadworld*.

Dream comic-book project: Superman's return.

✷ **Barry Dutter.** Marvel Entertainment, 387 Park Avenue South, New York, New York 10016.

Barry Dutter

Born: December 29, 1964, in Scotch Plains, New Jersey.

Biggest creative influences: Stan Lee, Frank Miller, Jack Kirby, and Alan Moore.

1993 projects: *Fury* graphic novel, stories for *Captain America Annual, Wonder Man Annual, Fantastic Four Unlimited, Marvel Comics Presents*, and *Mush* back-ups for Topps.

Past comics titles and related projects: *Nightcat, Captain Planet, Bullpen Bulletins, Marvel Tales*, a book: *Everything I Really Need to Know I Learned from Television, Hellraiser*, and *What The--?!*

Favorite comics not worked on: *Hulk, Warlock and the Infinity Watch, X-Factor, Groo, Spawn, Harbinger*, and *Batman: Legends of the Dark Knight*.

Dream comic-book project: *Mush* as a monthly series or *The Avengers*.

✷ **Leonard Dworkins (Leon Gordon).** c/o *CBG* Editorial Department, 700 East State Street, Iola, Wisconsin 54990.

Born: December 3, 1921, in Chicago, Illinois.

College or other education: (Student at Large) Lake Forest College, Columbia (Radio) Co., and Roosevelt Co.

Comics-related education: Assistant to Lt. Dick Calkins (*Buck Rogers*, adventure comic strip).

Biggest creative influences: *Mickey Mouse, Popeye, Tarzan, Buck Rogers, Flash Gordon, Prince Valiant* newspaper comic strips.

1993 projects: *Curley's Magic Pencil* (science fiction), *Sandra Sharon, Future City — Today* (science fiction), *Spaced Out — with Klink and Klutz* (comic strip) for newspaper syndication. (*Curley and Sandra* "C" books.)

Past comics titles and related projects: *Skyroads, Buck Rogers, Speed Spalding, Draftie (Lem and Oinie), Wade Cabot, Let's Explore Your Mind, Bang-Up Comics Book, Cappy Dick*, etc.

Favorite comics not worked on: *Tarzan, Flash Gordon*, and *Prince Valiant*.

Dream comic-book project: *Curley's Magic Pencil* and *Sandra Sharon*.

The Dynamic Duo Inc. (Arlen Schumer and Sherri Wolfgang)

✳ **The Dynamic Duo Inc. (Arlen Schumer and Sherri Wolfgang).** 95 Kings Highway South, Westport, Connecticut 06880.

Agent: Gerald and Ellen Rapp Inc.

Born: Arlen Schumer: June 6, 1958, in Detroit, Michigan. Sherri Wolfgang: September 2, 1961, in Queens, New York.

College or other education: Arlen Schumer: B.F.A., Graphic Design, Rhode Island School of Design (1980). Sherri Wolfgang: B.F.A., Carnegie Mellon University.

Comics-related education: Both worked at Neal Adams' Continuity Associates from Fall 1983-Winter 1985.

Biggest creative influences: Neal Adams, Jim Steranko, Carmine Infantino, Walt Simonson, Curt Swan, Murphy Anderson, and early '60s DC comics.

1993 projects: Series of comic book-style ads for Stridex Pads, *Zitfighters from Outer Space*, appearing in all Marvel Comics, spring/summer 1993.

Past comics titles and related projects: Series of ads for 3 Musketeers that appeared in Marvel and DC books, 1990-1992; ad illustration for HBO's TV series, *Tales from the Crypt*, 1991; wrote article for *Print* magazine's special comics issue (November/December 1988), *The New Superheroes*, and designed cover; presented multi-media slide show to New York City Art Director's Club, *Superhero to Antihero: Comic Book Art in the 1960s*, October 1992.

Dream comic-book project: To design and write a full-color, hardcover coffee-table art book about comics history.

✳ **Felipe Echevarria.** 3041 Sumac, #4, Fort Collins, Colorado 80526-5756.

Born: March 14, 1959, in San Diego, California.

College or other education: Joe Kubert School of Cartoon and Graphic Art graduate, 1990. Miscellaneous continuing education in Psychology, NLP, Human Potential Study, Science, Illustration.

Biggest creative influences: John Singer Sargent, Gustav Klimt, Andrew Wyeth, Edward Hopper, Burt Silverman, Charles Reid, John Blockley, Kent Williams, Dave McKean, George Pratt, Jon Muth, Joe Kubert, and Alex Toth.

1993 projects: Innovation: *Dark Shadows*

Felipe Echevarria

Book 3 #1-4, *Private Commissions*, my own book (top secret).

Past comics titles and related projects: *Alfred Hitchcock's Psycho*, Innovation, 1991-92, three issues. *Troubled Youth* (b&w), *Kodansha of Japan*, 1992, five stories. *Sinbad* #1-4 (1991), *Merlin* #3 (1990), *Vampyres* graphic novel (1991), and *Alien Nation* (1991) (covers for all, all from Malibu). Various background inking on *Flash, Tomorrow Knights, Barbie,* and *Power Pack Special*, 1991-93.

Favorite comics not worked on: *Cages* by Dave McKean.

Dream comic-book project: My own book — already in the works and a full-color pin-up gallery comic.

G. Raymond Eddy

✳ **G. Raymond Eddy.** 1202 Panama Road SE, Carrollton, Ohio 44615-9659.

Born: March 29, 1960, in Canton, Ohio.

1993 projects: *Crossways* for *Wildlife* (Antarctic Press).

Past comics titles and related projects: *Crossways* for *Wildlife* #1.

Favorite comics not worked on: *Albedo.*

Dream comic-book project: *Galen the Saintly* (guardian mouse angel).

✳ **Hy Eisman.** King Features Syndicate, 235 East 45th Street, New York, New York 10017.

Born: March 27, 1927, in Paterson, New Jersey.

College or other education: Army newspaper, World War II. Art Career School, New York City.

Comics-related education: Pencilled *Kerry Drake* for Alfred Andriola for three years. Pencilled thousands of love stories for Vinnie Colletta.

Biggest creative influences: Alex Raymond, Hal Foster, Chester Gould, Walt Disney, Albert Dorne, Al Capp, Will Eisner, Percy Crosby, Rudolph Dirks, Ernie Bushmiller, Bud Blake, etc.

1993 projects: Produce (write, pencil, ink, and letter) *Katzenjammer Kids* Sunday page for King Features. Sundry comic books for industry.

Past comics titles and related projects: Comic books: *Smokey Stover, Nancy and Sluggo, The Munsters, Tom and Jerry, Little Lulu, Katy Keene, Bunny Ball, Blondie, Archie,* and *Felix the Cat.* Children's Book: Ghosted Bud Blake's *Tiger.* Newspaper strips: *Kerry Drake, Bringing up Father, Mutt and Jeff, Little Iodine* (Sunday page for 17 years), *Katzenjammer Kids* (Sunday page since 1986).

Favorite comics not worked on: *Flash Gordon, Calvin and Hobbes, Hagar,* and *Prince Valiant.*

Dream comic-book project: My autobiography.

✳ **Mindy Eisman.** 19B Ackerson Road, Blairstown, New Jersey 07825.

Born: April 11, 1960, in Passaic, New Jersey.

College or other education: Pratt-Manhattan Center, Art Students League.

Comics-related education: Joe Kubert School.

Biggest creative influences: Hy Eisman.

Past comics titles and related projects: *Valkyrie!, Sky Wolf, New America, Hotspur, The Airmaidens, The Liberty Project, The Detectives, Dragonflight, Toadswart D'Amplestone, Fusion, Xanadu, The Dreamery*, Eclipse F/X series, Felix Comics, and Archie Comics.

✳ **Will Eisner.** 8333 West McNab Road, Tamarac, Florida 33321.

Born: March 6, 1917, in New York City.

College or other education: Art Students League.

Biggest creative influences: Segar, Harriman, Caniff, and Leyendecker.

1993 projects: Television/graphic novels.

Past comics titles and related projects: *The Spirit, Contract with God, Heart of the Storm, Comics and Sequential Art, Life Force*, and *New York, Big City*.

Tim Eldred

✳ **Tim Eldred.** Malibu Comics, 5321 Sterling Center Drive, Westlake Village, California 91360.

Born: June 9, 1965, in Grand Rapids, Michigan.

College or other education: Commercial Art vocational training.

Comics-related education: Non-accredited class given by Michael Gustovich, 1980-81.

Biggest creative influences: Japanese car-

toons and comics, specific American, Japanese, and European creators.

1993 projects: *Captain Harlock: The Machine People* and various *Robotech* series.

Past comics titles and related projects: *Broid* (writing, pencilling), *Mecha* (writing), *Ground Zero* (writing, pencilling), *Lensman* (pencilling), *Chaser Platoon* (writing, pencilling), *Captain Harlock* (pencilling, inking), *Cybersuit Arkadyne* (writing, pencilling, inking), *Grease Monkey* (writing, pencilling, inking), *Robotech: Invid War* (pencilling), and *Fathom* (pencilling).

Favorite comics not worked on: *Nausicaä, Sandman, Venus Wars, 2000 AD, Groo*, and *Nexus*.

Dream comic-book project: Adaptation of Japanese animation program *Armored Trooper Votoms*.

✳ **Robert S. Elinskas.** 1805 Girard Street, Utica, New York, 13501.

Born: March 15, 1972, in Utica, New York.

College or other education: Utica College of Syracuse University, B.S. — Public Relations (June '94).

Biggest creative influences: Scott McCloud and Doug Moench.

1993 projects: *Bloodmoon* mini-series, *Mister Mid-Nite Annual* #2, and *Small Press Feedback!*.

Past comics titles and related projects: Have written *Mister Mid-Nite* #1-7 and *Annual* #1. Edited/published *Small Press Feedback!* magazine from October 1992 to the present. Editor-in-chief Allied Comics.

Favorite comics not worked on: *Zot!, Bone, Detective Comics*, and *Batman: Legends of the Dark Knight*.

Dream comic-book project: Batman graphic novel.

✳ **Harlan Ellison.** c/o *CBG* Editorial Department, 700 East State Street, Iola, Wisconsin 54990.

Agent: Martin Shapiro, Shapiro-Lichtman Talent Agency.

Born: May 27, 1934, in Cleveland, Ohio.

College or other education: Thrown out of Ohio State after 1½ years of wretched matriculation resulting in (by record, to this day) the low-

Harlan Ellison

est point average in the history of the institution. Subsequently, I have been awarded half a dozen honorary "Doctor of Letters" degrees from various universities.

Comics-related education: Fan and reader of comics without cessation since 1939: a far more exhaustive "education" in comics than some night course for Ivy League parvenus.

Biggest creative influences: Percy Crosby, Will Eisner, C.C. Beck, Alex Raymond, Milton Caniff, George Carlson, Mark Twain, Franz Kafka, Jorge Luis Borges, Heinreich Kley, Shirley Jackson, Frederic Prokosch, Joseph Conrad, Julius Schwartz, Jack Cole, Alfred Bester, Ernest Hemingway, etc.

1993 projects: A major project I cannot, by clause of confidentiality in my contract, reveal at this time. But if I use the word *big*, I ain't talking a one-shot adaptation. Big.

Past comics titles and related projects: *The Hulk, The Avengers, Twilight Zone, Weird Tales, Mangle-Tangle Tales,* Kitchen Sink's *Li'l Abner* series, Batman in *Detective Comics,* Marvel's *Daredevil, Weird Science-Fantasy* (original EC version, not reprint), *X-Men Heroes against Hunger, Fire Sale, Images of Omaha* benefit book, *Swamp Thing, Fish Police,* etc.

Favorite comics not worked on: *Sandman Mystery Theater,* Gaiman's *Sandman, Hellblazer, Concrete, Justice Society of America,* Nancy Collins' *Swamp Thing, Sin City, The Ray,* and *The Spirit.*

Dream comic-book project: The one I'm doing that I can't talk about, that will no doubt be a cover story in *CBG* when the publisher deems the moment propitious. Big.

Randy Emberlin

✳ **Randy Emberlin.** c/o *CBG* Editorial Department, 700 East State Street, Iola, Wisconsin 54990.

Born: September 27, 1955, in Portland, Oregon.

College or other education: Two years liberal arts college.

Comics-related education: Five years full partner in a commercial animation studio. Five years illustrator for educational book company.

Biggest creative influences: Frank Miller, Jack Kirby, Steve Ditko, Terry Austin, and Klaus Janson.

1993 projects: *Amazing Spider-Man.*

Past comics titles and related projects: Marvel: *Alien Legion* (2½ years), *Doctor Strange* (2½ years), *Strange Tales* (1 year), *G.I. Joe* (5 years), *Amazing Spider-Man* (3 years), fill-ins on: *Punisher, X-Factor, Defenders, Cloak and Dagger, Avengers West Coast, Marvel Comics Presents,* and others. DC: One issue of *Batman.* First: *American Flagg!* (one year). Dark Horse: *The Mask, Dark Horse Presents* #1-4 and others, *Predator,* and *Predator 2.*

Favorite comics not worked on: *Daredevil, Batman, Wolverine,* and *X-Men.*

Dream comic-book project: It is currently in progress.

✳ **Mark Engblom.** c/o *CBG* Editorial Department, 700 East State Street, Iola, Wisconsin 54990.

Born: December 21, 1965, in Duluth, Minnesota.

College or other education: B.A. from College of Associated Arts in St. Paul, Minnesota.

Comics-related education: Twenty years of reading comic books, which has taught me the importance of having a headquarters, a sidekick, and a good costume.

Biggest creative influences: Bill Watterson, Paul Coker, Jack Davis, *The Ren & Stimpy Show*, Jack Kirby, and a lifetime of pop culture.

1993 projects: "Watchmen II" and cartoon contributions to *CBG* (editorial and spot illustrations).

Past comics titles and related projects: No comics, but I've contributed cartoons to *CBG* since 1986 and have no plans of quitting, despite a full freelance and salaried job and family-life thing. I don't want to make comics . . . I just want to make fun of them and all of us big geeks that still read them.

Favorite comics not worked on: *Sandman*, the Superman titles, *The Incredible Hulk, The Spectre*, and *Madman*.

Dream comic-book project: To write a Superman mini-series. I've got some ideas *nobody's* thought of.

✳ **Jim Engel.** 218 S. Craig Place, Lombard, Illinois 60148.

Born: October 20, 1956, in Oak Park, Illinois.

Biggest creative influences: Warner Bros. cartoons and the funny animal greats, Kelly, Hubbard, Bradbury, Eisenberg, etc.

1993 projects: Possibly another attempt at syndication, comics for *Non-Sport Update*, continued involvement with licensed character toy design for McDonalds and Disney Giftware designs for Enesco Corp.

Past comics titles and related projects: *Spotlight* covers, scattered funny animal stuff for DC,

Jim Engel

Dick Duck in *Comic Reader, Critters, Usagi Yojimbo* back-ups, Mickey Mouse Synd. in 1991, 3-D Zone. Product design and illustration for licensed properties including Teenage Mutant Ninja Turtles, Tiny Toons, Batman, Gumby, The Muppets, Peanuts, Garfield, ALF, Ronald McDonald, Mickey Mouse, Sesame Street, Super Mario Brothers, Bozo, The Simpsons, etc.

Favorite comics not worked on: Currently: *Usagi Yojimbo*, Rosa's Duck books, Mark Martin, and *The Ren & Stimpy Show*. Past: '60s Marvels, all the classic funny animals, and Eisner.

Dream comic-book project: A funny animal anthology title with original characters by myself, Tiefenbacher, Rosa, Sternecky, Shaw!, Bennett, and anyone else I admire who's not already dead.

✳ **Jack Enyart.** c/o *CBG* Editorial Department, 700 East State Street, Iola, Wisconsin 54990.

Born: January 1, 1950, in Los Angeles, California.

College or other education: Los Angeles City College, California Institute of Arts, Art Center.

1993 projects: Warner Bros. *Looney Tunes* and *Tiny Toons*.

Past comics titles and related projects: Western Publishing, *Looney Tunes*, Disney Comics, Hanna-Barbera comics, Disney's *Roger Rabbit*.

Favorite comics not worked on: My very own.

Dream comic-book project: My very own.

✳ **Steve Erwin.** P.O. Box 1562, Hurst, Texas 76053-1562.

Born: January 16, 1960, in Tulsa, Oklahoma.

College or other education: Tulsa County Vo-Tech, Oklahoma State Tech.

Biggest creative influences: Neal Adams, Gene Colan, Jim Aparo, Jim Steranko, and Tom Palmer.

1993 projects: *Deathstroke, the Terminator* (series); *Deathstroke Annual* (Bloodlines).

Past comics titles and related projects: *Grimjack* and *Shatter* (First). *Vigilante, Checkmate!, New Gods, New Titans, Hawk and Dove, Who's Who*, and *Batman Returns* (all DC).

Favorite comics not worked on: *Green Arrow, Calvin and Hobbes*, and *The Far Side*.

Dream comic-book project: To work with a favorite writer and do full art (pencil and ink) on a graphic novel or mini-series.

✳ **Ric Estrada.** 281 Venado Avenue, Thousand Oaks, California 91320.

Agent: Mike Friedrich/Star*Reach.

Born: February 26, 1928, in Havana, Cuba.

College or other education: B.A., two years of Drawing Color and Design, Art Students League, New York.

Comics-related education: Landon School of Cartooning (correspondence), Famous Artists School (correspondence), *Flash Gordon* (Dan Barry's assistant), Art Director for Famous Artists Schools, Instructor at Joe Kubert School.

Biggest creative influences: Milton Caniff,

Harold Foster, Albert Dorne, Robert Fawcett, Alex Toth, Joe Kubert, and Roy Crane.

1993 projects: *Jimmy Gunn, Jr. Spy; Tales of the Token; Star Force Terra; Timescape — Dragonchase* (all for Another Rainbow Publications).

Past comics titles and related projects: *Pony Tailers* (Disney Adventures), *Amethyst* (DC), *Bob Kanigher's Gallery of War* (DC), *Wonder Woman* (DC), *Legion of Super-Heroes* (DC), *Devilina* (Atlas), *Plop!* (DC), *Two-Fisted Tales* (EC), *Teen Romance* (DC), *Detective Comics* (Standard), *Romance* (St. John), *Alfred Hitchcock Mystery Magazine* (St. John), *Flash Gordon* (King Features), *Spider-Man* (daily strip, ghosted), *Superfriends* (DC), *Sgt. Rock* (DC), *The Gobots* (animated full-length feature, Hanna-Barbera), *Star Trek* (DC), and many others including *New Testament Stories for Children* (for the Mormon Church).

Favorite comics not worked on: *Apartment 3-G, The Shadow, Hagar the Horrible, Crock, Corto Maltese*, and anything by Moebius.

Dream comic-book project: (Are you ready for this?) A cross between Captain Easy and Little Nemo (that's one). The other would be *The Shadow* (updated and futuristic).

✳ **Michael Eury.** c/o *CBG* Editorial Department, 700 East State Street, Iola, Wisconsin 54990.

Born: September 28, 1957, in Concord, North Carolina.

College or other education: 1980 Bachelor of Music Education, East Carolina University, Greenville, North Carolina.

Comics-related education: Learned how to edit comics as Diana Schutz's assistant editor during Comico the Comic Company's glory days.

Biggest creative influences: Fun comics and TV cartoons of the 1960s, 1960s DC and Marvels, the work of Curt Swan, Stan Lee, Julie Schwartz, John Byrne, Neal Adams, and Denny O'Neil.

1993 projects: Currently writing *Sensational She-Hulk* for Marvel Comics and the adventures of G'Nort in *Green Lantern Corps Quarterly* for DC Comics.

Past comics titles and related projects: DC editor for three years: *Legion of Super-Heroes,*

Michael Eury

Legionnaires, Eclipso, Valor, Timber Wolf, Who's Who (co-designed looseleaf format), *Hawk and Dove, New Gods, Ambush Bug Nothing Special, Secret Origins*, and *Huntress*. Wrote: *Inside DC* column and *Cool World* movie adaptation and prequel mini-series. Was assistant to VP/Editorial Director Dick Giordano for one year. Prior to DC, Comico editor: *Elementals, The Maze Agency, Gumby's Winter Fun, Sam and Max: Freelance Police, Justice Machine, Bloodscent, Trollords, E-Man*, and more.

Favorite comics not worked on: All Superman titles, *Incredible Hulk, Tales from the Heart, Fantastic Four* (always loved 'em), *Swamp Thing, Concrete*, and *The Spectre*.

Dream comic-book project: I'd love to write the adventures of the original Captain Marvel (Shazam).

✱ **George Evans.** 203 Frederick Street, Mount Joy, Pennsylvania 17552.

George Evans

Born: February 5, 1920, in Harwood Mines, Pennsylvania.

College or other education: U.S. Air Force Air Mech Courses — unrelated to art/cartooning. About 1½ years of Art Student's League, then dropped out, no degree.

Comics-related education: Staff artist at Fiction House Inc., publisher of comics and pulp magazines. Freelance from end of FH tenure, with Fawcett, EC, Johnston and Cusing (advertising comics), numerous textbooks, including projects for all major faiths in comic/illustrative material. Thirteen years producing daily *Terry and the Pirates* for George Wunder, work on *Wash Tubbs, Dr. Rex Morgan, Secret Agent*, plus ads and illos of all types.

Biggest creative influences: For comics writing/illustrating: Roy Crane, Harold Foster, and Alex Raymond. For other types of work: the many fine illustrators in all media.

1993 projects: A thirteenth year of writing and producing *Secret Agent Corrigan* for King Features Syndicate, plus a steady run of commissioned art in all media based on past comic stuff and/or aviation themes. Stop-and-go work on a proposed book about life and work in the field.

Past comics titles and related projects: Just about all the then-major publishers, then independents. Pencilled episode of *Wash Tubbs and Captain Easy* for Les Turner; quit in disgust work on *Rex Migraine*. Thirteen years daily *Terry and the Pirates*, in thirteenth year on *Secret Agent Corrigan*. 1992 episode of *Tarzan* for Kure (pencils).

Topps: many kinds of work on various Topps projects, including *Star Wars* card for *Star Wars Special* upcoming series.

Favorite comics not worked on: *Calvin and Hobbes, Calvin and Hobbes, Calvin and Hobbes*, the only Golden Age quality strip now running. *Wizard of Id* and *Peanuts*.

Dream comic-book project: A graphic novel on World War I airmen, script, art, color, lettering, the entire works.

✳ **Mark Evanier.** P.O. Box 480265, Los Angeles, California 90048.

Agent: Douroux and Co.

Born: March 2, 1952, in Santa Monica, California.

College or other education: U.C.L.A.

Comics-related education: Apprenticed with Jack Kirby.

Biggest creative influences: George S. Kaufman, Laurel and Hardy, Stan Freberg, *Mad* magazine, Jack Kirby, Bugs Bunny, Yogi Bear, and masking tape.

1993 projects: *Groo the Wanderer, The Mighty Magnor*, and *DNAgents*.

Past comics titles and related projects: Tons of Disney, Warner Bros. (Bugs Bunny, *et al.*), Hanna-Barbera (*Flintstones, Scooby-Doo*), *Tarzan, Korak, Blackhawk, New Gods, Mr. Miracle, DNAgents*, and *Crossfire*.

✳ **Matt Feazell.** 3867 Bristow, Detroit, Michigan 48212.

Born: May 11, 1955, in Ames, Iowa.

College or other education: B.S., Communication and Fine Arts, Southern Illinois University, Carbondale, Illinois, 1977.

Biggest creative influences: Hank Ketchum, Stan Lee and Jack Kirby, Alex Toth, Tim Conrad, Elvis Costello, and The Ramones.

1993 projects: *Death of Antisocialman* graphic novel.

Past comics titles and related projects: *Zot!* (Eclipse Comics), *The Amazing Cynicalman* (Eclipse), *Munden's Bar Annual* (First Comics), *Ant Boy* (Steel Dragon Press), *Cynicalman, the Paperback* (Thunder Baas Press), and *Not Available Comics* (self-published).

Matt Feazell

Favorite comics not worked on: *Cud, Love and Rockets, Hate, Eightball, Raw, Morty the Dog, Beanworld*, and *Yummy Fur*.

Dream comic-book project: Nationally distributed weekly mini-comic in 7-11 stores and grocery stores.

✳ **Norman Felchle.** 64 East Mission Street, San Jose, California 95112.

Born: January 15, 1964, in San Jose, California.

College or other education: B.F.A., California College of Arts and Sciences.

Comics-related education: Assistant to Chuck Austen.

Biggest creative influences: Jim Starlin, Dr. Seuss, Rudolph F. Zallinger, Mike Mignola, and W. Heath Robinson.

1993 projects: *S.T.A.R.-C.O.R.P.S.* (DC Comics, six-issue mini-series).

Past comics titles and related projects: DC Comics: *The Griffin* and two issues of *Batman: Legends of the Dark Knight* yet to be published. Marvel Comics: *Darkhold* #4. Dark Horse Comics: *Aliens* mini comic (toy giveaway) # 1 "Bishop."

Favorite comics not worked on: *Sandman* (what a surprise!) and anything by Kyle Baker.

Dream comic-book project: A *Lizard* (Spider-Man villain) mini-series based in some lost corner of a swamp with monsters.

✳ **Phil Felix.** P.O. Box 94, Frenchtown, New Jersey 08825.

Born: December 23, 1954, in Phillipsburg, New Jersey.

College or other education: B.F.A., 1979, School of Visual Arts, New York City.

Comics-related education: Ten years assisting Harvey Kurtzman, two years in the Marvel Bullpen (1984-86), and miscellaneous freelance work.

Biggest creative influences: Harvey Kurtzman, Will Elder, Dan Crespi, Ben Oda, Gaspar Saladino, and Vince Lombardi.

1993 projects: *The 'Nam, Thor, Terror Inc., Alien Legion, Darkhold, Ravage 2099, Werewolves,* etc.

Past comics titles and related projects: 1979-88: Backgrounds and lettering on *Little Annie Fanny.* Marvel Comics: *Marshal Law, G.I. Joe Special Missions, Nick Fury, Agent of S.H.I.E.L.D., Plastic Forks,* etc. DC: *The Flash, Wonder Woman, Warlord,* etc. Also: work in *National Lampoon, Raw, Screw, American Splendor,* and the comics of Drew Friedman, and Topps bubble gum.

Favorite comics not worked on: Anything by Walt Simonson, John Byrne, and Rich Corben.

Sheryl L. Ferraro

✳ **Sheryl L. Ferraro.** c/o *CBG* Editorial Department, 700 East State Street, Iola, Wisconsin 54990.

Born: January 3, in Highland Park, Illinois.

College or other education: B.A., Columbia College, Chicago, Illinois.

Biggest creative influences: Van Gogh. I read once that he lashed himself and his canvas to trees so that he could paint during a storm. Perseverance.

1993 projects: *Mr. T and the T-Force, Green Hornet: Dark Tomorrow, Ghostbusters, Ralph Snart Adventures, Married with Children,* etc. I mostly do design and layout, so . . .

Past comics titles and related projects: I get to work on all the books to some degree. I work on ads, editorial pages, layout, and color for covers, *Speed Racer* video sleeves, and trading cards. I do Mac graphics and also traditional design and layout. My favorite ad I've done recently was for instant Mr. Lizard. I did the copy-writing for the ad too, which was fun. It was quite the "Now" collaboration. Everyone had fun with Mr. Lizard.

Favorite comics not worked on: *The Teenie Weenies* by William Donahey.

Dream comic-book project: The authorized version of Elvis comics, with fully-painted interiors (acrylics). Special editions would feature Elvis portrait covers. One would be on black velvet, of course, and I'd like to commission the artist who did the Elvis in glitter portrait that I saw at a Chicago gallery last February (1992). Also, Elvis computer-art covers.

✳ **Steve Firchow.** 719 West Wilson, #G-4, Costa Mesa, California 92627.

Born: June 30, 1966, in New Guinea.

College or other education: B.F.A. (specializing in Illustration) from Cal State Long Beach.

Biggest creative influences: Michael Whelan, Bros. Hildebrandt, Frazetta, Wrightson, Jim Lee, Simon Bisley, etc.

1993 projects: I am currently painting covers for *Fate Comics,* an independent quarterly published in Maine, and will possibly color *Stormwatch* trading cards.

Past comics titles and related projects: I have painted covers for two Nate Butler Studios titles, *Aida-Zee* and *Behold!* I've colored covers for Valiant Efforts, Hero Graphics, and Northridge Games. I recently had a piece (sequential) published by Zeitgeist Studios in their anthology.

Favorite comics not worked on: *The Maxx, Pitt, Digitek, Slaine, Conan,* etc.

Dream comic-book project: A story I've had for about three years that is screaming to be *painted* and published.

Favorite comics not worked on: *Sandman, Hellblazer, Stanley and His Monster, Hulk,* and some Batman stories.

Dream comic-book project: Captain Marvel, Plastic Man, or just about any of the 1940s Quality characters.

Sholly Fisch

✳ **Sholly Fisch.** Children's Television Workshop, One Lincoln Plaza, New York, New York 10023.

Born: September 3, 1962, in Teaneck, New Jersey.

College or other education: Ph.D. in Experimental Psychology, New York University.

Biggest creative influences: Ray Bradbury, Will Eisner, Lawrence Block, John Steinbeck, Stan Lee, Gardner Fox, Shelly Mayer, and others.

1993 projects: *What The--?!,* fill-ins on *She-Hulk, Doctor Strange Annual, Marvel Holiday Special 1993, Marvel Age,* and possibly *The Ren & Stimpy Show* fill-ins (still waiting for clearance from Nickelodeon).

Past comics titles and related projects: *What The--?!,* Clive Barker's *Hellraiser, Marvel Comics Presents, Marvel Holiday Special 1992, Hellraiser Holiday Special, Marvel Tales,* and *Marvel Age.* Also, I've been Director of Research for Square One TV at the Children's Television Workshop (where I've also worked on *3 2 1 Contact*).

Bill Fitts

✳ **Bill Fitts.** P.O. Box 60081, Florence, Massachusetts 01060.

Born: March 4, 1963, in Wellesley, Massachusetts.

College or other education: Basic B.A.

Comics-related education: Miscellaneous tutoring in watercolor painting, commercial art courses, etc.

Biggest creative influences: Vaughn Bodé, Robert Crumb, and Walt Kelly.

1993 projects: War story for Antarctic Press' *Furrlough* and a short story for *Teenage Mutant Ninja Turtles Adventures* for Archie Comics.

Past comics titles and related projects: *Miami Mice* #2-4 (Rip Off Press, assistant inker, filler stories and illustrations); *Gyro Force* #1-3 (Rip Off Press, assistant inker, toning, and colorist); *Cobalt 60* #2-4 (Tundra Publishing, colorist and pin-up art); *Teenage Mutant Ninja Turtles* #32, *Shell of the Dragon Color Special,* and *Time's Pipeline* (all from Mirage Publishing, colorist); *Teenage Mutant Turtles III: Turtles Back in Time* movie adaptation (Archie Comics, assistant colors).

Favorite comics not worked on: *Omaha, Bone, Maximortal, Cerebus,* and *Nexus.*

Dream comic-book project: To do a funny-animal story written by Alan Moore.

Mary Fleener

✳ **Mary Fleener.** P.O. Box 230079, Encinitas, California 92023-0079.

Born: September 14, 1951, in Los Angeles, California.

College or other education: California State University at Long Beach, Printmaking major.

Biggest creative influences: Robert Crumb, Egyptian art, *Mad* magazine (Bill Elder and Dave Berg), and Fleischer animation.

1993 projects: My solo title, *Slutburger* (published by Drawn and Quarterly), *Twisted Sisters* #2, *Das Magazin* (Switzerland), and *Striptease* section in *Heavy Metal*.

Past comics titles and related projects: *Hoodoo* (solo title, published by Ray Zone). Anthologies: *Weirdo* and *Strip AIDS USA* (Last Gasp); Rip Off Comix, *Heck!*, and *Wimmen's Comix* (Rip Off); *Grateful Dead Comix, Snarf,* and *Blab!* (Kitchen Sink); *Real Stuff, Real Girl, Prime Cuts,* and *Itchy Planet* (Fantagraphics); *Hyena* and *Heavy Metal* (Tundra); *Drawn and Quarterly* (Drawn and Quarterly); *Twisted Sisters* (Viking Penguin); *The Art of Mickey Mouse* (Hyperion

Press); *Pox* (Sweden); *Girl Frenzy* (England); *Das* (Switzerland); and *Surri Kurpitsa* (Finland).

Favorite comics not worked on: *Snake Eyes, Hate, Eightball, Love and Rockets,* and *Cud* (Fantagraphics); *Beer Nutz* and *Harvey the Hillbilly* (Tundra); and *Stickboy* (Starhead Comics).

Dream comic-book project: A collection of illustrated song lyrics, blues or rock 'n' roll.

✳ **Robert Loren Fleming.** 3 Maplewood Drive, Mount Kisco, New York 10549.

Born: November 5, 1956, in Batavia, New York.

College or other education: Some.

Biggest creative influences: Evelyn Waugh, Frank Capra, Stanley Kubrick, Robert Kanigher, John Williams, and Bernard Herrmann.

1993 projects: *Eclipso* and *Valor* monthly ongoing series, *Eclipso Annual* #1, *Batman: Legends of the Dark Knight* #51, and *Chigger and the Man* (new Vertigo mini-series).

Past comics titles and related projects: *Thriller, Ambush Bug, Underworld, Aquaman, Hell on Earth, Ragman, Eclipso: The Darkness Within, Eclipso, Valor* (all from DC); *Honeymooners* (from Triad); *Codename: Danger* and *March Hare* (from Lodestone); *Chigger and the Man* (Taboo); *Matt Champion* (Metro); various stories, *Veronica in the Soviet Union, Hawaii, Switzerland, Hong Kong,* Archie TV movie adaptation, *Teenage Mutant Ninja Turtles Special* #4 (Archie); "Buster the Ghost" (episode of *Ghostbusters* TV show).

Favorite comics not worked on: *Hate, Real Stuff, Yummy Fur,* anything by P. Craig Russell, *Bone, Reid Fleming,* and *Big Numbers.*

Dream comic-book project: *Thriller.*

✳ **Creig Flessel.** c/o *CBG* Editorial Department, 700 East State Street, Iola, Wisconsin 54990.

Born: February 2, 1912, in Huntington, New York.

College or other education: Grand Central Art School, New York City (1930-1932).

Comics-related education: Pratt Institute (night class, 1937-38), 1937-38, Assistant to John Striebel on *Dixie Dugan*. 1958-60, Assistant to Al Capp on *Li'l Abner.*

Creig Flessel

Biggest creative influences: Norman Rockwell, Chas DeFeo, Harvey Dunn, and Vic Forsythe (*Joe Jinx*).

1993 projects: Recreation of Golden Age comic book covers circa 1938-1943. A how-to-draw book for Doubleday out in '93.

Past comics titles and related projects: *More Fun Adventures* and *Detective Comics* (1937-1945). *Romantic Comics, Prez, Jungle Jim* (1937-39). Created *Speed Saunders, Steve Conrad, Hankes the Cowhand, The Bradley Boys.* Many of the first covers of Sandman and *Detective Comics.* Advertising comics in Sunday newspapers. *Boys' Life* covers. Covers for *Pictoral Review* (Hearst). Textbooks. SUDG Films storyboards. And, of course, in my dotage, I created *The Tales of Baron Von First in Bed* for *Playboy*, 1980-, and a Doubleday book on how to draw, soon to be published.

Dream comic-book project: I should tell you and Walter Winchell to steal my idea! No way!

✱ **J.A. Fludd.** 138 Benson Street, Albany, New York 12206.

Born: February 16 in Albany, New York.

College or other education: Rhode Island School of Design, Providence, Rhode Island, Illustration major. Russell Sage College Albany Campus, Albany, New York, Commercial Art major. A.A.S. degree.

Biggest creative influences: Stan Lee and Jack Kirby (*The Fantastic Four*), Gene Roddenberry (*Star Trek*), Carl Sagan (*Cosmos*), *Omni* magazine, and George Pérez.

J.A. Fludd

1993 projects: *Sentinel*, the ongoing super-hero adventure series in *Gay Comics*, with writer/editor Andy Mangels.

Past comics titles and related projects: *The FantaCo Chronicles* series: magazines on history and criticism of comics. Articles and drawings appeared in volumes on The X-Men, The Fantastic Four, Spider-Man, and The Avengers.

Favorite comics not worked on: *The Fantastic Four, The Avengers, The Uncanny X-Men, Legionnaires,* Baron and Rude's *Nexus,* and Colleen Doran's *A Distant Soil.*

Dream comic-book project: The formation of a comics company that would publish my own creations, produced according to my own personal vision.

✱ **Daniel Howard Fogel.** Cherry Comics, P.O. Box 11991, Berkeley, California 94701.

Born: December 5, 1965, in San Francisco, California.

College or other education: Bachelor's Degree in Dramatic Art (honors).

Comics-related education: Studied with underground cartoonist John J. Woznink, Master Class weekend intensive 1981 — Harvey Kurtzman, Burne Hogarth, and Gil Kane.

Biggest creative influences: August Strindberg, Hunter S. Thompson, Larry Welz, and Vaughn Bodé.

Daniel Howard Fogel

1993 projects: *Cherry* #14-16, *Cherry's Jubilee* #2-5, editor and contributing writer.

Past comics titles and related projects: *Cherry* #10 (1990), *Cherry* #12 (1991), *Cherry* #13 (1992), *Cherry's Jubilee* #1 (1992), *Cherry Mini* #1 (1992), *One-Fisted Tales* #3 (1991). Producer/director *Open Season: The Play*, 1989. Producer/director/actor *Open Season: The Rewrite*, 1990.

Favorite comics not worked on: *Cerebus, Grendel, Love and Rockets*, and *Gregory*.

Dream comic-book project: Create an original graphic-novel series, adapting plays and novels to comics.

✻ **T.C. Ford.** Obsidian Publishing, 24 Harborside Drive, #3, Milford, Connecticut 06460.

Born: February 9, 1964, in Bridgeport, Connecticut.

College or other education: Associates degree, Housatonic Community College, 1983.

Comics-related education: Background apprentice/assistant for Dick Giordano and Frank McLaughlin, 1979-1982.

Biggest creative influences: Dick Giordano, Neal Adams, Steve Ditko, Bernie Wrightson, and Frank McLaughlin.

1993 projects: *Team: Danger*, writing, lettering, pencilling; *Shockwave*, writing, art, lettering; *Steve Woron's Survivors*, editing; and *Star Knight*, writing and inking.

Past comics titles and related projects: *Charlton Bullseye* #4 (one-page story, art and lettering); *Charlton Bullseye Special* #1 (writing and inking, 10 pages); *Lugh, Lord of Light* #2 and 3 (lettering); *Omega/Omen* #1 (lettering); *Tales of the Ninja Warriors* #9 (lettering); *Murcielaga, the She-Bat* (back--up story, lettering). Connecticut area projects: *Total Comics* #1-10, *Cosmic Forces* #1, *Nyteside* — a serial about a rock band which ran in various issues of *Hip* magazine (to be concluded in *Shockwave*).

Favorite comics not worked on: *Strips, Cerebus, Archer & Armstrong, Mage, The Crow*, and *Watchmen*.

Dream comic-book project: A graphic novel of *The Greatest American Hero* or *Buckaroo Banzai*.

✻ **Dick Foreman.** c/o *CBG* Editorial Department, 700 East State Street, Iola, Wisconsin 54990.

Born: August 16, 1952, in Chippenham, Wiltshire, United Kingdom.

College or other education: University of Essex, B.A. (Literature).

Biggest creative influences: DC and Marvel comics of the 1960s, the best of the undergrounds, Alan Moore, and the best of the modern non-mainstream comics from Fantagraphics, Drawn and Quarterly, etc.

1993 projects: Scripting *Black Orchid* ongoing series for DC/Vertigo. Scripting *Rites of Alchemy*, a 12-issue series for DC/Vertigo.

Past comics titles and related projects: Single-issue fill-ins on *Hellblazer* (one) and *Swamp Thing* (three) for DC. Eight-page story, *Suburban Autopsies*, in *Taboo Especial* for Tundra. Eight-page story, "The Janitor," in *Miracleman Apocrypha* #2 for Eclipse. Three-page story, "Future Shock," for *2000 AD*, Fleetway U.K. Two four-page stories (series title: *On Earth as It Is . . .*) for *Blaam* (a now defunct U.K. magazine).

Favorite comics not worked on: *Hate, Love and Rockets, Sinner, Naughty Bits, Slutburger, Drawn and Quarterly, From Hell, Sandman*, (J.

Delano's) *Animal Man, Tantalizing Stories, Skidmarks*, and many more.

Dream comic-book project: Completing the *On Earth as It Is . . .* series (with John McCrea's art), a small project but close to my heart.

✳ **Tonne Forquer.** c/o *CBG* Editorial Department, 700 East State Street, Iola, Wisconsin 54990.

Born: June 30, 1970, in Louisiana.

College or other education: Advanced Laboratory Technology.

Biggest creative influences: Johnette Napolitano, Tori Amos, Graham Ingels, Cyndi Lauper, the cemetery, and silence.

1993 projects: *Tales from the Balcony* and various projects for Allied Comics.

Past comics titles and related projects: *Bloodklott, Manhandler*, and various horror shorts.

Favorite comics not worked on: *Tales from the Crypt, Death, The Haunt of Fear, Sandman*, and *Cry for Dawn*.

Dream comic-book project: To do a graphic novel with John Bolton.

Ron Fortier

✳ **Ron Fortier.** P.O. Box 265, Somersworth, New Hampshire 03878.

Born: November 5, 1946, in Rochester, New Hampshire.

College or other education: B.S. in Business Administration from New Hampshire College.

Biggest creative influences: Stan Lee, Ray Bradbury, and Forrest Ackerman.

1993 projects: *Green Hornet* (Now), *Chivalry* (Caliber), *Captain Hazzard* (Alpha Productions), *Britannia* (Heroic Publications), and *Mr. Jigsaw* (Alpha Productions).

Past comics titles and related projects: *Mr. Jigsaw* (Charlton), *Popeye* and *Street Fighter* (Ocean Comics), *Terminator* and *Green Hornet* (Now).

Favorite comics not worked on: *Justice Society of America, The Spider, The Rocketeer*, and *Magnus Robot Fighter*.

Dream comic-book project: Anything with Russ Heath.

✳ **Frank Fosco.** 1310 Prairie Avenue, Chicago Heights, Illinois 60411.

Born: July 23, 1956, in Merrysville, California.

Biggest creative influences: Kirby, Frazetta, Smith, Wrightson, and Jim Lee.

1993 projects: *Ethrian*, a back-up two-parter in *Vanguard* for Image Comics, © Erik Larsen.

Past comics titles and related projects: *Megaton* out of Elgin, Illinois. *Aida-Zee* for Nate Butler Studios.

Favorite comics not worked on: *WildC.A.T.S.*

Dream comic-book project: Ethrian in his own book, *Fantastic Four, New Gods*, or *Thor*.

✳ **Ronn Foss.** HCR 3, Box 40, Birch Tree, Missouri 65438.

Agent: Bill Schelly, biographer/Comic Fandom Archives.

Born: July 14, 1939, in Defiance, Ohio.

Comics-related education: High-school art scholarship.

Biggest creative influences: H. Foster, A. Raymond, J. Kubert, A. Toth, A. Williamson, F. Frazetta, E.R. Kinstler, W. Wood, R. Crandall, and W. Eisner.

1993 projects: Ongoing private collectors' fantasy strips and videotapes.

Past comics titles and related projects: *Not Brand Echh* #13, 1969, pencils, Marvel; *Good Jive* #1, 1971, script, Kitchen; *Wildman* #1, 1985, pencils, Miller; *Rip Off Comics* #19-21, and 30, 1989-91, script and art; *Sinnin'* #1, 1991, pen-

Ronn Foss

Brad W. Foster

cils, Eros; *Decorator* #1, 1992, script and art, Eros; EC negatives opaque, *Valor, Piracy, Psychoanalysis*, 1984-85, Russ Cochran; record album cover "Songs of Conscience," art, 1981; cassette audio tape cover, Led Zeppelin fan club, Ocean, 1989; dozens of rubber stamps, female figures, ongoing; adult art videotapes, ongoing serials; *Secrets of Comics*, how-to overview.

Favorite comics not worked on: *Batman*.

Dream comic-book project: *Cabinet of Dr. Caligari*.

✷ **Brad W. Foster.** Jabberwocky Graphix, P.O. Box 165246, Irving, Texas 75016.

Born: April 26, 1955, in San Antonio, Texas.

College or other education: Texas A & M University (Bachelors in Architecture). Two years art study, University of Texas.

Biggest creative influences: Graphic arts 1500-1800; Art Deco; Art Nouveau; Baroque; Victorian art and architecture.

1993 projects: *Adventures of Olivia* series; *Passions* series; background work on *Shadowhawk II*; various art print projects; and editing the *Goodies* anthology comics series.

Past comics titles and related projects: Created, wrote, and drew *Mechthings* for Renegade

Press. Cover colorist for *Fission Chicken* from Fantagraphics Books. *Adventures of Olivia, Bawdy Bible*, etc. from Jabberwocky Graphix. Contributor to *101 Other Uses for a Condom* from Apple Press. Back cover color for *Ultra Klutz* from Onward Comics. Article and illustrations for *Comics They Never Told You About*, Cavalier magazine.

Favorite comics not worked on: *Cerebus* and *Xenozoic Tales*.

Dream comic-book project: Continue editing my different-artist-every-page project, *Our Story Thus Far*, to get up to at least 1000 artists involved.

✷ **Bill Fountain.** 8425 Green Mound, Dallas, Texas 75227.

Born: January 18, 1965, in Dallas, Texas.

College or other education: Bachelors degree in Humanities (Master of Arts) M.A., graduated high honors, finishing Master's degree in Humanities.

Biggest creative influences: Will Eisner and Frank Miller.

1993 projects: *Sound of Coming Darkness* (a 42-page graphic novel for Blackbird). Graphic novel *The Final Cut* and second series, *Sinister Surges*.

Past comics titles and related projects: All

cartoons and layouts for a political economy book: *Longwave Rhythms in Economic Development.* For eight years syndicated comic strip in local Texas weekly papers.

Favorite comics not worked on: *Hard Looks* and *Concrete*.

Dream comic-book project: *Batman*.

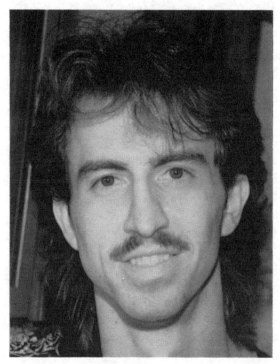

Franchesco

✱ **Franchesco.** 2025 N. 19th Avenue, Melrose Park, Illionis 60160.

Born: January 12, 1965, in Carbonara, Italy.

College or other education: Self-taught.

1993 projects: Co-created and illustrated Adam, the freshest Green Lantern to appear in the Corps (DC Comics). Co-created and illustrated *The Scavengers* for Triumphant Comics.

Past comics titles and related projects: Pencilled Mike Barr's *Maze Agency's Swansong*. Illustrated various covers, posters, and pin-ups for various publishers (Marvel, Malibu, DC, Comico, Triumphant, Innovation, Grey Productions, Personality, *Comics Buyer's Guide, Amazing Heroes, Wizard,* etc.).

Favorite comics not worked on: Alan Davis' *Excalibur, Sam and Max, Bone,* and *Groo*.

Dream comic-book project: Pencil the trials

and tribulations of Marvel's merry mutants and more Adam (the freshest Green Lantern).

✱ **Scott Alexander Frantz.** Rebel Studios, 4716 Judy Court, Sacramento, California 95841.

Born: October 24, 1966, in New Jersey.

College or other education: Tim Vigil artist course.

Comics-related education: Silverwolf Comics, ARC Adult Education Cartooning Course.

Biggest creative influences: Jack Kirby, Tim Vigil, Japanimation, Ditko, and Steranko.

1993 projects: *Darkstar II, Gotterdammerung,* and *Meccalopolis*.

Past comics titles and related projects: *Raw* media mags and *Darkstar*.

Favorite comics not worked on: *Justice League, Thor, Captain America*, and *Legion of Super-Heroes*.

Dream comic-book project: *Darkstar* as a graphic novel and continuing it until I die. P.S. And an animated film.

Frank Kelly Freas

✱ **Frank Kelly Freas.** Kelly Freas Studios, 7713 Nita Avenue, West Hills, California 91304-5546.

Agent: Laura Brodian Freas.

Born: August 27, 1922, in Hornell, New York.

College or other education: Art Institute of Pittsburgh.

Comics-related education: Six years on the staff of *Mad* magazine.

Biggest creative influences: Edd Cartier and Virgil Finlay.

1993 projects: *Star Trek: Deep Space Nine* — not finalized yet. TSR: *Buck Rogers* — still negotiating.

Past comics titles and related projects: *Mad* magazine, *Crazy* magazine, *National Lampoon*, Marvel Comics, DC Comics, and *XXXenophile*.

Dream comic-book project: A satire involving extraterrestrials trying to understand Earth people.

Fred Fredericks

✱ **Fred Fredericks.** Box 475, Eastham, Massachusetts 02642.

Born: August 9, 1929, in Atlantic City, New Jersey.

Comics-related education: 1953-54, nights at Cartoonists and Illustrators School (now known as School of Visual Arts), thanks to the G.I. Bill.

Biggest creative influences: Milton Caniff,

Chester Gould, Jack Kirby, and Mort Meskin.

1993 projects: Still drawing *Mandrake the Magician* daily and Sunday, plus inking many Marvel characters, *Iron Man, Ghost Rider, The Civil War*, etc.

Past comics titles and related projects: Inked: *The Punisher War Journal, Daredevil, The Destroyer* mini-series, *The Nth Man, Avengers, Quasar, Thor Annual, G.I. Joe, Silverhawks*, etc. for Marvel; *Catwoman* in *Showcase '93* for DC. Pencils, inks, and story for: *The Munsters, Mister Ed, Rocky and Bullwinkle, Daniel Boone, New Terrytoons, King Leonardo*, etc. for Dell/Gold Key.

Favorite comics not worked on: *Captain America* and *Punisher War Zone*.

Dream comic-book project: A Mandrake and Phantom mini-series for the Nineties, both characters in the same story.

✱ **George Freeman.** c/o Mike Friedrich (Star✱Reach), 2991 Shattuck Avenue, Suite 202, Berkeley, California 94705.

Born: May 27, 1951, in Selkirk, Manitoba, Canada.

College or other education: Commercial art course at community college.

Biggest creative influences: Carmine Infantino, Nick Cardy, Joe Kubert, Alex Toth, and Bernie Krigstein.

1993 projects: *Mr. Monster* graphic novel for Atomeka.

Past comics titles and related projects: *Captain Canuck, Batman, Wasteland, Marvel Fanfare, Jack of Hearts, Elric, Green Lantern, Chaos, Big Break, True North, Avengers West Coast*, and *Dinosaurs Attack*.

Favorite comics not worked on: Grant Morrison's *Doom Patrol, Herbie, Yummy Fur*, and *The Jam*.

Dream comic-book project: A mystery or historical graphic novel.

✱ **James W. Fry.** 553 Prospect Avenue, Brooklyn, New York 11215.

Born: May 18, 1960, in Brooklyn, New York.

College or other education: Two years at Dartmouth College.

Comics-related education: Marvel Comics'

Apprenticeship Program, September 1984-December 1985.

Biggest creative influences: Poverty, caffeine, and desperation.

1993 projects: *Moon Knight* (Marvel), *Silver Star* limited series (Topps).

Past comics titles and related projects: *Liberty Project* #1-8, *Total Eclipse* (Eclipse); *Atari Force Special* #1, *Doom Patrol Annual* #1, *Checkmate* #8, *Blasters* #1, *Star Trek V* adaptation, *Star Trek* #1-10 (DC); *Inhumanoids* #1 and 2, *West Coast Avengers Annual* #5, *Nomad* limited series #1-4, *Namor Annual* #1 and 2, *Excalibur* #53, *Slapstick* limited series #1-4, *Moon Knight* #45-present (Marvel); *Blood Syndicate* #2 (Milestone); *Vampirella Summer Nights* #1, *Creepy* #2 and 4 (Harris).

Favorite comics not worked on: *Sandman, Hellblazer, Milk & Cheese, Groo*, and *Nexus*.

Dream comic-book project: I dunno, something critically acclaimed, mind-numbingly profitable, and easy to draw, I hope.

✳ **Ed Furness.** 812 Burnham Thorpe Road, #1903, Etobicoke, Ontario, Canada M9C 4W1.

Born: May 11, 1910, in Yorkshire, England.

College or other education: A.O.C.A., Ontario College of Art (Toronto, Canada).

Comics-related education: Art Director, writer, cartoonist.

Biggest creative influences: *The Spirit* (Will Eisner), *Flash Gordon* (Alex Raymond), and *Prince Valiant* (Hal Foster).

Past comics titles and related projects: These were all published 1941-45 and were pioneers of comics industry in Canada. *Freelance, Robin Hood, Red Rover, Dr. Destine, The Purple Rider, Commander Steel*, the Canadian editions of *Captain Marvel, Bulletman, Spy Smasher* (all Fawcett publications, working with C.C. Beck and Pete Costanza).

Favorite comics not worked on: I don't work on any, now — just paint.

Dream comic-book project: A little kids' version of *Robin Hood*.

✳ **Neil Gaiman.** c/o *CBG* Editorial Department, 700 East State Street, Iola, Wisconsin

Neil Gaiman

54990. [Fans can contact a Neil Gaiman information service: The Magian Line, P.O. Box 170712, San Francisco, California 94117.]

Agent: Merrilee Heifetz, Writers House, 21 West 26th Street, New York, New York 10010.

Born: November 10, 1960, in Portchester, England.

1993 projects: *Sandman, Children's Crusade, Alice Cooper*, and *Miracleman*.

Past comics titles and related projects: Lots and lots and lots and lots . . .

Dream comic-book project: *Neil Gaiman's Comics and Stories*, I suppose.

✳ **Michael Gallagher.** c/o *CBG* Editorial Department, 700 East State Street, Iola, Wisconsin 54990.

Born: November 15, 1951, in Manhattan, New York City.

College or other education: B.F.A., Rider College, 1973.

Biggest creative influences: John Gallagher (father), Walt Kelly, E.C. Segar, Will Eisner, Johnny Hart, Harvey Kurtzman, and C.C. Beck.

1993 projects: Writer: *Guardians of the Galaxy, Sonic the Hedgehog, Archie* daily and Sunday strip, and *Looney Tunes* magazine.

Past comics titles and related projects: Writer: *ALF, Mighty Mouse, Betty, Veronica, Count Duckula, Flintstone Kids, Heathcliff, Care Bears, Madballs,* and *Impossible Man Summer Specials.*

Favorite comics not worked on: *Concrete, Judge Dredd, Groo, The Spirit,* and *Mai, the Psychic Girl.*

Dream comic-book project: *Mighty Mouse* (again).

✳ **Carlos Garzón.** P.O. Box 306, Callicoon, New York 12723.

Born: May 22, 1945, in Bogotá, Colombia.

College or other education: Three years in Bogotá, Columbia.

Comics-related education: A lot of training at home and working with top comic artists and the best companies.

Biggest creative influences: Harold Foster, Alex Raymond, and Al Williamson.

1993 projects: *Star Trek: The Next Generation* (cover), some *Team Titans* (DC Comics). *Archer & Armstrong* (Valiant Comics).

Past comics titles and related projects: *Ka-Zar, Star Wars, Star Trek, Cosmic Odyssey, Flash Gordon, Bugs Bunny, Yosemite Sam, Sylvester, Tweety, Hex, Hawkman, Legion of Super-Heroes, The Get Along Gang, Blade Runner, World of Krypton, The Jetsons, Bullwinkle and Rocky, Transformers,* and several *Creepy* and *Eerie* magazines.

Favorite comics not worked on: *Lone Ranger, Porky Pig,* and *Tarzan.*

Dream comic-book project: *Bugs Bunny, Sylvester, Daffy Duck, Batman,* and *Tarzan.*

✳ **David Gatzmer.** 293 N. Wilder, #14, St. Paul, Minnesota 55104.

Born: November 20, 1966, in Anoka, Minnesota.

College or other education: Minneapolis College of Art and Design (1½ years).

Biggest creative influences: Warner Bros. cartoons, *Ren & Stimpy,* Ted McKeever, Sam Kieth, Egon Shiele, and Robert Williams.

1993 projects: *Aesop's Desecrated Morals* (by Doug Wheeler), *Butch Butchwax* (ongoing), and *Hoox* limited series proposal.

Past comics titles and related projects: Spot

illos for *Cheval Noir* (Dark Horse), *Classics Desecrated* (Dark Horse, Rip Off), *Butchy Butchwax and His Transdimensional Winnebago,* and other spot illos and ads for local humor monthly *Funny Pages.* Storyboards for Lock and Load herbicide commercial.

Favorite comics not worked on: *The Maxx, Tank Girl, Savage Dragon, Spawn, The Mask, Lobo,* and *Metropol.*

Dream comic-book project: My own monthly title to tell a variety of different stories in.

Rick Geary

✳ **Rick Geary.** 701 Kettner Boulevard, #118, San Diego, California 92101.

Agent: David Scroggy Agency.

Born: February 25, 1946, in Kansas City, Missouri.

College or other education: University of Kansas, B.F.A. (1968), M.A. (1970).

Biggest creative influences: Edward Gorey and Gluyas Williams.

1993 projects: *Blanche Goes to Hollywood* (graphic novel — Dark Horse).

Past comics titles and related projects: Stories and illustrations for: Dark Horse Comics (1987-), *National Lampoon* (1979-92), *New York*

Times (1988-92), and *Heavy Metal* (1984-). Graphic novels: *A Treasury of Victorian Murder* (1987), *Blanche Goes to New York* (1992), and three adaptations for *Classics Illustrated*.

Favorite comics not worked on: *Flaming Carrot* (Bob Burden) and *Thirteen O'Clock* (Richard Sala).

Dream comic-book project: *Three Journeys* (graphic novel).

✶ **Joe Gentile.** 17126 South 71st Avenue, #11, Tinley Park, Illinois 60477, or A-F Books and Comics, 582 Torrence Avenue, Calumet City, Illinois 60409.

Born: June 2, 1963, in Chicago Heights, Illinois.

College or other education: B.A. in Broadcast Communications from Columbia College, Chicago.

Comics-related education: English/Writing minor, Columbia College.

Biggest creative influences: Neil Gaiman, Denny O'Neil, and Alan Moore.

1993 projects: Writer: *Cambion* and *Sherlock Holmes* for Northstar/Comico.

Past comics titles and related projects: Writer: *Fright Night* #1 and 2 (Now Comics), and *Sherlock Holmes Tales of Mystery and Suspense* #1-4 and ongoing (Northstar/Comico).

Favorite comics not worked on: *Sandman, Hellblazer, Animal Man, Daredevil,* and *Avengers.*

Dream comic-book project: Writing the *Avenger* or *Shadow* series.

✶ **Nat Gertler.** I-8 East Atlantic Avenue, Hi-Nella, New Jersey 08083.

Born: April 30, 1965, in Cinnaminson, New Jersey.

College or other education: B.A., Simons Rock College, December 1983.

Biggest creative influences: Alan Moore, Denny O'Neil, Daniel Keyes, and Mom.

1993 projects: *Elfquest: New Blood* #6 and *Summer Special.* Various Parody Press books including *1968 (Give or Take 25 Years).* Richard Petty graphic novel.

Past comics titles and related projects: Writer: *Speed Racer* #21 and 22 ("The Last

Nat Gertler

Lap"), *Grimjack* #57, *Intruder* #7-9, Nascar racing histories, *Grave Tales* #1 and 2, *Nascar Christmas Special, Elfquest: New Blood* #1, *Legends of Nascar* #12, *Dread of Night* #1 and 2, *R.I.P.* #3, 5, 7, and 8, *Images of Omaha* #1, articles for *Comics Buyer's Guide, Comics Career Newsletter,* and *Wizard. Stunt Dawgs* TV episode, "Freedom of Screech."

Favorite comics not worked on: *Bone, Cerebus, Sandman, Hulk, Archer & Armstrong,* and *Spectre.*

Dream comic-book project: *Life and Loves of the Average Panther,* ongoing color series.

✶ **Vincent Giarrano.** P.O. Box 1391, SMS, Fairfield, Connecticut 06430.

Born: November 17, 1960, in Buffalo, New York.

College or other education: Seven years Sculpture major, State University of New York at Buffalo, B.F.A.. Syracuse University, M.F.A.

Biggest creative influences: Jack Kirby, Frank Miller, and Jim Steranko.

1993 projects: *Batman, Spirits of Vengeance, Red Blade, Motorhead,* and *Pete and Moe Visit Professor Swizzle's Robots* (a children's book).

Past comics titles and related projects: *Dr. Fate, Haywire, Batman, Aquaman, Foolkiller, Spectre, Terminator, Doom Patrol, Grimjack, Whisper,*

Action Comics, Peter Parker (first job), *Conan*, and *Badlands*.

Favorite comics not worked on: Various Japanese manga. Mostly I have favorite artists instead of titles.

Dream comic-book project: *Redblade* is my own creation; it's the most fun job I've had.

Dave Gibbons

✳ **Dave Gibbons.** c/o *CBG* Editorial Department, 700 East State Street, Iola, Wisconsin 54990.

Born: April 14, 1949, in London, England.

College or other education: A.R.I.C.S.

Biggest creative influences: *The Eagle, Mad*, and Julius Schwartz comics of the '60s.

1993 projects: *Martha Washington's War Diaries, 1963, Aliens: Salvation*, and *Riftworld*.

Past comics titles and related projects: *Doctor Who, Dan Dare, Rogue Trooper, Green Lantern, Watchmen, World's Finest, Give Me Liberty*, and *Batman vs. Predator*.

Favorite comics not worked on: *Sin City, Blue Lily*, and *Nexus*.

Dream comic-book project: Don't start me talking.

✳ **Keith Giffen.** 261 Central Avenue, Box 14, Jersey City, New Jersey 07307.

Born: November 30, 1952, in Queens, New York.

Biggest creative influences: Jack Kirby, José Munoz, Alex Toth, and Dr. Seuss.

1993 projects: *Trencher* (art and writing), *Images of Shadowhawk* (art and plot), *Superpatriot* (plot), *Freak Force* (plot), *Bloodstrike* (plot), and, I guess, whatever else strikes my fancy.

Past comics titles and related projects: *Lobo* (various), *Legion of Super-Heroes, Eclipso, Ambush Bug, Justice League America, Justice League Europe, Justice League International Quarterly, Dr. Fate, L.E.G.I.O.N., Ragman, Emerald Dawn, Invasion, Aquaman, Heckler, Video Jack, Amethyst, Hex, Omega Men, Legionnaires 3, Wally Woods' T.H.U.N.D.E.R. Agents* (I know I've forgotten a bunch), and a whole slew of one-shots, inventories, and fill-ins.

Favorite comics not worked on: Anything by Ted McKeever, *Yummy Fur, Raw, Taboo, Sin City*, and Scott McCloud's indispensable *Understanding Comics*.

Dream comic-book project: *Catch 22* adapted into comic form.

✳ **Tom Gill.** P.O. Box 725, Rockville Centre, New York 11571-0725.

Born: June 3, 1913, in Winnipeg, Canada.

College or other education: Attended Fordham, Pratt Institute, New York Art Students League, and State University of New York.

Biggest creative influences: Milton Caniff, Hal Foster, and Noel Sickles.

1993 projects: How-to book on drawing from memory for art, illustration, and the comics called *Drawing by Association*. Also writing and drawing a dinosaur book.

Past comics titles and related projects: Art staff, *New York News* and *New York Times*. Comic strip in *New York Herald Tribune*, 1941-48. Golden Age love for DC, Harvey, and Timely. Western comics for Dell/Gold Key: *Bonanza, Hi-Yo, Silver, Tonto*, pencilled and inked *Lone Ranger* for 20 years, 1950-1970. Advertising, commercial, TV comics. 1948: Initial faculty Cartoonists and Illustrators School (C and I), then renamed School of Visual Arts in 1956, still associated with SVA as consultant. Also teach cartooning and Drawing by Association at Molloy College and Nassau Community College. Have helped train many top pros like Wally Wood, Joe Sinnot, Tom Darcy, Angelo Torres, and Sal Amendola.

Favorite comics not worked on: Horses, animal, nature stories like *Hi-Yo, Silver*, the Lone Ranger's horse as a colt, written by Gay DuBois. I did it for five years.

Dream comic-book project: Just what I'm doing now.

Jim Gillespie

✱ **Jim Gillespie.** c/o *CBG* Editorial Department, 700 East State Street, Iola, Wisconsin 54990.

Born: October 28, 1959, in Eldorado, Illinois.

College or other education: Two art classes.

Biggest creative influences: Bill Ward, John Byrne, Alan Davis, George Pérez, Tom LaSarro, Neal Adams, Jim Lee, Bart Sears, and many others.

1993 projects: A 10-page story for publisher LH-Art. The story will feature full-shaded pencil drawings.

Past comics titles and related projects: Jabberwocky Graphix's *Goodies* (former mini-comic, now a full-size, adults-only magazine) has published many of my pin-ups, one-panel cartoons, and one comics story. Two pin-ups appeared in

Jabberwocky's *Fever Pitch*, while several pin-ups have been included in LH-Art's *LH-Artist Folio*.

Favorite comics not worked on: *Excalibur, Faust, Cry for Dawn, The Batman Adventures, Wild-C.A.T.S,* and *Evil Ernie.*

Dream comic-book project: An "Anti-Crisis" crossover, which would restore (for the most part) the pre-Crisis DC Universe. Or edit or coordinate a comprehensive reprint collection of the erotic art and stories of Bill Ward.

Darren Goodhart

✱ **Darren Goodhart.** c/o *CBG* Editorial Department, 700 East State Street, Iola, Wisconsin 54990.

Born: September 24, 1962, in Hannibal, Missouri.

College or other education: Art Institute of Pittsburgh, Associate in a specialized technology degree (Visual Communications).

Biggest creative influences: The works of Frank Miller, John Byrne, Howard Chaykin, Jim Starlin, and too many more to mention.

1993 projects: Actually not due out until early 1994, I'm currently pencilling and inking, *. . . absolute power . . .*, co-created by myself and Daniel Wilson, to be published by Alpha Productions.

Past comics titles and related projects: *The Survivors* (with Steve Woron) for Prelude Graphics and Burnside Comics; *Femforce, the Armageddon Factor*, and *Untold Origin of Femforce* for AC Comics; *Rust* (with Fred Schiller) for Now Comics;

stories for *The Shattered Earth* (with Daniel Wilson), Keith Laumer's *Retief*, and *Blood of the Apes* (with Roland Mann); various covers for Malibu Graphics; various pin-ups and logo designs for Alpha Productions; spot illustrations for *Amazing Heroes*; a *Nightmark* short story (with Chris Mills) for *Undead Zombie Biker Chickens from Hell* for Alpha Productions.

Favorite comics not worked on: *Legion of Super-Heroes, Legionnaires, Incredible Hulk*, the Superman titles, *John Byrne's Next Men, Nexus, Sandman*, and *Shade, the Changing Man*.

Dream comic-book project: Well, I'm pretty much doing it, I co-created and co-own . . . *absolute power* . . . but I would also like to do some work for hire with a preference for DC's various Legion titles.

Darrell Goza

✳ **Darrell Goza.** 45 Lindsley Place, East Orange, New Jersey 07018-1109.

Born: August 21, 1955, in Queens, New York.

Comics-related education: Assistant to Neal Adams at Continuity Associates from 1982 to 1992. Placed on DC Ready to Work list 1986.

Biggest creative influences: Jim Steranko, Jack Kirby, and Neal Adams.

1993 projects: *Major Liberty* for Alpha Productions (art), *Scarlet Scorpion* for AC Comics (pencils), *Knight Hawks* for Scriptgraphics (story and art), *Muta* for Beatnik Productions, and *Star Angels and the Unseen* self-published.

Past comics titles and related projects: Assisted on backgrounds on *Crazyman, Megalith, The Revengers,* and many of Continuity's titles. Penciller on *Danse* for Blackthorne. Worked as a background artist on *The Ray* for DC Comics and *Icicle* for Heroic Publishing (both uncredited). Assisted Ernie Colon in coloring *Magnus* #15 for Valiant (uncredited).

Favorite comics not worked on: *Doom Patrol* and *Excalibur*.

Dream comic-book project: To write and draw *Cage* or *X-O Manowar* from Valiant or to illustrate *Doom Patrol*.

✳ **Miyako Matsuda Graham.** 8167 Park Avenue, Forestville, California 95436.

Born: January 11, 1960, in Yamaguchi Prefecture, Japan.

College or other education: College in Kyoto, Japan, and Los Angeles, California, 1980-1982.

1993 projects: Specializing in ink-water colors "kimono girls" and manga signed originals. Translating videotapes (manga) for international distribution and selling water colors at San Francisco area comic conventions. Also keep busy pressing flowers, writing in diary, corresponding with dozens of pen pals, and reading manga. Actively seeking inking and lettering jobs, can render Frazetta-like lines, beating deadlines is normal. Bud Plant Inc. is currently handling "kimono girl" artwork.

Past comics titles and related projects: Drew, inked, and sold comic strips to Japanese manga from 1975-1980, when I entered college. 1985-1990: Inks, lettering, coloring, and retouching of 1940s comic-book reprints for Eclipse Comics: Geo. Herriman, Walt Kelly, Frank Frazetta, Will Eisner, Jack Cole, Winsor McCay, etc. 1990-present: (see 1993 projects). Also, first to translate (with Toren Smith) manga videos into English from 1984-1986.

Neil Grahame

✳ **Neil Grahame.** Route 2, Box 49, Orma, West Virginia 25268.

Born: March 25, in Toronto, Ontario, Canada.

College or other education: I studied commercial and fine art under several private tutors in Florida, notably O. "Pat" Mitchell.

Biggest creative influences: Milton Caniff, Dave Graue and V.T. Hamlin (*Alley Oop*), Stan Lynde (*Rick O'Shay*), and Dick Moores (*Gasoline Alley*).

1993 projects: I am pencilling the Looney Tunes characters: Bugs Bunny, Daffy Duck, Wile E. Coyote, etc., for DC Comics/Warner Bros. International Publishing Department.

Past comics titles and related projects: 1989-93 Pencilled *The Real Ghostbusters* for Now Comics. 1992 Pencilled the graphic album *Read My Lips*, an unofficial cartoon biography of George Bush published by Malibu. 1990-91 Pencilled *New Kids on the Block* for Harvey Comics. 1986-87 Colored covers for Malibu/Eternity. 1981-92 Wrote, pencilled, inked, and lettered a wide variety of strips for Petersen Pub. *Cartoons* magazine.

Favorite comics not worked on: *Cerebus,*

Sandman, Batman Adventures, Dark Horse Presents, and *Cheval Noir.*

Dream comic-book project: I would love to do a wild, freewheeling cartoony adventure strip like *Captain Easy, Popeye,* and *Mickey Mouse* newspaper strips of the '30s and '40s.

Steven Grant

✳ **Steven Grant.** Red Fist Productions, 22845 NE 8th Street, Suite 146, Redmond, Washington 98053.

Born: October 22, 1953, in Madison, Wisconsin.

College or other education: B.A., Communication Arts, 1977, University of Wisconsin.

Biggest creative influences: Phil Ochs, Gil Kane, William Gaddis, and Karl Heinz Stockhausen.

1993 projects: Marvel: *The Punisher, Spectacular Spider-Man,* and *Nightstalkers.* DC: *Manhunter.* Dark Horse: *The Badlands Collection, Enemy,* and *X.* Malibu: *Edge.* Piranha: *Choose Your Own JFK Assassination Conspiracy Theory.*

Past comics titles and related projects: *Badlands, Whisper, Psychoblast, Punisher* miniseries, *Legends of the Dark Knight,* and *The Life of Pope John Paul II.*

Favorite comics not worked on: *Those Annoying Post Brothers, Hellblazer,* and *Deadface.*

Dream comic-book project: *Badlands;* I've already done my dream project and hope to do it again.

✳ **D. Alexander Gregory.** 320 East Victory Drive, Apartment #3, Savannah, Georgia 31405.

Born: February 5, 1972.

College or other education: Savannah College of Art and Design.

Biggest creative influences: Sargent, Abbey, Waterhouse, Klimt, Schiele, Williams, Pratt, Muth, Chiavello, Van Fleet, Sienkiewicz, McKean, Jones, Manara, Moebius, and life itself.

1993 projects: *Kilroy Is Here, The Twist,* and *The Comedy.*

Past comics titles and related projects: *Vampire II: Masquerade* and *Who's Who: Children of the Inquisition* (both Whitewolf).

Favorite comics not worked on: *Enigma, Shade, Death, Sandman, Madman,* and *Cages.*

✳ **Daerick Gröss Sr.** Studio G, 1340 North Indian Springs Road, Flagstaff, Arizona 86004.

Born: January 28, 1947, in Dayton, Ohio.

College or other education: Two years at Ohio University, two years at Central Academy of Design in Cincinnati.

Biggest creative influences: Al Hirschfeld, Bob Peak, Alphonse Mucha, Sid Mead, Neal Adams, Maxfield Parrish, and Joe Quesada.

1993 projects: *Necroscope, Batman/Two-Face, Reiki Warriors, Blackwatch, The Mythfits, The Jinni, Buck Naked,* and *Murciélaga/She-Bat.*

Past comics titles and related projects: *Vampire Lestat, Interview with a Vampire, Queen of the Damned, Forbidden Planet, Color of Magic, Robo-Warriors,* and *Tales of the Ninja Warriors.*

Favorite comics not worked on: Almost anything DC, *The Tick,* and *White Trash.*

Dream comic-book project: A graphic novel in which characters from all companies (including those in limbo) appear and interact.

✳ **David Gross.** 76 Sicard Street, New Brunswick, New Jersey 08901.

David Gross

Born: March 20, 1968, in Philadelphia, Pennsylvania.

College or other education: B.F.A. at Mason Gross School of the Arts/Rutgers University.

Biggest creative influences: Paul Gulacy, Michael Golden, and Chris Bachalo.

1993 projects: Pencilling *Rose* for Heroic Publishing and *The Key* for Marple Publishing.

Past comics titles and related projects: Heroic Publishing — *Rose* #5 (full book). Personality Comics — *New Crew* #5: Michael Dorn (five pages, 1992), *Sports Personalities* # 8: George Brett (full book, 1992), and *Baseball Sluggers* # 4: Don Mattingly (five pages, 1992).

Favorite comics not worked on: *Sandman, Shade,* and *Love and Rockets.*

Dream comic-book project: *Sandman, Shade,* or *Star Trek: The Next Generation.*

✳ **Peter Gross.** c/o *CBG* Editorial Department, 700 East State Street, Iola, Wisconsin 54990.

Born: March 7, 1958, in St. Cloud, Minnesota.

College or other education: Undergrad, St. Johns University (Minnesota), Painting/Art History. Graduate, University of Wisconsin-Superior, Painting, Printmaking, and Art History.

Biggest creative influences: Every comic book I read as a kid and printmaking.

1993 projects: Marvel: *Hellstorm* (inks). Inking on various Titans issues at DC. Breakdowns and inks for Vertigo's *Tim Hunter Annual*.

Past comics titles and related projects: *Empire Lanes, Swamp Thing, Doctor Fate, New Titans, Team Titans, Shade, the Changing Man*, and *Hellstorm*.

Favorite comics not worked on: *Legion of Super-Heroes, Hellblazer*, and *Sandman*.

Dream comic-book project: A new *Empire Lanes* series.

Paul Guinan

✳ Paul Guinan. c/o *CBG* Editorial Department, 700 East State Street, Iola, Wisconsin 54990.

Born: November 27, 1962, in Chicago, Illinois.

College or other education: School of the Art Institute of Chicago (majored in Film/Video).

Comics-related education: Three years staff artist for First Comics.

Biggest creative influences: Mom (who is an illustrator). In comics: Russ Heath, Gray Morrow, and John Severin.

1993 projects: *Aliens: Colonial Marines, Urban Legends, Indiana Jones and the Sargasso Sea*, and my wife's and my own project: *The Heartbreakers* (a women in combat mini-series).

Past comics titles and related projects: Chronologically: *Grimjack* (inked Tom Sutton's run), *Lone Wolf and Cub* (retouch artist), *Heartbreakers* (story and art and co-created with my wife, Anina Bennett), *Terminator* (inked Dark Horse's first series with Chris Warner), *Aliens* (story and art for *Dark Horse Presents* #42, 43 and *Dark Horse Presents Fifth Anniversary Special*), *Punisher* #52, *Hard Looks* #4, and *Aliens: Colonial Marines* (have finished #6 of 12 as of April 1993).

Favorite comics not worked on: *Cud* by Terry LaBan from Fantagraphics. Was honored to be part of the anthology *Urban Legends* from Bob Schreck at Dark Horse and Sung Koo of Chicago.

Dream comic-book project: A 192-page graphic novel of the conquest of Mexico — the most unique historical adventure story in Earth's history.

Nabile P. Hage

✳ Nabile P. Hage. Dark Zulu Lies Inc., 5401 Old National Highway, Suite 610, College Park,

Georgia 30334, or c/o Darris Gringeri, Parker Public Relations, 11500 West Olympic Boulevard, Suite 400, Los Angeles, California 90064.

Born: August 14, 1965.

College or other education: B.S. in Business Management.

Comics-related education: School of hard knocks and seat of pants.

Biggest creative influences: Man's inhumanity to man.

1993 projects: Ania, *Dark Zulu Lies, Motorbike Puppies*, and *Zwanna, Son of Zulu*.

Past comics titles and related projects: *Motorbike Puppies* and *Zwanna, Son of Zulu*.

Favorite comics not worked on: *Uncanny X-Men* (Nightcrawler should have his own book). *Fantastic Four*.

Dream comic-book project: *Motorbike Puppies* and *Zwanna, Son of Zulu*.

✳ **Lurene Haines.** Phoenix Rising Studio, P.O. Box 203, Mary Esther, Florida 32569.

Born: December 19, 1958, in Montreal, Quebec, Canada.

College or other education: B.S., Neuropsych major, Summa Cum Laude.

Comics-related education: July 1986-February 1988, assistant to Mike Grell.

Biggest creative influences: Frazetta, Kaluta, Jeff Jones, Vargas, Soroyama, and Dorman.

1993 projects: Fully painted; *Deep Space Nine: Hostage Situation*, six-issue *Cat People* series, and a variety of comics covers.

Past comics titles and related projects: *Green Arrow: The Longbow Hunters* (pencil, ink, color pencil), *Hellraiser* (painted, story), *Indiana Jones: Fate of Atlantis* (color), *Miss Fury, Reanimator, Baker Street, The Realm* (cover art), *Thumbscrew* (cover art, interior illustrations), *Femina: Dream Girls* (all artwork).

Favorite comics not worked on: *Cynicalman* by Matt Feazell.

Dream comic-book project: Many, but is fully painted *Elektra* graphic novel.

✳ **Matt Haley.** 2691 Woodstone Place, Eugene, Oregon 97405.

Matt Haley

Agent: Sharon Cho.

Born: June 10, 1970, in Houston, Texas.

Biggest creative influences: Steve Purcell (*Sam and Max*), Jerome Moore, Doug Gray (*Eye of Mongombo*), Mike Grell, and José Luis Garcia-Lopez.

1993 projects: *Phantom of Fear City, Squire*, and *Powermonger*.

Past comics titles and related projects: *Star Trek: The Next Generation* and *Tarzan the Warrior*.

Favorite comics not worked on: *Legion of Super-Heroes, Sam and Max: Freelance Police, Nexus, Alien Legion*, and *Tank Girl*.

Dream comic-book project: My own project, *Event Horizon*.

✳ **Cully Hamner.** Gaijin Studios, 5581 Peachtree Road, Atlanta, Georgia 30341.

Born: March 7, 1969, in Huntsville, Alabama.

Comics-related education: Assisted ex-Disney animator Don Howard for two years while also freelancing in commercial art.

Biggest creative influences: Will Eisner, Frank Miller, Mike Mignola, Rod Serling, and everyone at Gaijin Studios.

1993 projects: Currently pencilling *Firearm* for Malibu's Ultraverse; also plotting and pencilling the creator-owned *Brave* for the Dark Horse/ Gaijin Studios anthology *Ground Zero*.

Past comics titles and related projects: I was regular penciller on DC Comics' *Green Lantern: Mosaic* for eleven issues, pencilled *Silver Surfer #*83, pencilled part of *Namor Annual #*3, various pin-ups in *Amazing Heroes Swimsuit Special, Homage Studios Swimsuit Special*, and *Spawn*, and a couple of trading cards for DC and Homage Studios.

Favorite comics not worked on: Miller's *Sin City*, Eisner's *Invisible People, Incredible Hulk*, and *Legionnaires*, currently.

Dream comic-book project: A creator-owned project with writer Doug Wagner called *Magnum 357* or an updated comic-book version of *The Day the Earth Stood Still*.

Al Williamson, Will Eisner, Winslow Homer, and the Disney Studios.

1993 projects: *Uther, the Half Dead King* for Tundra (painted cover, pencils, and inks). *Vampirella* (inks and painted cover) for Harris Publications. *Quest*, S.A.T. review guide in comics format, and *The Thing in the Hole* (a children's book).

Past comics titles and related projects: *Alien Encounters, Epic Illustrated, Moon Knight, Swamp Thing, Thor Annual, New Mutants, Showcase, Luger, Lost Planet, Tapping the Vein, Viking Glory, Legend of Sleepy Hollow*, and *Hellraiser*.

Favorite comics not worked on: *Hate* and any of Eisner's books.

Dream comic-book project: William Goldman's *The Princess Bride* and *The Family of the Verdilak* by A.K. Tolstoy.

Bo Hampton

✱ **Bo Hampton.** c/o *CBG* Editorial Department, 700 East State Street, Iola, Wisconsin 54990.

Born: June 29, 1954, in High Point, North Carolina.

College or other education: B.F.A. School of Visual Arts, New York City.

Comics-related education: One year assistant to Will Eisner. Three months assistant to Al Williamson.

Biggest creative influences: Angelo Torres,

D. Larry Hancock

✱ **D. Larry Hancock.** 153 Woodington Avenue, Toronto, Ontario, Canada M4C 3K7.

Born: July 29, 1954, in Toronto, Ontario, Canada.

College or other education: Chartered

Accountant: Honors Bachelor of Mathematics, University of Waterloo, 1977.

Biggest creative influences: Fredric Brown, Henry Kuttner and C.L. Moore, and John Wyndham.

1993 projects: Wrote a *Suburban Nightmare* story entitled "Secrets" which will appear in *Cheval Noir* #42 to 46 from Dark Horse Comics (May to October 1993). Also have a new mini-series under development with Dark Horse, first issue expected to be on sale in January 1994.

Past comics titles and related projects: With Michael Cherkas, wrote *The Silent Invasion*, a 12-issue mini-series (1986-88) from Renegade Press. With Michael Cherkas and John van Bruggen, wrote *Suburban Nightmares*, a four-issue mini-series (1988) from Renegade Press. Both series have been reprinted in graphic albums (four volumes and one volume respectively) by NBM Publishing. With Michael Cherkas, wrote Dick Mallet stories in *Canadian Comics Annual* and *Cerebus*. With Michael Cherkas, had stories in two "fund-raising" books: *Quest for Dreams* and *The True North*.

Favorite comics not worked on: *Legion of Super-Heroes, Legionnaires, Groo, Sandman Mystery Theatre, Concrete*, and Don Rosa's duck stories.

Dream comic-book project: Writing a mystery novel in comic-book form and having it sell well.

✳ **Elizabeth Hand.** c/o *CBG* Editorial Department, 700 East State Street, Iola, Wisconsin 54990.

Agent: Martha Millard.

Born: March 29, 1957, in San Diego, California.

College or other education: B.A., Cultural Anthropology/Playwriting, Catholic University of America.

Biggest creative influences: Roky Erickson and Vladimir Nabokov.

1993 projects: *Anima*, revival of *The Forever People*.

Past comics titles and related projects: Science-fiction novels: *Winterlong, Aestival Tide*, and *Icarus Descending*. Horror: *Waking the Moon*. Numerous short stories, reviews, articles, etc.

Favorite comics not worked on: *Sandman, Hellblazer, Batman*, and *X-Men*.

Dream comic-book project: Graphic-novel versions of my science-fiction novels.

Marc Hansen

✳ **Marc Hansen.** 1107 Glengary Road, Walled Lake, Michigan 48390.

Born: February 15, 1963, in Roger Heights, Michigan.

College or other education: Associates degree, Commercial Art, Ferris State University.

Biggest creative influences: Harvey Kurtzman and Carl Barks.

1993 projects: *Weird Melvin* weekly strip for *CBG*. *Ralph Snart Adventures* latest monthly series. *Weird Melvin* stories for Tundra's *Crackaboom*. *Lawdog* back-up for Epic.

Past comics titles and related projects: *Ralph Snart Adventures*, 30 issues, 1986-92, Now Comics. *Dr. Gorpon*, three-issue mini-series, Malibu Graphics. *Roger Rabbit, Roger Rabbit's Toontown, Goofy Adventures,* and *Disney Adventures Digest*, Disney Publications. *Snarf* #10, Kitchen Sink. *Married with Children, Astro Boy, Rust*, and *Speed Racer*, Now Comics.

Favorite comics not worked on: *Eightball* and *Yummy Fur*.

Dream comic-book project: 1950s Superman gives Cable a swirly.

✳ **Jack F. Harris.** Visual Logic, 724 Yorklyn Road, Suite 325, Hockessin, Delaware 19707.

Agent: Lisa Harris.

Born: August 24, 1960, in Midland, Texas.

College or other education: B.F.A., Communication Arts and Design (Virginia Commonwealth University).

Biggest creative influences: Bernie Wrightson and Jack Kirby.

1993 projects: *Version* for Dark Horse Comics.

Favorite comics not worked on: *Spawn, Sin City, The Ray*, and anything by Kirby.

Dream comic-book project: *Forever People* on CD-ROM.

Everette Hartsoe

✳ **Everette Hartsoe.** London Night Studios, P.O. Box 5249, Hickory, North Carolina 28601.

Born: May 24, 1967, in Newton, North Carolina.

College or other education: Nothing after high school training.

Biggest creative influences: Frank Miller and Tim Vigil.

1993 projects: *Razor*, ongoing series and writing new series, *Morbid Angel*, both for London Night Studios.

Past comics titles and related projects: My first work was in *Midnight Screams* #2 from Mystery Graphix Press.

Favorite comics not worked on: *Cry for Dawn, Faust*, and *The Crow*.

Dream comic-book project: A crossover with *Razor* and James O'Barr's *The Crow*.

Dean E. Haspiel

✳ **Dean E. Haspiel.** 64 Thompson Street, #17, New York, New York 10012.

Born: May 31, 1967, in New York Hospital.

College or other education: SUNY, Purchase, New York. Studied Visual Arts and Film (did not complete).

Comics-related education: Art assistant to: Bill Sienkiewicz, Howard Chaykin, and Walt Simonson.

Biggest creative influences: Alex Toth, Howard Chaykin, Frank Miller, Bill Watterson, Walt Simonson, and Jack Kirby.

1993 projects: I am illustrating *The Ugly Man* written and co-created by Larry O'Neil to be published in *This Is Sick* by Silver Skull Studios.

Past comics titles and related projects: 1. Art assistant on: *American Flagg!, Thor, New Mutants,* and *Elektra: Assassin,* respectively. 2. Penciller/cover art: Bonus Book #5 in *Detective Comics* #589. 3. Artist/cover art: Bonus Book #13 in *Justice League International* #24. 4. Co-creator/illustrator of *The Verdict* mini-series (Eternity). 5. Co-plot/illustrator of *The Verdict* in *Caliber Presents.* 6. Co-plot/illustrator of *The Verdict: The Acolyte* one-shot (Caliber Press).

Favorite comics not worked on: *Batman: Legends of the Dark Knight,* Miller's *Daredevil* and *Sin City,* everything in the Vertigo line, and *Baker Street.*

Dream comic-book project: My own created, successful properties.

Steve Hauk

✳ **Steve Hauk.** 4853 Cordell Avenue, Unit 1501, Bethesda, Maryland 20814.

Born: August 4, 1954, in Washington, D.C.

College or other education: Self-taught.

Biggest creative influences: Will Eisner, Vaughn Bodé, Mike Ploog, Mike Hinge, George

Carlin, Monty Python, Douglas Adams, *Rocky and Bullwinkle,* and Robert Sheckley.

1993 projects: Developing a title for Parody Press, full art and story. *Emperor of Da Universe* back-up story in *Team Danger* #0 from Obsidian Publishing, inks on Marvel Comics' *Barbie Fashion* #29.

Past comics titles and related projects: Since issue #677 in November 1986 contributed editorial and other cartoons to *Comics Buyer's Guide.* Multiple logos for the Arrow/Caliber book *Deadworld.* Two contributions to the Apple Press book *101 Other Uses for a Condom* (mine were "Frog Partyhat" and "Emergency Airsickness Bag"). A *Fish Police* mini-series from Apple Press, *Fish Shticks,* six issues, all interior art, pencils, inks, and tones. Recently my inks over Dan Parent's cool pencils on *Barbie Fashion* #29 for Marvel (and on my first work for Marvel, my first work to see color, Michelle Wrightson does the coloring. Wow.). I've written gags for Don Martin and Larry "Bud" Melman.

Favorite comics not worked on: Any *Ambush Bug* comic, *2000 AD,* Epic Comics' *The Sleeze Bros.* and *Lance Barnes, Post Nuke Dick,* and Ostrander's *Grimjack.*

Dream comic-book project: Realistically, to ink a Keith Giffen pencilled *Ambush Bug* special (or any Giffen pencils; I especially like his silly side). Total fantasy, to have worked with Vaughn Bodé.

✳ **Glenn Hauman.** 1130 Willow Avenue, #3, Hoboken, New Jersey 07030-3222.

Born: March 4, 1969, in Port Jefferson, New York.

College or other education: New York University, B.S. in Communication Arts.

Comics-related education: Art course with John Buscema, 1983.

Biggest creative influences: Peter David, Harlan Ellison, J.R. "Bob" Dobbs, John Buscema, Denny O'Neil, Mark McKenna, Terry and Sue Ohlinger, and Brandy Phillips.

1993 projects: *101 Ways to Say I Love You; Gotcha!: Tales of Spite, Malice, Revenge, and the Fine Art of Getting Even.*

Past comics titles and related projects: *101*

Glenn Hauman

Other Uses for a Condom, Apple (writer/packager/designer). *Outer Space Babes*, Silhouette Studios (production/edits). DC Comics Production Department, August 1988-March 1989.

Favorite comics not worked on: *Sandman, Hulk, Hardware, Slapstick*, and *Hard Looks*.

Dream comic-book project: *Thunderbolt* or *The New Curiosity Shop*.

✳ **Michael R. Hawkins.** c/o *CBG* Editorial Department, 700 East State Street, Iola, Wisconsin 54990.

Born: October 14, 1965, in Chicago, Illinois.

College or other education: B.A., Art History from University of Illinois in Champaign/Urbana, English Literature minor.

Comics-related education: *Rex Dexter* comic strip published in the *Daily Illini* (University of Illinois school paper) during 1986-87 school year. Won first place Illinois College Press Association Award for Best Comic Strip, co-judged by *The Chicago Tribune* — what an education!

Biggest creative influences: Neal Sternecky, Bob Oksner, Kurt Schaffenberger, Nina Paley, Frank King, and Carl Barks, to name a few.

1993 projects: *Tiny Toon Adventures* for DC Comics/Warner Bros, International Publishing. *Mr. Lizard 3-D Special* — recently published by Now Comics.

Past comics titles and related projects:

Michael R. Hawkins

Inks: *Slimer* #10 (Now Comics). Pencils and inks: *Mr. Lizard* teaser in *Now What?* #10, *Mr. Lizard* four-page origin in *Ralph Snart* #26. Three *Rex Dexter Christmas Mini-Comics*. *Mr. Lizard* #1 and 2 (#1 now published as *Mr. Lizard 3-D Special*, #2 unpublished to date). [Sure, it's not impressive, but it's what I've done so far.]

Favorite comics not worked on: *Sandman, Uncle Scrooge, Legionnaires, X-O Manowar, Solar, The Hacker Files*, and *Elfquest*.

Dream comic-book project: Self-publishing *Rex Dexter Adventures* or writing/drawing a *Leave It to Binky* mini-series for DC Comics.

✳ **Drew Hayes.** Mulehide Graphics, P.O. Box 5844, Bellingham, Washington 98227-5844.

Born: July 20, 1969, in Los Angeles, California.

Biggest creative influences: Dave Sim, Bernie Wrightson, Simon Bisley, Gerhard (shading). In writing I'm influenced by everything I see, read, and go through (experience). I don't base my written work on anyone's style; I figure they've done or are doing their own thing; I'll go off to this side of the woods and do mine. Emotions are also a major factor. I tend to find the darker side of living quite fascinating.

1993 projects: *Necromancer* #3 (Anarchy Press), *Poison Elves, The Once Over Twice,* (benefit CBLDF Annual).

Favorite comics not worked on: *Cerebus, Sandman,* and *Bone.*

Dream comic-book project: I'm doing it already. Second up would be collaborating on something with Dave Sim, but I won't hold my breath on this dream.

✳ **Patrick Hayes.** 413 Marcia Street, Redlands, California 92373.

Born: November 9, 1967, in Pomona, California.

College or other education: B.A. in English and a California teaching certificate.

Biggest creative influences: Don Martin, Sergio Aragonés, Keith Giffen, and Carl Barks.

1993 projects: *It's Bound to Happen!* strips for *CBG.*

Past comics titles and related projects: *It's Bound to Happen!* for *CBG* and assorted minicomics in the Redlands area.

Favorite comics not worked on: *Legion of Super-Heroes, Legionnaires,* Disney duck books, and Batman titles.

Dream comic-book project: Draw one page for a Legion book or write an issue.

✳ **Steve Haynie.** c/o Haynie Auto Sales, 109 Pilgrim Drive, P.O. Box 5112, Easley, South Carolina 29640.

Born: April 16, 1964.

College or other education: Associate Degrees in Electronics Engineering and Automated Manufacturing Technologies.

Biggest creative influences: Todd Klein.

1993 projects: Lettering: *Shaman's Tears, Hardware, Static,* and *Green Arrow.*

Past comics titles and related projects: Lettered many titles for First Comics, Comico, DC Comics, Dark Horse Comics, and Milestone Media.

Doug Hazlewood

✳ **Doug Hazlewood.** 309 Dunbar, Victoria, Texas 77904.

Born: September 20, 1954, in Dallas, Texas.

College or other education: A.A., Fine Arts (Victoria College). B.S. in Commercial Art (SWTSU).

Biggest creative influences: Kirby, Kirby/Ayers, Kirby/Stone, Neal Adams, Gene Colan, Steranko, and Tom Palmer.

1993 projects: *Adventures of Superman.*

Past comics titles and related projects: DC: *Adventures of Superman, Doom Patrol* #42, and *Animal Man.* Marvel: *Nick Fury, Agent of S.H.I.E.L.D., What If?* #23, and *Daredevil* #286. First: *Sable.* Eclipse: *Liberty Project.* Wonder/Pied Piper: *Power Factor.* Eternity: *Pellestar.* Many cover inks for Eternity/Malibu and Quality Comics, *Hamster Vice* (Blackthorne), and *Nightveil* (AC).

Favorite comics not worked on: *Hulk, Superman: Man of Steel,* and *Reid Fleming.*

Dream comic-book project: *Hulk vs. Martian Manhunter?* (Something that excites me genuinely, is always welcome. Always liked Martian Manhunter and like doing Hulk faces . . . I don't know!)

John Heebink

✴ John Heebink. c/o *CBG* Editorial Department, 700 East State Street, Iola, Wisconsin 54990.

Born: January 2, 1958, in Palo Alto, California.

College or other education: BA, Communications major in Advertising, Michigan State University, 1980.

Comics-related education: Assistant to Mike Manley.

Biggest creative influences: Wally Wood, Neal Adams, Howard Chaykin, Alex Raymond, Al Williamson, and Mike Manley.

1993 projects: *Daredevil Annual #9* (Marvel).

Past comics titles and related projects: *Nick Fury, Agent of S.H.I.E.L.D., Darkhawk,* and *Deathlok* (Marvel). *Grave Tales* and *Dread of Night* (Gladstone/Hamilton). *MetaCops!* (Fantagraphics/Monster).

Favorite comics not worked on: *Eightball, Peep Show, Palookaville, Spider-Man 2099,* and *Tantalizing Tales.*

Dream comic-book project: *Batman.*

✴ Mark Heike. AC Comics, P.O. Box 1216, Longwood, Florida 32752.

Born: June 14, 1958, in Milwaukee, Wisconsin.

Biggest creative influences: Money.

1993 projects: *Femforce, Femforce up Close, Jungle Girls, Good Girl Art Quarterly,* all from AC Comics.

Past comics titles and related projects: *X-Men Annual, Nexus, Green Hornet, She-Hulk, Spider-Man,* and *Legion of Super-Heroes.*

Dream comic-book project: Doing it now, *Femforce* for AC Comics.

Topper Helmers (right)

✴ Topper Helmers. 225 South Lincoln Street, Burbank, California 91506.

Born: April 13, 1955, in Nashville, Tennessee.

College or other education: Youngstown State University.

Comics-related education: Apprenticed under Val Mayerik, *New Talent Showcase,* DC Comics.

Biggest creative influences: Hal Foster, Al Williamson, Victor de la Fuenta, and Jeff Jones.

1993 projects: *Caligula* and *The Black Kite* (Eclectus Comics).

Past comics titles and related projects: *Weird War Tales, Secret Six* (unpublished miniseries), DC Comics. *Sherlock Holmes and the Case of the Missing Martian, Shanghaied, Saga of the Black Kite,* Eternity. *Caligula* series, Eclectus Comics. *Savage Tales* magazine, Marvel.

Favorite comics not worked on: *Prince Valiant, Spawn, Peter Pan* — Loisel, and anything by Al Williamson.

Dream comic-book project: A story line with mountain men, pre-Revolution, mid-1750s.

✳ **Fred George Hembeck.** 83 Highland Avenue, Kingston, New York 12401.

Born: January 30, 1953, in New York City, New York.

College or other education: State University of New York at Farmingdale, 1971-73, B.A. in Advertising Art and Design. State University of New York at Buffalo, 1973-75, B.A. in Communications Design.

Biggest creative influences: Al Wiseman, Fred Toole, John Stanley, Jack Kirby, Stan Lee, Steve Ditko, Jim Steranko, Bob Bolling, Dan DeCarlo, Robert Crumb, Curt Swan, Kurt Schaffenberger, and Mort Walker.

1993 projects: *Mr. Mumbo Jumbo* for Topps, *Factoid Books* for DC/Piranha (art only), *Elvira* for Claypool (script only), *Marvel Age*, and my own 200-plus-page graphic novel, non-genre situation comedy I am 137 pages into, to be sold at the completion.

Past comics titles and related projects: *The Fantastic Four Roast, Fred Hembeck Destroys the Marvel Universe, Fred Hembeck Sells the Marvel Universe, What The--?!,* 100-plus issues of *Marvel Age, Petey, The Adventures of Peter Parker Loonng before He Became Spider-Man* (creator, sorta) for *Marvel Tales,* various *Spider-Man Annual* features, *Hembeck* feature in DC Comics' *Daily Planet* pages, *Zoot Sputnik* in *'Mazing Man, Flash* #300 featurette, *Mr. Monster* intro pages, *Batbabe, Wolverbroad, Superbabe,* and *Spider-Femme* origin stories for Personality Comics, *Munden's Bar, Spider-Ham, Dateline @!?#?!* for *The Buyer's Guide for Comics Fandom* (later *CBG*), collected into a series of books by Eclipse and FantaCo, *Amazing Heroes* #200, *Aesop's Fables,* and *Gates of Eden.*

Favorite comics not worked on: *Superman, Captain America,* and *Archie.*

Dream comic-book project: Reviving Dennis the Menace and/or Little Lulu in comic book form.

Marc Hempel

✳ **Marc Hempel.** Insight Studios, 7844 St. Thomas Drive, Baltimore, Maryland 21236.

Born: May 25, 1957, in Evanston, Illinois.

College or other education: B.F.A., Northern Illinois University.

Biggest creative influences: Chuck Jones, Charles Schulz, Walt Kelly, Geo. Herriman, Neal Adams, Wrightson, Ditko, Crane, and Kurtzman.

1993 projects: *Gregory III, Gregory IV,* and *Sandman: The Kindly Ones* (with Neil Gaiman).

Past comics titles and related projects: *Mars* (with Mark Wheatley), *Blood of the Innocent* (with Mark Wheatley and Rick Shanklin), *Breathtaker* (with Mark Wheatley), *Jonny Quest* (with Bill Loebs, Mark Wheatley, and Kathryn Mayer), *Gregory, Marvel Fanfare, Epic Illustrated, Heavy Metal, Hellraiser* (with Del Stone Jr.), *Challengers of the Unknown* (cover), *Who's Who, Tarzan the Warrior* (covers and inks), *Amazing High Adventure, Be an Interplanetary Spy* (paperback series, art and covers), *Honk!, Splat!, Eclipse,* and *Alien Encounters.* (I left some out at the end.)

Favorite comics not worked on: *Yummy Fur, Eightball, Raw, Drawn and Quarterly, Pogo, Calvin* *and Hobbes, Krazy Kat, Wash Tubbs, Polly and Her Pals*, and anything Jim Woodring does.

Dream comic-book project: I'm already doing it.

✳ Franz Henkel. c/o *CBG* Editorial Department, 700 East State Street, Iola, Wisconsin 54990.

Born: January 23, 1960, in Korea.

College or other education: B.A., English (Vassar), M.A., English/Creative Writing (University of California-Davis).

Biggest creative influences: Dostoevsky and Gogol.

1993 projects: *The Way of the Sorcerer*, two-issue mini-series from Marvel Epic, painted by Mike Dringenberg.

Past comics titles and related projects: *EO* (Rebel Studios); *Predator 2 — The Official Movie Adaptation* (Dark Horse); *Flesh Wounds* and *Bone Saw* (Tundra); *Forbidden Kingdom, Blackmask, Demon Warrior*, and *Trickster King Monkey* (Eastern Comics).

Favorite comics not worked on: *Cages, Sandman*, and *Yummy Fur*.

✳ Eric Hess. 211 Pauline Drive, Saltsburg, Pennsylvania 15681-8914.

Born: December 19, 1962, in Indiana, Pennsylvania.

College or other education: Art Institute of Pittsburgh, six months.

Biggest creative influences: '60s Hanna-Barbera cartoons, '60s and '70s Marvel comics, Doc Savage novels, and Dave Sim.

1993 projects: *Furies* mini-comics.

Past comics titles and related projects: *Caliber Presents* #2, 3, 5; *Profolio Volume 3* #1; *Tempest* #2 (mini); cartoons in *CBG, Zot!, Retief of the CDT, Comics Career Newsletter, Round House Comics; Aaiiieeeee!* #1 (mini); and *Fantaescape* # 1.

Favorite comics not worked on: *Cerebus*.

✳ Phillip Hester. 707 Oak, #12, Williamsburg, Iowa 52361.

Born: August 27, 1966, in Cedar Rapids, Iowa.

Phillip Hester

College or other education: B.F.A., University of Iowa, 1984-88.

Biggest creative influences: Eisner, Krigstein, Toth, Kirby, Wood, Munoz, Kojima, Miller, Rude, Colan, Zaffino, Newton, Rothko, and Bellows.

1993 projects: Pencilling: *Flash Annual* and *Swamp Thing* (DC), *By Bizarre Hands* (Dark Horse). Story and art: *Sponge* (Caliber) and *Underground* (Dark Horse short story).

Past comics titles and related projects: *Nightbreed, Dark Horse Comics (Timecop), Deadline USA, Freaks' Amour, Rust, Fringe, Taboo, Caliber Presents, A Modest Proposal, Namor* (backup), *Attitude Lad, Deadworld, The Real Ghostbusters, Ex-Mutants, Badger* (backups), *Nexus* (backups), *Bloodbrothers, Interactive Comics, Tales from Ground Zero*, and *'Port*.

Favorite comics not worked on: *Sandman, Sin City, Grendel, Rescue Comics, Nexus, Drawn and Quarterly, Yummy Fur, Hulk, Rubber Blanket, Superman*, and *Sin* (everything, I guess).

Dream comic-book project: *Ragman, Omac vs. Atlas, Grimjack*, or a full-length graphic novel about my childhood.

✳ Cathy Hill. 1632 Loma Crest, Glendale, California 91205.

College or other education: B.A. from UCLA.

Comics-related education: Freelance artwork.

Biggest creative influences: Carl Barks, Walt Kelly, Neal Adams, and Al Williamson.

1993 projects: *Mad Raccoons* #3.

Past comics titles and related projects: *Mad Raccoons* #1 and 2, published by MU Press, and *The Dreamery* published by Eclipse.

Favorite comics not worked on: *Weirdo, Naughty Bits, Hate,* and *Invisible People.*

Dream comic-book project: A graphic-novel style book of collected stories.

Joan Hilty

✳ Joan Hilty. 7 East 14th Street, #1011, New York, New York 10003.

Born: December 27, 1966, in Lexington, Kentucky.

College or other education: B.A. from Brown University, with training at Rhode Island School of Design.

Biggest creative influences: Junk food, country music, feminism, and *Krazy Kat.*

1993 projects: Work for *Women's Glib* #3, most of the usual suspects below, plus a strip, *Jitterbug Waltz,* for syndication.

Past comics titles and related projects: *Gay Comix, Wimmin's Comix* (Rip Off Press), *Real Girl* (Fantagraphics). 'Zines: *Girljock, Oh,* and a regular feature in *The Advocate.*

Favorite comics not worked on: *Love and Rockets* and *Drawn and Quarterly.*

Dream comic-book project: A graphic novel of Linda Niemann's raunchy railroad memoir, *Boomer.*

✳ Rick Hoberg. c/o *CBG* Editorial Department, 700 East State Street, Iola, Wisconsin 54990.

Agent: Stephen Donnelly.

Born: June 7, 1952, in Belton, Texas.

College or other education: B.A. in Fine Art from University of California, Irvine.

Comics-related education: Assistant to Russ Manning, 1975-76.

Biggest creative influences: Comics work of Jack Kirby, Russ Manning, Hal Foster, Gil Kane, Frank Frazetta, and Al Williamson.

1993 projects: *Strangers* for Malibu and an unannounced project with Mike Grell.

Past comics titles and related projects: *Tarzan* with Russ Manning, *What If?, Star Wars, Kull, Conan* at Marvel. Storyboard and character design on: *Godzilla Power Hour, Super Friends, Plastic Man, Thundarr, G.I. Joe, Jem, Ghostbusters,* and many more. Producer on: *Defenders of the Earth, X-Men* shows (as well as Art Director of Fox's *X-Men* show). *Batman, Justice League America, All-Star Squadron, Checkmate, New Gods, Green Arrow, Superman, Brave and the Bold,* all for DC Comics. *Star Wars* comic strip, *DC Cosmic Cards, Strangers* for Malibu, and storyboards for *Cyborg* and *Stephen King's It.*

Favorite comics not worked on: *Calvin and Hobbes, Sword of Azrael, Batman: Legends of the Dark Knight, Groo, WildC.A.T.S,* and *Shaman's Tears.*

Dream comic-book project: A graphic adaptation of *Lost Horizon* and a story of my father's World War II exploits.

✳ Bill Holbrook. 846 Arlington Drive, Tucker, Georgia 30084.

Agent: King Features Syndicate.

Born: October 17, 1958, in Los Angeles, California.

College or other education: B.A., Illustration and Visual Design, Auburn University, 1980.

Bill Holbrook

Biggest creative influences: Charles Schulz, Jack Davis, Mort Drucker, and Will Eisner.

1993 projects: Comic strips *On the Fastrack* and *Safe Havens* and a comic book on job training for the New Jersey Department of Labor.

Past comics titles and related projects: See strips listed above.

Favorite comics not worked on: *Calvin and Hobbes, Outland*, and *The Far Side*.

Dream comic-strip project: I'm doing it.

✳ **John Holland.** 104 Oak Court, Westwego, Louisiana 70094.

Born: July 12, 1959, in Millington, Tennessee.

1993 projects: *Diebold* from Conquest Press.

Past comics titles and related projects: *Critters, Death Rattle, Deathworld, Quantum Leap*, and *Lizards Summer Fun Special*.

✳ **Matthew Hollingsworth.** 2181 NW Glisan Street, #404, Portland, Oregon 97210.

Born: December 17, 1968, in Lakewood, California.

College or other education: Joe Kubert School of Cartooning and Graphic Art, graduated 1991.

Biggest creative influences: Steve Oliff, Lovern Kindzierski, Tatjana Wood, George Pratt, Dennis Corrigan, and Lynn Varley.

1993 projects: Colorist on: *Creature from the Black Lagoon* (Adams and Austin), *Pumpkinhead*

(S. McManus), *The Mummy* (Tony Harris), *Aliens: Labyrinth, Aliens: Colonial Marines, Predator: Race War, Comics' Greatest World, Hammer of God: Pentathlon (Nexus)*, and *Robocop: Mortal Coils.*

Past comics titles and related projects: Colorist on : *Lobo's Greatest Hits, Legends of the Dark Knight* (with McManus), *Punisher, Superman Annuals, Hellraiser, Judge Dredd, Judge Death, Magnus: Robot Fighter, Flash, Wonder Woman, Green Lantern, New Titans, Deathstroke: The Terminator, Ren & Stimpy, Classic Star Wars, Agent Liberty, Hawk and Dove, Hawkworld, Justice League Quarterly, The Ray #2, Sgt. Rock, The Shadow*, and *Cry for Dawn.*

Favorite comics not worked on: *Love and Rockets, Animal Man, Sandman*, anything Diana Schutz edits, any Kyle Baker stuff, *Mage*, and *Tank Girl.*

Dream comic-book project: *Bladerunner. Fracture* with Doselle Young.

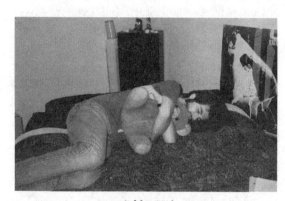

Ashley Holt

✳ **Ashley Holt.** 2474 Swallow Drive, Charleston, South Carolina 29414.

Born: December 4, 1968, in Charleston, South Carolina.

College or other education: Currently studying with Bo Hampton at the Savannah College of Art and Design, Savannah, Georgia.

Biggest creative influences: Hank Ketcham, Steve Ditko, Al Hirschfeld, Art Spiegleman (without the mice), and Jim Woodring.

1993 projects: *Detours*, the working title of the Savannah College of Art and Design's comic-book anthology. Various short stories for Slave Labor graphics.

Past comics titles and related projects:

1989 — *Screenplay*, written and drawn by me, published by Slave Labor Graphics. 1992 — *Portraits of Eddie*, written and drawn by me, published by Caliber Press' Iconographix line. 1990 to present — various naughty stories in *One-Fisted Tales*, written and drawn by Chico Ditko (me), published by Slave Labor Graphics.

Favorite comics not worked on: *Dirty Plotte, Eightball, Zoot, The Cowboy Wally Show*, and *Tantalizing Stories*.

Dream comic-book project: A dark, gritty examination of Big Boy (from the Big Boy restaurants).

✳ **Richard Howell.** 647 Grand Avenue, Leonia, New Jersey 07605.

College or other education: B.A. in English from Harvard.

Comics-related education: John Buscema's art seminar classes.

Biggest creative influences: Jack Kirby, Nick Cardy, Leonard Starr, Bill Everett, Mike Sekowsky, Thomas Hardy, Charles Dickens, and Jerome and Bridget Dobson.

1993 projects: Claypool Comics (editor), *Deadbeats* (writer, penciller), *Elvira* (writer), and *Soulsearchers and Co.* (co-plotter).

Past comics titles and related projects: *Flaxen* (penciller), *Vampirella, Creepy* (editor), *Dinosaurs* (penciller), *Marvel Masterworks* (colorist), *Vision and Scarlet Witch* (penciller), *Rick Jones, Scarlet Witch* (writer, penciller, inker, letterer, and colorist), *Inhumans* (penciller, colorist), *Hawkman* (penciller), *Green Lantern* (penciller, co-plotter), *All-Star Squadron* (penciller, inker), *Portia Prinz of the Glamazons* (writer, penciller, inker, and letterer), *Jonny Quest* (penciller), *Epic Illustrated* (letterer).

Favorite comics not worked on: *Legion of Super-Heroes*.

Dream comic-book project: The original, unlicensable *Dark Shadows, Inhumans*, and *Kamandi*.

✳ **Shon Howell.** Antarctic Press, 7272 Wurzbach, Suite #204, San Antonio, Texas 78240.

Born: February 11, 1962, in Portsmouth, Virginia.

Comics-related education: George Bridgeman and Jeff Jones.

1993 projects: *Furrlough, Wild Life, Genus, Hit the Beach*, and *Shanda the Panda*. (Also, currently the editor of Antarctic's anthropomorphic line, in addition to all-around artist).

Past comics titles and related projects: *Ninja High School, XXXenophile, Gunhed, Mighty Tiny, SB Ninja High School*, and *Windsor*.

Favorite comics not worked on: *Theonomachine Golver* by Rulia 046 (Kuba Shoten Publishing/Japan).

Dream comic-book project: Humorous comic history of the development of the Soviet Air Force 1917-88 (which was pretty comical in real life).

✳ **Lawrence D. Hubbard.** Real Deal Productions, P.O. Box 19129, Los Angeles, California 90019.

Born: August 14, 1960, in Los Angeles, California.

College or other education: Various classes at Otis Art Institute, Santa Monica College, no degrees.

Comics-related education: Have done freelance artwork on numerous underground comics, movie posters for independent productions, advertising, etc.

Biggest creative influences: Wally Wood, Jack Kirby, Joe Orlando, *Mad* magazine, X-Men comics, and *Heavy Metal*.

1993 projects: Drawing and publishing *Real Deal Magazine, Your Urban Terror Comic*. Working on getting one of the stories into studio development.

Past comics titles and related projects: *Too Raw of the Third Tier*.

Favorite comics not worked on: *X-Men, Heavy Metal, Mad, Swamp Thing*, EC reprints, and *Batman*.

Dream comic-book project: Rewrite the Marvel and DC Universes.

✳ **James D. Hudnall.** c/o *CBG* Editorial Department, 700 East State Street, Iola, Wisconsin 54990.

Born: April 10, 1957.

College or other education: A.S. in Computer Science.

Comics-related education: Read a lot of books on writing and English.

Biggest creative influences: Various book authors, movies, and Alan Moore.

1993 projects: *Hardcase, The Solution, Harsh Realm, Gangland, Hollyweird*, and *Streets*.

Past comics titles and related projects: *ESPers, Strikeforce: Morituri, Alpha Flight, Lex Luthor: The Unauthorized Biography, Interface, The Agent, The Psycho, Twister, Sinking, Legends of the Dark Knight* #31, *Superman*. Translating of: *Mai the Psychic Girl, Area 88, Firetripper, Pineapple Army, Gunhed, Macross II*, and *Silent Moebius*.

Favorite comics not worked on: *Hate, Eightball, Sanctuary, Ranma½*, and *Peep Show*.

Dream comic-book project: A maxi-series about pre-Crisis DC where I had *carte blanche*.

✱ **Rian Hughes.** The Coach House, Ealing Green, Ealing, London, England 1W5 5ER.

Born: November 20, 1963, in London, England.

College or other education: B.A., Honors, Graphic Design.

1993 projects: *Robo Hunter — 2000 AD*.

Past comics titles and related projects: *Really and Truly — 2000 AD, Dan Dare —* Revolver, *The Science Service, Tales from beyond Science — 2000 AD*, numerous design projects — various clients, *Goldfish* (Raymond Chandler) — Byron Preiss, etc.

Dream comic-book project: To design an imprint from scratch.

✱ **Chad Hunt.** 1158 SW Empire Street, Port St. Lucie, Florida 34983.

Born: May 28, 1965, in Winston-Salem, North Carolina.

Biggest creative influences: Joe Sinnott, Bob McLeod, Jim Starlin, Walt Simonson, and Jack Kirby.

1993 projects: *Femforce*.

Past comics titles and related projects: *Femforce, Captain Paragon, AC Annual, Femforce* trading cards, and *Good Girl Art Quarterly*.

Favorite comics not worked on: *Incredible*

Chad Hunt

Hulk, Superman, Batman, Aliens, and *Predator*.

Dream comic-book project: A Hulk outer space adventure.

WHAT A PHOTO OF GREG HYLAND MIGHT LOOK LIKE.

✱ **Greg Hyland.** Lethargic Comics, P.O. Box 85067, Burlington, Ontario, Canada L7R 4K3.

Born: April 28, 1969, in Oakville, Ontario, Canada.

College or other education: Sheridan College Art Fundamentals Diploma (1988) and Classical Animation Diploma (1991).

Biggest creative influences: Frank Miller, Dave Sim, Peter Bagge, and Evan Dorkin.

1993 projects: Drawing *Butt Biscuit* for Malpractice Graphics, writing and drawing *Tales of Lethargy* and *Lethargic Comics* for Alpha Productions, and pencilling *Felix the Cat* for Felix Comics.

Past comics titles and related projects: 12 issues of *Lethargic Comics Weakly* for Lethargic Comics. Back-up stories for *This is Sick* for Silver Skull Studios. Four-page story for *True North II*. Eight-page Lethargic Lad/Elfquest crossover for *Elfquest: New Blood*. Animation layouts for *Beetlejuice* syndicated series.

Favorite comics not worked on: *Archie, Green Lantern, Batman, Detective Comics*, and *Justice League*.

Dream comic-book project: More *Justice Society* or a *Gwar* comic.

Bob Ingersoll

✳ **Bob Ingersoll.** Cosmic Odysseys, P.O. Box 24314, Lyndhurst, Ohio 44124.

Born: October 13, 1952, in Cleveland, Ohio.

College or other education: B.A., Dartmouth College, 1975. J.D., Case Western Reserve University School of Law, 1981.

Comics-related education: None (unless you count my creative writing courses in college and my J.D., which allows me to write *The Law Is a Ass*.)

Biggest creative influences: Gardner Fox, Stan Lee, and Tony Isabella.

1993 projects: *The Law Is a Ass.* Outstanding proposals and plots galore, but nothing greenlighted yet. Tony and I have two proposals at Topps Salicrup wants to do and I have one at Now Caputo wants to do, but they're stalled. If they go forward, I'll let you know.

Past comics titles and related projects: *The Law Is a Ass. Hero Alliance, Quantum Leap, Lost in Space, Power Factor* for Innovation. *Tales of the Green Hornet* for Now. *Vigilante* and *House of Mystery* for DC. *Marvel Super-Heroes* (Moon Knight) for Marvel. *Justice Machine* for Comics. *Death Rattle* for Kitchen Sink.

Favorite comics not worked on: *Batman, Sandman, Superman* (Oh, the list goes on and on and on . . .)

Dream comic-book project: There's this super-hero team book proposal of mine under consideration at DC.

✳ **Sheldon Inkol.** 5-593 St. Clair Avenue West, Toronto, Ontario, Canada M6C 1A3.

Born: August 8, 1965, in St. Catharines, Ontario, Canada.

College or other education: B.F.A., Film Production and Screenwriting (York University, Toronto, Canada).

Biggest creative influences: Alan Moore, Frank Miller, and Chester Brown.

1993 projects: More *Nut Runners* and a few other original projects I plan to shop around.

Past comics titles and related projects: Writer, *Nut Runners* #1 and 2 (Rip Off, 1991/1992). Writer, *Single Page, Cerebus Bi-Weekly* #1 (1990). Writer, *Headcheese* #1-3 (1988/1989) (an anthology series with other contributors).

Favorite comics not worked on: *Yummy Fur, Sandman, Eightball*, and *Miracleman*.

Dream comic-book project: An unlimited series *accurately* reconstructing the Kennedy assassination.

✳ **Tony Isabella.** P.O. Box 1502, Medina, Ohio 44258.

Tony Isabella

Born: December 22, 1951, in Cleveland, Ohio.

Comics-related education: Editorial assistant, associate editor, and editor for Marvel Comics under Stan Lee, Roy Thomas, and Sol Brodsky from 1972-1975. Story editor for DC Comics, 1976.

Biggest creative influences: Stan Lee and Roy Thomas.

1993 projects: *Black Lightning* (DC Comics). *Satan's Six* (Topps Comics).

Past comics titles and related projects: *Ant-Man, Avengers, Black Goliath, Black Lightning, Captain America, Captain Universe, Chamber of Chills, Champions, Crazy, Daredevil, Deadly Hands of Kung Fu, DC Comics Presents, Defenders, Doc Savage, Dracula Lives, Fantastic Four, FOOM* magazine, *Freedom Fighters, Ghost Rider, Giant-Size Chillers, Giant-Size Dracula, Green Arrow, Grim Ghost, Haunt of Horror, Hawkman, Incredible Hulk, Iron Fist, It, the Living Colossus, Justice Machine, Korak, Legends of the Stargrazers, Legion of Monsters, Living Mummy, Man-Monster, Manphibian, Man-Thing, Man-Wolf, Marvel Team-Up, Marvel Two-in-One, Monster Madness, Monsters of the Movies, Monster Times, Monsters Unleashed, Moon Knight, Mystery in Space,* 1976 *Marvel Bicentennial Calendar, Planet of the Apes, Plop!, Power Man, Power Man and Iron Fist, Rocket Racer, Sandman, Satana, Sgt. Fury, Sons of the Tiger, Spider-Man, Star Trek, Super-Team Family, Super-Villain Team-Up, Tales of the Zombie, Tarzan Family, Teen Titans Spotlight, Thongor, Tigra, Unknown Soldier, Unknown Worlds of Science-Fiction, Vampire Tales, War Is Hell, Welcome Back Kotter, Werewolf by Night, What If?,* and *Young Love.*

Favorite comics not worked on: *Superman* and *Usagi Yojimbo.*

Dream comic-book project: A Batman or Superman graphic novel.

Geof Isherwood

✳ **Geof Isherwood.** P.O. Box 1746, Place du Parc, Montreal, Quebec, Canada H2W 2R7.

Born: December 4, 1960, in Quantico, Virginia.

College or other education: B.F.A.

Comics-related education: Larry Hama: On-the-job training at Marvel.

Biggest creative influences: J. Buscema, G. Kane, B. Windsor-Smith, B. Wrightson, G. Colan, P. Gulacy, and many more minor influences.

1993 projects: *Doctor Strange, Doctor Strange Annual.* Also writing for *Doctor Strange.*

Past comics titles and related projects: First comic: *Bizarre Adventures* #31. *New Talent Showcase* #2 (DC), *Daredevil* # 203, *Power Man/Iron*

Fist, *G.I. Joe* #20, 96, *Swords of the Swashbucklers* #6-12, *Conan the King* #22-31, 50-55, *Conan the Barbarian* #191-208, *Peter Parker the Spectacular Spider-Man* #100, *West Coast Avengers Annual* #3, *Web of Spider-Man* #7 and 8, *The 'Nam* #15-41, *Suicide Squad* #33-66, *Doctor Strange*, various *Tales of Vishanti*, full-time *Doctor Strange* #37-51, continuing, *Annual* #3, *Mighty Thor* #366, *Tales of Asgard* in #452-459, and other things I can't remember off the top of my head.

Favorite comics not worked on: *Batman*, *Spider-Man*, and *Conan*.

Dream comic-book project: A Conan graphic novel, or a creator-owned, near-future adventure.

Michal Jacot

✳ **Michal Jacot.** 1045 North US 23, East Tawas, Michigan 48730.

Born: June 4, 1957, in Marlette, Michigan.

Biggest creative influences: Keith Giffen and Hembeck.

Past comics titles and related projects: *Comics Buyer's Guide* spot cartoons and *Single Page* for *Cerebus*, Aardvark-Vanaheim.

Favorite comics not worked on: *Swamp Thing, Animal Man, Superman*, and *Ambush Bug*.

Dream comic-book project: An ongoing comedy series in the same vein as *Ambush Bug* and *Heckler*.

✳ **Verzell Keith James.** Jam Graphics and Publishing, 1719B McDaniel, Evanston, Illinois 60201-3342.

Born: May 26, 1961, in Harvey, Illinois.

College or other education: B.A., Visual Communications, School of the Art Institute of Chicago.

Comics-related education: First Publishing, production and trafficing departments.

Biggest creative influences: Every single comic and art book I've ever read, whether or not I liked them.

1993 projects: 1. *Reaper* mini-series for Jam Graphics. 2. *The Gift* for Culture Press.

Past comics titles and related projects: 1. *The Edge* anti-drug comic with Tim Truman. 2. *Edventure Comic* for Jam Graphics. 3. Associated Reading Service.

Favorite comics not worked on: I read a lot of comics, but I don't have any real favorites.

Dream comic-book project: I am doing it with *The Reaper*, which will be published this fall after 10 years' planning.

✳ **Dennis Janke.** P.O. Box 278, Seymour, Connecticut 06483.

Born: April 13, 1950, in Cleveland, Ohio.

College or other education: B.F.A., Cleveland Institute of Art.

Biggest creative influences: Ditko, Kirby, Frazetta, G. Herriman, and Edward Lear.

1993 projects: *Superman: Man of Steel* (monthly) and *Clark Kent: Under a Red Sun* (graphic novel).

Past comics titles and related projects: *Captain America* #300-320, *Daredevil* #226, *Electric Warrior*, and various Superman titles since 1987.

Favorite comics not worked on: *Sandman*.

Dream comic-book project: Personal project.

✳ **Michael Jantze.** 4211 Vincennes Place, New Orleans, Louisiana 70125-2744.

Agent: Mike Friedrich.

Born: March 19 in Middletown, New York.

College or other education: B.A. in Radio-Television-Film.

Biggest creative influences: Will Eisner, Charles Schulz, Walt Kelly, Frank Miller, Garry Trudeau, and Lynn Johnston.

1993 projects: DC Comics' Piranha Press:

Three-part full color original graphic novel titled *Rave On*, no completion date set.

Past comics titles and related projects: *Normal U.S.A.*, a comic-strip collection published by Harvest Moon Publications, 1988. In 1992, a development contract for *Normal* with United Media Syndicate in New York. Currently working on *Normal* and a new property for syndication.

Favorite comics not worked on: *The Batman Adventures, Madman, The Spirit, Calvin and Hobbes, For Better or for Worse*, and many more.

Dream comic-book project: Original works dealing with themes generally not well presented in comics.

✳ **Phil Jimenez.** DC Comics, 1325 Avenue of the Americas, New York, New York 10019.

Born: July 12, 1970, in Los Angeles, California.

College or other education: I attended the School of Visual Arts for two years and was expelled for financial reasons.

Comics-related education: I worked briefly with the folks at Valiant Comics before I started working at DC Comics.

Biggest creative influences: George Pérez and my three roommates Jeff, Mark, and Trevor.

1993 projects: *Team Titans*.

Past comics titles and related projects: *The New Titans, Showcase '93, Cosmic Cards*, and *Bloodlines* trading cards.

Favorite comics not worked on: *Sandman*.

Dream comic-book project: I just submitted the proposal; I'll let you know.

✳ **Brad Johnson.** P.O. Box 411172, San Francisco, California 94110.

Born: July 17, 1959, in Fort Collins, Colorado.

Biggest creative influences: Underground comics, pop culture, etc. (Milt Gross, Emmett of *Punch*, William Hogarth, Hairy Who, etc.)

1993 projects: I'm developing a weekly strip. (The rest is secret.)

Past comics titles and related projects: *Weirdo, Hyena, Snake Eyes, Chemical Imbalance, Nancy's*, and various self-published novelties.

Favorite comics not worked on: Not too many: *Kaktus Valley, Eightball, Dirty Plotte*.

Dream comic-book project: Exactly what I'm doing, only I'd get paid.

✳ **Dave Johnson.** Gaijin Studios, 5581 Peachtree Road, Atlanta, Georgia 30341.

Born: April 4, 1966, in Pittsburgh, Pennsylvania.

College or other education: Art Institute of Atlanta, Portfolio Center of Atlanta.

Biggest creative influences: Michael Golden, Masamune Shirow, Mike Mignola, Moebius, Jack Kirby, and Otomo.

1993 projects: *Chain Gang War* (DC), *Super Patriot* (Image), and *Namor Annual* (Marvel).

Past comics titles and related projects: *After Apocalypse Earth Boys* (*Dark Horse Presents*), *The Demon Annual #1* (DC), *Iron Man Annual # 13* (Marvel), and *Wonder Woman Annual # 3* (DC).

Favorite comics not worked on: *Appleseed, Akira, Sin City, 1963*, and *The Dirty Pair*.

Dream comic-book project: *S.H.I.E.L.D./ Iron Man*, done my way.

Gerard Jones

✳ **Gerard Jones.** 942 Noe Street, San Francisco, California 94114.

Born: July 10, 1957, in Cutbank, Montana.

Biggest creative influences: Everything I've ever done, seen, read, and heard. I yam jest a sponge.

1993 projects: *Prime, Freex,* and *Solitaire* (for Malibu). *Green Lantern, Green Lantern: Mosaic, Legends of the Dark Knight:* "Bop," and *Justice League International* (for DC). *Hulk 2099* and *Wonder Man* (for Marvel). *The Trouble with Girls* (for Epic).

Past comics titles and related projects: *Martian Manhunter: American Secrets, Batman: Run, Riddler, Run, Guy Gardner Reborn, Guy Gardner* (regular series), *El Diablo, The Shadow Strikes!, Green Lantern: Emerald Dawn I and II* (all for DC). *The Score* (Piranha Press). *Shanna:* "The Bush of Ghosts" (Marvel). *Idol* (Epic). *The Trouble with Girls, Lester Girls, The Lizard Lady, The Big Prize,* and *Monsters from Outer Space* (Malibu). *Timedrifter* (Innovation). *Real Girl* (Fantagraphics). *Death Rattle* (Kitchen Sink). *Tommy and the Monsters* (New Comics). etc.

Favorite comics not worked on: Carl Barks reprints and *Hate.*

Dream comic-book project: *Fantastic Four.*

✳ **Ken L. Jones.** 425 N. Kodiak Street, Apartment B, Anaheim, California 92807.

Born: August 22, 1951, in Sioux City, Iowa.

College or other education: California State Junior College at Cypress (A.A. degree in Literature/History, Cal State-Long Beach. (Achieved Junior year in pursuit of B.A. in Lit/History).

Comics-related education: Graduated Magna Cum laude from the school of hard knocks.

Biggest creative influences: Walt Disney, William S. Burroughs, Alfredo Alcala, Sparky Moore, Jimi Hendrix, and Winsor McCay.

1993 projects: (Tom Luth) *The Lab Rats,* a *Tape Worm* graphic novel: *We Belong Dead Stilts,* several possible Disney stories for Gladstone.

Past comics titles and related projects: Past titles: Comics: 1. *Heroman* (Dimension Graphics) writer/editor/creator. 2. *Chuck Morris the Karate Kat* and *The Conscience* in *Launch!* (Elsewhere Productions) writer/editor/co-creator. 3. *World Wrestling Federation* inventory stories (Black-

thorne Press). 4. Various *Donald Duck* inventory stories for Disney Comics (written with Dan Slavin). 5. Various *New Kids on the Block* stories (Harvey Comics). Related projects: 1. Several dozen articles, editorials, and interviews for *The Comics Journal, Amazing Heroes,* and *Comics Interview.* (I was the West Coast Editor for *Comics Interview* for a while.) 2. Associate Producer/Head Writer for the comic-book-related cable show *Star Pilot.* 3. Worked in the story development "think tank" of Hollywood director Brian Yuzna. 4. Various tentative stabs at selling original licensable characters with my cohorts Sparky Moore and Alfredo Alcala.

Favorite comics not worked on: *Mr. Monster, Doctor Strange,* Bob Foster's *Myron Moose Comics,* and anything by Russ Heath.

Dream comic-book project: A monthly full-color comic book version of Sparky Moore and my *Chuck Morris the Karate Kat.*

R.A. Jones

✳ **R.A. Jones.** c/o *CBG* Editorial Department, 700 East State Street, Iola, Wisconsin 54990.

Born: March 12, 1953, in Tulsa, Oklahoma.

College or other education: Associate Degree in Journalism, B.A. in History.

Biggest creative influences: Probably the early '60s Marvels written by Stan Lee and Roy Thomas.

1993 projects: *Protectors, Ferret, Witch,* and *White Devil Book II.*

Past comics titles and related projects: *Dark Wolf, Scimidar, Pistolero, Fist of God, Merlin, Straw Men, White Devil, Debbie Does Comics,* and *Airman.*

Favorite comics not worked on: *Incredible Hulk* and *Animal Man.*

Dream comic-book project: Working in comics at all is my biggest dream come true.

Cyril Jordan

✳ **Cyril Jordan.** Artlab, 537 Jones Street, #1850, San Francisco, California 94102.

Agent: Tom Andre.

Born: August 31, 1948, in San Francisco, California.

College or other education: Self-taught.

Comics-related education: Disney-Gladstone Comics (G. Blum).

Biggest creative influences: Frank Kelly Freas, Frank Frazetta, and Carl Barks.

1993 projects: Busts of The Old Witch, The Vault Keeper, and The Crypt Keeper for Russ Cochran and large carved wood frames featuring the Ghoul-lunatics.

Past comics titles and related projects: Cover art for *Gladstone Album #17: Mickey Mouse in the World of Tomorrow.* Cover art for Sire Records CD: *Groovies' Greatest Grooves* (mouse with guitar). Cover art for National Records CD: *Rock Juice* (inspired by Frank Kelly Freas' "Fool Aid" *Mad* painting). Commissioned color paintings: *The Phantom* for Tom Andre and others.

Favorite comics not worked on: *Uncle Scrooge, Mad, Walt Disney's Comics and Stories,* and *Cracked.*

Dream comic-book project: I would love to commission J. Craig, Basil Gogos, Kelly Freas, and Al Feldstein to do color painting for an EC-style publication.

✳ **Dan Jurgens.** 4906 Bruce Avenue, Eding, Minnesota 55424.

Born: June 27, 1959, in Ortonville, Minnesota.

College or other education: B.F.A., Minneapolis College of Art and Design.

Biggest creative influences: Neal Adams, Jack Kirby, Gene Colan, Irv Novick, and John Byrne — because he's been there every month for his entire career. A study in professionalism.

1993 projects: *Superman* and *Justice League America.*

Past comics titles and related projects: *Warlord* — artist; *Sun Devils* — artist, writer, and co-creator; *Booster Gold* — creator, writer, artist; *Flash Gordon* — artist; *Superman* — writer, artist; *Justice League America* — writer, artist; and *Armageddon 2001* — artist, co-creator.

Favorite comics not worked on: *Fantastic Four, Spider-Man, Sandman, Solar, Hulk,* and *Archer & Armstrong.*

Dream comic-book project: Own DC Comics.

✳ **Barbara Kaalberg.** 1440 Jasper Circle, Sun Prairie, Wisconsin 53590.

Born: February 13, 1959, in West Liberty, Iowa.

College or other education: Advertising

Barbara Kaalberg

Design, Iowa State University.

Biggest creative influences: Wendy Pini, George Pérez, and Dick Giordano.

1993 projects: Various Barbie titles — Marvel. *Married with Children* titles — Now Comics. *New Blood Summer Special* — Warp Graphics. *Buck Godot* — Palliard Press. Others to be announced.

Past comics titles and related projects: Adventure Comics — *Planet of the Apes* #1-11. Eternity Comics — *Tiger-X* #3 and 4, *Jack the Ripper* #1-3. TSR Inc. — *13: Assassin* #10. Innovation Corp. — *Power Factor* #3, *Equinox Chronicles* #1, *Child's Play* #5, *Freddy's Dead* #1-3, *Lost in Space* #9, *Lost in Space Annual* #1 and 2, *Lawnmower Man: The Movie* graphic novel, short stories, and covers. Palliard Press — *XXXenophile* #7. Now Entertainment — *Twilight Zone* #4, 7, and 10, all *Speed Racer* video sleeves, *Tales of the Green Hornet* #2, *Green Hornet* #14, *Married with Children Flashback Special* #1 and 2. DC Comics — *Star Trek* #33, *Green Lantern Corps Quarterly* #3-5, Impact's *The Web* #14. Marvel Comics — *Captain Ultra* short for *1991 Marvel Holiday Special, What The--?! Wolverina* short in #20, *Barbie Fashion* #25 and 26, *Barbie* #29.

Favorite comics not worked on: *Justice League America, Elfquest, Elfquest: New Blood, New Titans, Robin* series, *Omaha the Cat Dancer*, and *Sandman*.

Dream comic-book project: A *Sandman* mini-series written by Neil Gaiman, pencilled by Bernie Wrightson, and inked by me.

✱ **Len Kaminski.** c/o *CBG* Editorial Department, 700 East State Street, Iola, Wisconsin 54990.

Born: October 20, 1962, in Bangor, Maine.

Comics-related education: Various staff positions at Marvel Comics, 1984-1992.

Biggest creative influences: Harlan Ellison, Alvin Toffler, Steve Gerber, The Ramones, and Traci Lords.

1993 projects: *Iron Man, Sensational She-Hulk*, and *War Machine*.

Past comics titles and related projects: *Iron Man, Morbius, Doctor Strange, Slapstick* limited series, *Avengers*, and various other Marvel stuff.

Favorite comics not worked on: *Sandman, Spectre*, and *Flaming Carrot*.

Dream comic-book project: Either a monthly *Creeper* series pencilled by James Fry or *Amy Fisher — Sky Marshal of the Universe*.

Mike Kanterovich

✱ **Mike Kanterovich.** P.O. Box 51, Hollis, New Hampshire 03049.

Born: April 15, 1961, in Hollis, New Hampshire.

Biggest creative influences: Stan Lee (my formative influence), too many more to mention.

1993 projects: *Fight! Miori Yamada* for Antarctic Press, with artist/co-creator Frank Strom.

Past comics titles and related projects: *Mighty Mouse* #5 (*Bat-Bat* backup story), *Count Duckula* #14 and 15, *Double Dragon* #5 and 6, *Bill and Ted's Excellent Comic Book* #8, the 1992 *Amazing Spider-Man, Spectacular Spider-Man, Web of Spider-Man, Iron Man,* and *Incredible Hulk Annual*s (various back-up features), *The Punisher Back to School Special* (10-page story), *The Sleepwalker Holiday Special,* and *Marvel Year in Review 1992,* all with co-author Tom Brevoort, published by Marvel Comics.

Favorite comics not worked on: *For Better or for Worse, Wolff and Byrd, 'Mazing Man, Zot!,* anything by Lee and Kirby, too many more to mention.

Dream comic-book project: *The 3-D Man* (hey, why not?).

✳ **Carlos Kastro.** 10 Rue Pasteur, Anieres, France 92600.

Born: November 3, 1966, in El Salvador.

College or other education: Parsons, Paris.

Biggest creative influences: John Nordland II, Dave McKean, Alberto Breccia, Kent Williams, Bilal, Edward Gorey, and Bernie Wrightson.

1993 projects: *Spare Parts* for Blackbird, *Night of the Living Dead: London* story for Tropo.

Past comics titles and related projects: *Night of the Living Dead, Night of the Living Dead: London, Omnibus* (*Scales* story), *Where-wolf* story in *Heroes* #5, *Daughter of Fly in the Eye,* layouts for *Just Friends* back-up in *Heroes* #6, back cover of *Heroes* #6, and pin-ups for *Heroes.*

Favorite comics not worked on: *Tropo, Heroes, Sandman, Love and Rockets, Cages,* and *Enigma.*

Dream comic-book project: *Chiarscuro* (work in progress), *Sandman* or anything with Neil Gaiman, anything with Lewis Shiner, P. Craig Russell, or anything "dark."

Gary T. Kato

✳ **Gary T. Kato.** c/o Sharon Cho (Star*Reach Productions), 2991 Shattuck Avenue, Suite 202, Berkeley, California 94705.

Agent: Sharon Cho (Star*Reach Productions).

Born: December 9, 1949, in Honolulu, Hawaii.

College or other education: B.F.A. from University of Hawaii, 1971.

1993 projects: Story for *Elfquest: New Blood, Mr. Jigsaw, Boston Bombers, Captain Hazzard,* and *Streetfighter.*

Past comics titles and related projects: *Destroyer Duck, Thunderbunny, Ms. Tree, Streetfighter, Popeye, Mr. Jigsaw, Peter Pan, Return to Centaur, Boston Bombers,* and *Retief.*

✳ **Mike Kazaleh.** c/o *CBG* Editorial Department, 700 East State Street, Iola, Wisconsin 54990.

Born: March 9, 1962, in Detroit, Michigan.

Biggest creative influences: Lots and lots of people in animation too numerous to mention, mostly from UPA, Warner Bros., Jay Ward, Walt Lantz, and Hanna-Barbera. Lots and lots of comic book artists . . . I'll mention but a few . . .

Harvey Kurtzman, Walt Kelly, Jim Tyer, Bob Oksner, Geo. Herriman, and Bob Crumb are all I can think of offhand.

1993 projects: All I know for sure right now is *The Ren & Stimpy Show* at Marvel.

Past comics titles and related projects: *Dope Comix* #5 (one-page gag), Kitchen Sink Press. Various stories and gags in *Critters*, Fantagraphics. *Adventures of Capt. Jack* #1-12, *Har*Har* #1 and 2, *A K Q J, Mean Green Bondo Machine* (complete issue), MU Press. *Doomsday Squad* # 5, *Anything Goes* #3, short color stories. Pencilled Archie's *Mighty Mutanimals* #2-7 and 9. Spotty work for Disney Comics, *Goofy, Donald Duck*, and *Roger Rabbit*. Pencilling on Marvel's *Mighty Mouse* #3, 5, and 10. Complete eight-page story in Marvel's *Epic Lite*, pencil and ink *The Ren & Stimpy Show* for Marvel. Did entire *Critters* #42: "Not the Adventures of Capt. Jack." I also work in animation.

Favorite comics not worked on: Old or new?

Dream comic-book project: To just be able to write and draw my own stories whenever I please.

Edward K. Keller

✳ **Edward K. Keller.** 1806 Harmony Way, Evansville, Indiana 47720.

Born: December 23, 1963, in Evansville, Indiana.

College or other education: Indiana Law Enforcement Academy.

Biggest creative influences: Stan Lee, Alan Moore, Neil Gaiman, Matt Wagner, Jim Valentino, and a cast of thousands.

1993 projects: *The Apex Project, The Blues, True Police Stories*.

Past comics titles and related projects: *The Apex Project, Web-Man*.

Favorite comics not worked on: *Sandman, Grendel, Miracle Man, Omaha, Spawn, Animal Man, Elfquest, Detective Comics,* Avengers titles, *The Ren and Stimpy Show, Captain America,* Superman titles, and too many others.

Dream comic-book project: To take over either *Captain America* or one of the Avengers titles and be given a free hand in trying to recapture readers.

Cam Kennedy

✳ **Cam Kennedy.** c/o *CBG* Editorial Department, 700 East State Street, Iola, Wisconsin 54990.

Born: October 15, 1944, in Glasgow, Scotland, United Kingdom.

1993 projects: *Lobo: Unamerican Gladiators,* Judge Dredd/Batman crossover, *Star Wars: Dark Empire 2, Star Wars Hardware Manual,* and *Star Wars*.

Past comics titles and related projects: *Rogue Trooper, Judge Dredd, V.C.'s, Daredevil, Spectre, Punisher, Light and Darkness War, Outcasts, Star Wars: Dark Empire, Batman, Bogie Man, War Dog,* and *Clash of the Guards*.

Favorite comics not worked on: *Ecosse Libre*.

Dream comic-book project: A pictorial exposé of all the evil and exploitation bestowed by England on Scotland.

✳ **Karl Kesel.** c/o *CBG* Editorial Department, 700 East State Street, Iola, Wisconsin 54990.

Born: January 7, 1959, in Rochester, New York.

College or other education: Just missed getting a B.A. at the Hartford Art School, Hartford, Connecticut.

Comics-related education: One year at the Joe Kubert School.

Biggest creative influences: Milton Caniff, Roy Crane, and Jack Kirby.

1993 projects: *Strange 2099* — writing and inking (Marvel), *Adventures of Superman* — writing (DC), *Indiana Jones and the Sargasso Pirates* — writing, pencilling, and inking (Dark Horse).

Past comics titles and related projects: Various Newsboy Legion stories here and there — writing, pencilling, and inking. *Hawk and Dove* — co-write with Barbara Randall Kesel. *Terminator: Secondary Objectives* — inking (Dark Horse). *World's Finest* — inking (DC). *Superman* — inking (DC). *Suicide Squad* — inking (DC). Also: inked or pencilled and inked art on all of Bantam's young adult *Star Wars* books.

Favorite comics not worked on: *Sandman, Love and Rockets, Flash,* and *Steve Canyon* reprints.

Dream comic-book project: *The Challengers of the Unknown* (a strong possibility for 1994).

✳ **Avido Khahaifa.** c/o *CBG* Editorial Department, 700 East State Street, Iola, Wisconsin 54990.

Born: August 5, 1963, in New York, New York.

College or other education: B.S. in Journalism, Florida A & M University.

Biggest creative influences: Orshii Boldiis, Ken Falana, Rembrandt, da Vinci, Gene Colan, Frank Miller, and Bernie Wrightson.

1993 projects: *Sojourn* (Caliber) and *Black Mist.*

Past comics titles and related projects: *Shackles* (self-published). *Marco the Metamorphic Manatee.*

Avido Khahaifa

Favorite comics not worked on: *Sandman, Eightball, Yummy Fur, Cerebus, Watchmen, Sin City,* and *Shade, the Changing Man.*

Dream comic-book project: To write and illustrate a graphic novel based on my work as a newspaper reporter covering a race riot.

Bill Kieffer

✳ **Bill Kieffer.** 308 Barton Avenue, Port Pleasant, New Jersey 08742-2112.

Born: December 12, 1963, in Jersey City, New Jersey.

College or other education: Ocean City College (freshman).

Comics-related education: Ten years' worth of rejections from Marvel and DC.

Biggest creative influences: Roy Thomas and Alan Moore.

1993 projects: *Billy Joe Van Helsing: Redneck Vampire Hunter* from Alpha Productions. *Barnaby Rex: Affections of a Dragon* currently seeking a home.

Past comics titles and related projects: Some back-ups in *Rock 'n' Roll Comics* from Revolutionary Comics. Also some stories in *Tipper Gore's Comics and Stories* and *Alpha Illustrated*. Some interviews in *Comics Interview*. Worked on two issues of *Teen Enforcers* for a Texas concern that vanished, and I'm seeking information on Imagi-Mation.

Favorite comics not worked on: *Sandman, Swamp Thing,* and *Animal Man*. I really miss *All-Star Squadron*.

Dream comic-book project: I'd love to wrest control of the *Fantastic Four* from Tom DeFalco

✳ **Lovern Kindzierski.** Digital Chameleon, 61 Gertie Street, Winnipeg, Manitoba, Canada R3A 1B5 or c/o Mike Friedrich, Box 2328, Berkeley, California 94702.

Born: July 29, 1954, in Arborg, Manitoba, Canada.

College or other education: University of Manitoba, B.F.A., honors degree Graphic Design.

Comics-related education: Assistant animator at Canadian Broadcasting Corporation. Assistant to George Freeman.

Biggest creative influences: Carravagio, N.C. Wyeth, and Frazetta.

1993 projects: Coloring: *Sandman* #50, *Batman: Legends of the Dark Knight, Lobo Annual* and mini-series, and *Trencher*. Writing *Shame, Tarzan,* and *Inferno*.

Past comics titles and related projects: Colored: *Sword of Azrael, Fairy Tales of Oscar Wilde, Black Widow/Coldest War,* and *Private Files of the Shadow*. Wrote and colored: *Within Our Reach*.

Favorite comics not worked on: *Sandman Mystery Theatre, Sandman,* and *Animal Man*.

Dream comic-book project: To write a story for Francois Boucq.

✳ **Leonard Kirk.** c/o *CBG* Editorial Department, 700 East State Street, Iola, Wisconsin 54990.

Born: December 6, 1966, in Quincy, Illinois.

College or other education: B.A. in Fine Arts, Brock University, 1989.

Comics-related education: Self-taught.

Biggest creative influences: Jack Kirby (who doesn't put his name down) and, more recently, Dave Gibbons and Dale Keown.

1993 projects: *Dinosaurs for Hire* (Malibu), *Switchblade* (Caliber), *The Men in Black* (Castle Graphics), and *The Resistance* (Caliber).

Past comics titles and related projects: *The Eliminator* (Malibu), *Alien Nation: The Skin Trade* (Malibu), *Galaxina* (Malibu), *Planet of the Apes: The Forbidden Zone* (Malibu), *Sports Superstars* # 6, 10, 12, and 13 (Revolutionary), and *Baseball Superstars Annual* #1 (Revolutionary).

Favorite comics not worked on: *Star Trek* and *Star Trek: The Next Generation* (more for nostalgia than anything else) and anything drawn by Dave Gibbons.

Dream comic-book project: An adaptation of a Stephen King book. *Any* Stephen King book.

✳ **Richard Klaw.** P.O. Box 16066, Austin, Texas 78761-9998.

Born: December 22, 1967, in Brooklyn, New York.

Comics-related education: Interned editing with Blackbird.

Biggest creative influences: Lewis Shiner, Philip K. Dick, Ray Bradbury, Alan Moore, Raymond Chandler, Edgar Allan Poe, Alfred Hitchcock, Rod Serling, Richard Matheson, and Michael Moorcock.

1993 projects: *Wings: Learning to Fly* (writing). Editing *Omnibus*.

Past comics titles and related projects: Editor of *Children with Glue*. Edited *Omnibus: Modern Perversity*. Writer of *Wings: Learning to Fly* (mini-series started by MU Press, now by Blackbird).

Favorite comics not worked on: *Tropo, Signal to Noise, Animal Man,* and *Hate.*

Dream comic-book project: To do a book with an artist the caliber of Dave McKean.

Todd Klein

✳ **Todd Klein.** c/o *CBG* Editorial Department, 700 East State Street, Iola, Wisconsin 54990.

Born: January 28, 1951, in Plainfield, New Jersey.

College or other education: School of Visual Arts, New York City. Kansas City Art Institute (no degrees).

Comics-related education: Production Artist 1977-1982, DC Comics. Assistant Production Manager, 1982-1987, DC Comics.

Biggest creative influences: Lettering: Gaspar Saladino, John Workman, John Constanza, and Tom Orzechowski. Writing: Marv Wolfman and Alan Moore.

1993 projects: Lettering: *Jonah Hex: Two-Gun Mojo* (DC Comics), *Dark Joker* (DC), *Sandman* (DC), *Hitchhiker's Guide to the Galaxy* (Byron Preiss), *Sweeney Todd* (Taboo), *Galactic Girl Guides* (Tundra), and others.

Past comics titles and related projects:

Writing: *Tales of the Green Lantern Corps* (DC) 1980-84, *Omega Men* (DC) 1984-85. **Lettering:** Tons of thousands of pages for DC from 1978-present, including *Batman: Year One, Batman/Dredd: Judgment on Gotham, Detective Comics, Sandman, Books of Magic, Black Orchid,* and many others. Also several thousand covers and several hundred cover logos for DC, as well as Marvel, Disney, Dark Horse, Tundra, and other publishers, as well as occasional stories lettered for them.

Favorite comics not worked on: *Nexus, Zot!, John Byrne's Next Men, Miracleman, Pogo and Albert,* Don Rosa's ducks, *Spawn,* and well-written comics.

Dream comic-book project: Adapting a classic children's novel for comics, one involving magic and real kids.

Bill Knapp

✳ **Bill Knapp.** 1031 Allston Road, Cleveland Heights, Ohio 44121.

Born: July 21, 1962, in Cleveland, Ohio.

Comics-related education: Figure drawing classes — Art Students' League in New York, past assistant to Val Mayerik.

Biggest creative influences: Marvel comics from the '60s and early '70s.

1993 projects: *Green Hornet* #18 (completed). Currently working on *Out of the Frying Pan* (writer/artist) about a newspaper reporter fighting the mob in late '30s New York.

Past comics titles and related projects: *Green Hornet* #18 (pencils), covers to *Green Hornet* #15 and 16 (all for Now). *Aliens* mini-comic #7 (Dark Horse). Bonus Book for *Flash* #19 (DC). Various stories for *American Splendor* #8-12 and 15.

Favorite comics not worked on: *Hellblazer, Sandman, Nexus, Aztec Ace,* non-mainstream comics.

Dream comic-book project: Writing and drawing non-super-hero stories, telling a good story for its own sake.

✴ **George Kochell.** P.O. Box 2629, Laurel, Maryland 20709.

Born: March 1, 1957, in Reading, Pennsylvania.

Comics-related education: I've worked with Mark Wheatley and Marc Hempel at Insight Studios off and on since 1986. John Buscema School of Comic Book Art, 1975-76, New York City.

Biggest creative influences: Jack Kirby, Jack Davis, Alex Niño, and Alicia Austin.

1993 projects: As writer: *The Super Image Catalog* (currently at DC Comics — status uncertain).

Past comics titles and related projects: *Starlog. Adventures of Baron Munchausen,* Now Comics, colorist. *Rotten to the Core,* Eclipse card set, pencils on part of the set. *Lone Wülf* mini-comics, artist/writer. *Hard Boiled Animal Comics* #1, artist/writer. *Tales Mutated for the Mod* #1, artist only (more).

Favorite comics not worked on: Historically: *Metal Men, Magnus, T.H.U.N.D.E.R. Agents.* Currently: *Crying Freeman.*

Dream comic-book project: Write a new *Metal Men* or produce an interactive CD-ROM comic.

✴ **Jim Korkis.** c/o *CBG* Editorial Department, 700 East State Street, Iola, Wisconsin

Jim Korkis

54990.

Born: August 15, 1950, in Tulsa, Oklahoma.

College or other education: B.A. (Occidental College). M.A. (Occidental College, graduated with honors). Secondary school and junior college teaching credentials.

Comics-related education: I appeared as a cartoon character in *Dynomutt* #2 (Marvel Comics, January 1977), *Groo the Wanderer* #7 (Pacific Comics, February 1984), and *The Phantom* #6 (DC Comics, August 1989). Does that count?

Biggest creative influences: Stan Lee, Chuck Jones, Jack Kirby, Will Eisner, Mort Walker, and Michael Maltese.

1993 projects: Three-part series for Malibu on '60s rock and roll, more *Tiny Toons* scripts for Warners International.

Past comics titles and related projects: Historical introductions to over 50 Malibu Graphics comic book titles including *I Love Lucy, Polly and Her Pals, Uncensored Mouse, Peter Rabbit, Sherlock Holmes, Three Stooges, Mighty Mouse,* etc. (1989-1992). Wrote 12-part *History of the Comic Books* for Adventure Comics (1992). Co-authored the following books: *Encyclopedia of Cartoon Superstars* (Pioneer, 1990), *How to Create Animation* (Pioneer, 1990), *Cartoon Confidential* (Malibu

Graphics, 1991), *Animation Art Buyer's Guide* (Malibu Graphics, 1991). Co-edited the first newsstand animation magazine, *Cartoon Quarterly* (Gladstone, 1988). Wrote scripts for *Tiny Toons* comic book for Warners International Publishing including "Homework Hysteria," "Bad Luck Bunny," "The Big Mooch," "Future Shock," "Great Pluckin'," etc.

Favorite comics not worked on: *Captain America, Superman, Xenozoic Tales, Mickey Mouse,* and *Spirit*.

Dream comic-book project: A three-part mini-series called *The Toonville Murders* where I get to solve the mystery of who is killing off the great black-and-white animated stars.

Barry Kraus

Photo: Phin Dali

✳ **Barry Kraus.** Karl Art Publishing, P.O. Box 525, Hewlett, New York 11557.

Born: June 27, 1964, in Far Rockaway, New York.

College or other education: Fashion Institute of Technology and School of Visual Arts.

Comics-related education: School of Visual Arts, studied under Will Eisner, Harvey Kurtzman, Joe Orlando, Carmine Infantino, and Jerry Moriarty. Apprenticed under Joe Orlando for DC Comics.

Biggest creative influences: Parents, Bob Kane, EC Comics, 1960s toys, 1960s television shows and cartoons, movies by Orson Welles and others.

1993 projects: *Dimension X, Space Bananas, The Adventures of Amethyst Welles, The Steel Empire, Captain Action, Thrilling Fiction Mysteries, Boomer Magazine,* and *Epoch — Saga of the Ages*.

Past comics titles and related projects:

Dimension X, The Shadow Annual #1, Model and Toy Collector magazine, and *Gateways* magazine.

Dream comic-book project: Film adaptations of my creations and merchandising.

Robert A. Kraus

✳ **Robert A. Kraus.** 241 East Thornton Street, Akron, Ohio 44311.

Born: March 26, 1959, in Canton, Ohio.

College or other education: University of Akron. Worked in commercial art studio since I was 17 years old.

Comics-related education: On-the-job training with my own company but with the help of a *strong* graphic design/commercial art background.

Biggest creative influences: Frank Frazetta, Gustave Doré, Barry Windsor-Smith, and Bernie Wrightson.

1993 projects: *Chakan II, RAK Rampage, RAK Graphic Noize, RAK #1,* and *The Art of Robert Kraus*.

Past comics titles and related projects: *Thundermace #1-7, Chakan the Forever Man* graphic novel, *Chakan the Forever Man* concept work for Sega of America's video game, *Stephen Darklord the Survivor #1-3, RAK Presents #1, Evolution of the Mind, Straight From the Sketchbook,* and *Aliens of the Cosmos*. Also, T-shirt designs, posters, and prints of the various creations.

Favorite comics not worked on: *Sin City* by Miller.

Dream comic-book project: *Chakan* in painted colors or *Chakan vs. Conan the Barbarian*.

Gary Kwapisz

✴ **Gary Kwapisz.** 3758 Hollow Corners, Dry Den, Michigan 48428.

1993 projects: *Punisher War Journal.*

Past comics titles and related projects: *Savage Sword of Conan, Airboy,* a story with Harvey Pekar, *Hawkworld,* and *Moon Knight.*

Favorite comics not worked on: *Law Dogs, Batman,* and *Conan.*

Dream comic-book project: *Parts Unknown* with Beau Smith.

✴ **Steve Lafler.** P.O. Box 576, Hudson, Massachusetts 01749.

Born: March 16, 1957, in Batavia, New York.

College or other education: University of Massachusetts at Amherst, B.F.A., 1979.

Comics-related education: None, except daily strip at U Mass.

Biggest creative influences: Robert Crumb, Jack Kirby, Jerry Garcia, and Will Eisner.

1993 projects: *Buzzard* (anthology), *Dog Boy* (continuing character), *Bug House* (new story and characters).

Past comics titles and related projects: *Buzzard,* an anthology. *Dog Boy,* 17 issues of a solo book. *Femme Noire,* two issues of a solo book.

Steve Lafler

Duck and Cover, two issues of a collaborative series. *Mean Cat,* a one-shot. *Guts* (three issues, mostly my work). Contributor to a stack of other comics.

Favorite comics not worked on: *Dangle* (*Drawn and Quarterly*), *Trailer Trash* (Roy Tompkins, Tundra), *Hate* (P. Bagge, Fantagraphics).

Dream comic-book project: *Bug House,* my down 'n' dirty, urban be-bop fantasy.

✴ **Ray Lago.** P.O. Box 36, Jersey City, New Jersey 07303.

Born: July 1, 1958, in Jersey City, New Jersey.

College or other education: B.A. from Kean College of New Jersey.

Biggest creative influences: Frank Frazetta, Neal Adams, M.W. Kaluta, Jeff Jones, George Pratt, Burt Silverman, Barry Smith, Bernie Wrightson, Alan Lee, Alphonz Mucha, the Pre-Raphaelites, David Levine, John Sloan, J.S. Sargent, J.M. Whistler, and Scott Hampton.

1993 projects: Covers featuring Predator and RoboCop for *Dark Horse Comics,* an eight-page story for Tundra's *Skin-Tight Orbit,* cover and graphic novel *Strange Tales* for Marvel. All the above are fully painted covers and pages.

Past comics titles and related projects: *Hellraiser* #19 (cover and 15-page story,

Ray Lago

painted) for Epic; *Hellraiser* #18 (frontpiece and endpiece, painted) for Epic; Predator covers for *Dark Horse Presents* #68 and 69 (painted) for Dark Horse Comics; Predator cover for *Dark Horse Presents* #7 (ink and pencils) for Dark Horse; RoboCop cover for *Dark Horse Comics* #10 (painted) for Dark Horse; Marvel's adaptation of *Hook* (eight pages, pencils; two pin-ups, pencils on both, inks on one); *Ivanhoe* (cover and insides, entire book, painted) for *Classics Illustrated*/First Publishing; *Lone Wolf and Cub* #45 (cover, painted) for First; *Open Space* #1, 2, and 4 (painted insides and one cover) for Marvel.

Favorite comics not worked on: *Sandman, Shade, the Changing Man, Ring of Roses, Cages, Wolverine* (because of "Tex"), *Big Numbers, Hellstorm,* and *Dark Knight.*

Dream comic-book project: Would be late as all heck.

✳ **Mark Landman.** 365 Maple Avenue, Cotati, California 94931.

Born: December 12, 1953, in San Francisco, California.

College or other education: Art and computer skills (such as they are) self-taught.

Comics-related education: None specifically oriented towards comics. In fact, the best advice for aspiring artists and writers would be to orient their education to things outside the comics industry, so they can hopefully bring something fresh to the field.

Biggest creative influences: All the usual suspects.

1993 projects: Just completed a "Martian comic-book cover" for Mark Martin's section in *Heavy Metal.*

Past comics titles and related projects: Anthology work appearing in numerous comics including: *Weirdo, Snarf, Suburban High Life, Centrifigal Bumble-Puppy,* and *Blab.* Edited, designed, and appeared in *Buzz* #1-3 for Kitchen Sink. Teamed with Jim (*Kings in Disguise*) Vance to do the infamous *Republicans Attack!* trading card set. Have done illustration work for *Mondo 2000, M, Time, Audio-Video Interiors, Verbum,* and *Car Audio/Electronics.*

Favorite comics not worked on: *Tantalizing Stories, Thirteen O'Clock, Trailer Trash, Eightball, Hate, Sandman, Xenozoic Tales,* and *Fat Dog Mendoza.*

Dream comic-book project: *The Return of Buzz* or something like it, in a gorgeous thick, full-color format, with a healthy budget to pay artists and production costs.

✳ **Erik Larsen.** P.O. Box 20760, Oakland, California 94620.

Agent: This is comics. Anybody with an agent is an idiot.

Born: December 8, 1962, in Minneapolis, Minnesota.

Biggest creative influences: Kirby, G. Kane, W. Simonson, Byrne, Miller, and Sienkiewicz.

1993 projects: *The Savage Dragon, SuperPatriot, Vanguard,* and *Freak Force.*

Past comics titles and related projects: *Graphic Fantasy, Megaton, Sentinels of Justice, DNAgents, The Doom Patrol, Punisher, Marvel Comics Presents, Amazing Spider-Man,* and *Spider-Man.*

Favorite comics not worked on: *Sin City, Zot!, Spawn, Youngblood,* and *Trencher.*

Dream comic-book project: *The Savage Dragon, SuperPatriot, Vanguard,* and *Freak Force.*

✳ **Batton Lash.** 832 Fifth Avenue, Suite 3, San Diego, California 92101.

Batton Lash

Born: October 29, 1953, in Brooklyn, New York.

College or other education: School of Visual Arts (New York City), B.F.A.

Comics-related education: Assistant to Howard Chaykin (1977).

Biggest creative influences: Steve Ditko, Will Eisner, Harvey Kurtzman, Milton Caniff, Johnny Craig, Donald Westlake, Geo. Kaufman, and Peter DeVries.

1993 projects: Untitled project for Piranha Press, *Aesop's Desecrated Morals* (Rip Off Press), the third collection of *Wolff and Byrd* strips (Sidebar Books).

Past comics titles and related projects: *Wolff and Byrd, Counselors of the Macabre*, weekly newspaper strip 1979 to present, *National Law Journal, Brooklyn Paper Publications, CBG; Mr. Monster* (Eclipse, 1987); *Munden's Bar* (First, 1990); *Panorama* (st.EVE, 1991); *CD Comics* (Hi-Test, 1989); *Frankie's Frightmares* (Cat's Paw, 1992); *Wolff and Byrd, Counselors of the Macabre* (collected strips, Andrion, 1988); *Supernatural Law* (Sidebar, 1992); *Grave Tales, Dread of Night, Maggots* (Hamilton Comics, 1991); *Satan's Six* #1 (Topps, 1993).

Favorite comics not worked on: *Cerebus, Love and Rockets, Eightball, Steve Canyon* and *Li'l Abner* collections, *Spirit, Deadface, Mr. Monster, Ms. Tree*, and anything by Alan Moore.

Dream comic-book project: What else? A monthly *Wolff and Byrd* comic, black-and-white

and *one* color, with guest artists and characters. The law was never this much fun.

Carol Lay

✻ **Carol Lay.** c/o *CBG* Editorial Department, 700 East State Street, Iola, Wisconsin 54990.

Born: September 15, 1952, in Whittier, California.

College or other education: B.A. from UCLA.

Biggest creative influences: Kurtzman, Crumb, Segar, Herriman, and Capp.

1993 projects: A short story, *Clio's Problems*, for the next *Taboo*; a short piece, *Panty Raid*, for the next *Young Lust*; a weekly strip that appears in the *LA Weekly*, the *NY Press*, the *San Diego Reader*, and the *San Francisco Examiner*. A book collection of the strips is coming out in September through Kitchen Sink Press.

Past comics titles and related projects: *Good Girls* #1-6, various underground short stories in *Weirdo, Rip Off Magazine, Wimmen's Comix, Cannibal Romance, Viper, Pontiac Tempura, Zomoid Illustrations, Honk!, Heck!*, the *LA Reader*, and ¼ page in *Raw* #5. I've also done comics work for Mattel, Hanna-Barbera, and DC. Reprints have appeared in *Pox* (Sweden), *El Vibora* (Spain), and

Twisted Sisters — an anthology of Bad Girl art from Penguin Viking Press.

Favorite comics not worked on: *Hate* and *Love and Rockets*.

Dream comic-book project: I'm pretty much doing my dream project already by doing my weekly strip and collecting the strips in book form. What would be better is more papers to put it in, a producer sees them and makes movies out of the stories, I become fabulously wealthy and keep working till I drop anyway just because I like it.

Gary Leach

✳ **Gary Leach.** c/o *CBG* Editorial Department, 700 East State Street, Iola, Wisconsin 54990.

Born: May 15, 1957, in Columbia, Missouri.

College or other education: A.A. degree at Maricopa Technical Community College.

Comics-related education: Pure field experience as Art Director/colorist/scripter for Gladstone/Disney/Egmont.

Biggest creative influences: Carl Barks, Jack Kirby, Nick Cardy, Arthur C. Clarke, and the Marx Brothers.

1993 projects: Gladstone's Disney comics

and *The Carl Barks Library in Color, Mr. Monster's Gal Friday, Kelly*, Egmont Disney comics.

Past comics titles and related projects: The original series of Gladstone Disney comics and comic albums, *Spawn* giveaway for Stabur, Gladstone EC comics, Hamilton horror magazines, *The Carl Barks Library, The Little Lulu Library, Mickey Mouse in Color*, Disney's Disney comics, *Uncle Scrooge in Color*, and Another Rainbow's series of Carl Barks lithographs.

Favorite comics not worked on: *Desert Peach, Elfquest, Bone, Lost in Space*, and *Xenozoic Tales*.

Dream comic-book project: A revival of the 1960s *Teen Titans* with Nick Cardy.

Ken Leach

✳ **Ken Leach.** 12536 East Jefferson, Mishawaka, Indiana 46545.

Born: November 1, 1947, in Dowagiac, Michigan.

College or other education: B.S. degree, cinema animation artist — studio co-owner.

Comics-related education: Joe Kubert seminars. Ran graphic arts studio for 12 years. TV art director for eight years.

Biggest creative influences: Joe Kubert and Will Eisner.

1993 projects: *Tales from the Morgue* (32 pages, black-and-white), Kineticom. Lettering work for Parody Press.

Past comics titles and related projects: *Frankie's Frightmare*, packaged entirely for publication by Cat's Paw Comics. Logo and lettering work for numerous Malibu Graphics comics. Lettering for Viz Communications, DC Comics (Warner Bros. International Publishing), Comico, Parody Press, and other independents. 3-D separation work. Hand-separated color work. Logo design.

Favorite comics not worked on: Disney/ Gladstone comics.

Dream comic-book project: A "Universal" '30s horror/sci-fi graphic novel.

Susan Daigle-Leach

✳ **Susan Daigle-Leach.** c/o *CBG* Editorial Department, 700 East State Street, Iola, Wisconsin 54990.

Born: November 11, 1960, in Norristown, Pennsylvania.

College or other education: B.F.A., Kutztown University, 1983.

Comics-related education: No direct comics education, but many years of art and production experience prior to becoming production manager at Another Rainbow/Gladstone.

Biggest creative influences: N.C. Wyeth, Vermeer, and three outstanding professors: John K. Landis, Rosemarie Sloat, and George Sorrels.

1993 projects: Primary colorist for *Carl Barks Library in Color* album series; colorist and color supervisor for new Gladstone Disney comics; colorist for Egmont (Denmark) Disney albums of Al Taliaferro's Donald Duck.

Past comics titles and related projects: Colorist for original Gladstone Disney comics (1986-1990); also Disney's Disney comics (1990-1993). Production assistant, production manager, and assistant editor for Another Rainbow's *Carl Barks Library* and *Little Lulu Library*. Colorist for Gladstone's *Felix the Cat* and *Dick Tracy* albums. Have lost count of how many thousands of Disney pages I've colored, but it is several. Recently colored Mike Gilbert's *Mr. Monster's Gal Friday, Kelly* for Tundra. Also dialogue and lettering work on Gladstone's Disney comics.

Favorite comics not worked on: Donna Barr's *Stinz* and *Desert Peach*, Jeff Smith's *Bone*, Baron and Rude's *Nexus* (and spin-offs), *Love and Rockets*, the now-defunct *Dreamery* and *Fusion* from Eclipse, and Phil Foglio's *Buck Godot*.

Dream comic-book project: To write, pencil, and ink my own space opera — and have somebody *else* color it.

✳ **Brian LeBlanc.** c/o *CBG* Editorial Department, 700 East State Street, Iola, Wisconsin 54990.

Born: July 8, 1971, in West Jefferson Hospital, Harvey, Louisiana.

Biggest creative influences: Mitch Byrd, Steven Butler, Bernie Wrightson, Simon Bisley, nature, and metaphysics.

1993 projects: *Bloodmoon* (Allied Comics), *Tales from the Balcony* #1 and 3 (Allied Comics), various work from Succeed Comics.

Past comics titles and related projects: *The Balcony* #1, *Blood Klott, Manhandler,* and *Horror Shorts.*

Favorite comics not worked on: *Grendel, Sandman, Spawn, WildC.A.T.S,* and *Death.*

Dream comic-book project: A classic adventure based on two female bounty hunters. Violent.

✳ **Jim Lee.** Homage Studios, 106068 Camino Ruiz, Suite 209, San Diego, California 92126.

Agent: Dan Adler, Creative Artists Agency.

Born: August 11, 1964, in Seoul, South Korea.

College or other education: Psychology degree, Princeton University.

Jim Lee

1993 projects: *WildC.A.T.S, Deathblow*, and *Deathmate* crossover with Valiant.

Past comics titles and related projects: *X-Men* and *Alpha Flight*.

✻ Stan Lee. 1440 South Sepulveda Boulevard, Los Angeles, California 90025.

Born: December 28, 1922, in New York City.

College or other education: DeWitt Clinton High School, City College of New York (about six months).

Biggest creative influences: William Shakespeare, *The Bible*, various legends and classics, H.G. Wells, Mark Twain, O. Henry, Poe, *Tarzan*, and Sir Arthur Conan Doyle.

1993 projects: Comic-book version of *Riftworld* (with Bill McKay), tying in *Spider-Man* strip and comic, possible comic based on a new Danny DeVito movie, possible comic based on new Don Johnson TV series.

Past comics titles and related projects:

Stan Lee

Golden Age: *Captain America* (and other Timely titles). 1950s: *Marvel Tales, Strange Tales, Journey into Mystery, Millie the Model* (and other Atlas titles). 1960s: *Fantastic Four, The Incredible Hulk, The Amazing Spider-Man, Daredevil, X-Men, Avengers, The Mighty Thor, Silver Surfer, Sgt. Fury and His Howling Commandos*, stories about Doctor Strange, Captain America, Iron Man, Sub-Mariner, and many others. 1970s: Silver Surfer graphic novel, *Origins of Marvel Comics, Spider-Man* comic strip (until present). 1980s: *Silver Surfer: A Parable*. 1990s: *Ravage 2099*.

Favorite comics not worked on: Have no time to read comics (like *Groo*, though).

Dream comic-book project: I've already done 'em.

✻ Wendi Lee. P.O. Box 1007, Muscatine, Iowa 52761.

Agent: Barb Puechner (for novels).

Born: February 29, 1956, in Minneapolis, Minnesota.

College or other education: Three years of college: Beloit College in Wisconsin, University of Massachusetts, Boston.

Biggest creative influences: Will Eisner.

1993 projects: *Elfquest: New Blood*.

Past comics titles and related projects: *Elf-quest: New Blood Summer Special* #1, *Eclipse Monthly* #9, and press liaison for Renegade Press 1986-87.

Favorite comics not worked on: *Little Lulu, Mr. Monster, Omaha the Cat Dancer, Angel and the Ape* (the original only), *Ms. Tree, Silent Invasion, Deadface, Eightball*, and *Bone*.

Dream comic-book project: An updated *Little Lulu* or adaptations of novels and movies.

Mike Leonard

✳ Mike Leonard. R.D. #2, Box 214, Cherry Tree, Pennsylvania 15724.

Born: August 10, 1972, in Spangler, Pennsylvania.

College or other education: Art Institute of Pittsburgh, left to write novel, *The Muse*, unpublished as of yet.

Biggest creative influences: Stephen King, Clive Barker, Neil Gaiman, Chris Claremont, Frank Miller, and Peter David.

1993 projects: *Wiindows* #5: *Masterpiece in Bone*, Cult Press. *Doorman*, full-color monthly starting in June, Cult Press.

Favorite comics not worked on: *Wolverine, Sandman, Faust, Spawn*, and *Batman*.

Dream comic-book project: An all-new *Buckaroo Banzai* series, and/or a Doorman/Spawn crossover.

✳ Linda Lessman. 2030 Harrison Street, Evanston, Illinois 60201.

Born: June 18, 1948, in Chicago, Illinois.

College or other education: Graduated Stephens College, 1970; A.A. degree (1968), B.F.A. (1970).

Comics-related education: Began work in offices of Marvel Comics doing production work, August 1973. Phased into coloring on staff a few months later.

Biggest creative influences: Marie Severin, Glynis Oliver, Barry Windsor-Smith, Bill Reinhold, and the wonderful *Rupert* books by Bestall.

1993 projects: Coloring *Spyke*, a four-issue mini-series for Epic (Heavy Hitters) by Mike Baron, drawn and inked by Bill Reinhold.

Past comics titles and related projects: Coloring numerous Marvel titles circa 1973-75 including: *Man-Thing, Tomb of Dracula, Werewolf by Night, Fantastic Four, Amazing Spider-Man*, etc. 1985-87 for First Comics: *American Flagg!, Grimjack*, and *Badger*, also the graphic novel *Time Beavers*. 1989: Punisher graphic novel, *Intruder*, drawn and inked by Bill Reinhold. 1990: *Punisher* #38 and 43. 1991: *Hellraiser* #7: *Under the Knife*, Silver Surfer graphic novel: *Homecoming*.

Favorite comics not worked on: *Cerebus, Beanworld*, and I'd love to color *Barbie* for Marvel, believe it or not.

Dream comic-book project: I'd love to publish a book of Oogle stories; he's a little furry creature that I invented back in 1965.

✳ Ken Lester. P.O. Box 495, Coloma, Michigan 49038.

Born: November 25, 1963, in St. Joseph, Michigan.

College or other education: Art at Central Michigan University. Business at Western Michigan University and Lake Michigan College.

Biggest creative influences: John Buscema.

1993 projects: *Red Thunder* and the *Crime Killers*. Also, inker on *The Knight Wolf*.

Favorite comics not worked on: *Fantastic Four, Captain America*, and *The Savage Dragon*.

Dream comic-book project: I *am* doing my dream project. I've started national distribution of Five Star Comics.

✳ **Mark A. Lester.** P.O. Box 240, Coloma, Michigan 49038.

Born: April 20, 1965, in Berrien Springs, Michigan.

College or other education: Dropped out of college in second year after disagreement with art teachers.

Comics-related education: Just reading and drawing since the age of 4 or 5.

Biggest creative influences: Mike Grell's '70s *Legion of Super-Heroes* and Jim Aparo's *Brave and the Bold*.

1993 projects: *Knight Wolf* — an ongoing series by new small black-and-white publisher — Five Star Comics (creator, pencils, and script). Pencilling for (one of many pencillers) Doug Wheeler, done for Rip Off Press: *Aesop's Desecrated Morals*.

Past comics titles and related projects: Pencils and inks on an English story, *The Invisible Boy*, with writer Tim Quinn. The story was one in an anthology title I do not believe ever saw print.

Favorite comics not worked on: Any.

Dream comic-book project: The original Captain Marvel.

Robert Lewis

✳ **Robert Lewis.** Feather Fall Press, 723 Greenridge, Battle Creek, Michigan 49015.

Born: March 6, 1971, in Grand Rapids, Michigan.

College or other education: B.F.A. Painting at Western Michigan University.

Comics-related education: Independent study on comics layout and design with Professor Curtis Rhodes.

Biggest creative influences: Richard Sala, Bill Sienkiewicz, Dave Sim, Bill Plympton, and Maurice Sendak.

1993 projects: *Gill, Ned, Loonacy, The Silent Theatre*.

Past comics titles and related projects: Self-publisher of mini-comics including two volumes of *Ned, Gill the Clownfish of the North Pacific Railroad*, and *Loonacy*, a cartoon humor anthology.

Favorite comics not worked on: *From Hell, Cages*, and *Cerebus*.

Dream comic-book project: *Classics Illustrated, The Harp of Burma*.

Jean-Marc Lofficier, Randy Lofficier

✳ **Jean-Marc Lofficier.** P.O. Box 17270, Encino, California 91416.

Born: June 22, 1954, in Toulon, France.

✳ **Randy Lofficier.** P.O. Box 17270, Encino, California 91416.

Born: February 3, 1953, in Philadelphia, Pennsylvania.

✳ **Aaron A. Lopresti.** Artfarm, 3407 S.W. Corbett Avenue, Portland, Oregon 97201.

Born: January 7, 1964, in Portland, Oregon.

College or other education: University of Southern California (USC), Film Production.

Comics-related education: I teach a class in Comic Book Art at the Pacific Northwest College of Art, Portland, Oregon.

Biggest creative influences: Bernie Wrightson, Neal Adams, Brian Bolland, Michael Golden, and Frank Frazetta.

1993 projects: *Sludge* (penciller on this new series from Malibu's Ultraverse line). *Amazing*

Aaron A. Lopresti

Spider-Man Annual #12 (pencils), *Darkhawk Annual* #2 (pencils), *What The--?!* # 25 and 26 (pencils, inks, writing) (all for Marvel).

Past comics titles and related projects: *Amazing Spider-Man* #365, 368, 370-372, and 375, *Amazing Spider-Man Annual* #26, *Spectacular Spider-Man Annual* #12, *Web of Spider-Man Annual* #8, *New Warriors Annual* #8, *What If?* #34, and *What The--?!* #8, 12, 14, 16, 18, 20, and 22-24.

Favorite comics not worked on: *Batman: Legends of the Dark Knight, Batman: The Killing Joke, Pitt*, and *Amazing Spider-Man*.

Dream comic-book project: A Batman/ Swamp Thing team-up.

Mark Lucas

❋ **Mark Lucas.** P.O. Box 491744, Los Angeles, California 90049.

Born: August 24, 1966, in Columbia, South Carolina.

College or other education: B.A. (USC), M.A. (Antioch, expected June 1994).

Biggest creative influences: Self-publishing boom of mid-'80s.

1993 projects: *The Art Spectrum* for Caliber's *Negative Burn, Comics Critics Cavalcade* (publisher), magazine for aspiring creators.

Past comics titles and related projects: *Single Page* (with Michal Jacot) for *Cerebus* # 24, more than 500 letters published in comics, interviews for *Comics Interview*, articles for San Diego Convention Programs, founding member Mad Hatter Studios, *Comics Critics Cavalcade, State of Comics* in *Minnesota Comics and Stories, Pun-isher* strips (with Michal Jacot) in *Comics Buyer's Guide*, "Comics Are Coming to the Big Screen" in *Graphic Comments* #20, and interviewed in *Comics Interview* #107. Member CAPA-Alpha since 1988 and Marvel Zombie Society since 1990 (Central Mailer, 1993).

Favorite comics not worked on: DC's Vertigo comics (*Sandman, Shade, Death, et al.*), *Cerebus, The Spectre*, and *'Mazing Man*.

Dream comic-book project: Writing and publishing a book of commercial and artistic merit (non-super-hero project).

❋ **Eric Lurio.** 250 West 15th Street, New York, New York.

Agent: Madeline Morel.

Born: February 23, 1957, in Newark, New Jersey.

College or other education: B.F.A., Pratt Institute.

Biggest creative influences: Vaughn Bodé, James Gillray, Garry Trudeau, Winsor McCay, and Maurice Sendak.

1993 projects: *The Day after the Dinosaurs*.

Past comics titles and related projects: *The Cartoon Guide to the U.S. Constitution* (1987). *Plato for Beginners* (1989). *A Fractured History of the Discovery of America* (1992). *The I Hate Unicorns Book* (1984).

Favorite comics not worked on: *Pogo, Barnaby, Fritz the Cat*, and *Marcel Gotlib*.

Eric Lurio

Dream comic-book project: *Ashreah, the Further Adventures of God's Ex-Wife.*

John Lustig

✴ **John Lustig.** c/o *CBG* Editorial Department, 700 East State Street, Iola, Wisconsin 54990.

Born: January 25, 1953, in Seattle, Washington.

College or other education: B.A. in English and a B.A. in Communications (Journalism). Several years as a newspaper reporter and columnist.

Biggest creative influences: Carl Barks, William Van Horn, John Stanley's *Little Lulu,* and P.G. Wodehouse.

1993 projects: Writing various Disney comics for Egmont Publishing in Europe.

Past comics titles and related projects: Writer of: *Donald Duck Adventures, Uncle Scrooge, DuckTales,* and *Daffy Duck.*

Favorite comics not worked on: *Groo, The Desert Peach, Bone,* and *Mr. Monster.*

Dream comic-book project: Revival or updating of *Supersnipe* or *Little Lulu.* Also light-humor/adventure series based on my own characters.

Tom Lyle

✴ **Tom Lyle.** P.O. Box 301, Newfield, New York 14867-0301.

Born: November 2, 1953, in Jacksonville, Florida.

College or other education: B.A. in Art (Advertising Design), University of Florida, Gainesville, Florida.

Comics-related education: School of hard knocks — I'm pretty much self-taught.

Biggest creative influences: Jack Kirby, Gil Kane, and Barry Windsor-Smith.

1993 projects: Regular artist on *Spider-Man*

(the unenhanced title) and a *Venom/Punisher* mini-series.

Past comics titles and related projects: All three *Robin* mini-series, *The Comet, Starman,* and *Total Recall* for DC. *Strike!* and *Skywolf* (mini-series and back-ups in Airboy) for Eclipse. Various and sundry stories and covers for others such as Quality Comics, Wonder Comics, AC Comics, and so on.

Favorite comics not worked on: *Daredevil.*

Dream comic-book project: Write and draw my own book (*Spider-Man* or *Daredevil*, preferably).

Jay Lynch

✳ **Jay Lynch.** 2019 West Potomac, Chicago, Illinois 60622.

Born: January 7, 1945, in East Orange, New Jersey.

College or other education: School of the Art Institute of Chicago. Roosevelt University.

Comics-related education: Taught comix class at School of the Art Institute of Chicago in the early '70s.

Biggest creative influences: Kurtzman, Elder, Wood, Davis, Lenny Bruce, Vince Fago, Alfred Korzybski, and Stan Freberg.

1993 projects: No comics, only sticker albums, *Little Mermaid, Teenage Mutant Ninja Turtles III,* and *Super Mario Bros.*

Past comics titles and related projects: *Bijou Funnies, Bazooka Joe, Give 'Em an Inch* (*Playboy*), Topps bubblegum cards, early underground comix, *Nard 'n' Pat.* Stickers and sticker album sets of licensed characters for Diamond Publishing including: Teenage Mutant Ninja Turtles, Simpsons, Archie, Nintendo, NFL, and most popular licenses of the last decade. *Phoebe and the Pigeon People* comic strip.

Favorite comics not worked on: Crumb books, EC reprints, and *Eightball.*

Dream comic-book project: Newsstand (as opposed to comics shop) distributed 1990s version of 1952 *Mad*, for mass audience rather than comics-shop audience.

Stan Lynde

✳ **Stan Lynde.** Cottonwood Graphics Inc., 2340 Trumble Creek Road, Kalispell, Montana 59901-6713.

Agent: Publisher: Lynda Brown Lynde.

Born: September 23, 1931, in Billings, Montana.

College or other education: University of Montana, Missoula, Montana, 1949-1951 (no degree).

Comics-related education: Art Instruction Inc. (didn't complete). School of Visual Arts, New York City, 1956-1957.

Biggest creative influences: Other professionals: Hal Foster, Al Capp, J.R. Williams, Fred Harman, and Walt Kelly.

1993 projects: Currently at work on (text)

novel. Printing of reprint material from comic strips *Rick O'Shay* (Sunday pages), *Latigo* (dailies, Book 3). Second graphic novel in series *The New Adventures of Rick O'Shay and Hipshot.* Projected length, 64 to 72 pages, present title undecided.

Past comics titles and related projects: Syndicated newspaper strips: *Rick O'Shay*, creator, author, artist, 1958-1977. *Latigo*, creator, author, artist, 1979-1983. Self-syndicated panel: *Grass Roots*, creator, author, artist, 1984-1985. Reprint books: *Rick O'Shay, Hipshot, and Me*, 1990. *A Month of Sundays*, 1985. *Latigo Book One*, 1991. *Latigo Book Two*, 1992. Original graphic novels: *Rick O'Shay and Hipshot: The Price of Fame* Books 1 and 2, 1992. *Pardners* Books 1 and 2, 1990 and 1991.

Favorite comics not worked on: Have to date worked on own material only. No particular current favorites. Admirer of John Severin's work on old *Two-Fisted Tales, Watchmen*, Miller's *Dark Knight.* Like strips *Calvin and Hobbes* and *For Better or for Worse.*

Dream comic-book project: I'm one of those lucky ones who *has. Price of Fame* Books 1 and 2. Plan to continue to explore and develop the Western form through *Rick O'Shay*, possibly *Latigo* graphic novels.

✱ **Scott McCloud.** P.O. Box 798, Amherst, Massachusetts 01004-0798.

Born: June 10, 1960, in Boston, Massachusetts.

College or other education: B.F.A. Illustration, Syracuse University, 1978-1982.

Comics-related education: DC Comics production job 1982-1983.

Biggest creative influences: Osamu Tezuka, Art Spiegelman, Will Eisner, Jack Kirby, and Hergé.

1993 projects: *Understanding Comics* (Tundra), 224-page comic book about comics.

Past comics titles and related projects: *Zot!*, 1984-1985, 1987-1991 (Eclipse), 36 issues. *Destroy!!*, 1986 (Eclipse), giant one-shot. *A Day's Work*, 1991 (published in *Taboo Especial*), first of the 24-hour comics (24-page story done in 24 hours). *Small Press Watch* column in *Amazing Heroes*, 1986, 10 installments.

Favorite comics not worked on: Anything by Eisner, Spiegelman, Marder, and Woodring. Others: *Bone, Eightball, Sandman, Cages*, and *Yummy Fur.*

Dream comic-book project: My next one.

✱ **Rick McCollum.** 440 Warner Street, #1, Cincinnati, Ohio 45219.

Born: November 19, 1954, in Winchester, Indiana.

College or other education: B.F.A., major in Drawing/Painting from the College of Design, Art, and Architecture, University of Cincinnati. Also some graduate work in Art History.

Comics-related education: The school of hard knocks.

Biggest creative influences: Symbolist/decadent movements.

1993 projects: *Robert E. Howard's Blood and Thunder* — total art, story adaptations (Conquest). *The Excruciator* — co-scripting, layouts (Conquest).

Past comics titles and related projects: *Teenage Mutant Ninja Turtles, Taboo Especial, Turtle Soup, Tundra Sketchbook: Screaming Masks, Gore Shriek, Autumn: Earth, Barbaric Tales, Horde, Dimension Z, Omicron, Dark Regions, Mangazine, Comico Primer*, and many more. I was writer/artist on all, although Bill Anderson inked many of my projects.

Favorite comics not worked on: *Swamp Thing, Doom Patrol, Sandman, Spectre, Animal Man*, and *Hellblazer.*

Dream comic-book project: Adaptations of Robert E. Howard's Conan stories which were actually true to the text. The same for Lovecraft and the Doc Savage series.

✱ **Bruce McCorkindale.** 619 South 37 Street, #305, Omaha, Nebraska 68105.

Born: December 27, 1960, in Omaha, Nebraska.

College or other education: University of Nebraska at Omaha, B.F.A., Creative Writing.

Comics-related education: Studio Art (three years) U.N.O.

Biggest creative influences: Beatles, Dr.

Bruce McCorkindale

Seuss, Marvel Comics of the '60s and early '70s, The Studio artists (Wrightson, etc.).

1993 projects: Inking *Dinosaurs for Hire*, ongoing color series from Malibu Comics.

Past comics titles and related projects: All inking: Eternity: *Plan 9 from Outer Space* (graphic novel), *Scimidar, Twilight Avenger.* Adventure: *Merlin, Sinbad, Planet of the Apes: Blood of the Apes, Strange Sports Stories.* Malibu: *Dinosaurs for Hire.* Pencils and inks: Eternity: *Halloween Terror.* Monster Comics: *Tor Johnson — Hollywood Star.*

Favorite comics not worked on: *Sandman, Epicurus the Sage,* and *Watchmen.*

Dream comic-book project: To write and illustrate a comics story that would comfort and/ or inspire someone the way my favorite comics stories did me.

✱ **Paul McCusker.** 97 Eaglewood Boulevard, Mississauga, Ontario, Canada.

Born: December 12, 1953, in Halifax, Nova Scotia, Canada.

College or other education: Sueridan College (three years) Illustration program graduate.

Comics-related education: Sheridan College, Media Arts Cartooning graduate (two years).

Biggest creative influences: *Mad* magazine, early Marvels, Curt Swan, Murphy Anderson,

Kirby, Ditko, pre-Raphaelites, and Rubens (not that any of this shows up in my works).

1993 projects: Currently working on a series of Canadian historical works authored by Pierre Berton for adolescents.

Past comics titles and related projects: A piece in *Heavy Metal*, work for Vortex Comics, comics work for Toronto Blue Jays baseball team, cartoons for newspapers, nature comic book for children's science text. Work in the early ill-fated *Orb Magazine* (a Canadian comic). Animation storyboards, layouts, and colorist on *Ali Baba. Sheerluck Holmes* strip.

Favorite comics not worked on: *Sandman, Watchmen,* early Ditko *Spider-Man*, anything by Dave McKean, Mike Cherkas, and Larry Hancock.

Walter Antonio McDaniel

✱ **Walter Antonio McDaniel.** c/o *CBG* Editorial Department, 700 East State Street, Iola, Wisconsin 54990.

Born: January 1, 1971, in St. Thomas, Virgin Islands.

College or other education: DC New Talent Program, Joe Kubert School, School of Visual Arts.

Biggest creative influences: Gil Ashby, Drew Strusan, Rich Buckler, Neal Adams, and Norman Rockwell.

1993 projects: *Deathlok* #16-23, covers #16-25, *X-Men Annual, Punisher back to School Special, Ghost Rider* cover #15, *Morbius Revisited* covers

#2 and #5, *Marvel Comics Presents*, Milestone Media covers, *Youngblood* back-up, and *Cain #3*.

Past comics titles and related projects: *Earth 4* (Continuity Comics).

Favorite comics not worked on: *X-Men, Uncanny X-Men, X-Force, X-Factor, Youngblood, CyberForce, Savage Dragon*, and *Shadowhawk*.

Dream comic-book project: My own creator-owned project *Final Phase*.

Heidi D. MacDonald

✳ **Heidi D. MacDonald.** *Disney Adventures Magazine*, 500 South Buena Vista, Burbank, California 91521-6020.

Born: November 15, in Buffalo, New York.

Biggest creative influences: Carl Barks, John Stanley, J.R.R. Tolkien, and E.B. White.

1993 projects: *Disney Adventures, Secret Teachings of a Comic Book Master*, and *Tales from the Freezer*.

Past comics titles and related projects: *The Comics Journal, Amazing Heroes, Amazing Heroes Preview Special, CBG*, comics reviewer for *L.A. Weekly, Boris the Bear, Sidekicks at Large* (*Reflex* magazine).

Favorite comics not worked on: *Love and Rockets, Hate, Eightball, Dirty Plotte*, and *From Hell*.

Dream comic-book project: An anthology of humorous/whimsical/fantastic continuing strips that would be a cross between *Zap* and *Walt Disney's Comics and Stories*.

Clint McElroy

✳ **Clint McElroy.** 1107 Tenth Street, Huntington, West Virginia 25701.

Born: August 10, 1955, in Ironton, Ohio.

College or other education: Bachelor's degree in Broadcasting from Marshall University.

Biggest creative influences: Rowan Atkinson, Stephen R. Donaldson, Chuck Dixon, Timothy Truman, Archie Goodwin, Mike Royko, Brian Donleavy, and Beau Smith.

1993 projects: *Green Hornet: Dark Tomorrow* and *Blood Is the Harvest 2*.

Past comics titles and related projects: *Blood Is the Harvest, Freejack, Universal Soldier, Green Hornet, Illegal Aliens*. Co-producer of *Comicast*, an audio fanzine done with Beau Smith. Host of *Comics Vision* video series. Columnist for *Comic Book Week*.

Favorite comics not worked on: *Legionnaires, Xenozoic Tales, Nomad, Law Dog*, Superman titles, *Pendragon II, Archer & Armstrong*, and the Titans books.

Dream comic-book project: *King of the USA*: an alternate history about the United States as a monarchy.

Todd McFarlane

❋ **Todd McFarlane.** Image Comics, 2400 East Katella Avenue, Suite 1065, Anaheim, California 92806.

College or other education: University of Eastern Washington, B.S., Graphic Design.

Biggest creative influences: Kirby, Miller, and Byrne.

1993 projects: *Spawn* regular series, Spawn/Batman crossover.

Past comics titles and related projects: *Amazing Spider-Man, Spider-Man, Batman, Hulk, Coyote, Scorpio Rose, Infinity Inc.,* numerous *Marvel Tales* and other covers.

Favorite comics not worked on: All Image!

Dream comic-book project: *Bedrock* one-shot! © Rob Liefeld.

❋ **Ed McGeean.** c/o *CBG* Editorial Department, 700 East State Street, Iola, Wisconsin 54990.

Born: December 22, 1928, in Oak Park, Illinois.

Comics-related education: Chicago Academy of Fine Arts, studied cartooning under the late Martin Garrity, gag cartoonist.

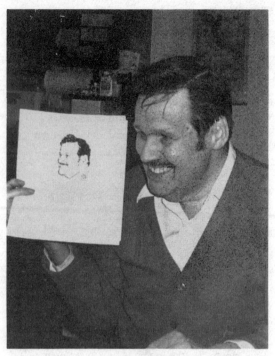

Ed McGeean

Biggest creative influences: Milton Caniff, Hal Foster, Will Eisner, Wally Carlson, Rick Yager, Hank Ketcham, Joe Kubert, S.R. (Bob) Powell, and many more.

Past comics titles and related projects: None. I was a staff cartoonist with *The Chicago Sun-Times* and also worked on the now-defunct *Chicago Daily News*. At 64 I am enjoying my semi-retirement by writing a monthly column on comics news (*Ink Blots*) for the Comics Art Professional Society (CAPS). Doing book reviews for CAPS, National Cartoonists Society (NCS), and, when they use them, *CBG*. Enjoy helping younger cartoonists, as I was helped.

Favorite comics not worked on: *Calvin and Hobbes, B.C., Wizard of Id, Motley's Crew, Herb and Jamaal,* and *Bound and Gagged.*

Dream comic-book project: Adapting Louis L'Amour's Western novels and other works.

❋ **Mark McKenna.** c/o *CBG* Editorial Department, 700 East State Street, Iola, Wisconsin 54990.

Born: April 19, 1957, in Flushing Hospital, Queens, New York.

College or other education: A.A., Suffolk

Mark McKenna

Community College. B.F.A., School of Visual Arts.

Comics-related education: Art corrections at Marvel Comics under John Romita Sr. (Romita's Raiders).

Biggest creative influences: Brian Bolland, Jerry Ordway, and John Beatty.

1993 projects: *Punisher War Zone, X-Factor Annual, X-Men Unlimited, Deathlok Annual, Punisher Annual, Rack and Pain* mini-series (Dark Horse), *Bubblegum Crisis* (Dark Horse), *Nova* ongoing (?), *Spider-Woman* mini (?).

Past comics titles and related projects: *Dr. Fate* #1-6, *Legion '89-'90* #4-18, *Doom Patrol* #36-46, *Griffin* mini-series #1-6, *Nomad* mini-series #1-4, *Doctor Strange* #26-33, *Nomad* (regular series) #1-13, *Darkhold* #1-5, *Punisher Summer Special* #2, *Punisher War Zone* #12-16, *Thor Annual* (Terminus Factor), *Fantastic Four Annual* (Volcana), *Deathlok* #20, *Dai Kamikaze* #1-6 (Now), *Rust* #3 and 4 (Now), *Nexus* #61 (First), *Swords of Texas* (mini) #1-4 (Eclipse), *Marvel Comics Presents*: Red Wolf (#15), Red Wolf (#72), Devil Slayer (#46-49), Werewolf by Night (#98), Doctor Strange (#79).

Favorite comics not worked on: *Warlock* and *Silver Surfer.*

Dream comic-book project: A Judge Dredd graphic novel (with Brian Bolland or Mike McKone).

✳ **Marc McLaurin.** Marvel Comics, 387 Park Avenue South, New York, New York 10016.

Born: October 4, 1964, in Springfield, Massachusetts.

College or other education: Pratt Institute, B.F.A., Illustration and Communications Design.

1993 projects: *Cage* (writer), *Punisher* (pencilling), *Ectokid, Hyperkind, Saint Sinner, Hokum and Hex, Marvels, The Harrowers* (editor).

Past comics titles and related projects: *Atomic Ace, Alien Legion, Akira, Moebius, Punisher, Alpha Flight, Hellraiser, Nightbreed, Groo, Power Pack, Justice, Marvel Universe Handbook,* and *Spider-Man.*

Favorite comics not worked on: *Sandman* and *Death.*

Dream comic-book project: Writing and drawing a comic on real life made interesting.

✳ **John MacLeod.** P.O. Box 671, Guelph, Ontario, Canada N1H 6L3.

Born: April 24, 1957, in Brantford, Ontario, Canada.

College or other education: B.A. Fine Art, M.A. Sociology (half of a Ph.D. Sociology).

Biggest creative influences: Chester Brown, Los Bros Hernandez, Scott McCloud, and Japanese comics.

1993 projects: Back-up strip for Topps, science-fiction one-shot possibly for Fantagraphics, *Dishman* #11, untitled graphic novel, and Dave Frishberg tribute.

Past comics titles and related projects: *Dishman* #1-10 (self-published), *Dishman* #1 (Eclipse reprint anthology), *Cheese Heads* #5, *Ultra Klutz* #28, *Street Music* #2, *1980 Comics Annual, Comic Book Newsletter/Citizen Publishing Digest/Comicist* (commentary column), and various small-press titles.

Favorite comics not worked on: *Love and Rockets, Desert Peach, Stinz, Concrete, Cheese Heads, Buz Sawyer, 2001 Nights, Zot!,* and *Mai.*

Dream comic-book project: Everything I'm currently working on (especially untitled graphic novel).

✳ **Darwin McPherson.** c/o *CBG* Editorial Department, 700 East State Street, Iola, Wisconsin 54990.

Born: October 6, 1966, in Buffalo, New York.

College or other education: B.S. in Business.

Biggest creative influences: British TV dramas: *East Enders, Tenko.* U.S. TV: *China Beach, thirtysomething, M.A.S.H.* Comics: Claremont/Byrne, Wolfman/Pérez, Gaiman, Moore, Miller. Books: F. Scott Fitzgerald.

1993 projects: *Green Lantern Corps Quarterly* story and promotional copy for DC Comics.

Past comics titles and related projects: Writer/reviewer for *Amazing Heroes.* Production artist for Dragon Lady Press (*Wash Tubbs, Alley Oop, Terry and the Pirates*). Ghost writer on the DC trading cards (Series One and Two). Various journalistic endeavors for numerous clients, Homage Studios, Steve Jackson Games, etc.

Favorite comics not worked on: *Shade, the Changing Man, Sandman, Hellblazer, Xenozoic Tales,* Superman (all), *Next Men, Ms. Tree, The Trouble with Girls,* and *Love and Rockets.*

Dream comic-book project: An ongoing serial featuring normal people living normal lives or the *real Legion of Super-Heroes.*

✳ **Kelly McQuain.** 1334 Rodman Street, Philadelphia, Pennsylvania 19147.

Born: February 5, 1967, in Elkins, West Virginia.

College or other education: M.A. in Creative Writing, Temple University. B.A. in English, Temple University.

Comics-related education: School of hard knocks is the only one.

Biggest creative influences: John Byrne, Jim Lee, William Faulkner, R.E.M., Neil Gaiman, and *Watchmen.*

1993 projects: *Ratman: Fields of Blood* for Comico. Various other projects.

Past comics titles and related projects: *Elementals Sex Special.* Various projects for Personality Comics and Comics Zone.

Favorite comics not worked on: X-titles, *Animal Man, WildC.A.T.S,* and Batman and/or Robin projects.

Dream comic-book project: A movie of *Watchmen* or *Bat-Mite the Motion Picture* (just kidding).

✳ **Robert E. McTyre.** *Michigan Chronicle,* Virtual Reality page, 479 Ledyard, Detroit, Michigan 48201, or c/o *CBG* Editorial Department, 700 East State Street, Iola, Wisconsin 54990.

Born: August 2, 1955, in Detroit, Michigan.

College or other education: Wayne State University, Detroit College of Business (Journalism, Management).

Comics-related education: Writer/business assistant, Foundation Studios (Gauntlet), Detroit, Michigan.

Biggest creative influences: Dennis O'Neil and Neil Gaiman.

1993 projects: *U.N. Force Files,* writer. Editor/columnist of *Michigan Chronicle*'s *Virtual Reality, the Science and More Page.*

Favorite comics not worked on: *Sandman, Green Lantern: Mosaic,* and *Thunderbolt.*

Dream comic-book project: A comic book about my experiences as a fire department paramedic.

Jon Macy

✳ **Jon Macy.** c/o *CBG* Editorial Department, 700 East State Street, Iola, Wisconsin 54990.

Agent: John Nordland II (Blackbird Comics).

Born: September 11, 1964, in San Jose, California.

College or other education: A.A. in

Philosophy from DeAnza College, Cupertino, California.

Comics-related education: None (except for drawing Tippi the Turtle but I never sent it in).

Biggest creative influences: San Francisco gay scene and *Love and Rockets*.

1993 projects: Continue *Tropo*, a *Tropo* collection, a short erotic series about devils and angels, *Penetrating Heaven*, and *Sartoria*.

Past comics titles and related projects: *Venus Castina*, the art of gender, the ever fab drag queen zine. *Spirits of Procrastination*, the play, adaptation for the stage.

Favorite comics not worked on: Robyn Scott's *Homozone 5*, Steve Purcell's *Sam and Max*, Michael Allred's *Madman*, and Neil Gaiman's *Sandman*.

Dream comic-book project: I'm doing it now.

Larry Mahlstedt

✳ **Larry Mahlstedt.** 1001 Easton Road, Apartment 215M, Willow Grove, Pennsylvania 19090.

Born: April 22, 1956, in Amityville, Long Island, New York.

Comics-related education: John Buscema's comic art workshop 1975-76, otherwise, self-taught.

Biggest creative influences: John Buscema, Neal Adams, Joe Rubinstein, Klaus Janson, Joe Sinnott, and Terry Austin.

1993 projects: *The New Warriors*, Warriors poster, Warriors trading cards, *Night Thrasher* #1 (back-up), *Marvel Super-Heroes*. All are inking jobs for Marvel. Also, inks on a Mark Bagley cover for *Wizard*.

Past comics titles and related projects: Marvel: *Incredible Hulk Annual*, *Marvel Tales* and *Marvel Age* covers. DC: *Flash*, *Legion of Super-Heroes*, *Legion of Super-Heroes* poster, *Dr. Fate* (back-up series in Silver Age *Flash*), *Green Arrow* (in *World's Finest*), *Adam Strange* (back-up in Silver Age *Green Lantern* series), *Dial "H" for Hero* (in *Adventure Comics*), *DC Challenge*, plus tons of jobs for DC's Silver Age anthology titles such as *House of Mystery*, *Weird War Tales*, etc.

Favorite comics not worked on: *Amazing Spider-Man*, *Deathlok*, *Fantastic Four*, *Batman*, *Spawn*, and *Incredible Hulk*.

Dream comic-book project: To ink a John Buscema project (over full pencils), his work has such power and majesty. To be able to ink him after first salivating over his stuff as a teen-ager and then learning under his tutelage would really bring things full-circle for me and be a definite highlight in my career.

Seppo Makinen

✳ **Seppo Makinen.** R.R. #2, Indian River, Ontario, Canada K0L 2B0.

Biggest creative influences: Hogarth's *Tarzan*, Alex Raymond, Neal Adams, and Richard Corben.

1993 projects: *Dark Destiny* with Martin Powell for Alpha Comics. Airbrushed covers.

Past comics titles and related projects: *Sherlock Holmes, Dracula, Three Musketeers* for Eternity Comics. *Pilgrim's Progress* for Marvel, etc. Lots of small publishers, amateur publishing associations.

Myke Maldonado

✱ **Myke Maldonado.** 27 Village Green Way, Hazlet, New Jersey 07730.

Born: June 16, 1964, in New York City (Manhattan).

Biggest creative influences: Enki Bilal, Moebius, and Guy Davis.

1993 projects: *Splice* (Rebel Studios), *The Dick* (Rebel Studios), *Medusa Rising* (Atomeka), and *Nightvision*, short story (Rebel Studios).

Past comics titles and related projects: *New Humans* (Eternity), *Solo Ex-Mutants* (Eternity), various short stories for Eternity, *Northstar*, Alpha. *Bambi and Friends* (Friendly). *Flesh Wounds* (Tundra). Main profession: Tattoo artist at Rising Dragon Graphics.

Favorite comics not worked on: *Baker Street* and *Cerebus*.

Dream comic-book project: *Splice*.

Andy Mangels

✱ **Andy Mangels.** 2167 SW Yamhill, Suite #6, Portland, Oregon 97205 or A.M. Productions, P.O. Box 3226, Portland, Oregon 97208-3226.

Born: December 2, 1966, in Polson, Montana.

College or other education: Two years college, Flathead Valley Community College, Kalispell, Montana, A.A. degree. One year college, Portland State University, Portland, Oregon.

Comics-related education: None. However, I have worked as a comics journalist since 1985. My writing career began in the second year of college, at 18. A contributor to *Focus on George Pérez* (Fantagraphics), I was given freelance assignments at comics news magazine *Amazing Heroes* shortly thereafter (#94). After writing hundreds of articles and interviewing most of the comics industry, I moved into new territory, creating the TV/movie news column *Backstage*, a popular feature that ran in *Amazing Heroes* #159-204. Spin-off columns included *Reel Marvel* in *Marvel Age* magazine, and *Behind the Camera* for the British *Fantazia*. My column, *Hollywood Heroes*, for *Wizard* magazine and the Italian *Edizione Star*, appears regularly.

Biggest creative influences: L. Frank Baum,

J.M. Barrie, Howard Cruse, Clive Barker, George Lucas, George Pérez, Armistead Maupin, Piers Anthony, Edgar Allan Poe, Alphonse Mucha, and Charles Dickens.

1993 projects: *Jason Goes to Hell: The Final Friday*, Topps Comics (three issues, July-September). *Elfquest: Blood of Ten Chiefs*, Warp Graphics (#2-on, September). *The Hidden: Gene War*, Millennium (three issues, fall). *The Batman Adventures*, DC (one issue, fall/winter). *Gay Comics*, Gay Comics (ongoing, editor and contributor). Also stories in *Star Trek: The Next Generation* and *Justice League Quarterly*, both from DC Comics.

Past comics titles and related projects: August 1985, Fantagraphics, *Focus on George Pérez* (contributor, non-fiction book). October-December 1990, Innovation, *Child's Play 2* #1-3 (writer). 1990-1991, Rip Off, *Annie Sprinkle Is Miss Timed* #1-4 (writer). May-December 1991, Innovation, *Child's Play The Series* #1-5 (writer; issue #4 is my favorite). October-December 1991, Innovation, *Freddy's Dead* #1-3, *3-D*, and trade paperback (writer). January-March 1992, Innovation, *Child's Play 3* #1-3 (writer). September 1991-June 1992, Innovation, *Nightmares on Elm Street* #1-6 (writer). Summer-Fall 1992, Innovation, *A Nightmare on Elm Street: The Beginning* #1 and 2 (writer). January-February 1993, Innovation *Quantum Leap* #8 (last page), and 9 (writer on both, #9 is my favorite)). Winter 1991-present, *Gay Comix* #14, *Special* #1, *Gay Comics* #15-17 (editor and writer). Also work appearing in Fantagraphics' *Amazing Heroes* from March 1986-July 1992, *Marvel Age* magazine from December 1990-present, and *Wizard: The Guide to Comics* from December 1991-present. Became the first openly gay mainstream comics writer in June 1988, in an article for *Amazing Heroes* #143 and 144: *Out of the Closet and into the Comics*. Following in the footsteps of underground star Howard Cruse, became a committed presence for gay rights in the comics world, chairing convention panels on the topic of gays in comics, starting gay comics clubs, and featuring gay characters in various stories (most notably *Quantum Leap* #9). In late 1991, took over the editorship of *Gay Comix* with #14, changing the name to *Gay Comics* with #15, and created *Sen-*

tinel, a gay super-hero strip.

Favorite comics not worked on: *Sandman, Naughty Bits, Hellblazer, Tales of the Closet, Omaha the Cat Dancer, Ren & Stimpy, From Hell*, and *Animal Man*.

Dream comic-book project: *Star Wars, Teen Titans, Vartox Returns* (old *Superman* character), *Wizard of Oz, Wonder Woman*, and *Aquaman*.

Michael Manley

✳ **Michael Manley.** 430 Spruce Avenue, Upper Darby, Pennsylvania 19082.

Born: October 19, 1961, in Detroit, Michigan.

College or other education: All self-taught. Worked in a commercial art studio from 15-17 years old. Freelance commercial artist. Art Director for an alternative newspaper in Detroit.

Biggest creative influences: Alex Raymond, Frank Robbins, Al Williamson, Wood, Kirby, Moebius, Kubert, and classic American illustration.

1993 projects: *Batman, Spirits of Vengeance,* Wolverine mini-series, *Akira* tribute story, *Elvira* story, Spider-Man/Deathlok series.

Past comics titles and related projects: *Quasar, Alpha Flight, King Conan, Transformers, Jon Sable, Dr. Zero, Darkhawk, Sleepwalker, Punisher: War Zone*, and *Deathlok*. Lots of work for Western Publishing: coloring books, children's books. Work for Henson.

Favorite comics not worked on: *Eightball, Xenozoic Tales, Sin City, Cheval Noir*, lots of European stuff like *Torpedo*, etc.

Dream comic-book project: To produce some European albums, do a *Challengers of the Unknown* series, more science-fiction-oriented work, or *The Fantastic Four*.

✳ **Marvin Perry Mann.** 1205B Santa Clara Avenue, Alameda, California 94501.

Born: October 7, 1953, in Goshen, Indiana.

College or other education: No degrees. Attended Indiana University, UCLA, and Cal State-Long Beach.

1993 projects: *The Drakes of Wrath*.

Past comics titles and related projects: *The Trouble with Girls, Ape City, Lizard Lady*, and *Flesh Gordon*.

Dream comic-book project: *Legion of Super-Heroes*.

✳ **Roland Mann.** Malibu Comics, 5321 Sterling Center Drive, Westlake Village, California 91361.

Born: November 1, 1964, in Memphis, Tennessee.

College or other education: B.S. in English from University of Southern Mississippi, 1988.

Biggest creative influences: Stan Lee, H.G. Wells, and Isaac Asimov.

1993 projects: Editor on: *Protectors, Ex-Mutants, Dinosaurs for Hire, The Ferret, Man of War*, and *Gravestone*. Writer on: *Ex-Mutants* #11 and 12 and *Widowmaker*.

Past comics titles and related projects: All as writer: *Cat and Mouse* (Aircel/Malibu), *Vortex* (Comico), *Planet of the Apes: Blood of the Apes* (Adventure), *Miss Fury* (Adventure), *Rocket Ranger* (Adventure), and *The Arrow* (Malibu).

✳ **Francis J. Mao.** Infotainment World/*Gamepro* magazine, 951 Mariner's Island Boule-

vard, Suite 700, San Mateo, California 94404.

Born: February 4, 1966, in Taipei, Taiwan.

College or other education: B.A. English Literature, two years Law (uncompleted).

Biggest creative influences: John Byrne, George Pérez, Howard Chaykin, and José Luis Garcia Lopez.

Past comics titles and related projects: *Teenage Mutant Ninja Turtles — Turtle Soup*. Creative director and illustrator for: *Gamepro* magazine, *S.W.A.T.Pro* magazine, *Sega Visions* magazine, and *Street Fighter II Strategy Guide*.

Favorite comics not worked on: *X-Men, Team Titans, Justice League America*, and *Midnight Sons*.

Dream comic-book project: *Nova* limited series, favorite character from childhood.

✳ **Timothy T. Markin.** 1207 East 117th Street, #5, Kansas City, Missouri 64131.

Born: January 2, 1968, in Cherry Point, North Carolina. Raised in Toledo, Ohio.

College or other education: Art instruction schools, Marine Corps Personnel Administration course.

Comics-related education: Art instruction schools, two-day seminar of the Joe Kubert School.

Biggest creative influences: William Overgard on *Steve Roper and Mike Nomad*, Steve Ditko, and Alex Toth.

1993 projects: Creator/producer of *Breakneck Boulevard*, to be released fall 1993.

Past comics titles and related projects: Gag cartoons in *CBG, Leatherneck* magazine, and *Quantico Sentry*; military continuity strip in *Forum Four* magazine; *Hazard* #1 (May 1993): Inking, lettering on *Runaway*; writer, artist on *Breakneck Boulevard*. Small-press comics, *Urban Angst* (1990), *GFI's Greatest Hits* (1990), and *Blame It on Elvis* (1991) (all published under the Graphic Fiction Illustrated imprint).

Favorite comics not worked on: *Eightball, Madman*, Disney comics, and *The Maxx*.

Dream comic-book project: Comic-book version of the *Mike Nomad* comic strip.

✳ **Bill Marks.** Vortex Comics Inc., P.O. Box 173, Sanborn, New York 14132.

Agent: Dan Ostroff.

Born: April 10, 1962, in Toronto, Canada.

College or other education: Ontario College of Art, President's Council.

1993 projects: *Stock Car Legends, Food, Nocturnal Emissions*, and *Mister X*.

Past comics titles and related projects: *Mister X, Doc Chaos, Yummy Fur, Bloodlines, Black Kiss, Kaptain Keen and Company, Kelvin Mace, Post Brothers, Vortex* magazine, *Savage Henry, Stig's Inferno, Legends of Nascar, Badlands*, and *Nascar Adventures*.

Favorite comics not worked on: *Hate.*

Dream comic-book project: *Hate.*

✻ **Don Markstein.** Etienne's Type Shop, 14836 North 35th Street, Phoenix, Arizona 85032.

Born: March 21, 1947, in New Orleans, Louisiana.

College or other education: Louisiana State University.

Biggest creative influences: Carl Barks, for pacing, characterization, use of language, the best.

1993 projects: Disney comics.

Past comics titles and related projects: Disney comics for Gladstone, Egmont, Disney/Burbank. Horror stories for a couple of publishers. Editor, *Comics Revue*. Editor, *A Prince Valiant Companion*. Production, *Comics Interview*.

Favorite comics not worked on: *Sandman, Prince Valiant*, and *Li'l Abner*.

Dream comic-book project: I've been pecking away at a mini-series taking a sideways look at super-heroes, it would be great to see it published.

✻ **Charles Marshall.** 8203 Poplar Pike, Germantown, Tennessee 38138.

Born: May 28, 1963, in Memphis, Tennessee.

College or other education: B.S. in English from Memphis State University.

1993 projects: Malibu's new *Ex-Mutants* (beginning with issue #13).

Past comics titles and related projects: Adventure's *Planet of the Apes* (#1-24), Adventure's *Strange Sports Stories*, Innovation's *Quantum Leap*, Hamilton Publishing — *Dread of Night*, Adventure's *Ape Nation* and *Ape City*, Innovation's *Angry Shadows*, Caliber Press' *Fugitive*.

Favorite comics not worked on: Too many to name.

Dream comic-book project: Probably something with The Flash.

John Talbot Marshall

✻ **John Talbot Marshall.** Marshall Comics, P.O. Box 283, Rancocas, New Jersey 08073-0283.

Born: October 2, 1964, in Valley Stream, Long Island (New York).

College or other education: Sarah Lawrence College, 1983-85, Brooklyn College, 1985-88, B.A. Radio/Television.

Comics-related education: Well, I did contact the Kubert School about student submissions but I never got any.

Biggest creative influences: *Mad* magazine, the *Batman* TV show (1966), and a high sugar diet.

1993 projects: *Mortar Man*, premiering May 1993, a bimonthly title. A second title begins in February 1994, to be published on the alternate months.

Past comics titles and related projects: I am, or was, or sort of am, an honorary member of Shop Talk APA, which I joined in 1991.

Favorite comics not worked on: *Hate, Flaming Carrot* up to issue #19, Silver Age DC and Golden Age everything.

Dream comic-book project: A Mortar Man/ Flaming Carrot team-up.

Don Martin

✳ **Don Martin.** c/o Norma Haimes, P.O. Box 1330, Miami, Florida 33243.

Agent: Norma Haimes.

Born: May 18, 1939, in Passaic, New Jersey.

College or other education: Newark (New Jersey) School of Fine and Industrial Arts; Pennsylvania Academy of Fine Arts.

Biggest creative influences: Charlie Chaplin, Laurel and Hardy, Sylvester the Cat, and artists from Giotto to Paul Klee; writers like Kafka and Ambrose Bierce.

1993 projects: *Cracked* magazine.

Past comics titles and related projects: *Mad* magazine and *Cracked* magazine.

Favorite comics not worked on: *Edika* (Europe).

Dream comic-book project: *The Adventures of Captain Klutz.*

✳ **Gary Martin.** 3314 SW Marigold Street, Portland, Oregon 97219.

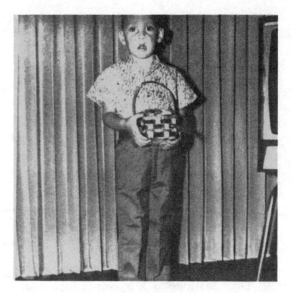

Gary Martin

Born: April 12, 1956, in Newport Beach, California.

College or other education: West Valley Junior College, San Jose State University.

Biggest creative influences: Frazetta, Walt Kelly, Raymond, Austin, Bolland, and Golden.

1993 projects: *Nexus: Alien Justice* (Dark Horse), *Sludge* (Malibu Comics), *Berzerkers* miniseries (Image), inks on all.

Past comics titles and related projects: *Nexus: Origin* (Dark Horse) — inks. *Captain Crusader, Dark Horse Presents* — story, pencils, and inks. *Mickey Mouse Adventures, Darkwing Duck,* and *Little Mermaid* (Disney) — inks. *The Olympians, Shanna the She-Devil* in *Marvel Comics Presents, Conan* graphic novel (Marvel) — inks. *Doom Patrol* and *Blue Devil* (DC) — inks.

Favorite comics not worked on: *Xenozoic Tales, Sam and Max, Excalibur* by Davis. Anything by Golden, Bolland, Russell, Mignola, Nolan, Garcia Lopez, J. Hernandez, Gibbons, Ordway, and D. Williams.

Dream comic-book project: A creator-owned project with David Williams, with my plot and inks (currently in the works).

✳ **Mark Martin.** 2 Briar Hill Road, Williamsburg, Massachusetts 01096.

Born: January 21, 1956, in Leeds, Alabama.

Biggest creative influences: Walt Kelly, Salvador Dali, George Herriman, and Harrison Cady.

1993 projects: *Tantalizing Stories, Underwhere,* and *Strip Tease.*

Past comics titles and related projects: *Gnatrat, 20 Nude Dancers 20, Ralph Snart, Hyena, Teenage Mutant Ninja Turtles,* and *Lillian Spencer Drake Catalog of Values.*

Favorite comics not worked on: *Cud, Dangle,* and *Eightball.*

Dream comic-book project: Art for art's sake.

✳ **Don Martinec.** 8856 Ridge Road NE, Kinsman, Ohio 44428.

Born: September 17, 1958, in Youngstown, Ohio.

Comics-related education: *The Comic Book Guide for the Artist,* writer, letterer (Charlton Comics), *How to Draw Comics the Marvel Way.*

Biggest creative influences: Early Hanna-Barbera cartoons, Steve Ditko, Jack Kirby, Artie Simek, and Monty Python.

Past comics titles and related projects: Cartoons for *CBG, Amazing Heroes, Comics Journal,* and many fanzines. *Adam and Eve, A.D.* — letters, edits, back-ups; *Heroic* — letters, art, inks. Writing letters and logos for Spotlight Comics. *FantaCo Chronicles Series* — writing, art, letters. *Giant-Size Mini-Comics.* Lettering for Innovation. Inks for *Cap'n Oatmeal, Desert Storm, Maze Agency.* Art restoration: *Walt Kelly's Santa Claus Adventures.*

Favorite comics not worked on: *Justice Society of America* and *Fantastic Four.*

Dream comic-book project: Drawing *Quick Draw McGraw,* inking Kirby or Ditko (at least once).

✳ **Tom Mason.** Malibu Comics, 5321 Sterling Center Drive, Westlake Village, California 91361.

Born: July 10.

Biggest creative influences: The Marx Brothers, P.G. Wodehouse, John D. MacDonald, Dashiell Hammett, Bob Hope, and H. Allen Smith.

1993 projects: *Dinosaurs for Hire, Prototype,* and *Man of War.*

Tom Mason

Past comics titles and related projects: *Dinosaurs for Hire, Ex-Mutants, Robotech II: The Sentinels,* and *Zillion.*

Favorite comics not worked on: *Bone* by Jeff Smith.

Dream comic-book project: I'm already there, Malibu's Ultraverse.

✳ **Nathan Massengill.** c/o *CBG* Editorial Department, 700 East State Street, Iola, Wisconsin 54990.

Born: March 5, in Hickory, North Carolina.

College or other education: Two years at Joe Kubert's School of Art.

1993 projects: *Fenry* graphic novel from Raven Publications, which I am painting in watercolor. Also writing and producing *Conceptual Heroes* #1 (publisher to be announced).

Past comics titles and related projects: *Poets Prosper* from Caliber's Tome Press (writing, some art).

✳ **Steve Mattsson.** 414 NE 53rd Avenue, Portland, Oregon 97213-3018.

Born: December 16, 1959, in Salt Lake City, Utah.

College or other education: B.S. in Secondary Art Education at Western Oregon State College.

Comics-related education: Assistant to Paul Gulacy.

Biggest creative influences: Richard Debencorn and David Hockney — art; Jorge Luis Borges and Franz Kafka — writing.

1993 projects: *Chain Gang War* — color; *Green Lantern Corps Quarterly* — color, writer; *Green Lantern: Mosaic* — color; *L.E.G.I.O.N. '93* — color; *The Trouble with Girls* — color; and *Wonder Woman* — color.

Past comics titles and related projects: *Black Panther* — color; *Boris the Bear* — writer, color; *Doc Abstruse, the Vitruvian Man* in *Dark Horse Presents* — writer; *Idol* — writer, color; *Shanna the She-Devil* in *Marvel Comics Presents* — color.

Favorite comics not worked on: *Flaming Carrot* and *The Spirit*.

Dream comic-book project: An adaptation of the diary I kept during the summer of 1985.

✳ **Roger May.** P.O. Box 1271, Grass Valley, California 95945.

Born: September 6, 1947, in Chicago, Illinois.

College or other education: High school graduate; the last of the self-taught Renaissance men. Always liked books better than teachers. Currently an expert in 3-D photography and art.

Comics-related education: Lifelong observation of the medium; working in the printing industry since 1966; The Ground Under Cartoonists — 1975, a 10-month weekly encounter of a dozen artists in San Francisco, concentrating on upgrading graphic skills; The Hygraders — 1985, 20 seminars in Nevada City, California with Dan O'Neill on writing for comics; self-publishing since 1973 (one learns by doing); teaching self-publishing and cartooning to kids (one learns from instruction); member: National Stereoscopic Association, the International Stereoscopic Union.

Biggest creative influences: People: Maynard G. Krebs, Steve Allen, Harvey Kurtzman

Roger May

and Bill Elder, Will Eisner, Steve Ditko, Raymond Loewy, Raymond Chandler, Paul Krassner, Harlan Ellison, Salvador Dali, Frank Zappa, George Carlin, Bob Dylan, Warren Murphy and Richard Sapir, Brennan Totten, Bill Watterson, Alan Moore, Frank Miller, Brian Bolland, Rand Holmes, Kyle Baker, Mark Schultz, Howard Chaykin, and Moebius. Things: Silkscreen printing, photocopy machines, saddle stapler, stereo photography, single-frame film-making, and figure drawing.

1993 projects: *Cadillacs and Dinosaurs 3-D Poster*; the second in a series of 3-D serigraphs; a set of 3-D trading cards; two convention minicomix; *Betty Page: Queen of Hearts*, based on photos I discovered; *Sturdy Women, Glamour Extremist*, and other self-published monographs; and *Grateful Dead Comix in 3-D*.

Past comics titles and related projects: *All Atomic Comics, Underground Classics #12 — Gilbert Shelton in 3-D, The Adventures of Billy Broccoflower in 3-D, Cherry #11 in 3-D, Cadillacs and Dinosaurs in 3-D, Stereographix 1986, Bewildering Intimacies #1-4, Vibratory Provincial News #1-3,* and *Nips on Parade.* Editor and publisher of over

80 titles in small press. Hand-screened fine art prints in 3-D (#1, Fabulous Furry Freak Brothers).

Favorite comics not worked on: God, there's so many — *Calvin and Hobbes, Stray Toasters, American Flagg!, Batman*, hundreds more, I can't think . . .

Dream comic-book project: As much as I want to do *Doctor Strange in 3-D* (Ditko!!) and a Phillip Marlowe *noir* comic book, my heart lies with a Kurtzman-style *Mad* comic made for 3-D, with all the funniest artists in the field — the funniest 3-D comic of all time. *Forbidden Planet* graphic novel in 3-D or *Teenage Mutant Ninja Turtles in 3-D.*

✳ **Mark Mazz.** 82 Teed Street, Huntington Station, New York 11746-4533.

Born: September 24, 1962, in Franklin Square, New York.

College or other education: Bachelor's Degree, Illustration, School of Visual Arts, New York City.

Comics-related education: Student — Art Spiegelman.

Biggest creative influences: Alex Raymond — inks, Miller — storytelling, Will Eisner — over-all stories, Richard Bruning — book design, Moebius and Amand — everything else.

1993 projects: 1. Horror anthology to be self-published, more information forthcoming when done. 2. *Plasma Babies*, Caliber mini-series — book design.

Past comics titles and related projects: *Revolutionary Comics* #9 — inks. *Utterly Strange Publications* — creative director. Caliber, *Plasma Baby* #1-3 — book design/logo design. Cry for Dawn Publications — book design — *Girl: Rule of Darkness* #1, *From the Darkness* #1. *Faust* #7 — book design.

Favorite comics not worked on: *Nexus, Archer & Armstrong, Grendel, Turok, Hellstorm*, and *Legion of Super-Heroes.*

Dream comic-book project: Working with Jack Kirby on anything.

✳ **David Mazzucchelli.** Rubber Blanket Press, P.O. Box 3067, Uptown Station, Hoboken, New Jersey 07030.

Born: 1960, in Providence, Rhode Island.

College or other education: B.F.A. (Painting), Rhode Island School of Design.

Comics-related education: Lots of hard work.

Biggest creative influences: Art history, literature, film, friends, and former teachers.

1993 projects: *Rubber Blanket* #3. Stories for: *Drawn and Quarterly, Nozone, Nickelodeon Magazine.* Published in 1993: Cover, *Cheval Noir* #40; story, *Snake Eyes* #3.

Past comics titles and related projects: *Rubber Blanket* #1 and 2, *Drawn and Quarterly* #9, *The New Yorker, Esquire, Nickelodeon Magazine, Snake Eyes* #1, *Nozone* #3, *Batman: Year One, Marvel Fanfare* #40, *Daredevil: Born Again, X-Factor* #16, and *Daredevil* (1984-1986).

Favorite comics not worked on: Work by: Herriman, Schulz, Kurtzman, Kirby, Segar, Gould, Crumb, *Julius Knipl* — Katchor, *Optic Nerve* — Tomine, and *Way out Strips* — Swain.

Dream comic-book project: Write, draw, edit, and publish my own . . . hey, wait a minute!

✳ **Angel Medina.** 909 Kane Street, Aurora, Illinois 60505.

Born: March 25, 1964, in Bronx, New York.

College or other education: Northern Illinois University, Waubonsee Community College.

Biggest creative influences: Bernie Wrightson, Sal Buscema, Frank Frazetta, and Eleuteri Serpieri.

1993 projects: *Warlock and the Infinity Watch.*

Past comics titles and related projects: *Megaton, Dreadstar, Badger, Incredible Hulk, What The--?!,* and *Soviet Super Soldiers.*

Favorite comics not worked on: *Love and Rockets, Nexus, Excalibur, WildC.A.T.S,* and *Sandman.*

Dream comic-book project: It's a secret 'cuz I may do it in the next year or so.

✳ **Erich Mees.** c/o *CBG* Editorial Department, 700 East State Street, Iola, Wisconsin 54990.

Born: May 8, 1970, in Atlanta, Georgia.

College or other education: Emory University, 1988-1992, B.A., English.

Biggest creative influences: Peter David, Grant Morrison, Richard Linklater, Evan Dorkin, and Kyle Baker.

1993 projects: *Virtual Images* APA (contributing writer/artist), *Amazing Heroes Swimsuit Special* (have submitted three illustrations), possible articles and illustrations for *Scary Monsters Magazine*.

Past comics titles and related projects: *Rip Off* #30 (Spring 1991, inked three-page story *Global Warning*). *Comics Buyer's Guide* #986 (October 9, 1992, inked Thanos/Death illustration).

Favorite comics not worked on: *Sandman, Doom Patrol* (Grant Morrison's run), *Incredible Hulk, Pirate Corp$!, Love and Rockets,* and *Eightball*.

Dream comic-book project: A book featuring realistic characters, whether the situations are commonplace or extraordinary.

✴ **Chuck Melville.** 824 NE 45th Street, #11, Seattle, Washington 98105.

Born: July 25, 1953, in Rochester, New York.

College or other education: Art courses through continuing education programs at Rochester Institute of Technology.

Comics-related education: Production artist, gofer, editor at MU Press.

Biggest creative influences: Too many to list, but a few are: Carmine Infantino, Walt Kelly, and Gil Kane.

1993 projects: *Champion of Katara, The Furkindred, Princess Karanam and the Djinn of the Green Jug,* and *Mezari's Wish* (a graphic album), all for MU Press.

Past comics titles and related projects: *Champion of Katara* and *The Furkindred*. (*Champion of Katara* is my own book, while *The Furkindred* is a shared-world project that I edit and contribute to.)

Favorite comics not worked on: *Bone, Usagi Yojimbo, Superman, Rhudiprrt,* and *Groo*.

Dream comic-book project: *Champion of Katara* as a series of graphic albums.

✴ **Rachelle A. Menashe.** c/o *CBG* Editorial Department, 700 East State Street, Iola, Wiscon-

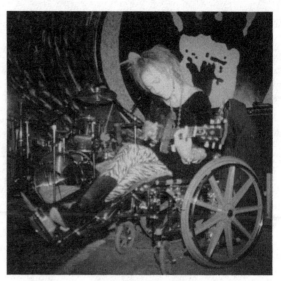

Rachelle A. Menashe

sin 54990.

Born: May 26, 1961, in Portland, Oregon.

College or other education: One year P.C.C., one year P.S.U.

Comics-related education: Assistant to Chris Chalenor, production manager of Dark Horse Comics, for two years.

Biggest creative influences: Lynn Varley and Steve Oliff.

1993 projects: *Virus* — Dark Horse, *Icon* #1 — Milestone Media, *Predator vs. Magnus* — Dark Horse/Valiant, *The Safest Place,* one-shot — Dark Horse, and more.

Past comics titles and related projects: *Terminator, Predator: Cold War, Aliens, Young Indiana Jones, RoboCop vs. Terminator, Dark Horse Comics* (*Time Cop, Mad Dogs, X*), *Predator vs. Magnus Robot Fighter* #2, *Virus, Godzilla Color Special,* and lots of covers including: *Secret of the Salamander, Tardi, Nina Paley,* etc.

Favorite comics not worked on: *Spawn*.

Dream comic-book project: Find the greatest artist and writer and color it myself with full creative control (Yeah, right!). Pretty vague description, I know, but I've already worked on so many great projects that it's hard to think of what my "dream" would be. Still waiting . . .

✴ **William Messner-Loebs.** Turning Point Studios, P.O. Box 558, Pinckney, Michigan 48169.

Born: February 19, 1949, in Detroit, Michigan.

College or other education: B.A. in History, honors.

Biggest creative influences: Will Eisner, Bernie Wrightson, E.C. Segar, Walt Kelly, Neal Adams, and Denny O'Neil.

1993 projects: *The Maxx, Wonder Woman, Aesop's Desecrated Morals, War Drums*, Marvel's history of the Civil War, and *The Maxx* trading cards.

Past comics titles and related projects: *Journey, Jonny Quest, Wastelands, Flash, Batman* newspaper strip, *Jaguar, Dr. Fate, Epicurus the Sage, Welcome to Heaven*, and *Dr. Franklin*.

Favorite comics not worked on: *The Spirit, Cud, Uncle Scrooge, Wash Tubbs, Sandman*, and *Bizarre Heroes*.

Dream comic-book project: The history of Blackbeard the pirate, as it *should* have happened.

✳ **Jeff Meyer.** 8307 Huguenard Road, Fort Wayne, Indiana 46818.

Born: June 8, 1971, in Fort Wayne, Indiana.

1993 projects: *Stupid-Man: Burial for a Buddy* and *1968 Give or Take 25*.

Favorite comics not worked on: *Eightball, Yummy Fur, Rubber Blanket, Love and Rockets*, etc.

✳ **Ken Meyer Jr.** 13227 Wimberly Square, #261, San Diego, California 92128.

Agent: Steve Donnely (Creative Interests).

Born: February 12, 1957, in Isabella, Puerto Rico.

College or other education: Four years, Weber State College. One year, University of Utah.

Biggest creative influences: Mid-'70s comics, commercial art mid-'70s to present (John Buscema, Steranko, Adams, F. Miller, and Bob Peak).

1993 projects: *Midnight Sons* #3 (Marvel), mini-series for Cry for Dawn comics, miscellaneous covers for Revolutionary Comics and Parody Press, miscellaneous art for White Wolf Games (interiors and covers).

Past comics titles and related projects: *Hamster Triumphant* #1 and 2 (Eclipse), *Adoles-*

Ken Meyer Jr.

© 1992 Ken Meyer Jr.

cent Radioactive Black Belt Hamsters #9, *American Summer Special* (Dark Horse), *Open Space* # 4, *Toxic* #30 and 31, *Cry for Dawn* #8 (all of preceding is interior work, traditional or painted). Covers: Parody Press — *X-Cons* #1 (three covers), *Hamsters* (reprint) # 2 and 3, *Rye* (*Rai* parody). Revolutionary Comics — *Jimmy Connors, Casey Stengel, Jim Abbot, Lou Gehrig, Jim Thorpe/ Jesse Owens, Charles Barkley, Patrick Ewing, Black Sox, Genesis, Image Comics, McCartney*. White Wolf Games — *Vampire, The Masquerade, The Sabbat*. Mayfair Games — *Demons* and *Chilled to the Bone* (cover). *Amazing Heroes Swimsuit Special 1993, Sandmadame and Dame Patrol* (Personality) — cover coloring. Coloring assist: *Weaveworld* #3 (Marvel), *Black Panther* graphic novel, 1991 (Marvel).

Favorite comics not worked on: *Cerebus, Love and Rockets, Milk & Cheese, Sandman, Nexus*, anything by McKean, Sienkiewicz, Gaiman, and Miller.

Dream comic-book project: A *real* story with real emotions/people by someone like Gaiman or Moore.

✳ **Bernie Mierault.** (Art signature: BEM) 5269 Waverly, Montreal, Quebec, Canada H2T 2X6.

Born: June 27, 1961, in France (Canadian Armed Forces Base).

Comics-related education: None. I learned by doing it.

Biggest creative influences: Comic art: Harvey Kurtzman, Jack Kirby, P. Craig Russell, Frank Miller, Klaus Janson. Music: Jonathan Richmond, The Feelies.

1993 projects: *The Jam*, super-hero parody of sorts, created, written, and drawn by myself, from Dark Horse in November 1993. Colorist (with Kathryn Delaney) on *Grendel: War Child* and *Grendel: Devil by the Deed*.

Past comics titles and related projects: *Mackenzie Queen*, collected by Caliber Press (black-and-white). *The Jam* # 1-5, Slave Labor (black-and-white), Tundra (color version). DC: "When is a Door" (written by Neil Gaiman) *Secret Origins Special* #1; "Clayface II" in *Secret Origins* #44 (Clayface issue). Stories in *Taboo* # 1 and 3, "Cable" and "Poker Face." *Grendel* #13-15 (pencils/inks), # 27-29 (inks), # 30-40 (color). Other short stories in a variety of publications too tedious to list.

Favorite comics not worked on: Anything drawn by Frank Miller. Some local Montreal stuff. I'm trying to show some of the brilliant work around here through back-up stories in *The Jam*.

Dream comic-book project: I'm already doing it working on *The Jam*. In my dreams, it sells big-time.

✳ **Michael J. Mignola.** c/o *CBG* Editorial Department, 700 East State Street, Iola, Wisconsin 54990.

Born: September 16, 1960, in Berkley, California.

College or other education: B.F.A. degree (Illustration), California College of Arts and Crafts.

1993 projects: *Aliens: Salvation*, one-shot 48-page book from Dark Horse written by Dave Gibbons.

Past comics titles and related projects: *Faf-

Michael J. Mignola

hrd and the Grey Mouser* (Epic), *Ironwolf* (DC), *Cosmic Odyssey* (DC), *Dracula Movie Adaptation* (Topps), *Corum* (First Comics), *Rocket Raccoon, Wolverine Jungle Adventure, Doctor Strange-Dr. Doom* graphic novel (Marvel), *Gotham by Gaslight, Superman* (DC).

✳ **Ralph Ellis Miley.** P.O. Box 3001, Santa Fe Springs, California 90670.

Born: March 1, 1956, in Los Angeles, California.

College or other education: Teaching credentials, Cal State-Los Angeles. A.A., Art/Science, El Camino College. B.A., Advertising Illustration, Cal State-Fullerton.

Biggest creative influences: Jack Kirby, John Byrne, and Joe Chiodo.

1993 projects: *Aida-Zee 3-D*, Nate Butler Studios; Legacy Comics; *Christian Tract*, Discovery Press; new comics line, Immanuel Productions.

Past comics titles and related projects: *Aida-Zee* #1, *Valiant Efforts* #1 and 2, and *Humants* #4.

Favorite comics not worked on: *The Tick* and *Xenozoic Tales*.

Dream comic-book project: Start my own line of comic books.

Frank Miller

✳ **Frank Miller.** c/o *CBG* Editorial Department, 700 East State Street, Iola, Wisconsin 54990.

Born: January 27, 1957, in Olney, Maryland.

Biggest creative influences: Will Eisner, Johnny Craig, Wallace Wood, Jack Kirby, Mickey Spillane, and so many others, it's ridiculous.

1993 projects: *Sin City: A Dame to Kill For, Martha Washington Goes to War, The Big Guy and Rusty the Boy Robot,* and *Man without Fear.*

Past comics titles and related projects: *Daredevil, Give Me Liberty, Wolverine, Sin City, Ronin, Hard Boiled, The Dark Knight Returns, Elektra: Assassin, Elektra Lives Again, RoboCop vs. Terminator.* Movies: *RoboCop 2* and *RoboCop 3.*

Favorite comics not worked on: *Concrete, Next Men, Madman, Hellblazer, Xenozoic Tales, Big Baby,* and *Suburban Nightmares.*

Dream comic-book project: *Sin City.*

✳ **Jill (Beth) Miller.** c/o *CBG* Editorial Department, 700 East State Street, Iola, Wisconsin 54990.

Born: December 4, 1965, in Marshfield, Wisconsin.

College or other education: Uh, my academic transcripts read like a rap sheet; you don't wanna know.

Comics-related education: Member Stevens Point, Wisconsin, Comics Club.

Biggest creative influences: Kirby, Ditko, and Jensen.

1993 projects: "Work?" What is this strange animal "work"? I'm writing a novel. Yeah, that's it. A novel. What was the question again?

Past comics titles and related projects: *One-Fisted Tales* (Slave Labor), *Slave Labor Stories,* and *Nanite* (unsold as I write this).

Favorite comics not worked on: *Sparky the Dog, Tales from the Heart, Legion of Super-Heroes, Hellblazer, Sandman, Martyr Man,* and *Stanley and His Monster.*

Dream comic-book project: Heh, heh, heh, House of Ambush! (Keith? Al? Tequila time?).

✳ **Pat Mills.** c/o *CBG* Editorial Department, 700 East State Street, Iola, Wisconsin 54990.

Born: July 3, 1949, in Ipswich, Suffolk, England.

1993 projects: *Slaine, Kamikazes,* and *Marshal Law.*

Past comics titles and related projects: *Marshal Law, Slaine, Charley's War, Metalzoic,* and *Third World War.*

✳ **Mark Miraglia.** 867 Coburn Court, Apartment D, San Leandro, California 94578 or c/o Steve Donnelly, Creative Interests Agency, 106 South B Street, San Mateo, California 94401.

Agent: Steve Donnelly, Creative Interests Agency.

Born: January 22, 1959, in Walnut Creek, California.

College or other education: Junior college, A.A.

Biggest creative influences: Al Williamson, Alex Raymond, Mac Raboy, Steve Rude, John Prentice, and the E.C. artists.

1993 projects: Currently working on *Green Arrow* for DC.

Past comics titles and related projects: Two

covers for *Tales of the Green Hornet* and a story in the upcoming *Black Beauty Special*.

Favorite comics not worked on: *Captain America, Justice Society*, and *Sandman*.

Dream comic-book project: A Justice Society Golden Age story or any DC or Timely Golden Age characters.

✱ **Dan Mishkin.** 404 Northlawn, East Lansing, Michigan 48823-3119.

Born: March 3, 1953, in Mineola, New York.

College or other education: B.A., Michigan State University.

1993 projects: *Star Trek: Captain Sulu*.

Past comics titles and related projects: Co-creator of *Blue Devil* and *Amethyst, Princess of Gemworld. Wonder Woman, DC Comics Presents, The Brave and the Bold, Advanced Dungeons and Dragons*, and *Dragonlance*.

Moebius (Jean Giraud)

✱ **Moebius (Jean Giraud).** P.O. Box 17270, Encino, California 91416.

Born: May 5, 1938, Nogent, St. Marne, France.

✱ **Victor Ramon Mojica.** Eugenus, 3635 Hill Boulevard, Suite 520, Jefferson Valley, New York 10535.

Born: May 15, 1949, in Manhattan, New York.

College or other education: Two years of college, Animation and Cartooning.

Comics-related education: Studied one semester with Ralph Reese and another with Jerry Robinson.

Victor Ramon Mojica

Biggest creative influences: Ken Longtempts, Leo and Diane Dillon, and Glenn Dodds.

1993 projects: *Eugenus* #4 and 5.

Past comics titles and related projects: Since 1992, I've been producing and publishing *Eugenus* #1-3. this has been my sole contribution to the comics world thus far. I have illustrated other commercial products such as T-shirts, lithographs, and children's books.

Favorite comics not worked on: *Batman, Conan, Spider-Man*, and the old version of the *Fantastic Four*.

Dream comic-book project: *Eugenus*.

✱ **Sheldon "Shelly" Moldoff.** 3710 Inverrary Drive, 1W, Lauderhill, Florida 33319.

Born: April 14, 1920, in New York City.

College or other education: Attended W.P.A. life drawing classes (1930s).

Comics-related education: Practice, practice, practice.

Biggest creative influences: Alex Raymond, Hal Foster, and Willard Mullin.

1993 projects: Re-issue of full-length animated feature I created and produced, *Marco Polo Jr.*

Sheldon "Shelly" Moldoff

Past comics titles and related projects: *Hawkman, Black Pirate, Flash, Green Lantern, Kid Eternity, Moon Girl and the Prince, Commander Battle and the Atomic Sub, Tygra, The Black Terror, Mr. District Attorney, Blackhawk, Sea Devils, Batman, Legion of Super-Heroes, This Magazine Is Haunted,* and *Worlds of Fear.*

Favorite comics not worked on: The Walt Disney animated films.

Brad Moore

✳ **Brad Moore.** 910 West Sycamore, #8, Carbondale, Illinois 62901.

Born: September 19, 1960, in El Dorado, Illinois.

College or other education: A.A., B.A., Bachelor of Education.

Comics-related education: I worked under Herbert Fink, winner of 1971 American Illustrators Award for Book Illustrations, 1980-1984.

Biggest creative influences: Ray Harryhausen, Ken Russell, foreign films, pre-Raphelite and surrealist painters.

1993 projects: *Bathory* for Boneyard Press, 32 pages. *Concussion* for Fathom Press, 32 pages. *Medusa, the Party Zombie* for London Nights Publications, 32 pages. *Cadaver* (anthology) for Fathom Press, ongoing.

Past comics titles and related projects: *Dark Visions* #1, *Tipper Gore's Comics and Stories* #1, *Barbaric Tales* #2, *World of Fandom* #13, 15, and 16, *Cadaver* #0 and 1, *Bloodreign* #2 and 9, *Art Flux* #1, *Fever Pitch* #8, *Black Market* #10, *Thrasher* magazine, *Outlaw Biker, Sheet Metal* #8, *Uncle Fester* #13 and 14. Plus, over 17 album and cassette covers, rock T-shirts, fliers, and posters, designs and storyboards for film and TV commercials, etc.

Favorite comics not worked on: *Trailer Trash, Skull, Slow Death, Heavy Metal,* and *Lobo's Back.*

Dream comic-book project: It changes every day, but it would have to be a splatter-goth-cyber-punk-death culture/horror/fantasy epic with two fast-acting ingredients against hair and grease.

✳ **Charles Moore.** 117 Golden Hills Drive, Woodstock, Georgia 30188.

Born: August 26, 1967, in Atlanta, Georgia.

Biggest creative influences: Andrew Vachss, Flannery O'Connor, and the Cohen brothers.

1993 projects: Writer: *Dominique and the Chairman* for Dark Horse, *Predator, Green Lantern.* Co-editing *Negative Burn: An Anthology, Illuminator, Matrix* 7.

Past comics titles and related projects: *Dragonlance* and *Doc Savage.*

Favorite comics not worked on: *Hard Looks* and *Fantastic Four.*

Dream comic-book project: To bear Kevin Dooley's love child.

✳ **Lisa Moore.** c/o *CBG* Editorial Department, 700 East State Street, Iola, Wisconsin 54990.

Born: March 22, 1967, in Mineral Wells, Texas.

College or other education: Bachelor's degree, Public and Social Services.

Biggest creative influences: Mary Gentle and Madeline L'Engle.

1993 projects: *Dominique* for Dark Horse (writer/co-creator).

Past comics titles and related projects: *Dragonlance*.

Favorite comics not worked on: *Hawkworld*.

Dream comic-book project: *Hawkworld* illustrated by Craig Hamilton.

✳ **Morgan.** 2507 Audubon Place, Austin, Texas 78741.

Comics-related education: School of hard knocks.

Biggest creative influences: Dagas, Sandorfi, Leffel, Francis Bacon, and Marshal Arisman.

1993 projects: Covers for *Wings: Learning to Fly*, stories for *Omnibus* and Lewis Shiner compilation with Lewis Shiner and Franz Henkel.

Past comics titles and related projects: Ad for Caliber, cover and interior art for *Omnibus: Modern Perversity*, and cover for *Wings: Learning to Fly*.

Favorite comics not worked on: *Animal Man '93* and *Tropo*.

Dream comic-book project: *Batman* with Joe Lansdale.

✳ **Bill Mumy.** c/o *CBG* Editorial Department, 700 East State Street, Iola, Wisconsin 54990.

Agent: Manager: Susan Dietz — Multi-Talent.

Born: February 1, 1954, in California.

College or other education: Two years Santa Monica City College, studied music, no degrees.

Comics-related education: 34 years of work

Bill Mumy

in fantasy/science-fiction television, such as *Twilight Zone, Lost in Space*, etc.

Biggest creative influences: On comic book work: Jack Kirby, Stan Lee, Jerry Siegel and Joe Shuster, Bob Kane, and Gardner Fox.

1993 projects: Writing *Lost in Space* for Innovation, *Voyage to the Bottom of the Soul*, parts 1-13. Also, co-writing *Lost in Space Annual #2* with Peter David.

Past comics titles and related projects: *The Comet Man*, six-issue mini-series for Marvel, 1986-87, co-created and scripted. *The Dreamwalker*, 1988, Marvel graphic novel, co-created and scripted. *Trypto, the Acid Dog*, 1989, Renegade Press, co-created and scripted. For Marvel Comics have also written: Spider-Man, The Hulk, Iron Man, She-Hulk, Comet Man, and Wonder Man stories. Co-wrote three issues of *Star Trek* with Peter David for DC, *Hellraiser* for Epic, *Trypto, the Acid Dog* (again) for Atomeka, and many issues of *Lost in Space* for Innovation. As an actor I have been in the following "comic book" productions: *Twilight Zone* (4), *Lost in Space, The Flash, Superboy* (3), and *Captain America*.

Favorite comics not worked on: The Batman titles, *Sandman*, and *Groo*.

Dream comic-book project: I'd love to write a Justice Society of America project, or a Batman, or Superman.

✳ **John Mundt.** 1411 South 14th Street, Prairie du Chien, Wisconsin 53821.

Born: December 8, 1965, in Richland Center, Wisconsin.

Comics-related education: One year (1984-1985) at the Joe Kubert School of Cartoon and Graphic Art Inc.

Biggest creative influences: C.C. Beck, Will Eisner, Charles Dana Gibson, Jack Kirby, Frank Miller, Bill Sienkiewicz, Alex Toth, and Wally Wood.

Past comics titles and related projects: Creator and artist on: *The Adventures of Monkey: Chicago Comicon Special* #1, 1992. *The World of Monkey Trading Cards Series 1*, 1993. *John Woe* comic strip, University of Wisconsin-La Crosse, 1986-1987. Also, assistant inker for Dennis Jensen on various things including a Wolverine story in *Marvel Comics Presents*. Also, many advertising illustrations and other illustrations for local groups.

Favorite comics not worked on: Jeff Smith's *Bone*, Michael Allred's *Madman*, DC's Superman titles, and almost anything touched by Alan Moore, Neil Gaiman, and Mike Mignola.

Dream comic-book project: I would love to, somehow, create comics that kids, as well as kids-at-heart adults, could enjoy without having their intelligence insulted. Nice dream, huh?

✳ **Doug Murray.** 1810 East Anchor Drive, Deltona, Florida 32725.

Born: November 13, 1947, in Brooklyn, New York.

College or other education: B.A. (History), Columbia University.

Biggest creative influences: Will Eisner, Larry Hama, Jim Shooter, and Jack Kirby.

1993 projects: *Medal of Honor* (new Dark Horse series), *Flying Tigers* (Tundra), and various *Disney Adventures*.

Past comics titles and related projects: *The 'Nam* (creator and writer), *The Merc, Adventure of the Missing Martian, Justice Machine, Hellraiser,* *Iron Man, Batman: Digital Justice, Hearts and Minds, The War, Conan,* and *Nick Fury, Agent of S.H.I.E.L.D.*

Favorite comics not worked on: *Batman, Captain America,* and *Concrete.*

Dream comic-book project: Realistic science fiction, literate stuff.

✳ **Will Murray.** P.O. Box 2505, Quincy, Massachusetts 02269.

Born: April 28, 1953, in Boston, Massachusetts.

College or other education: B.A. English, University of Massachusetts at Boston.

Biggest creative influences: Stan Lee, Lester Dent, Walter B. Gibson, and H.P. Lovecraft.

Past comics titles and related projects: *The Destroyer* (Marvel), *The Punisher,* and *Marvel Super-Heroes.*

Favorite comics not worked on: *Fantastic Four, Flaming Carrot, The Shadow,* and *The Green Hornet.*

Dream comic-book project: *Squirrel Girl* limited series.

✳ **Vince Musacchia.** 24 Second Place, Brooklyn, New York 11231.

Born: May 7, 1952, in Columbus Hospital, New York City.

College or other education: Albert Pels School of Art, School of Visual Arts.

Comics-related education: Colorist on Sunday strips of *Dr. Kildare* by Ken Bald for King Features.

Biggest creative influences: Bob Kane, Jack Kirby, Steve Ditko, Jack Davis, Wally Wood, Harvey Kurtzman, Will Elder, Mort Drucker, J.C. Leyendecker, Haddon Sundblom, Will Eisner, Ken Bald, and Chuck Jones.

1993 projects: I'm currently doing storyboards and animatics for advertising and developing my own comic-book project.

Past comics titles and related projects: Creative Director, penciller, inker, and colorist for *The Honeymooners* comic book in partnership with Triad Publications. *Popeye* ads and billboard art for *U.S. News and World Report. Hagar the Horrible* point of purchase and in-store advertising art for Pepsi's Mug Root Beer.

Favorite comics not worked on: *Spider-Man, Batman, Daredevil*, and *Mr. Monster*.

Dream comic-book project: A *Honeymooners* graphic novel or limited series with Robert Loren Fleming.

✴ **John Nadeau.** 27934 Tammi Drive, Tavares, Florida 32778.

Born: December 16, 1971, in Syracuse, New York.

College or other education: Embry-Riddle Aeronautical University (one year).

Biggest creative influences: Mike Golden, Frank Frazetta, Katsuhiro Otomo, Ingres, James Cameron, and Syd Mead.

1993 projects: *Aliens* mini-comics for Kenner toys, *Aliens: Colonial Marines*.

Past comics titles and related projects: *Femforce, Captain Paragon* (AC Comics). *Marvel Mutant Update* (TSR). *The Edison Adventure* (Animated Industrial).

Favorite comics not worked on: *The 'Nam* (Golden issues), *Akira*, and *Elektra: Assassin*.

Dream comic-book project: Technically and politically accurate modern war thrillers, miniseries about Operation Barbarossa.

✴ **Larry Nadolsky.** P.O. Box 1489, Lac du Bonnet, Manitoba, Canada R0E 1A0.

Born: April 7, 1959, in Pine Falls, Manitoba, Canada.

Comics-related education: Self-taught.

Biggest creative influences: Frazetta, Pérez, Bolland, and Russ Heath.

1993 projects: *Motorhead, Shaquille O'Neal* for Revolutionary, other titles for Revolutionary's *Hard Rock, Rock 'n' Roll*, and sports series.

Past comics titles and related projects: *Hey Boss* (a parody of Bruce Springsteen), *Curse of the She Cat, Galaxy Girl, Guns N' Roses* (original), *Bon Jovi, Metallica, Motley Crue, Def Leppard, Faith No More, Ugly Kid Joe, Stan Back*, various things for *Barf!, Pantera, Aerosmith II, Kareem Abdul Jabbar, Ted Williams, Shaquille O'Neal, Joan Jett/Lita Ford*, and *Motorhead*.

Favorite comics not worked on: *Batman* and *Superman*.

Dream comic-book project: Batman graphic album. Western comic.

✴ **Dan Nakrosis.** Dano Graphics, 50 Sanford Avenue, 2nd Floor, Kearny, New Jersey 07032.

Born: July 4, 1963, in Bayonne, New Jersey.

College or other education: Sophia University, Japan, S.V.A., Joe Kubert School.

Comics-related education: Kubert School Saturday night classes.

Biggest creative influences: Sergio Aragonés and Scott Shaw!.

1993 projects: *Conservation Corps*, Marvel coloring books, and *Ultra-Man*.

Past comics titles and related projects: *Sonic the Hedgehog, Little Archie, Slimer*, and Disney comics.

Favorite comics not worked on: *Sandman, Hate*, and *Concrete*.

Dream comic-book project: *Dauna*, a graphic novel.

Nelson

✴ **Nelson.** c/o *CBG* Editorial Department, 700 East State Street, Iola, Wisconsin 54990.

Born: February 17, 1969, in New York City.

College or other education: B.A. in Fine Arts from the School of Visual Arts in New York City.

Comics-related education: Assisted Carmine Infantino.

Biggest creative influences: Byrne, Adams, both Buscemas, Romita, Colan, Infantino, and Wrightson.

1993 projects: Created *The Eudaemon* and the entire line of Manta Comics characters. Pencilling, inking, and writing *The Eudaemon* mini-series.

Past comics titles and related projects: Painted covers for *Ghost Rider* #18, *Punisher G-Force*, *RoboCop: Prime Suspect* (all four), and *Wizard* #13.

Favorite comics not worked on: *Terror Inc.*

Dream comic-book project: I'm working on it now. (I'm a lucky guy.)

Michael Netzer

✻ **Michael Netzer.** 141-02 Jewel Avenue, Flushing, New York 11367.

Born: October 9, 1955, in Detroit, Michigan.

College or other education: Wayne State University, 1973-75, two years of advanced art courses, no degree.

Comics-related education: Initial training 1974-75 under internship with Greg Theakston. Unofficial internship 1975-77 with Neal Adams.

Biggest creative influences: Neal Adams, Jack Kirby, Jim Steranko, and Frank Miller.

1993 projects: *Huntress* mini-series. *Legend* (Chaykin's adaptation of Philip Wylie's *Gladiator*). Adapting Israeli comic hero for American market.

Past comics titles and related projects: *Kamandi, Legion of Super-Heroes, Green Arrow, Black Canary, Isis, Kobra, Wonder Woman, Supergirl, Martian Manhunter, Batman, Flash, Black Lightning, Dr. Fate, Shazam!, Spider-Man, Megalith, Armageddon: Alien Agenda, Armageddon: Inferno, Team Titans, Batman/Green Arrow: Poison Tomorrow, Legends of the Dark Knight Annual, Detective, Ms. Mystic, Comet, Star*Reach, Hot Stuff, Uri-On* (Israeli), and *Shadow.*

Favorite comics not worked on: Anything that Frank Miller writes.

Dream comic-book project: An autobiography in comic book form.

Bill Neville

✻ **Bill Neville.** 506 Oakdale Road, Jamestown, North Carolina 27282.

Born: December 18, 1952, in Sanford, North Carolina.

College or other education: University of North Carolina and Guilford Tech.

Comics-related education: Interfan.

Biggest creative influences: Walt Kelly, Will Eisner, Harvey Kurtzman, Jack Kirby, Neal Adams, Al Capp, and Tex Avery.

1993 projects: *Elfquest: New Blood* (*Summer Special* #2, also issue #8). Other projects may print in 1993, but *Elfquest* is the sure thing.

Past comics titles and related projects: *Captain Paragon* (AC); *Southern Knights, Missing Beings* (Comics Interview); *Bugs Bunny/Looney Tunes Magazine* and *Tiny Toon Adventures Magazine* (DC Comics); *Tiny Toon Comics* (Warner Brothers International Publishing), *Elfquest: New Blood Summer Special* #1 (Warp); *Little Archie* (Archie); *Images of Omaha* (Kitchen Sink).

Favorite comics not worked on: *Bone, The Inferior 5, Uncle Scrooge,* and *She-Hulk.*

Dream comic-book project: Either an *Inferior 5* revival or a *Mad* type comic, Kurtzman style.

✱ **Mindy Newell.** Marvel Entertainment Group Inc., 387 Park Avenue South, New York, New York 10016.

Born: October 24, 1953, in Brooklyn, New York.

College or other education: Quinnipac College, Hamden, Connecticut. Beth Israel Medical Center School of Nursing, B.S.N.

Comics-related education: Everything I've ever read, watched, and done in terms of forming my opinions, etc. Began my freelance career working under Karen Berger and Paul Levitz at DC; at the beginning of my career, Karen was the biggest help and greatest teacher.

Biggest creative influences: Alan Moore, Neil Gaiman, Edna Ferber, Marion Zimmer Bradley, John Le Carré, Robert Heinlein, and Julian Barnes.

1993 projects: Assistant editor: *Deathlok, Marvel Masterworks, Official Handbook of Marvel Universe,* and various licensing and special projects; Editor: *The Marvel Masterpiece Collection.* Writing: *Daredevil Custom Comic, Black Widow* graphic novel (in proposal stage).

Past comics titles and related projects: DC:

New Talent Showcase, Tales of the Legion of Super-Heroes, Tales of the Green Lantern Corps, Superman, Legionnaires Three, Amethyst — ongoing series, *Amethyst* — four-issue mini-series, *Lois Lane* mini-series, *Wonder Woman* (pre- and post-Crisis), *Catwoman* mini-series. Eclipse: *The New Wave.* First: *American Flagg! Strip-AIDS, Heroes for Hunger.* Marvel: Black Widow story for *Marvel Comics Presents,* assistant editor on *Deathlok, Official Handbook of Marvel Universe,* and *Marvel Masterworks;* Editor on *Marvel Masterpiece Collection.*

Favorite comics not worked on: *Sandman, Shade, the Changing Man, Hellblazer, Death* mini-series, most of the Vertigo line.

Dream comic-book project: Writing about my illness (depression) and getting better, maybe someday.

✱ **Bill Nichols.** P.O. Box 426, Elizabethtown, Kentucky 42702-0426.

Born: August 14, 1961, in Elizabethtown, Kentucky.

College or other education: B.A. (1984) and M.A. (1985) from Morehead State University, majoring in Theatre and Communications, respectively.

Biggest creative influences: APA-5, John Byrne, Terry Austin, Frank Miller, Wendy Pini, and Neal Adams.

1993 projects: Inker: *Tempered Steele* and *Dead Kid* (both mini-series from Sky Comics), *The Immortal Three* (from Promethean Studios).

Favorite comics not worked on: *Cerebus, Nexus, Love and Rockets,* and *Elfquest.*

Dream comic-book project: *Amalgam,* an anthology of strips featuring my own assorted creations.

✱ **Jeff Nicholson.** Bad Habit, 2085 Mulberry Street, Chico, California 95928.

Born: October 5, 1962, in Walnut Creek, California.

College or other education: B.A., Communications, 1986.

Biggest creative influences: Jack Kirby and Dave Sim.

1993 projects: *Lost Laughter,* an examination/

Jeff Nicholson

exploration of the doom and gloom trend in comics.

Past comics titles and related projects: *Ultra Klutz* #1-31, 1986-1990. *Through the Habitrails*, serialized in *Taboo* #5-7 and *Taboo Especial* and forthcoming in *Total Taboo, Taboo* #8-10.

Favorite comics not worked on: *Cerebus.*

Dream comic-book project: Participate in a G-rated, successful humor magazine with top humorists in the field, creating a renaissance in the humor genre.

✳ **Troy Nixey.** 3119 Calder Place, Saskatoon, Saskatchewan, Canada S7S 4W8.

Agent: Dan Vado.

Born: April 12, 1972, in Lethbridge, Alberta, Canada.

Comics-related education: Zippo. Learned everything from advice from others and trial and error and successes.

Biggest creative influences: John Byrne, George Pérez, Neil Vokes, Todd McFarlane, Moebius, and Frank Frazetta.

1993 projects: *Bill the Clown* (Slave Labor), penciller. Covers for *Deadworld* (Caliber Press). Some cover work here and there.

Past comics titles and related projects: *Prey* from Monster Comics (was my first comic work

and isn't very good). Two prior issues of *Bill the Clown* from Slave Labor. Two sports covers and a couple of spot illustrations for Comic Zone. A few covers for Slave Labor Graphics. Some projects that never saw the light of day. A short list, I know, but I'm working on it.

Favorite comics not worked on: *Grendel, The Crow, Concrete, Alvarmax,* loved the *Blueberry* series, *Next Men, White Trash,* and, of course, anything Dan Vado writes.

Dream comic-book project: To work on an *Aliens* book in some capacity (painted covers or interiors). I would also love to do a fully painted book sometime.

Carrie and Martin (Mart) Nodell

✳ **Martin (Mart) Nodell.** c/o *CBG* Editorial Department, 700 East State Street, Iola, Wisconsin 54990.

Born: November 15, 1915, in Philadelphia, Pennsylvania.

College or other education: Chicago Academy of Fine Arts, Pratt Institute (Brooklyn, New York), and Chicago Art Institute.

Biggest creative influences: Charlie Chaplin and Harold Lloyd.

Past comics titles and related projects: Aside from *Green Lantern*, two years on staff at Timely Comics working on titles such as *Sub-Mariner, Human Torch,* and *Captain America* from 1948-50. Prior to *Green Lantern*, from 1938-40 worked on Fawcett titles; Ace Books; *Dr. Doom,* Fox Publishing (major ad agency art director 1950-1976).

Dream comic-book project: New art combining Golden Age artists in crossover stories of their original characters.

✳ **John Nordland II.** 1202 Levison Street, Albert Lea, Minnesota 56007.

Born: July 29, 1958, in Albert Lea, Minnesota.

Biggest creative influences: Way too many to mention: Just about everyone I've come in contact with influences me. My cousin, Daniel Nittag, who started me drawing is probably the biggest influence and, of course, Pink Floyd.

1993 projects: *Heroes*, second compilation volume (writing, drawing, lettering, printing, etc.); lettering on *Wings: Learning to Fly*. Both books from Blackbird.

Past comics titles and related projects: *Heroes*, series written, drawn, lettered, published, and printed. Printing and publishing various titles for Blackbird and other publishers including: *Children with Glue, Omnibus: Modern Perversity, Tropo*, and *Crazy Bob* for Blackbird and printed books from Nightwynd, Absolute Comics, B.S. Productions, Caliber Press, Dog Soup, Blazer Studios, and many others.

Favorite comics not worked on: Anything Alan Moore or Neil Gaiman have penned, *Cerebus*, and *Legion of Super-Heroes*.

Dream comic-book project: I am doing it, just might like to get paid better. Also anything written by Alan Moore or Neil Gaiman or to collaborate with Barry Windsor-Smith, Dave Mc-Kean, or George Pratt.

✳ **Phil Normand.** c/o *CBG* Editorial Department, 700 East State Street, Iola, Wisconsin 54990.

Born: November 9, 1945, in Vallejo, California.

College or other education: University of Colorado, Fine Arts.

Comics-related education: Assisted Bob Layton on one *Hercules* issue.

Biggest creative influences: Early 20th-century illustrators, Pyle, Wyeth, Hal Foster, and Will Eisner.

Past comics titles and related projects:

1967-68, *Aquara Muldoon*, comic strip in Denver underground newspaper. 1982-84, animation layouts for Hanna-Barbara series: *The Smurfs, The Monchichis*, and *The Snorks*. 1987-88: *The Wizard of 4th Street* #1 and #2, character designs, layouts, pencils, inks, and lettering.

Rick Norwood

✳ **Rick Norwood.** Manuscript Press, P.O. Box 336, Mountain Home, Tennessee 37684.

Born: August 4, 1942, in Monroe, Louisiana.

College or other education: Ph.D., Math, University of Southwest Louisiana, 1979.

Biggest creative influences: Hal Foster.

1993 projects: Editor: *Prince Valiant — An American Epic*. Writer: *The Best of the Best*.

Past comics titles and related projects: *Comics Revue Magazine*, editor. *Comics Buyer's Guide* columnist. *A Prince Valiant Companion*, editor. *Prince Valiant — An American Epic*, editor. Articles in: *Nemo, The Menomonee Falls Gazette, Comics Feature*, etc.

Favorite comics not worked on: *Sandman*.

Dream comic-book project: *Prince Valiant, Lance, Flash Gordon*, and *Tarzan*, all full-size, full color.

✳ **Bill Oakley.** Wilber Park Apartments, Apartment #2, Oneonta, New York 13820.

Born: April 1, 1964, in Oneonta, New York.

College or other education: One year in Kubert School of Cartoon and Graphic Art.

Comics-related education: Three-four years on Marvel Comics' production staff.

Biggest creative influences: A little bit of everyone and everything (I'm just a letterer).

1993 projects: *X-Men, Spirits of Vengeance* (for Marvel). *Chain Gang War, Lobo PG-13*, and *Kamandi: At Earth's End* limited series (for DC). *Marshal Law* limited series (for Dark Horse).

Past comics titles and related projects: Marvel: *Avengers, Daredevil, Darkhawk, Nightbreed* (to present), *Fantastic Four, West Coast Avengers, Havok and Wolverine: Meltdown* series. DC: *Action Comics, Superman: Man of Steel* (to present), *World's Finest* limited series, *Psycho* limited series, *Lex Luthor: The Unauthorized Biography, Power of the Atom*. Also various logos for Marvel and DC.

Favorite comics not worked on: *Sandman, Hellblazer*, and *Shade, the Changing Man*.

Dream comic-book project: Anything written by Moore or Gaiman; anything illustrated by Bisley or Sam Kieth.

✳ **Michael O'Connell.** Box 1489, Sudden Valley, Bellingham, Washington 98226.

Born: October 30, 1968, in Portland, Oregon.

College or other education: B.A. in English, minor in Computer Science from Gonzaga University.

Biggest creative influences: Alan Moore, Neil Gaiman, Frank Miller, Kurt Vonnegut, Tom Robbins, e.e. cummings, and T.S. Eliot.

1993 projects: *Necromancer, Doctor Faustus, Nightfall* (Anarchy Press), *Poison Elves* # 11 (Mulehide Graphics).

Favorite comics not worked on: *Miracleman, Big Numbers, From Hell, Sandman, Animal Man, Shade, the Changing Man, Xenozoic Tales*, and *Omaha*.

Dream comic-book project: A graphic novel with either Dave McKean or Bill Sienkiewicz.

✳ **Mitch O'Connell.** 6425 North Newgard, Chicago, Illinois 60626.

Born: March 26, 1961, in Boston, Massachusetts.

College or other education: School of the Art Institute of Chicago and The American Academy of Art.

Mitch O'Connell

Biggest creative influences: Alex Toth, Frank Fruzyna (not Frazetta), Big Daddy Roth, J.C. Leyendecker, and George Petty.

1993 projects: A book collecting my art, titled *Good Taste Gone Bad*.

Past comics titles and related projects: In comics: covers for Marvel, DC, Comico, Charlton, Dark Horse, First, etc. Plus work for *The Chicago Tribune, Spy, Playboy, TV Guide, National Lampoon, Advertising Age*, McDonalds, Coke, etc.

Favorite comics not worked on: *Little Lulu* and *Eightball*.

✳ **Glynis Oliver.** c/o *CBG* Editorial Department, 700 East State Street, Iola, Wisconsin 54990.

Born: October 26, 1949, in Cowes, Isle of Wight, England.

College or other education: A.A.S., SUNY, Farmingdale.

Comics-related education: Production, DC Comics.

1993 projects: *Excalibur, Namor, Hulk, She-Hulk, X-Factor, Punisher War Journal, Darkhold*, and *X-Men Unlimited*.

Past comics titles and related projects: *X-Men* (150 issues), *Wolverine, Avengers, Daredevil,*

Spider-Man, Marvel Comics Presents, Conan, Epic (John Byrne's *The Last Galactus Story*), *New Mutants, Elfquest, Superman, Power Pack, Swamp Thing, Thor, Cloak and Dagger, Fantastic Four, Batman, Black Panther, Slapstick, DC/Marvel Crossover Classics,* and various Marvel posters.

Favorite comics not worked on: None.

Dream comic-book project: Silver Surfer in a blizzard at the North Pole.

Turtel Onli

✴ **Turtel Onli.** 5121 South Ellis Avenue, Chicago, Illinois 60615.

Born: January 25, 1952, in Chicago, Illinois.

College or other education: B.F.A., Art Education, 1978. M.A.A.T., Art Therapy, 1989, from Art Institute of Chicago. Sorbonne, Centre Pompidou, Atelier Pont Royal, Paris, France, 1977-1983.

Comics-related education: Assorted freelance clients in USA and Paris, France.

Biggest creative influences: African art, Jimi Hendrix's music, and Jack Kirby.

1993 projects: Establishing the black age of comics as a logical expansion of the international comics business that is respected and supported by all fans. First black age of comics mini-con.

Past comics titles and related projects: 1993, Kamite Comics, *Numidian Force* #4 and 5,

pencils and inks. 1993, Onli Studios, *Malcolm 10* #2-4, *Sustah Girl* #1-3, *Natasha* #1. 1982, published *Future Funk* #1-5 (Black Bande-Dessineé), Educational Graphics. 1981, published *Nog, the Protector of the Pyramids.* 1980, published *Papers* (Black Bande-Dessineé), an anthology. Album covers: 1984, *You Shouldn't uf Bit Fish,* George Clinton. 1983, *Rap to the Wise,* Curtis Blow. 1979, *Captain Sky,* The Captain. 1978, censored *Some Girls,* Rolling Stones. I coined the term and concept "the black age of comics" in 1980.

Favorite comics not worked on: *Cat Claw, Hip-Hop-Heaven, M-C Squared,* and *Electro-X,* along with *The Sectornauts.*

Dream comic-book project: A full-color anthology of the black age of comics, 1974-1993, glossy-embossed and appropriately capitalized. A crossover of my black age characters and mainstream black characters with me as the writer and artist. One each with Marvel, DC, and Image.

Jerry Ordway

✴ **Jerry Ordway.** c/o *CBG* Editorial Department, 700 East State Street, Iola, Wisconsin 54990.

Born: November 28, 1957, in Milwaukee, Wisconsin.

College or other education: High school — Milwaukee Technical High School — three year commercial art degree. One year college, Milwaukee Area Technical College.

Comics-related education: Worked at a typography studio, Milwaukee, 1976-1978. Worked at advertising arts studio, Milwaukee, 1978-1981.

Biggest creative influences: Jack Kirby, Neal Adams, Wally Wood, Alex Raymond, John Byrne, Roy Thomas, Frank Miller, and Roy Crane.

1993 projects: *Wildstar* and *Captain Marvel*.

Past comics titles and related projects: *All Star Squadron*, finisher/penciller (DC) 1981-83; *Infinity Inc.,* penciller, co-creator, (DC) 1983-84; *Fantastic Four*, inker, (Marvel) 1984-85; *Crisis on Infinite Earths*, finisher, (DC) 1985; *Superman*, penciller, inker, writer, (DC) 1986-93; *Batman* movie adaptation, artist, (DC) 1989; *Wildstar*, co-creator, penciller, (Image) 1993; *Captain Marvel* graphic novel, (DC) 1992-93.

Favorite comics not worked on: *Archer & Armstrong*/Valiant; *Akira*/Marvel; *Savage Dragon*/Image; *Marvel Masterworks*/Marvel; *Wash Tubbs*/Flying Buttress.

Dream comic-book project: *The Messenger*, an old creation of mine.

✳ **James A. Owen.** 1750 South Alma School, #119, Mesa, Arizona 85210-3017.

Born: November 11, 1969, in Mesa, Arizona.

College or other education: Undergraduate double major of Physics and Philosophy (abandoned to be a cartoonist).

Comics-related education: I'm making it up as I go along.

Biggest creative influences: Barry Windsor-Smith, Bernie Wrightson, Dave Sim, Gerhard, Neil Gaiman, and Alan Moore.

1993 projects: The other self-published monthly comic book, *Starchild*. Anthologies, monographs, and tapestries. Various prints and illustrations.

Past comics titles and related projects: *Pryderi Terra*, Fantasy West, 1986, writer, illustrator. Limited-edition print series, Fantasy West, 1985-87, illustrator. Illustration/design

work, 1987-1991, for two publishing companies that went bankrupt and two entertainment conglomerates who didn't.

Favorite comics not worked on: *Cerebus, Sandman, Taboo, Bone, Maximortal*, and *Peter and Wendy*.

Dream comic-book project: *Starchild*, so far, so good.

✳ **Bob Palin.** Ocean Comics Inc., P.O Box 9665, Warwick, Rhode Island 02889-9665.

Born: February 19, 1953, in Central Falls, Rhode Island.

College or other education: B.S., Business Management, 1975, Providence College, Providence, Rhode Island.

Past comics titles and related projects: Writer: *Guerrilla Gorillas: Reality Check* in *The Greatest American Comic Book* #1, November 1992, Ocean Comics.

✳ **Kathy Palin.** Ocean Comics Inc., P.O. Box 9665, Warwick, Rhode Island 02889-9665.

Born: September 4, 1953, in Warwick, Rhode Island.

College or other education: B.S., Biology, 1975, Providence College, Providence, Rhode Island.

Past comics titles and related projects: Colorist: *Street Fighter* #1-4, 1986-87; *Popeye Special* #1 and 2, 1987-88; cover, *Mr. Jigsaw Special* #1, 1988; cover, *The Greatest American Comic Book* #1, 1992; all for Ocean Comics.

✳ **Terry Pallot.** 45 Levis Street, Upstairs Apartment, Sudbury, Ontario, Canada P3C 2G8.

Born: August 6, 1966, in Sault Ste. Marie, Ontario, Canada.

College or other education: Diploma: Illustration with Book Design major.

Biggest creative influences: Frank Miller, P. Craig Russell, Dave Sim, Bruce Jones, Moebius, and Kelley Jones.

1993 projects: *Paul the Samurai*.

Past comics titles and related projects: *Dinosaurs for Hire* (first series), *Tom Corbett, Space Cadet, Planet of the Apes, Ape Nation, Alien Nation:*

The Skin Trade, Subspecies, Galaxina, Flesh Gordon, Rock 'n' Roll Comics: Rush, Hard Rock Comics: Pearl Jam/Soundgarden, Alien Nation: The Lost Episode, Paul the Samurai, Aliens: Colonial Marines, and *Aliens* in *Dark Horse Comics.*

Favorite comics not worked on: *Peep Show, Faust, Shade, the Changing Man, Cerebus, Black Orchid* (mini-series), *Grendel,* and *Dirty Pair.*

Dream comic-book project: I wrote it, I drew it, I enjoyed it, I made big $$$; or adapt *The Legacy of Herot.*

Louis Paradis

✳ **Louis Paradis.** c/o *CBG* Editorial Department, 700 East State Street, Iola, Wisconsin 54990.

Born: July 6, 1959, in Montmagny, QC, Canada.

College or other education: D.E.C. Cégep de Rivière-du-Loup (Graphism)

Biggest creative influences: Hergé, Hogarth, Foster, Kirby, Moebius/Gir, and Caniff.

1993 projects: *Rock-Fun-Poutine/Les Apôtres/Le Vampire du Sahara. Les Saigneurs du Royaume Blanc.*

Past comics titles and related projects: *Tony Bravado/Trouble Shooter* I and II (Renegade Press), ink. *Necromancer* I (Anarchy Press), ink. *Clara* (Édition du Lombard, Belgium), pencil and ink. *Aventure sur Mars* (Édition Otto Publika), ink.

Sextant I, II, III, and IV. (Sextant Éditeur), pencil and ink. *Abraham et Moïse* (Édition Anne Sigier), color, pencil, and ink. *Ma Nature en Harmonie* I, II, and III (I.P.A.Q. Éditeur), pencil and ink.

Favorite comics not worked on: *Tarzan, Prince Valiant, Fantastic Four, Blueberry,* and *Conan.*

Dream comic-book project: A full-color graphic album.

Lisa Trusiani Parker

✳ **Lisa Trusiani Parker.** c/o *CBG* Editorial Department, 700 East State Street, Iola, Wisconsin 54990.

Born: January 22, 1959, in Portland, Maine.

College or other education: B.A., Sociology and Studio Art, Bowdoin College, Brunswick, Maine.

Comics-related education: Assistant Editor to Sid Jacobson at Marvel. Co-director Barking Dog Studios.

Biggest creative influences: Ted Geisel, Margaret Wise Brown, Robert McCloskey, Gabriel Garcia Marquez.

1993 projects: Write and draw storyboards for *Barbie* (Marvel) and *The Liquid Cat* (graphic novel).

Past comics titles and related projects: Written and drawn storyboards for *Heathcliff, New Kids on the Block, Barbie Fashion, Barbie,* and

Rex Morgan M.D. (King Features).

Favorite comics not worked on: *Bossmen* strip for *Marvel Age, Little Nemo, Maus* I and II, and *Calvin and Hobbes*.

Dream comic-book project: *The Liquid Cat.*

R.PARKER 3·29·93

Rick Parker

✱ **Rick Parker.** c/o *CBG* Editorial Department, 700 East State Street, Iola, Wisconsin 54990.

Agent: Ling Lucas.

Born: August 31, 1946, in Miami, Florida.

College or other education: B.F.A., Painting/Drawing, University of Georgia, 1972. M.F.A., Printmaking, Pratt Institute, 1975.

Comics-related education: Marvel Comics bullpen 1977-1983.

Biggest creative influences: Wood, Elder, Wolverton, Davis, Crane, Freas, Berg, Addams, Wilson, Kliban, Price, Steinberg, Poe, and Kurtzman.

1993 projects: *The Bossmen,* Marvel Comics' *The Bullpen Bullseye* cartoon; various other projects; and *The Bossmen* one-shot.

Past comics titles and related projects: *The Toxic Crusader, The Destroyer, What The--?!, The Bossmen,* Marvel Comics. *Everything I Really Need to Know I Learned From Television,* illustrated humor book for Applause Books, New York City.

Favorite comics not worked on: *Eightball, Hate, Trailer Trash,* anything by Jim Woodring, *White Trash, Hup, The Bojeffries Saga,* and others too numerous to mention.

Dream comic-book project: *The Bossmen* graphic novel.

Ande Parks

✱ **Ande Parks.** c/o *CBG* Editorial Department, 700 East State Street, Iola, Wisconsin 54990.

Born: October 1, 1964, in Emporia, Kansas.

College or other education: Attended University of Kansas.

Biggest creative influences: Dick Giordano, Josef Rubinstein, Neal Adams, and Jack Kirby.

1993 projects: *Wonder Woman,* Dark Horse's *Monster* (part of *Comics' Greatest World*), *Predator* mini-series — all as inker.

Past comics titles and related projects: *Rust* (Malibu), *Freaks Amour* (Dark Horse), *Action Comics, Wonder Woman Annual, L.E.G.I.O.N. '93* (DC) — as inker.

Favorite comics not worked on: *1963, Sandman, Sin City,* and anything else by Moore, Gaiman, Miller, or Mignola.

Dream comic-book project: A Kirby-faithful version of *OMAC.*

✱ **Mik Pascal (Mike Pascale).** Schism Comics, 19785 West 12 Mile, Suite 190, Southfield, Michigan 48076.

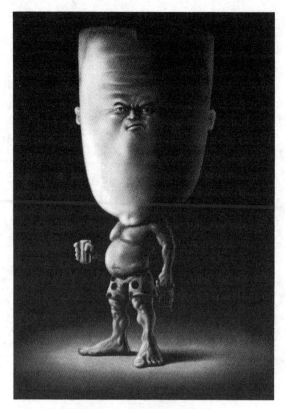

Mik Pascal (Mike Pascale)

Born: November 3, 1963, in Detroit, Michigan.

College or other education: B.F.A., Center for Creative Studies College of Art and Design, Detroit, Michigan.

Comics-related education: The Joe Kubert School of Cartoon and Graphic Art; the G/T Pacer independent study program, 1980-81, for narrative art.

Biggest creative influences: Michaelangelo (not the turtle!), Frazetta, Kirby, Wrightson, and Armstrong.

1993 projects: Penciller/writer on *Bru-Hed* and *Transylvania 90210*, for Schism Comics.

Past comics titles and related projects: Artist/writer on *Bru-Hed, Gold Star Showcase* (Gold Star Comics), *Fantasy World, Alpha Notes*, and artist on *Star Wreck* (a 1977 *Star Trek* parody).

Favorite comics not worked on: Wrightson's *Captain Sternn*, anything by Kirby, *Groo, Reid Fleming*, Disney comics, and *Captain America*.

Dream comic-book project: Bru-Hed meets Captain America.

✻ **Mark Pate.** 625 Avenue H, Westwego, Louisiana 70094.

Born: July 27, 1972, in New Orleans, Louisiana.

College or other education: C.A.D., Industrial Art Design.

Biggest creative influences: Various.

1993 projects: *Tales from the Balcony* #1.

Favorite comics not worked on: *The Vampire Lestat* and *Interview with a Vampire*.

Frederick Patten

✻ **Frederick Patten.** 11863 West Jefferson Boulevard, Culver City, California 90230-6322.

Born: December 11, 1940, in Los Angeles, California.

College or other education: UCLA, 1958-1962. UCLA School of Library Service (Master of Library Science), 1962-1963.

Biggest creative influences: Carl Barks, Don Arr (Don R. Christiansen), Hergé, Andre Franquin, Osamu Tezuka, Edmond Hamilton, Milton Caniff, and Harold Gray.

1993 projects: Writer, *The Second Wish*, short story for back-up in Antarctic Press' *Albedo* (tentatively scheduled for #10, late 1993); writer, "Heigh-Ho, Heigh-Ho . . . ," short story for back-up in *Albedo* (tentatively scheduled for #12 or 13).

Past comics titles and related projects: Writer, *Beyond the Mountain of Glass*, 15-page story in Antarctic Press' *Mangazine Volume 2* #1 (1989); *The Dynamic World of Go Nagai*, introduction in First's *Mazinger* (1988); *The Manga Story* #1, introduction in Viz/Eclipse's *Mai, the Psychic Girl* #3 (1987); reviews of comic books in Fantagraphics' *Amazing Heroes* (1988-1992); co-author (with Randy and Jean-Marc Lofficier) of the series *The Great European Comic Heroes* in Fantagraphics' *Nemo* (1985); various articles on Japanese comics, e.g. *A New Wind From the East*, *Amazing Heroes* #118 (1987) and *Mangamania!*, *The Comics Journal* #94 (1984). I wrote *Angela*, a 60-page story illustrated by Doug Wildey in 1978; it was commissioned and paid for by Sanrio but never published. The above list includes projects for which I was paid and which (with the exception of *Angela*) were published. It does not include many articles and reviews which were published but for which I was not paid (such as reviews of comic books for *Wittyworld* magazine) or comics and related projects which were never published or sold.

Favorite comics not worked on: Most of these are creator-controlled, such as Jeff Smith's *Bone*, Masamune Shirow's *Orion*, and Dwight Decker's *Rhudiprrt*.

Dream comic-book project: A hardbound anthology of *good* original science-fiction short stories in comic-art format. They are rare, but there have been enough over the years, throughout the world, to fill an anthology.

✳ **Bruce Douglas Patterson.** c/o *CBG* Editorial Department, 700 East State Street, Iola, Wisconsin 54990.

Born: January 6, 1953, in South Gate, California.

College or other education: Halfway through art school.

Comics-related education: Assistant to Neal Adams (Continuity Associates).

Biggest creative influences: Gahan Wilson, Kevin O'Neill, Charles Rodriegez, Antonio Vargas, Olivia, and H.P. Lovecraft.

Bruce Douglas Patterson

1993 projects: *Alpha Flight*, *RoboCop: Mortal Coil*, and *Marvel Universe Series IV* trading cards.

Past comics titles and related projects: *Captain Marvel*, *Master of Kung-Fu*, *Legion of Super-Heroes*, *Camelot 3000*, *Green Lantern*, *Alpha Flight* — inking. *E-Man*, *Sunspot* — coloring. Various titles — lettering. *E-Man* — co-writing. *Alien Sex/Monster Lust* — everything.

Favorite comics not worked on: *Marshal Law*, *Akira*, *Spawn*, *CyberForce*, *X-Men*, and anything by Dave Cooper.

Dream comic-book project: Something with nude or partially-clad women and Cthulhu-type monsters.

✳ **Eric Pavlat.** 106 Enchanted Hills Road, #103, Owings Mills, Maryland 21117.

Born: September 24, 1969, in Silver Spring, Maryland.

College or other education: B.A. in English from University of Maryland.

Comics-related education: Five years in retail comic-book sales.

Biggest creative influences: Peter David,

Eric Pavlat

Alan Moore, Henry James, J.M. DeMatteis, James Joyce (short stories), and Carl Barks.

1993 projects: *Messiah* mini-series, *I Dream a God* one-shot.

Past comics titles and related projects: I wrote *Wheelbarrow* in *Thumbscrew* #3 (Caliber).

Favorite comics not worked on: *Sandman, Cages, Incredible Hulk, Ren & Stimpy Show, Doom 2099, Icon, Cerebus,* and *A Distant Soil.*

Dream comic-book project: An extended Avengers/Silver Surfer storyline or a biblical/historical project with Stefano Gaudiano called *The Three Days.*

✳ **Bill Pearson.** P.O. Box 1013, Mayer, Arizona 86333.

Born: July 27, 1938, in Belle Fourche, South Dakota.

College or other education: School of Visual Arts, New York City, 1958-59.

Comics-related education: Off and on informal assistant to Wallace Wood, which included writing, lettering, coloring, and production work, 1965-1981.

Biggest creative influences: 20th Century popular culture, W.C. Fields, Fred Astaire and Sheena, Queen of the Jungle.

1993 projects: Writing scripts for Gladstone, lettering for several companies, and editing a series of Wally Wood reprint comics for Fantagraphics.

Past comics titles and related projects: For the past decade I have worked primarily as a letterer, freelancing for almost every major publisher.

Favorite comics not worked on: Classic comic strips, 1930-1960.

Dream comic-book project: I'd like to edit and design a comic book titled *Witzend* on a monthly schedule.

✳ **Jason Pearson.** Gaijin Studios, 5581 Peachtree Road, Atlanta, Georgia 30341.

Born: August 29, 1970, in Los Angeles, California.

Biggest creative influences: Michael Golden, Alex Toth, Paul Smith, Yukito Kishiro, Patrick Nagel, John Romita Jr., Frank Miller, Masamune Shirow, Katsuhiro Otomo, Milo Manara, Kevin Nowlan, Mike Mignola, and Rick Leonardi.

1993 projects: A *Bedrock* story for Liefeld, *Ground Zero,* and *Batman: Legends of the Dark Knight.*

Past comics titles and related projects: *Legion of Super-Heroes, Uncanny X-Men, Justice League Quarterly, Green Lantern Corps Quarterly, Starman, Who's Who, Spawn,* and *Homage Swimsuit Issue.*

Favorite comics not worked on: *Sin City, Akira, Appleseed, Battle Angel Alita, Love and Rockets,* and *Uncanny X-Men.*

Dream comic-book project: Comic-book adaptation of *La Femme Nikita.*

✳ **Harvey Pekar.** P.O. Box 18471, Cleveland Heights, Ohio 44118.

Born: October 8, 1939, in Cleveland, Ohio.

Biggest creative influences: Many prose fiction writers from the mid-19th Century to today.

1993 projects: *American Splendor* #18.

Past comics titles and related projects: *American Splendor* Volumes 1-17.

Joyce Brabner and Harvey Pekar

Dream comic-book project: I'm doing what I want to be doing in comics.

✻ **Laughland Pelle.** 140-19 Einstein Loop, Apartment 19E, Bronx, New York 10475.

Born: June 21, 1969, in Bronx, New York.

Comics-related education: One year internship with DC Comics.

1993 projects: Currently working on *Predator: Race War* #3 and 4, after that unemployed (that means desperately looking for work).

Past comics titles and related projects: Variety of biographical comic books: Kareem Abdul Jabbar, Frank Thomas, Dave Justice, all for either Revolutionary Comics or Personality. One Wonder Woman inventory story. Nothing really worth mentioning.

✻ **Ken Penders.** P.O. Box 982, Hudson, New Hampshire 03051-0982.

Born: September 28, 1958, in Buffalo, New York.

College or other education: Art Institute of Boston.

Comics-related education: DC Apprentice-

Ken Penders

ship Program (Dick Giordano).

Biggest creative influences: Jack Kirby, Jim Steranko, Will Eisner, Neal Adams, Dick Giordano, Gil Kane, and Carmine Infantino.

1993 projects: *Captain Hazzard* (Alpha Productions), *Britannia* (Heroic), *Shadowblade, Task Force Alpha* (Alpha Productions), *Star Trek* and *Star Trek: The Next Generation* (DC).

Past comics titles and related projects: *Star Trek: The Next Generation, Who's Who in Star Trek, Captain Atom, Forgotten Realms, Advanced Dungeons and Dragons* (DC); *Jaguar* and *Comet* (Impact); *Savage Sword of Conan* and *Transformers Digest* (Marvel); *Legend of Zelda* (Valiant); *Racer X* and *Green Hornet: Solitary Sentinel* mini-series (Now); *Southern Knights* (Fictioneer); *G.I. Mutants* (Eternity); *Shadowblade* (Hot); *The Man from U.N.C.L.E.* (TE Publications).

Favorite comics not worked on: *Batman, Solar*, and *Fantastic Four*.

Dream comic-book project: A full-color graphic novel featuring either a *Star Trek* story taking place during an untold era between the old and new generations, or a personal creation that deals with balancing personal/professional obligations and responsibilities in a way yet unseen in comics.

✷ **Mark Pennington.** Rural Route 2, Box 70, Bushkill, Pennsylvania 18324.

Born: September 29, 1959, in Cleveland, Ohio.

Comics-related education: Joe Kubert School of Comic Art.

Biggest creative influences: Frank Frazetta, Joe Kubert, and Neal Adams.

1993 projects: *X-Men, Violator, Batman: Legends of the Dark Knight,* and *Spawn Annual.*

Past comics titles and related projects: *Shade, the Changing Man, Hellblazer, Eclipso, Fright Night II, X-Force, Punisher, Animal Man, Judge Dredd, Slaine the Berserker,* and *Rogue Trooper.*

Favorite comics not worked on: *Tarzan* and *Conan.*

Dream comic-book project: Pencil, ink, and write an action-type book.

Shea Anton Pensa

✷ **Shea Anton Pensa.** 1921 Estudillo Street, Martinez, California 94553.

Born: March 18, 1968, in Crown Street, Sydney, N.S.W., Australia.

College or other education: Two years of Life Drawing (mandatory), one year of Advanced Drawing.

Biggest creative influences: Stephen Hickman, Frank Miller, Bill Sienkiewicz, Jim Steranko, Charles Dana Gibson, and Gustave Doré.

1993 projects: *Hammer of God, Nexus*-related mini-series for Dark Horse (pencils and inks), and *Sandman* #55.

Past comics titles and related projects: *The Butcher* mini-series, *Green Arrow, The Brave and the Bold, Punisher,* and *Ms. Tree Quarterly.*

Favorite comics not worked on: *Swamp Thing* and *Heavy Metal.*

Dream comic-book project: A painted science-fiction epic with sweeping operatic overtones, self-written, of course.

✷ **Andrew Pepoy.** P.O. Box 148524, Chicago, Illinois 60614.

Born: May 13, 1969, in Dearborn, Michigan.

College or other education: 1991, B.A. cum laude, Fine Arts/Honors from Loyola University, Chicago (with a minor in history). Further studies at the Art Institute of Chicago.

Comics-related education: Summer comics art courses, 1981 and 1982. Assistant (sort of) to Bill Reinhold and Linda Lessmann.

Biggest creative influences: François Shuiten, Brian Bolland, Gene Day, Maxfield Parrish, Enki Bilal, Umberto Eco, Norvell Page, Allain and Souvestre, Ildiko Enyedi's *My 20th Century* (film).

1993 projects: *Darkman* mini-series and *Morbius* #13-18 for Marvel; *Star Trek: Deep Space Nine* #1 and #2 (maybe more) for Malibu; Golden Age Green Lantern in *Green Lantern Corps Quarterly* for DC (all are inking credits).

Past comics titles and related projects: Inking: *Iron Man, Spider-Man, The New Warriors, X-Men Adventures, X-Factor, Doctor Strange, What If?, Cage,* and others for Marvel; *Justice League Quarterly, Flash Annual, Suicide Squad,* and others for DC; *Blood Syndicate* for Milestone; *X-O Manowar* for Valiant; *Alien Nation* for Malibu. Others: *Caliber Presents* #6 (art) and #14 (story and art), *Elementals Pin-Up Special* (art), and *Boots of the Oppressor* (art).

Favorite comics not worked on: *Sandman, Doom Patrol, Oblivion City, Cerebus, Bone, 2000 AD Weekly,* and *À Suivre.*

Dream comic-book project: A graphic novel written and drawn (or painted) by me, hardcover on good paper, and translated and sold around the world.

✸ **George Pérez.** c/o *CBG* Editorial Department, 700 East State Street, Iola, Wisconsin 54990.

Agent: Art Agent/Appearing Agent: Spencer Beck. Lawyer/Business Agent: Harris Miller.

Born: June 9, 1954, in The Bronx, New York.

Comics-related education: Assistant to Rich Buckler (1973-1974).

Biggest creative influences: Curt Swan, Neal Adams, Jack Kirby, John Buscema, Alphonse Mucha, Norman Rockwell, Barry Windsor-Smith, etc.

1993 projects: *Jurassic Park*, inks over Gil Kane. *Sachs and Violens*, penciller and inker. *Breakthrough*, Ultraverse crossover, scripter and penciller.

Past comics titles and related projects: *The Avengers, The Fantastic Four, Man-Wolf, The Sons of the Tiger, The Beatles Story, Logan's Run, Justice League, The New Teen Titans, Crisis on Infinite Earths, Wonder Woman, War of the Gods, Infinity Gauntlet, The Inhumans, Action Comics, Hulk: Future Imperfect*, and others.

Favorite comics not worked on: *Watchmen* and *Bone*.

Dream comic-book project: The Avengers/Justice League crossover.

Faye Perozich

✸ **Faye Perozich.** 4 Spanish Manor, Oglebay Park, Wheeling, West Virginia 26003.

Agent: Tony Gardiner/The Tantleff Office.

Born: April 27, 1963, in Pittsburgh, Pennsylvania.

Biggest creative influences: Harlan Ellison, Clive Barker, Stephen King, and Anne Rice.

1993 projects: *Queen of the Damned* and *Interview with the Vampire*.

Past comics titles and related projects: *The Vampire Lestat, The Mummy, Weird Tales, Hellraiser, Shadowman, Magnus Robot Fighter*, and *Angry Shadows*.

Favorite comics not worked on: *Sandman* and *Deadman*.

Dream comic-book project: *Bloodchilde* — series I created for DC.

✸ **Fred Perry.** Antarctic Press, 7272 Wurzbach Suite, #204, San Antonio, Texas 78240.

College or other education: Marine corporal, three years combat engineer, four years armored personnel (AAV driver). Working on Bachelor's degree in Computer Science.

Biggest creative influences: *Ninja High School* #4.

1993 projects: *Gold Digger* (monthly series).

Past comics titles and related projects: *Gold Digger* (four-issue Antarctic mini-series). *Mangazine* #11-14 (original *Gold Digger*). *Mangazine* #5-7 (*Gear*). Pencilled *Tom Corbett*, eight issues. Inking: *Robotech: Invid War, Robotech: Cyberpirates, Robotech: Malcontents*, and *Kid Cannibal* (four issues).

Favorite comics not worked on: *Ninja High School* and *G.I. Joe*.

Dream comic-book project: *Street Fighter*.

✸ **Barry Daniel Petersen.** 1056 Thacker, Des Plaines, Illinois 60016.

Born: June 21, 1961, in Chicago, Illinois.

College or other education: Miscellaneous underground courses.

Biggest creative influences: Walt Kelly and Charles Schulz.

1993 projects: Art Director of all Now Comics titles.

Past comics titles and related projects: *MirrorWalker* (the first comic book ever to use photographic backgrounds throughout the entire issue), *Slimer!*, and *The Real Ghostbusters*.

Barry Daniel Petersen

Dream comic-book project: A comic book on *Pogo* or another *MirrorWalker*.

✱ **Brandon C. Peterson.** c/o *CBG* Editorial Department, 700 East State Street, Iola, Wisconsin 54990.

Born: October 14, 1969, in Madison, Wisconsin.

College or other education: B.F.A. from the University of Wisconsin.

Biggest creative influences: Jim Lee, Marc Silvestri, Whilce Portacio, Art Adams, and Michael Golden.

1993 projects: *Strykeforce*, a new Image Comics ongoing series out in September.

Past comics titles and related projects: Most recent: *Uncanny X-Men, X-Men, X-Factor*, 1992-present. Various DC projects: *Legion of Super-Heroes, Star Trek, Star Trek: The Next Generation*, 1991-92.

Brandon C. Peterson

Favorite comics not worked on: *Bone, Cerebus, Sandman, Hellblazer, Spawn*, and *Savage Dragon*.

Dream comic-book project: Something of my own with a great writer.

✱ **Stefan Petrucha.** 75 Putnam Drive, Port Chester, New York 10573.

Born: January 27, 1959, in New York City.

College or other education: B.A. in Literature, certificate in Video Production from Center for Media Arts.

Biggest creative influences: Alan Moore, Philip Dick, Shakespeare, Dickinson, Faulkner, and Elizabeth Bishop.

1993 projects: *Lance Barnes: Post Nuke Dick* (Epic), *Counterparts* (Tundra), and *Last Action Hero* (Topps).

Past comics titles and related projects: *Squalor, Meta-4*, and *Nexus, the Liberator*.

Dream comic-book project: Something called *The Bandyman* with art by an unknown artist named Grant Fuhst.

✱ **Bob Pinaha.** c/o *CBG* Editorial Department, 700 East State Street, Iola, Wisconsin 54990.

Bob Pinaha

Born: July 26, 1953, in South Amboy, New Jersey.

College or other education: Art school (Design, Illustration, Comic Art, and Commercial Art).

Comics-related education: Just practice, practice, practice, and then, when you've got it right, *more* practice!

Biggest creative influences: Frank Thorne, Rudy Nebres, John Workman, Joe Rosen, Tom Orzechowski, and wife, Agnes.

1993 projects: *Star Trek, Star Trek: The Next Generation, Valor, Justice Society, Justice League Task Force, Legion of Super-Heroes, Modesty Blaise, Tiny Toons,* and *Looney Tunes.*

Past comics titles and related projects: *Robotech, Mage, Grendel, Justice Machine, A Distant Soil* (both Warp and Donning versions), *Starman, The Phantom, Debt of Honor, Hawk and Dove, New Gods, Thor,* plus others which I'm sure I've forgotten (such as *Elementals, Ginger Fox,* etc.).

Favorite comics not worked on: *Batman* and *X-Men.*

Dream comic-book project: Working on a photo project with Frank Thorne.

✳ **Richard Pini.** Warp Graphics Inc., 5 Reno Road, Poughkeepsie, New York 12603.

Born: July 19, 1950, in New Haven, Connecticut.

College or other education: M.I.T. (B.S., Astronomy).

Richard and Wendy Pini

Biggest creative influences: Keith Laumer and Robert B. Parker.

1993 projects: *Elfquest: New Blood, Elfquest: Blood of Ten Chiefs, Elfquest: Wavedancers, Jink* (all Elfquest Universe titles).

Past comics titles and related projects: Original *Elfquest* series (1978-84), *Siege at Blue Mountain* (1986-88), *Kings of the Broken Wheel* (1990-92).

✳ **Wendy Pini.** Warp Graphics Inc., 5 Reno Road, Poughkeepsie, New York 12603.

Born: June 4, 1951, in San Francisco, California.

Biggest creative influences: Tezuka, Erte, Chuck Jones, Rackham, and Doug Wildey.

1993 projects: *Elfquest: Hidden Years, Jink, The Rebels* (all Elfquest Universe titles).

Past comics titles and related projects: Original *Elfquest* series (1978-84), *Siege at Blue Mountain* (1986-88), *Kings of the Broken Wheel* (1990-92), *Beauty and the Beast* graphic novels (*Portrait of Love* and *Night of Beauty*), *Superman* #400, *Jonny Quest* #2, and *Red Sonja* #6.

✳ **Sandy Plunkett.** P.O. Box 745, Athens, Ohio 45701.

Born: October 18, 1955, in Williamsburg, Pennsylvania.

Biggest creative influences: Larry Ivie.

1993 projects: Work for the Conan titles, including cover paintings.

Past comics titles and related projects: Lots of covers for Marvel, various fill-in stories as artist and writer (*Ant-Man, Spider-Man*, and *Black Panther*).

Favorite comics not worked on: *Walt Disney Comics and Stories* (Carl Barks reprints).

Rachel Pollack

✳ **Rachel Pollack.** c/o *CBG* Editorial Department, 700 East State Street, Iola, Wisconsin 54990.

Agent: Ellen LeVine.

Born: August 17, 1945, in Brooklyn, New York.

College or other education: B.A., New York University. M.A., Claremont Graduate School.

Biggest creative influences: Grant Morrison, Carl Barks, Jack Kirby, Alan Moore, Neil Gaiman, and Peter Milligan.

1993 projects: *Doom Patrol.*

Past comics titles and related projects: *Vertigo Visions — The Geek.*

Favorite comics not worked on: *Shade, the Changing Man* and *Sandman.*

Dream comic-book project: Aside from *Doom Patrol*, which I'm already doing, *Wonder Woman* as a Vertigo comic or surreal graphic novels based on dreams and shamanism.

Carl Potts

✳ **Carl Potts.** c/o Marvel Comics, 387 Park Avenue South, New York, New York 10016.

Born: November 12, 1952, in Oakland, California.

College or other education: Three years of college, A.A. in Commercial Art.

Biggest creative influences: Comics: Stan Lee, Steve Ditko, and Jack Kirby. Outside of comics: Harper Lee, Dean Cornwell, Andrew Loomis, and Joseph U. Mascelli.

1993 projects: Wolverine/Punisher limited series *Damaging Evidence*, Venom/Punisher limited series *Funeral Pyre.*

Past comics titles and related projects: *Punisher War Journal, Shadowmasters, Alien Legion,*

Spellbound, Last of the Dragons, Moon Knight, Doctor Strange, and *Marvel Fanfare*.

Favorite comics not worked on: Does this mean as a creator or as an editor, too? *Sam and Max, Untamed, Midnight Men, Lawdog* (all the Epic Heavy Hitters titles), *Spider-Man 2099*, and *Groo*.

Dream comic-book project: Combine classic Ditko characters in one book (Spider-Man, Doctor Strange, Creeper, so on).

✳ **Paul S. Power.** c/o *CBG* Editorial Department, 700 East State Street, Iola, Wisconsin 54990.

Born: November 5, 1954, in Walthamstow, London, England.

College or other education: Alexander Mackie School of Art (Sydney, Australia). Bankstown Tech (life, watercolor, and calligraphy classes at night school).

Comics-related education: 1973, assistant to Alex Toth, *Superfriends* cartoon for Hanna-Barbera. Too many to mention. John Dixon, *Air Hawk* Sundays ghost.

Biggest creative influences: Alex Toth, John Dixon, Jack Kirby, Byrne Hogarth, Frank Bellamy, Alex Raymond, and Milton Caniff.

1993 projects: *Bob* TV show, actor/artist. *The Rock Warrior*.

Past comics titles and related projects: Worked with Dave Stevens. Ghosted John Dixon's *Air Hawk* in 1977. *Professor Om* Sunday strip 1977-78 for Rupert Murdoch. Animation super-hero *i.e., Superfriends*, 1973, *The Thing*, 1979. Lots of super-hero-type films, *i.e., The Road Warrior*, the first *RoboCop* and *Predator*. Now Bob Newhart's *Bob* TV show, the only comic-book TV series. If it's got real cartoonists on the show, then I got them on.

Favorite comics not worked on: *Spawn, WildC.A.T.S*, and *CyberForce*.

Dream comic-book project: My own series, *East Meets West, Professor Om, The Rock Warrior*, and to direct a real super-hero film.

✳ **Daniel Presedo.** P.O. Box 77086, Baton Rouge, Louisiana 70816.

Daniel Presedo

Born: April 15, 1970, in Baton Rouge, Louisiana.

College or other education: Louisiana State University, 1988-1990. Baton Rouge Fine Arts Academy, 1990-1992 (graduated — diploma).

Biggest creative influences: John Byrne, Steve Ditko, and John Buscema.

1993 projects: *Dream Wolves* #1 (writing/drawing), *Morbid Angel* #1 (drawing), *Razor* #4 (pencilling), *Practice in Pain* #1 (writing/drawing), *Razor Special* #1 (drawing), all publishing under London Night Studios.

Past comics titles and related projects: *Razor* #1 and #2, *Nightshades* #1, *Dark Angel: Death Dreams* #1, *Razor Tour Book '92, Fiends* #1, *Street Rat* #1, *Calculated Risk* #1, and *Razor: Dangerous Portfolio '92*.

Favorite comics not worked on: *Sandman, Swamp Thing*, and *Spider-Man*.

Dream comic-book project: A Spider-Man story written by Clive Barker and drawn by me.

Richie Prosch

✶ **Richie Prosch.** 305 Pinehaven Ext. #44, Laurens, South Carolina 29360.

Born: March 9, 1966, in Denver, Colorado.

College or other education: B.A., Commercial Art/English, Dana College, Blair, Nebraska.

Biggest creative influences: Ray Bradbury, Charles Schulz, Mike Grell, and Gardner Fox.

1993 projects: *The Peregrine* with Hal Milam, *'Lectric Man* custom comic book, *Farmboy/Open Range* series of projects.

Past comics titles and related projects: *Comix Wave* mini-series and *Comix Wave* magazine with Geerdes (1984-86). *Jorgen's Rainbow* for *The American Dane* magazine (1987-present). *American Heroes* #1: Martin Luther King Jr. for Personality Comics (1992). *Kiss: Satan's Music?* #1 for Personality Comics (1992).

Favorite comics not worked on: *Sandman*, *Bone*, and *Justice League America*.

Dream comic-book project: Work with Gardner Fox on a Justice Society story.

✶ **Jerry Prosser.** Dark Horse Comics, 10956 S.E. Main, Milwaukie, Oregeon 97222.

Born: September 9, 1963, in Cove d'Alene, Idaho.

College or other education: Master of Social Work.

1993 projects: *Skin Graft* — DC Comics, *Comics' Greatest World* — Dark Horse, and *Predator* — Dark Horse.

Past comics titles and related projects: *Exquisite Corpse* — Dark Horse. *Aliens: Hive* — Dark Horse. *Cyberantics* — Dark Horse.

James Pruett

✶ **James Pruett.** Madhatter Studios International/Krünchy Frogg Studios, P.O. Box 672162, Marietta, Georgia 30067-0037.

Born: January 8, 1966, in Valdosta, Georgia.

College or other education: University of Georgia.

Comics-related education: Associate editor of *Negative Burn* from Caliber Press.

Biggest creative influences: Eddie Campbell, Frank Miller, and Richard Bach.

1993 projects: Writer of *The Apparition* and *Sojourn* appearing in *Negative Burn* from Caliber Press. Writer of *Black Mist* from Caliber Press.

Past comics titles and related projects: *Negative Burn: An Anthology* — Associate Editor.

Favorite comics not worked on: *Deadface, Grendel, Miracleman, Enigma,* and *Adventures of Luther Arkwright.*

Dream comic-book project: To work on a painted hardcover graphic novel involving my own creation.

Joe Pruett

✳ **Joe Pruett.** P.O. Box 672162, Marietta, Georgia 30067-0037.

Born: January 8, 1966, in Valdosta, Georgia.

College or other education: English degree from the University of Georgia.

Comics-related education: Assistant to Bob Burden on *Flaming Carrot Comics* since 1989 (still do in my spare time, because it's fun).

Biggest creative influences: Bob Burden, Alan Moore, Dan Simmons, William Faulkner, Frank Miller, and Dave Sim.

1993 projects: *Kilroy Is Here* (writer/creator) and *Negative Burn: An Anthology* (co-editor) — both from Caliber Press; *Flaming Carrot* from Dark Horse.

Past comics titles and related projects: *Flaming Carrot Comics* (#21-29) from Dark Horse; *Calibrations* #1 from Caliber Press.

Favorite comics not worked on: *Cerebus, Shade, the Changing Man, Bone, Baker Street, Sandman, Concrete,* and *Love and Rockets.*

Dream comic-book project: My own self-published graphic novel illustrated by Brian Bolland.

Brian Pulido

✳ **Brian Pulido.** 11333 Moorpark Street, Suite #147, Toluca Lake, California 91602.

Born: November 30, 1961, in Newark, New Jersey.

College or other education: B.F.A., New York University-Film School.

Comics-related education: I work as assistant director for commercials and music videos. I am constantly exposed to storyboards.

Biggest creative influences: Jack Kirby, pop culture, music, and Frank Miller.

1993 projects: *Evil Ernie: The Resurrection* (May) for Chaos! Comics. *Rack and Pain,* four-issue mini-series for Dark Horse (September). *The Crawler,* one-shot for Dark Horse. *Detonator,* revisionist super-hero one-shot for Dark Horse (late '93). *Lady Death* micro-series. Interviews for Buffalo Books' *Comic Talk* (includes Erik Larsen and Sam Kieth).

Past comics titles and related projects: *Evil Ernie,* five-issue mini-series from Malibu. Music videos for Queensryche, Kiss, Heavy D, C and C Music Factory. Commercials for Coca Cola, Sprite, and Volkswagen, among others. Movies: *Bright Lights, Big City, Batteries Not Included*, and *Big Business*, among others.

Favorite comics not worked on: *Incredible Hulk, Marshal Law, X-O Manowar*, Dark Horse titles, *Lobo*, and *Spawn*.

Dream comic-book project: *The Fantastic Four* with Jack Kirby or *Iron Man*.

✱ **Deborah Purcell.** 222 East 80th Street, #12D, New York, New York 10021.

Born: December 14, 1952, in New Rochelle, New York.

College or other education: Cornell University, 1974, B.S.

Biggest creative influences: Classic and contemporary novelists and short story writers and many film genres.

1993 projects: Defiant Comics Universe, including *Plasm*.

Dream comic-book project: Exactly what I'm involved in now.

Gordon Purcell

✱ **Gordon Purcell.** c/o College of Comic Book Knowledge, 3151 Hennepin Avenue South, Minneapolis, Minnesota 55408.

Born: February 14, 1959, in Traverse City, Michigan. Raised in Antigo, Wisconsin.

College or other education: B.A.'s in Theatre and Studio Arts, University of Minnesota/ Twin Cities, 1983.

Comics-related education: School of hard knocks? Seriously, good advice from many people including Dan Jurgens, Greg Guler, and Fabian Nicieza.

Biggest creative influences: John Buscema, Neal Adams, Garcia-Lopez, Giordano, Ordway, Chuck Jones, and the movies.

1993 projects: *Mad Dog* #1-6 (Marvel), *Avengers* #362, *Wonder Man Annual* #2 (Marvel), *Star Trek Annual* # 4 (DC), *Star Trek: Deep Space Nine* #1 and 2 (Malibu), *Young Indiana Jones* #11 and 12 (Dark Horse). That takes me to May . . .

Past comics titles and related projects: *Star Trek* (three years' worth at DC), also *Flash* and *Gammarauders, War of the Gods* #4, and various fill-ins for DC. *Wonder Man* #12, *Cage* #11 (Marvel). *Young Indiana Jones* # 7 and 8 (Dark Horse). Plus work for Hero, Slave Labor (stories), First, Americomics, and three cartoons for *CBG*.

Favorite comics not worked on: *New Titans* and *Superman* (DC). *Incredible Hulk, Sensational She-Hulk*, and *Spider-Man 2099* (Marvel). *Next Men, WildC.A.T.S, Nexus*, and *Calvin and Hobbes.*

Dream comic-book project: I love superhero group books like *New Titans, Justice League America*, or the *Avengers*. Also, I really like Elongated Man and The Beast.

✱ **Joe Quesada.** c/o Laurie Bradach, 1340 West Irving Park Road, #222, Chicago, Illinois 60613.

Agent: Laurie Bradach.

Born: January 12, 1962, in New York City.

College or other education: School of Visual Arts.

Biggest creative influences: Miller, Mignola, Mazzucchelli, Toth, and Raymond.

1993 projects: *X-Factor* (monthly), *X-O Manowar* #0, Image/Valiant crossover, cover and costume design for *Batman* #500.

Past comics titles and related projects: *Batman: Sword of Azrael, X-Factor Annual* #8, and *The Ray*.

Favorite comics not worked on: *Sin City, Watchmen, Dark Knight Returns, V for Vendetta*, and *Miracleman*.

Dream comic-book project: Anything with Frank Miller, Alan Moore, or Neil Gaiman.

Ed Quinby

✳ Ed Quinby. 497 Leo Drive, Tallahassee, Florida 32310.

Born: December 15, 1952, in Orlando, Florida.

College or other education: B.F.A. from University of Florida.

Comics-related education: Same as above and, of course, high-school newspaper artist. Brief stint in proofreading.

Biggest creative influences: Wally Wood, Gene Colan, Steve Ditko, Al Williamson, and Steve Rude.

1993 projects: Eight-page story for Parody Press, 11-page story for Heroic Publishing, four-page story for Comic Zone, all just art; and a five-page science-fiction story, no publisher yet, art and story.

Past comics titles and related projects: Comic Zone Productions: *The Zodiac Detroit Child Murders* and various single-page illustrations, just art. Miller Publishing: *A Trip in Time, Cross of Ages*, art and story; also cover and two single-page illustrations. Eclectus Publishing: *Airlock #1, Have It Your Way*, art and story, one-page story and back cover. Malibu Graphics: *Scum of the Earth*, three covers.

Favorite comics not worked on: *Concrete, Nexus, Sandman, Hellblazer, Doom Patrol, Legion of Super-Heroes*, and *Mr. Monster*.

Dream comic-book project: To take a title I enjoyed as a kid (*Spider-Man, Fantastic Four, Green Lantern*, etc.) and, by virtue of hard work and three times the talent I now possess, bring it to a new Golden Age. Well, it's a dream, y'know.

✳ David Quinn. 101 North Wallace, Ypsilanti, Michigan 48197.

Agent: Star*Reach Productions (Sharon Cho).

Born: December 14, 1959, in Fort Wayne, Indiana.

College or other education: Amherst College, B.A., 1982. Brooklyn College, CUNY, M.F.A.

Comics-related education: Associate Publisher, Freelance for Rebel Studios; that's education the hard way.

Biggest creative influences: Eisner and Feiffer, Lee and Kirby, plus playwrights O'Neill and (August) Wilson.

1993 projects: *One Life, One Stand, Nightvision, Cain, Wet Metal Suites, The Dick*, and *Metamythics*, plus an Image project to be announced.

Past comics titles and related projects: *Omen, Faust, Utterly Strange Stories, Freedom Project, I Am the Public*, Fast Forward's "Arona", *Green Lantern Corps Quarterly, Two Guys in Hell, Raw Media Mags, This Year's Girl*, and the ongoing column *Writing at the Edge* in *Wizard*.

Favorite comics not worked on: *Doom Patrol, Grendel, The Spirit, Krazy Kat*, and vintage *Fantastic Four*.

Dream comic-book project: My kid's book *Speedogs*, sigh, someday.

✳ Keith Quinn. Brainstorm Comics, 457 Main Street, Suite 162, Farmingdale, New York 11735.

Born: August 28, 1966, in Bayshore, New York.

College or other education: SUNY at Buffalo, Illustration.

Biggest creative influences: Matt Wagner, Wendy and Richard Pini, Alan Davis, John Byrne, George Pérez, and Bill Willingham.

1993 projects: *Heroes Incorporated* and *Funny Animals out for Blood.*

Past comics titles and related projects: Personality Comics, Spoof Comics (including *Bloodskirt* and *Spiderfemme 2088*).

Favorite comics not worked on: *Legion of Super-Heroes, Excalibur, Grendel: War Child,* and *Sam and Max.*

Dream comic-book project: A *Legion of Substitute Heroes* series.

✳ **Dan Raga.** 5129 Wilcox Road, Whitesboro, New York 13492, or Allied Comics, 180 South Girard Street, Utica, New York 13501.

Born: September 23, 1963, in Utica, New York.

Biggest creative influences: All those cheesy monster movie matinee chiller theatre shows watched during my youth.

1993 projects: *Tales from the Balcony*, a bimonthly terror anthology.

Favorite comics not worked on: *Animal Man, Sandman,* and *Zot!.*

Dream comic-book project: A line of children's (young adult) comics that are on the same "level" with kids (young adults), not looking down at them.

✳ **Rich Rainey.** c/o *CBG* Editorial Department, 700 East State Street, Iola, Wisconsin 54990.

College or other education: SUNY at Plattsburgh, B.S.

Comics-related education: Worked as creator/contributor to several adventure novel series. Translates well to comics.

Biggest creative influences: C.S. Lewis, Kenneth Patchen, John Keel, Moore, Miller, and manga.

1993 projects: 1. Several issues of *The Punisher*. 2. *Flesh Crawlers* mini-series for Kitchen Sink. 3. Developing comics adaptation of *The 4th Tower of Inverness* radio series.

Past comics titles and related projects: I've written several *Executioner* novels which seem to have high recognition in the comics field and helped me land *Punisher* writing assignments, about a year's worth so far.

Favorite comics not worked on: *Flaming Carrot, Nick Fury, Wonder Woman, The Creeper, Iron Man, Daredevil,* and *Deathlok.*

Dream comic-book project: Ongoing series of *The 4th Tower of Inverness/Adventures of Jack Flanders.*

David Rawson

✳ **David Rawson.** c/o *CBG* Editorial Department, 700 East State Street, Iola, Wisconsin 54990.

Agent: Star*Reach.

Born: September 24, 1949, in Los Angeles (Windsor Hills), California.

College or other education: A variety of college study related to Electronic Engineering, Computer Science, Communications, and Media. Edited an alternative collegiate newspaper. Prepared coursework material for undergraduate and graduate studies programs. Communications consultant for local municipalities.

Biggest creative influences: From the late

'60s to the early '80s, I voluntarily spent my time and resources dealing with folks outside the "system" who needed shelter, crisis intervention, or hard-drug counseling. These experiences are inseparable from my creative well-spring. The following are also seminal for me: Henry Miller's *Tropic of Capricorn*, Esdras' curtain speech in Maxwell Anderson's *Winterset*, Charles Bukowski, Eugene O'Neill's interlocked character's psychology in *Long Day's Journey into Night*, Joseph Heller's *Catch-22*, Susan Keller's concepts of the "Strategic Elite," Gregory Bateson's *Ecology and Flexibility in Urban Civilization* from his *Steps to an Ecology of Mind*, Viktor Frankl's *Man's Search for Meaning*, the Sanskrit game of Leeja as explained in the commentaries of Harish Johari, G. Spencer Brown's existential calculus from *Laws of Form*, Dane Rudhyar's comprehensive Jungian system of interactive symbolism, Dreyfus' system of cross-cultural meta-glyphs, the socio-politico syllogisms of Thomas Szaz and R.D. Laing, Salvador Dali, the slo-mo dance of converging technologies, the reminder of self that comes from an errant hammer blow to one's thumb, and Solomon's injunction to above all be celebratory and awed.

1993 projects: As of March 28, 1993, projects include: *Chiaroscuro*, a multi-part Vertigo limited series about Leonardo da Vinci edited by Karen Berger. *Fighting American*, a six-part mini-series of Simon and Kirby's "epic tales of idiocy and intrigue." *Indiana Jones and the Golden Fleece*, a two-parter for Dark Horse. *Heat Wave*, a 24-page J'onn J'onzz story for *Justice League Quarterly*. It is about the church bombings in 1963 Alabama. *Home Work*, a 14-page Donald Duck story commissioned by the German affiliate of Egmont Publishing. This was in response to the Rostock riots and deals with issues of bigotry and racism. *On the Ball*, a 16-page Donald Duck and Mickey Mouse story for Egmont Publishing. This is the first time in almost a half century these two characters have been paired in the same story. *Fluffy's Back*, a 24-page story for the black-and-white anthology, *Wiindows*, for Cult Press. *A Collector, a Cobbler, a Bright and Yellow Ocher*, a 12-page Scrooge McDuck story for Egmont Publishing. *Clean Sweep*, a 10-page Mickey Mouse story for

Egmont Publishing. *Bugs, the Magician*, an eight-page Bugs and Daffy story for Warner Brothers International.

Past comics titles and related projects: A dozen Donald Duck (including a 129-page epic) or Scrooge McDuck scripts for Egmont Publishing; four *Justice League Quarterly* scripts for DC; three *Black Hood* scripts and three *Comet* plots for DC/Impact; a *Tarzan* script for Semic/Malibu; and a *Sebastian the Crab* script for Disney.

Favorite comics not worked on: *A1, Cerebus, Cheval Noir, Dirty Plotte, Eightball, From Hell, Grendel, Groo, Hate, Heavy Metal, Love and Rockets, Omaha, Sandman, Taboo, Usagi Yojimbo, Vietnam Journal*, and *Yummy Fur*.

Dream comic-book project: Probably *Tales from Regent Street*, stories from my experience of the coffee house/crisis intervention scene of the Los Angeles/Inglewood area from the late '60s to mid-'70s.

Barb Rausch

✳ **Barb Rausch.** c/o Star*Reach — Sharon Cho, P.O. Box 2328, Berkeley, California 94702.
Agent: Star*Reach (Sharon Cho).
Born: June 7, 1941, in Indianapolis, Indiana.
College or other education: B.A., Art Education, MSU, 1963. M.A., Art, MSU, 1967.
Comics-related education: Storyboard apprentice, Marvel Animation, 1985; Assistant, Chaykin Studio, 1989.

Biggest creative influences: Bill Woggon, Arn Saba, Romeo Tanghal, Howard Chaykin, Mike Vosburg, and Donna Barr.

1993 projects: Regular penciller on various issues of *Barbie* and *Barbie Fashion* for Marvel.

Past comics titles and related projects: *Neil the Horse Comics and Stories, Cutey Bunny, California Girls, Vicki Valentine, Jem* (animation), *The Scorpio Connection, Wonder Woman Annual* #2, *Cloak and Dagger, Wimmen's Comix, Renegade Romance, The Desert Peach, Barbie, Barbie Fashion, Strip AIDS, Images of Omaha* (Reed Waller benefit comic book).

Favorite comics not worked on: Kitchen Sink's *Li'l Abner* reprints and *Naughty Bits*.

Dream comic-book project: A historical romance with lots of adventure and fabulous costumes.

✳ **James Reddington.** c/o Steve Donnelly, 106 South B Street, San Mateo, California 94401.

Agent: Steve Donnelly.

Born: November 29, in New York City.

Biggest creative influences: Life, Bob Peak, Bernard Fuchs, Mark English, life, Alphonse Mucha, Winsor McCay, Norman Rockwell, and life.

1993 projects: *Hey, Kids! It's Satan!, The Warren Report*, and illustrating stories written by Joe Lansdale, Doug Wheeler, and Phil Nutman.

Past comics titles and related projects: Short stories for Pacific Comics, *House of Mystery, Avengers, West Coast Avengers.* Cover designs for DC, covers for Charlton reprints, *Who's Who, Who's Who in Star Trek, Marvel Handbook, Marvel Comics Presents, April Horrors, Sleepwalker, Punisher, Cracked*, the ill-fated super-hero line from Blackthorne, *Jonny Quest*, the ill-fated revival of the Archie super-hero line from Archie, and the ill-fated line of comics from TSR.

Favorite comics not worked on: *Sandman, Spawn, Magnus*, and *Shadow*.

Dream comic-book project: Drawing stories by Raymond Chandler and Mickey Spillane.

✳ **Daniel A. Reed.** Blazer Studios Inc., 101 West 12th Street, #4G, New York, New York 10011.

Born: January 26, 1960, in Springfield, Massachusetts.

College or other education: Miami Dade Community College (full scholarship). However, I am mostly self-taught through books on anatomy and perspective, history, and art history (and how they interrelate), logic, and advancements in the thought processes of mankind.

Comics-related education: Internship with C.C. Beck. Lessons from Bob McLeod on inking and Mike Zeck on pencilling. Having my work published by *Charlston Bullseye* and in *Megaton* #1 and seeing how my early work looked in print was a whole education in itself.

Biggest creative influences: Jack Kirby, Arthur C. Clarke, Robert Rauschenberg, Moebius, Stan Lee, movies, animation, and man's exploration of space.

1993 projects: Blazer Studios Inc.'s production of *New World Order.* Cover for *Berzerker* #3. Reprint of earlier work from *Megaton* #1 in *Berzerker* #1. Five-page story in *This Is Sick* #3.

Past comics titles and related projects: *Charlton Bullseye, What If?, Indiana Jones, Transformers* (both American and British), *Incredible Hulk, Incredible Hulk Annual, Marvel Comics Presents, Punisher* magazine, *House of Mystery, Forgotten Realms TSR Annual, TSR Worlds Annual, Alpha Flight, Rebels* (Paris), *Megaton, Berzerker, Fun Comics* (AC), *Amazing Heroes, El Hombre Mosca* (Central and South America), *Official Handbook of the Marvel Universe*, four-page strip, *Vision*, and 11-page strip, *Subatomica*, for Miami-Dade newspaper.

Favorite comics not worked on: *Grendel*.

Dream comic-book project: I'm working on my dream project. I have always wanted to write, ink, pencil, and letter my own work and treat it like the true art form it is.

✳ **Wayne R. Reid.** 2003 Farm Street, Henderson, North Carolina 27536.

Born: May 4, 1937, in Henderson, North Carolina.

Biggest creative influences: Frank Frazetta, Al Williamson, Alex Raymond, Norman Rockwell, and Louis S. Glanzman.

1993 projects: Lovecraft adaptation by Ste-

Wayne R. Reid

ven Jones for Caliber; *True Crime Stories* for Comic Zone; perhaps a series for Cult Press, still in the discussion stage.

Past comics titles and related projects: *Man from U.N.C.L.E.*, Entertainment Pub. *Werewolf*, Blackthorne. *Gringo, El Cid, Zulunation, Camelot Eternal, Sinergy*, Caliber. *M.C. Hammer, David Robinson, Michael Jordan*, various others for Personality. *Psycho Killers*, various issues for Comic Zone. *Airlock*, Eclectus. *Wiindows*, Cult Press.

Favorite comics not worked on: Any full painted graphic novel with a good story.

Dream comic-book project: Fully-painted concept of anything by James Fenimore Cooper or Robert Louis Stevenson.

✸ **Bill Reinhold.** 2030 Harrison Street, Evanston, Illinois 60201.

Born: March 18, 1955, in Chicago, Illinois.

College or other education: Three-year attendance at The American Academy of Art, Chicago, Graphic Arts Associate Degree, 1982.

Biggest creative influences: Artistic: Jack Kirby, Gil Kane, Steve Ditko, Alex Toth, Andrew Loomis, Joe Kubert, Ruben Pellejero, Jordi Bernit, and José Ortiz.

1993 projects: Penciller and inker/co-creator of *Spyke* mini-series for Epic, inking Adam Kubert on *Spirits of Vengeance* for Marvel, working on the Punisher bookshelf, *The Empty Quarter*, pencils and inks for Marvel.

Past comics titles and related projects: 1981: *Justice Machine*, Noble Comics. 1984-1988: *The Badger*, First Comics. 1988-1990: *Punisher*, 12 monthly issues, *Annual #*2, and Punisher graphic novel, *Intruder*, Marvel Comics. 1991: Clive Barker's *Hellraiser #*7, Epic Comics and Silver Surfer graphic novel: *Homecoming*.

Favorite comics not worked on: *Torpedo, Tor, Nexus, Corto Maltese, Sin City, Death: The High Cost of Living, Unsupervised Existence*, and *Sinner*. Favorite characters: Batman, Spider-Man, Hulk, Iron Man, Green Lantern, and Daredevil.

Dream comic-book project: Stories based on experiences and people in my life.

✸ **Steve Remen.** 169 Park Row South, Hamilton, Ontario, Canada L8H 4E9.

Born: November 17, 1969, in Hamilton, Ontario, Canada.

College or other education: Animation diploma (Sheridan College).

Biggest creative influences: Dave Sim, Steve Ditko, Woody Allen, and Groucho Marx.

1993 projects: *Tales of Lethargy*, three-issue mini-series for Alpha Productions. *Him* from Lethargic Comics, published by Alpha Productions, as well.

Past comics titles and related projects: *Him*, strip from *Lethargic Comics, Weakly*, published by Lethargic Comics.

Favorite comics not worked on: *Cerebus, Milk and Cheese, Nexus, Justice Society of America, Justice League*, and *Legionnaires*.

Dream comic-book project: A monthly title devoted to *Him* from Lethargic Comics.

✸ **Kay Reynolds.** 3719 Granby Street, C-4, Norfolk, Virginia 23504.

Agent: Sharon Jarvis (Toad Hall Inc.).

Born: January 6, 1951, in Norfolk, Virginia.

College or other education: Four years of college, no degree, English History, Art History major, Library Science minor.

Comics-related education: Went from fandom into using business and education history to become (eventually) Senior Editor at Donning for Starblaze Editions/Graphics.

Biggest creative influences: Charles Dick-

Kay Reynolds

ens, Rudyard Kipling, Fritz Leiber, Sam Delany, Aubrey Beardsley, and pre-Raphaelites.

1993 projects: Who knows right now? There's stuff going on, but since the contracts aren't signed, I can't really talk about them.

Past comics titles and related projects: Editor and marketing for *Elfquest* color volumes. Initiated sale of graphic novel into major chain bookstores and distributors including Waldenbooks, B. Dalton, and Ingrams. Developed and implemented graphic novel line for Starblaze Graphics including *Myth Adventures, Thieves World, Elfquest, Duncan and Mallory,* etc. Wrote graphic novel *Fortune's Friends, Hell Week.* Wrote and edited *Robotech Art I* and *Robotech Art II.* Currently negotiating contract with Transylvania Press for limited edition of my novel, *American Vampire,* to feature comic illustrators. Also initiated concept of comic artists as illustrators for novels including Phil Foglio, P. Craig Russell, Michael Kaluta, and Charles Vess.

Favorite comics not worked on: *Sandman.*

Dream comic-book project: Honestly? I'd like to work on translations and marketing of some of my favorite Japanese comics — the ones that are *not* being done. Would like to market projects I like to the general public.

✱ **Mike Richardson.** Dark Horse Comics, 10956 SE Main, Milwaukie, Oregon 97222.

Born: June 29, 1950, in Portland, Oregon.

College or other education: B.S. in Art, Portland State University.

Biggest creative influences: Kirby, Ditko, Frazetta, Harryhausen, Hitchcock, etc.

1993 projects: *Comics' Greatest World* and *Aliens.*

Past comics titles and related projects: Comics: *Aliens, Wacky, Boris the Bear,* others — *The Mark, Godzilla.* Movies: *Dr. Giggles* and *Time Cop.*

Favorite comics not worked on: *Hate, Sin City, Kings in Disguise, Concrete, Next Men,* and others.

Dream comic-book project: *Tarzan* with Frazetta.

Tom Richmond

✱ **Tom Richmond.** 13872 Alabama Avenue South, Savage, Minnesota 55378.

Born: May 4, 1966, in La Crosse, Wisconsin.

College or other education: B.F.A., Illustration major, School of the Associated Arts, St. Paul, Minnesota.

Biggest creative influences: Jack Davis, Mort Drucker, Wally Wood, and Hilary Barta.

1993 projects: *Married with Children 2099* mini-series; *Ralph Snart* short stories; assorted covers for Now Comics (pencils, some inks).

Past comics titles and related projects: Now's regular *Married with Children* title (pencils and covers); *Mr. Lizard 3-D* cover, specialize in caricature.

Favorite comics not worked on: *Incredible Hulk, Archer and Armstrong, Sandman,* and *Miracleman.*

Dream comic-book project: *The Batman Adventures,* DC Comics.

✳ **John Ridgway.** 1 Taunton Drive, Farnworth, Bolton, Manchester, United Kingdom.

Born: May 4, 1940, in Swinton, Manchester, United Kingdom.

College or other education: Mechanical Engineering.

Biggest creative influences: Frank Hampson, Hal Foster, and Burne Hogarth.

1993 projects: *Chiller,* a two-part series for Epic. *Prince Valiant,* a four-part series for Marvel.

Past comics titles and related projects: *Doctor Who, Commando War Stories, Transformers, Incredible Hulk, Solomon Kane, Luke Kirby, Judge Dredd, Hellblazer, My Name Is Chaos, Marvelman, Harsh Realm* (inking), *Punisher,* and *Dan Dare.*

Favorite comics not worked on: *Tarzan,* Malibu. *Twin Earths.*

Dream comic-book project: *Prince Valiant* and a decent version of *Dan Dare.*

✳ **Leonard Rifas.** EduComics, Box 45381, Seattle, Washington 98145-0831.

Born: April 16, 1951, in Washington, D.C.

College or other education: B.A., Philosophy, 1973, University of California-Berkeley; M.A., Communications, 1991, University of Washington-Seattle; currently in doctoral program, School of Communications, University of Washington-Seattle.

Comics-related education: Assistant Editor, Kitchen Sink, 1978.

Biggest creative influences: Underground comix.

1993 projects: Graphic introduction to *Critical Thinking,* comic-strip biographies of Antonio

Gramsci, Walter Benjamin, Roland Barthes, Stuart Hall, Michel Foucault, etc., for a local arts paper.

Past comics titles and related projects: *AIDS News, Itchy Planet, Food First Comics, Food Comics, All-Atomic Comics, Energy Comics, Corporate Crime Comics,* publisher of Keiji Nakazawa's *I Saw It* and *Gen of Hiroshima.*

Favorite comics not worked on: Small-circulation comics in general.

Trina Robbins

✳ **Trina Robbins.** 1982 15th Street, San Francisco, California 94114.

Born: Born in Brooklyn, New York.

College or other education: Two years of college, no degrees.

Biggest creative influences: The Stan Lee-written and edited teen comics of the '40s and '50s (*Patsy Walker, Millie the Model,* etc.); Will Eisner's *Spirit;* Wally Wood's E.C. fantasy and science fiction.

1993 projects: *A Century of Women Cartoonists,* history for Kitchen Sink Press; *Hawaii High,* a CD-ROM for Sanctuary Woods.

Past comics titles and related projects:
Edited and published *Choices*, a pro-choice benefit
book; co-edited *Strip AIDS USA*, an AIDS bene-
fit book; co-wrote *Women and the Comics* with Cat
Yronwode; two teen series for young girls: *Meet
Misty*, Marvel; *California Girls*, Eclipse; *The Leg-
end of Wonder Woman*, four-part mini-series for
DC; currently one of the writers and inkers for
Marvel's Barbie books.

Favorite comics not worked on: *Love and
Rockets* and *Groo*.

Dream comic-book project: A long-running
series for young girls.

✳ **Dave Roberts.** c/o *CBG* Editorial Department, 700 East State Street, Iola, Wisconsin
54990.

Born: February 20, 1960, in Wrexham,
North Wales, United Kingdom.

College or other education: University of
East Anglia, Norwich, England.

Comics-related education: None, just reading them.

Biggest creative influences: Mark Heike,
George Pérez, Alan Davis, John Byrne, Steve
Englehart, and Keith Giffen, to name but a few.

1993 projects: *Femforce* (AC Comics), pencils
for whole or part of #60-62, and #66-68 to
date. Co-plotting #62.

Past comics titles and related projects: Pencils: AC Comics: *Femforce* (1993), *Femforce: Up
Close* #1-3 (1991-92), and *Good Girl Art Quarterly* #7 (1991). Inks: Harrier Comics: *Barbarienne* #7 and 8 (1988).

Favorite comics not worked on: *Wonder
Woman, The Avengers, Justice League, Silver Surfer,*
and *Black Canary*.

Dream comic-book project: Recreating the
original Ms. Marvel (plot and pencils); I already
have the idea.

✳ **Lon Roberts.** 3078 Phipps Court, Lafayette, Indiana 47905.

Born: July 7, 1947, in Lafayette, Indiana.

College or other education: B.A., Visual
Design, Purdue University and Art Instruction
Schools, Minneapolis.

Comics-related education: Many courses
and workshops in writing, art, design, etc.

PHOTOGRAPH OF
LON ROBERTS
MARCH 1993

Biggest creative influences: Jack Davis,
Franklin Booth, Gustav Klimt, Howard Chaykin, and Pink Floyd.

1993 projects: Illustrations for short-story
projects — format similar to *Beautiful Stories for
Ugly Children* — and several experimental writ-
ing/illustration comic-style projects.

Past comics titles and related projects: Letterer for Oklahoma artist Tom Simonton. Many
projects for: Nightfall Publishing Ltd., United
Kingdom; Revolutionary Comics Press, California; Alpha Productions; Caliber Press; Whispers
Press; and Alpha-Omega APA.

Favorite comics not worked on: *Classics
Illustrated* and *Blackhawk*.

✳ **Neil A. Robertson.** 1142 Broadway, Rockford, Illinois 61104-1406.

Born: May 19, 1954, in Norman, Oklahoma.

College or other education: Began college
but was unable to complete.

Biggest creative influences: Julius Schwartz,
Piers Anthony, Rumiko Takahashi, and *Star
Trek*.

1993 projects: Regular contributor to *Rumic
America* series of comics for Japan.

Past comics titles and related projects:
Cheerleaders from Hell, one-shot from Caliber Press
(writer). *Ranma in America*, story in the magazine
of the same name published in Japan. First
American-created magazine ever sold in Japan's

comics market (writer/letterer). *Carry Me Away,* story in *Rumic America I,* a follow-up annual series to *Ranma in America* (co-plotter/letterer).

Favorite comics not worked on: *Groo, Bone, XXXenophile, Zot!, Ranma½, Maison Ikkoku, Ninja High School* (among the current titles).

Dream comic-book project: I'd love to work in the romantic/action/comedy field (commercially speaking, fat chance!).

✳ **Andrew C. Robinson.** 214 West Bolton, Apartment C, Savannah, Georgia 31401.

Born: October 9, 1970, in St. Augustine, Florida.

College or other education: B.F.A. in Illustration from Savannah College of Art and Design.

Biggest creative influences: Moebius, Egon Schiele, Gustav Klimt, Walt Simonson, Kent Williams, Paolo Eleutcri Serpieri.

1993 projects: *Kilroy's Here* and *The Chairman* in *Dark Horse Presents.*

Favorite comics not worked on: *Tank Girl, Sin City,* and *Heavy Metal.*

✳ **James Robinson.** c/o *CBG* Editorial Department, 700 East State Street, Iola, Wisconsin 54990.

Born: April 1, 1963, in Altringhan, Cheshire, England.

College or other education: Polytechnic of Central London, B.A. (honors), Filmmaking, degree.

Comics-related education: Editor Titan Books.

Biggest creative influences: Archie Goodwin, Will Eisner, Tom Waits, Alan Rudolph, Seth Morgan, R.L. Stevenson, R. Chandler, Hitchcock, P. Straub, and C. Dickens.

1993 projects: *The Golden Age, The Vigilante, Batman: Legends of the Dark Knight, Witchcraft* (3 Witches), *Grendel Tales, Bluebeard, Tales of Suspense* (Captain America and Iron Man) graphic novel, and *Firearm.*

Past comics titles and related projects: *London's Dark, Terminator: Secondary Objectives, Terminator: One Shot, Terminator: Endgame, 67*

Seconds graphic novel, and *Batman: Legends of the Dark Knight.*

Favorite comics not worked on: *Grendel,* any Frank Miller, *Sandman, Legion of Super-Heroes, Legionnaires,* Carl Barks monthly albums, *Bone,* and *Usagi Yojimbo.*

Dream comic-book project: *Captain Action.*

✳ **Scott Rockwell.** 4 Spanish Manor, Oglebay Park, Wheeling, West Virginia 26003.

Born: July 13, 1958, in Wheeling, West Virginia.

College or other education: B.S., honors, Commerical Art.

Biggest creative influences: Robert A. Heinlein, Rembrandt, Gene Wolfe, Degas, William Gibson, Will Eisner, Shakespeare, and George Carlson.

1993 projects: *Lost in Space, Quantum Leap, Dark Shadows, Nightmares on Elm Street, The Executioner,* and *On a Pale Horse.*

Past comics titles and related projects: *Cyberpunk, Mangle Tangle Tales, Hero Alliance, The Vampire Lestat, Child's Play 2 and 3, Maze Agency, Lunatic Fringe, The Colour of Magic, The Light Fantastic, Shadow of the Torturer, Freddy's Dead, Masques, On a Pale Horse,* and *Ex-Mutants.*

Favorite comics not worked on: *Sandman, Hate, Concrete,* Carl Barks and Don Rosa *Uncle Scrooge.*

Dream comic-book project: Finish adapting and coloring *Shadow of the Torturer.*

✳ **Denis Rodier.** 170 Ch. du lac Boileau Est., L'Annonciation, RR3, Quebec, Canada, J0T 1T0.

Born: June 24, 1963, in Nominingue, Quebec, Canada.

College or other education: Lionel-Grouly College (Fine Arts), Ahuntsic College (Graphic Design/Illustration).

Biggest creative influences: Jean Giraud, Hugo Pratt, Hermann, Giger, and N.C. Wyeth.

1993 projects: Superman in *Action Comics* (inks), *Hitchhiker's Guide to the Galaxy* (inks), Byron Preiss Publications, and *The Demon* (painted covers).

Past comics titles and related projects: *The*

Demon (ink on issue # 1-13 and painted covers). Art on "L.E.G.I.O.N. '67" in *L.E.G.I.O.N. '93* #50. *Arzach* portfolio (painting for the European edition, yet to be published). *Aliens* mini-comics for Dark Horse (for the Kenner toy line). *Legacy of Superman* (pencils). *Supergirl/Team Luthor Special* (pencil and ink). Various one-shots (ink): *Wonder Woman* #64, *New Gods, Sleepwalker, L.E.G.I.O.N. '93*, etc.

Favorite comics not worked on: *Lieutenant Blueberry* (Gir), *Corto Maltese* (Pratt).

Dream comic-book project: My own graphic-novel series.

✳ **Bud Rogers.** 10810 Willowmist Drive, Houston, Texas 77064.

Born: May 25, 1963, in Holyoke, Massachusetts.

Biggest creative influences: Carl Barks, Harvey Kurtzman, Chuck Jones, and Dr. Seuss.

1993 projects: *Awesomedude* comic-book series.

Past comics titles and related projects: *Awesomedude* comic strip in *Comics Buyer's Guide*. Editorial cartoons in *Comics Buyer's Guide*.

Favorite comics not worked on: *Groo, Usagi Yojimbo, Sandman, Cerebus*, and *Xenozoic Tales*.

Dream comic-book project: Working in or developing a line of humor, adventure, and/or historical Christian comics.

✳ **John S. Romita Jr.** Marvel Entertainment Group, 387 Park Avenue South, 10th Floor, New York, New York 10016.

Born: August 17, 1956, in Brooklyn, New York.

College or other education: Farmingdale University, Farmingdale, New York.

Biggest creative influences: John Romita Senior, John Buscema, Jack Kirby, Katsuhiro Otomo, Moebius, and one million illustrations from this old book in my closet.

1993 projects: Daredevil limited series (begins August 1993, finished working on it April 1991), *Uncanny X-Men* #300 and monthly, *Hearts of Darkness II*.

Past comics titles and related projects: *Punisher, Iron Man* (twice), *Daredevil, X-Men* (twice

(currently)), *Spider-Man* (twice), *Cable* limited series, and *Hearts of Darkness*.

Favorite comics not worked on: Any work by Byrne, Miller, Simonson, Chaykin, *et al*.

Dream comic-book project: Anything with my father.

Don Rosa

✳ **Don Rosa.** 9711 Dawson Hill Road, Louisville, Kentucky 40299.

Born: June 29, 1951, in Louisville, Kentucky.

College or other education: B.A. in Civil Engineering, University of Kentucky.

Biggest creative influences: Carl Barks, *Mad* magazine artists/writers, and various movie directors.

1993 projects: Writing and drawing Donald Duck and Uncle Scrooge comics. 1994-2020: (same answer).

Past comics titles and related projects: Fanzine work (free stuff): 1973-78, *The Pertwillaby Papers, Captain Kentucky*. Comic strips, Information Center, a question and answer column, various spot illustrations.

Favorite comics not worked on: *Asterix*.

Dream comic-book project: *Exactly* what I'm doing *right now*.

Scott Rosema

✳ **Scott Rosema.** c/o *CBG* Editorial Department, 700 East State Street, Iola, Wisconsin 54990.

Born: June 2, 1958, in Muskegon, Michigan.

College or other education: Kendall School of Art and Design, graduated Illustration major, Advertising minor.

Comics-related education: Self-taught. (But I've taught comics classes locally for 14 years. Brian Douglas Ahern was one of my first students. *That* was an education.)

Biggest creative influences: John Buscema, Neal Adams, Frank Frazetta, Andrew Loomis, Chuck Jones, Haddon Sundblom, Mucha, Alex Toth, and Yoshikazu Yasuhiko.

1993 projects: *The Dark Fire Saga* for *Dragon* magazine; *Tiny Toons* and *Looney Tunes* for Warner Bros.; various work for Disney; and a variety of personal projects in preparation for submission into the marketplace.

Past comics titles and related projects: Full Circle Comix: *Amazing Stories, Elecktra.* Second Generation Productions: *Errantry.* Pied Piper: *Beast Warriors of Shaolin, Power Factor, Cookie Pirates.* Big Shot Comics: *Bad Blood, Shark.* DC/Warner Bros.: *Tiny Toons, Looney Tunes.* Malibu Comics: *Airman, Thrasher, Robotech: The Sentinels, Robotech: Invid War, Ninja High School, Gigantor, Ex-Mutants, Rock It Comics.* Miscellaneous: *Bump-kin Buzz* in *CBG, Amazing Heroes, Cybersuit Arkadyne* — Ianus Pub., and Majestic Cards.

Favorite comics not worked on: *Excalibur, Nexus, Usagi Yojimbo, Green Lantern, Bone, Warlock, Superman,* and *Hulk.*

Dream comic-book project: Three of them: A comics adaptation of *Enter the Dragon*; a team book with Captain America, Black Panther, Iron Fist, and Daredevil; an ongoing *Space Ghost* series (and some personal projects too involved to list here, but give me a call, we'll talk).

Bob Rozakis

✳ **Bob Rozakis.** DC Comics, 1325 Avenue of the Americas, New York, New York 10019.

Born: April 4, 1951, in Manhattan, New York.

College or other education: B.B.A., Public Accounting, Hofstra University.

Biggest creative influences: Julius Schwartz, Ed McBain, *Hill Street Blues, M.A.S.H.,* and my 11th-grade English teacher.

1993 projects: Executive Director-Production of DC Comics.

Past comics titles and related projects: *'Mazing Man, Hero Hotline, Mister E, Superman, Batman, Robin, Batgirl, Man-Bat, Freedom Fighters, Secret Society of Super-Villains, Centurians, Superboy, Dial "H" for Hero, Air Wave, Aquaman, Atom, DC Comics Presents, Hawkman, Weird War Tales, Krypto, Superbaby, Teen Titans* (and a lot more I don't remember).

Favorite comics not worked on: *Justice League* (the original version).

Dream comic-book project: Years and years of *'Mazing Man*.

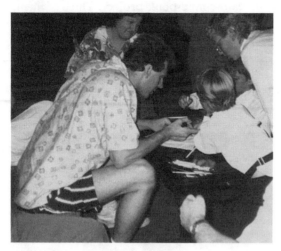

Steve Rude

✳ **Steve Rude.** c/o *CBG* Editorial Department, 700 East State Street, Iola, Wisconsin 54990.

Born: December 31, 1956, in Madison, Wisconsin.

College or other education: Milwaukee School of Art, two years. Madison Area Technical College, three years. University of Wisconsin in Madison, three semesters. Pas. Art Center, one semester. Art Institute of California, currently.

Biggest creative influences: Jack Kirby, Paul Gulacy, and Alex Raymond.

1993 projects: New *Nexus* mini-series.

Past comics titles and related projects: *Mr. Miracle*, *Space Ghost*, *Nexus/Next Nexus* mini-series, *World's Finest*, *Surge* mini-series, and *Teen Titans*.

Favorite comics not worked on: Related, *Nexus* as an animated cartoon. Have been working on selling it as a prime-time show.

Dream comic-book project: I've been doing it for 12 years. The best is yet to come.

✳ **P. Craig Russell.** c/o *CBG* Editorial Department, 700 East State Street, Iola, Wisconsin 54990.

Born: October 30, 1951, in Wellsville, Ohio.

1993 projects: *Sandman* #50: *Ramadan, The Young King* (an Oscar Wilde fairy tale), and "From Beyond" (story in Tundra's *The Illustrated H.P. Lovecraft*, scheduled for fall).

Past comics titles and related projects: Worked on *Amazing Adventures' Killraven/War of the Worlds* series, Marvel Comics, 1974-76. *Doctor Strange Annual* #1, Marvel Comics, 1976. *Parsifal* in *Star*Reach Magazine* #8 and #10 and later collected separately by Star*Reach, 1978. *The Avatar and the Chimera* in *Imagine* #2 and 3, 1978. Works in *Epic Illustrated* including *Siegfried and the Dragon*, 1980, *Isolation and Illusion*, 1981, *Elric — While the Gods Laugh*, 1982, and *Ein Heldentraum (A Hero's Dream)*, 1985. *The Chimera*, Eclipse, 1982. *Elric — The Dreaming City* graphic novel, Marvel Comics, 1982. *Killraven, Warrior of the Worlds* graphic novel, Marvel Comics, 1983. Work in *National Lampoon* including *King of the Castle*, 1983. Adaptations of various opera pieces in *Night Music*, Eclipse Comics, 1984-88. *Pelleas and Melisande*, two-issue adaptation of Debussy's opera based on Maurice Maeterlinck's play, Eclipse, 1985. *Elric of Melnibone* limited hardcover, Graphitti Designs, 1986. *Ariane and Bluebeard*, Eclipse, 1989. Clive Barker's *Tapping the Vein Book One*, Eclipse, 1989. *The Magic Flute*, Eclipse, 1990. *P. Craig Russell's Book of the Opera*, Eclipse, 1990. *Within Our Reach: Gift of the Magi*, Star*Reach Productions, 1991. *Tom Swift 3000* (unpublished, released as *Robin 3000* by DC Comics, 1992). *Ray Bradbury Chronicles* Volume 1: *The Golden Apples of the Sun*, Bantam Spectra Books, 1992. *The Fairy Tales of Oscar Wilde*, NBM Publishing, 1992. *A Voyage to the Moon*, Marvel/Epic, 1992 (currently unpublished). *Batman: Legends of the Dark Knight: Hothouse*, a two-part story published by DC Comics, 1992.

✳ **Scott Saavedra.** 19411 San Marcos Road, Saratoga, California 95070.

Born: February 4, 1960, in Los Angeles, California.

Biggest creative influences: Harvey Kurtzman, Jack Kirby, Jack Cole, Jack Benny, Ernie Kovacs, the Macintosh computer, and my Dad.

1993 projects: *Dr. Radium, Man of Science; Java Town*, both for Slave Labor.

Scott Saavedra

Past comics titles and related projects: *Chip 'n' Dale Rescue Rangers, Goofy Adventures*, and *Roger Rabbit's Toontown*, Disney Comics. *Epic Lite*, Marvel/Epic. *Twisted Tales*, Eclipse. *Graphic Story Monthly*, Fantagraphics. *It's Science with Dr. Radium*, Slave Labor Graphics.

Agent: John Gertz Productions.

Born: 1947, in Vancouver, Canada.

Biggest creative influences: Carl Barks, all Disney work; Milton Caniff, early newspaper strips; also, musical theatre and jazz/slow dance, especially Fred Astaire.

1993 projects: (Guess what?) *Neil the Horse* graphic novel (to be published late 1993) and a *Neil the Horse* musical comedy for stage, to be produced December 1993 in San Francisco at Theatre on the Square (writing book, music, and lyrics).

Past comics titles and related projects: Mostly *Neil the Horse* newspaper strips and comics since 1975. The *Neil the Horse* comic from Aardvark-Vanaheim and Renegade was published 1983-1988. Have been doing *Neil* animation development and occasional comics since then. Also have done my *Eureka Street* stories in a few places. Did comics-related journalism and radio in Canada, 1977-1983. Have continued to work in music and musical theatre.

Favorite comics not worked on: Barks!, Stan Lynde, *Modesty Blaise*, Terry LaBan, Crumb!!!, Alison Bechdel, Trina Robbins, lots more, I forget!

Dream comic-book project: Endless series of *Neil* graphic novels, with my original songs, and a CD enclosed (of the music).

Arn Saba

✳ **Arn Saba.** 484 Lake Park Avenue, #374, Oakland, California 94610.

Stan Sakai

✳ **Stan Sakai.** c/o *CBG* Editorial Department, 700 East State Street, Iola, Wisconsin 54990.

Agent: Mirage Licensing.

Born: May 25, 1953, in Kyoto, Japan.

College or other education: University of Hawaii, B.F.A. Art Center College of Design.

Biggest creative influences: Steve Ditko, Sergio Aragonés, and Akira Kurosawa.

1993 projects: *Usagi Yojimbo* ongoing series, *Space Usagi* mini-series, short story for *Plastron Cafe* (all from Mirage).

Past comics titles and related projects: Story/art: *Albedo* #1-4 (Thoughts and Images); *Critters* (Fantagraphics); *Usagi Yojimbo* # 1-38, *Usagi Yojimbo Color Specials*, *Usagi Yojimbo* trade paperback series, *Usagi Yojimbo Summer Special* (all Fantagraphics); *Turtle Soup, Shell Shock, Space Usagi* mini-series, *Usagi Yojimbo* (all Mirage Publishing). Lettering: *Groo the Wanderer, Legend of Kamui, Spider-Man* Sunday newspaper strip.

Favorite comics not worked on: *Sandman.*

✳ **James L. Sanders III.** c/o *CBG* Editorial Department, 700 East State Street, Iola, Wisconsin 54990.

Born: May 18, 1963, in Holyoke, Massachusetts.

Biggest creative influences: Dick Dillin, Dave Cockrum, Bob McLeod, Neal Adams, and John Beatty.

1993 projects: *Spider-Man Unlimited* and *Dragonlines.*

Past comics titles and related projects: *Incredible Hulk, Sensational She-Hulk, Doom Patrol, Doctor Strange, Silver Sable, Star Force Six, Fun Comics, Sentinels of Justice,* and *Silverhawks.*

✳ **Holly M. Sanfelippo.** 5225 West Byron Avenue, Chicago, Illinois 60641.

Agent: Joseph J. Gorro.

Born: November 3, 1953, in Milwaukee, Wisconsin.

College or other education: B.F.A. and M.F.A.: University of Wisconsin.

Biggest creative influences: Elvira, Olivia de Berardinis, Vargas, Avedon, and Diane Arbus.

1993 projects: *Green Hornet, Married with Children, Twilight Zone,* and *Ralph Snart.*

Past comics titles and related projects: *Re-Animator, Monolith, Mr. T and the T-Force, Green*

Holly M. Sanfelippo

Hornet, Little Monsters, Racer X, Speed Racer, The Real Ghostbusters, Terminator, Leatherface, Fright Night, Bats, Cats and Cadillacs, Slimer, Alias, and *Ralph Snart.*

Favorite comics not worked on: *Big Black Kiss.*

Dream comic-book project: Handpainting and airbrushing Olivia/Vargas-type females in exotic and seductive costumes.

✳ **Jay Allen Sanford.** 6948 Amherst Street, San Diego, California 92115.

Born: February 18, 1960, on the third planet from the Sun.

Comics-related education: Ran retail comics shop at 16 years old, worked in distribution and production for Pacific Comics and Diamond Comics Distributing, managed retail comics shop in San Diego, freelance writer for various comic and non-comic projects.

Biggest creative influences: Arthur Conan Doyle, Rod Serling, George Clayton Johnson, Alan Moore, Mark Twain, and Alan Dean Foster.

1993 projects: *Deepest Dimension,* terror anthology with George Clayton Johnson; *Woodring,* horror-based character series; *Heavy Metal*

Monsters for Ray Zone Productions; *Cult TV* series for Comic Zone; and upcoming titles from Heroic Publishing.

Past comics titles and related projects: *UFO and Alien Encounters* and *Cult TV* for Comic Zone. More than 50 issues of *Rock 'n' Roll Comics, Hard Rock Comics, Contemporary Bio-Graphics, Sports Legends*, and various other titles for Revolutionary. Celebrity interviews and feature articles for magazines including *Starlog, Midnight Marquee, Filmfax, Soundwaves, In the Midnight Hour*, etc. Wrote for television anthology *Possible Dreams.*

Favorite comics not worked on: *Sandman, Beanworld, Concrete, Shade, the Changing Man, Watchmen, Swamp Thing, V for Vendetta, Vampire Lestat, Hellraiser*, and *Rip Off Comics.*

Dream comic-book project: Writer of a psychological horror series based in real world for DC, with art by Bernie Wrightson, inks by Scott Pentzer, edited by Karen Berger, and covers by Charles Vess.

✴ **Charles Santino.** c/o Jane Otte, The Otte Company, 9 Goden Street, Belmont, Massachusetts 02178.

Agent: Jane Otte.

Born: May 27, 1955, in New York City, New York.

College or other education: B.A., English/ Journalism, State University of New York at Albany, 1977.

Biggest creative influences: Ray Harryhausen, Topps' *Mars Attacks* cards, Stan Lee, and Jack Kirby.

1993 projects: *Captain Stone and the Dinosaurs* (DC Comics) (co-plotted and pencilled by Val Semeiks).

Past comics titles and related projects: *Conan the Barbarian, Savage Tales, What The--?!* (all Marvel); *Aesop's Fables* (Fantagraphics); *Toplin* (Dell/Abyss) (horror novel collaboration with Michael McDowell, author of *Beetlejuice*).

Favorite comics not worked on: *Lobo PG- 13, Guy Gardner, Spawn*, and *Hate.*

Dream comic-book project: Whatever I'm currently working on.

✴ **Kurt Schaffenberger.** 65 Regent Lane, Brick Township, New Jersey 08723.

Born: December 15, 1920, in Germany.

College or other education: Pratt Institute, Brooklyn, New York.

1993 projects: Retired.

Past comics titles and related projects: *Captain Marvel, Superman*, and *Superman Family.*

Favorite comics not worked on: Anything done by José Garcia-Lopez.

✴ **Christopher Richard Schenck.** c/o Sharon Cho, Star*Reach, 2991 Shattuck Avenue, Suite 202, Berkeley, California 94705.

Agent: Sharon Cho (Star*Reach).

Born: January 16, 1963, in Escondido, California.

College or other education: University of San Francisco (B.F.A.). Academy of Art College (San Francisco, B.F.A.).

Comics-related education: Assistant to Mark Bodé, Paul Mounts, and Val Jones.

Biggest creative influences: Mike Mignola, J.C. Leyendecker, Bernie Fuchs, Bill Watterson, and Sarah Byam.

1993 projects: *Enemy* (Dark Horse), written by Steven Grant. *Colors in Black* by Scott Tolson. Various really cool things with Sarah Byam.

Past comics titles and related projects: *Miracleman, Tarzan, Robin Hood, Miami Mice*, coloring Marvel trading cards (with Paul Mounts), *Aquaman* (with Ken Hooper). Art Director new comics group.

Favorite comics not worked on: Mignola's *Fafhrd and Gray Mouser, Batman: Year One, Xenozoic Tales* by Mark Schultz.

Dream comic-book project: Dr. Doom kills everybody and takes over the universe.

✴ **Diana Schutz.** Dark Horse Comics, 10956 SE Main Street, Milwaukie, Oregon 97222.

Born: February 1, 1955, in Montreal, Canada.

College or other education: B.F.A., 1976, Creative Writing major.

Comics-related education: Currently working on Master of Arts in Communication Studies (to be completed in 1994). M.A. thesis on female comics artists.

Diana Schutz

Biggest creative influences: Trina Robbins, Cat Yronwode, Dave Sim, Frank Miller, and Will Eisner.

1993 projects: As editor: *Grendel: War Child, Grendel Tales, 1001 Nights of Bacchus, Aliens/Predator, Batman/Grendel, The Jam*, and *American Splendor*.

Past comics titles and related projects: As contributing writer: *Born to be Wild, True North II, Robotech: The Macross Saga*. As editor: *Mage, Grendel, Jonny Quest, Rio, Ginger Fox, Robotech, The Fish Police, Justice Machine, Batman vs. Predator, Aliens vs. Predator, Aliens: Earth War, Predator: Big Game, Terminator, Billi 99, Night and the Enemy, Deadface, Moebius #0* graphic album, *The Eyeball Kid, The Secret of the Salamander, Nina's All-Time Greatest Collector's Item Classics*.

Favorite comics not worked on: *Cerebus, Love and Rockets, Tales of the Beanworld, Dirty Plotte*, and *Naughty Bits*.

Dream comic-book project: A monthly romance comic, in the vein of the old Simon and Kirby *Young Romance*.

✳ **Fred Schwab.** 411 East 53 Street, New York, New York 10022.

Born: August 25, 1920, in New York City.

Fred Schwab

College or other education: New York Art Students League.

Comics-related education: I read many books on art to learn anatomy, perspective, and color. Also books on plotting and storytelling.

Biggest creative influences: Jack Cole and I worked at adjacent desks for a year for Harry "A" Chesler. We tried to out-do each other at drawing.

1993 projects: I'm doing cartoons for several ad agencies.

Past comics titles and related projects: During the Golden Age I worked for three "shops," Funnies Inc., Harry "A" Chesler, and the Eisner and Iger shop. My work was published by Timely, DC, Fiction House, Dell, Centaur, Fox, Globe, and Columbia. Did *Lady Luck* strip for the Eisner *Spirit* section, a syndicated weekly comic section. Had four cartoon books published. The most recent was *The Last Damn Cat Book*.

Favorite comics not worked on: *Groo the Wanderer* and *Mad* magazine.

✳ **Julius Schwartz.** 80-35 Springfield Boulevard, #2N, Queens Village, New York 11427.

Born: June 19, 1915, in The Bronx, New York.

College or other education: College of the City of New York, 1936, B.S.

Photo: Beth Gwin

Julius Schwartz

Biggest creative influences: Science fiction.

Past comics titles and related projects: Started at DC Feb. 23, 1944. 1940s: *All-American Comics, Green Lantern, Flash Comics, All-Flash, All-Star Comics*, and *Comic Cavalcade*. 1950s: *All-Star Western, Western, Jimmy Wakely, Big Town, Charlie Chan, Showcase, Brave and Bold, Strange Adventures, Mystery in Space*, and *Danger Trail*. From the start of the Silver Age: *Flash, Green Lantern, Justice League of America, Hawkman*, and *Atom*. From 1964: *Batman* and *Batman Family*. From 1971: *Action, Superman, Superman Family*, and *Superman vs. Muhammad Ali* (there may be others!).

✳ **Steven T. Seagle.** 460 East Palm Avenue, Apartment A, Burbank, California 91501.

Born: March 31, 1965, in Biloxi, Mississippi.

College or other education: B.S., Advertising/Journalism, University of Colorado, 1988; M.A., Speech Communication, Ball State University.

Comics-related education: Training from reading and creative writing courses. Taught a course in popular culture with heavy comics focus.

Biggest creative influences: François Truffaut, Samuel Beckett, Alan Rudolph, Frank Miller, Ron Carlson, and my return to comics mentor James Robinson.

1993 projects: *Jack O'Lantern* (DC); *Grendel Tales* (Dark Horse); Bill Kaplan monthly (DC — currently titled *Primal Force*); *My Vagabond Days* (Dark Horse); *Captain Satan* (Millennium); and *Monthly* (Premiere).

Past comics titles and related projects: *Kafka*, 1987-88, Renegade. *The Amazon*, 1989, Comico. *Jaguar Stories*, 1990, Comico — not published. *Kafka*, 1990, Caliber. *Grafik Muzik*, 1991, Caliber — typesetting only #3 and 4. *In Thin Air*, 1992, Caliber. *Grendel* #40, 1990, Comico — *Grendel Tales* (flip comic).

Favorite comics not worked on: Eddie Campbell's work and *Eightball*.

Dream comic-book project: *Daredevil, Doom Patrol* (old and new), and any number of non-super-hero projects I can't place.

✳ **N. Blake Seals.** 818 Route 25A, Suite #107, Northport, New York 11768.

Born: July 31, 1970, in Huntington, New York.

College or other education: School of Visual Arts.

Comics-related education: Occasional assistant to Mike Esposito.

Biggest creative influences: My four cats, Bill Sienkiewicz, and Helen Frankenthaler.

1993 projects: *This Is Sick, Brain Wave Comics*, and *Zen Comics*.

Past comics titles and related projects: *Leaf, Utterly Strange, Zen, Vortex*, and *This Is Sick*.

Favorite comics not worked on: *Brought to Light, Stray Toasters*, and *Fast Forward*.

Dream comic-book project: A totally abstract, completely insane exercise in self-indulgence.

✳ **David Seidman.** 645 North Westmount Drive, #308, West Hollywood, California 90069.

Born: June 8, 1958, in Los Angeles, California.

College or other education: B.A., English, UCLA.

Comics-related education: Various courses in art criticism, illustration, comedy writing, etc.

Biggest creative influences: 1960s and 1970s DC Comics and Julius Schwartz.

1993 projects: Wrapping up the last Disney Comics.

Past comics titles and related projects: Virtually all Disney Comics (Editor and Senior Editor) including: *Chip 'n' Dale Rescue Rangers, Donald Duck Adventures, Mickey Mouse Adventures, Goofy Adventures, Roger Rabbit, Roger Rabbit's Toontown, Walt Disney's Comics and Stories, Uncle Scrooge, The Little Mermaid, Sebastian, Colossal Comics Collection*, plus the graphic novels *Aladdin, Beauty and the Beast, The Little Mermaid, Arachnophobia, Peter Pan, The Prince and the Pauper, The Jungle Book, Super Goof, The Secret Casebook*, etc.

Favorite comics not worked on: *Bone.*

Dream comic-book project: Building a massive, comprehensive graphic-novel library/study center.

✱ **Val Semeiks.** P.O. Box 315, Sand Lake, New York 12153.

Born: February 5, 1955, in Catskill, New York.

Biggest creative influences: Kirby, Hal Foster, Moebius, and Warner Bros. cartoons.

1993 projects: *Lobo Special* #1 — *Portrait of a Victim; Captain Stone and the Dinosaurs; L.E.G.I.O.N. '93* #56; and *Lobo* monthly.

Past comics titles and related projects: *King Kull* in *Savage Sword of Conan. Conan the Barbarian* (#191-200, #202-220). *Detective Comics Annual* #2. *Dr. Fate* #12. *Aesop's Fables* (Fantagraphics).

Favorite comics not worked on: *Judge Dredd, Batman, Fantastic Four, Hulk*, and *Warlock.*

Dream comic-book project: See above.

✱ **Eric Shanower.** c/o Mike Friedrich, Star*-Reach Productions, 2991 Shattuck Avenue, Suite 202, Berkeley, California 94705.

Born: October 23, 1963, in Key West, Florida.

Comics-related education: Joe Kubert School of Cartoon and Graphic Art Inc.

Biggest creative influences: L. Frank Baum, John R. Neill, Eloise McGraw, Frederick Richardson, Robert Graves, and H. Rider Haggard.

Past comics titles and related projects: DC Comics: *New Talent Showcase* #13 and 16, one page in *Who's Who* #21 (first series), *Secret Origins* #32 *(Justice League of America)* and #47, *Christmas With the Super-Heroes* #2, one entry each in the looseleaf *Who's Who* #3, 5, and 12, *Conqueror of the Barren Earth* #2-4, *Elvira's House of Mystery* #7, *Action Comics Weekly* #642, and *The Legend of Aquaman*. First Comics: *Nexus* #8-17, *The Enchanted Apples of Oz* (and advertising poster), *The Secret Island of Oz, Badger* #29, 37, *The Ice King of Oz, The Forgotten Forest of Oz, Badger Goes Berzerk* #3, *Warp* #18 and 19, *Starslayer* #25 and 26, and *Nexus Legends* #8-17 (reprinted *Nexus* #8-16). Harris Publications: *Creepy* #146. Armstrong State College Press: *The Third Book of Oz*. Eclipse: *The New Wave* #13 and *Alien Worlds*. Avalon Editions: *Polychrome, the Rainbow's Daughter* (limited to 300 copies), Comico: *Fish Police* #17. Marvel/Epic: *Marvel Comics Presents* #48, *The Elsewhere Prince* #1-6, and fashion designs for *Meet Misty* #5. Les Humanoïdes Associés: *Le Prince Impossible, Les Quatre Royaumes*, and *Le Retour du Jour* (French printings of *The Elsewhere Prince* #1-6 (two issues in each book) [also reprinted in Portugese in single issue books and in German]. Star*Reach: *Within Our Reach: Home for Christmas*. Tundra: *Legends of Arzach Gallery Two*. Dark Horse: *Dark Horse Presents* #65-67: *An Accidental Death* and *The Blue Witch of Oz*. Apple Comics: *Eagle* #18. Mayfair Games: *JLA/JLI Supplement* for *DC Heroes Roleplaying Game* (unpublished cover). Also, *Mother Goose Nursery Rhymes, Peter Pan Coloring Book* #860 and work for the PBS series *Ghostwriter*.

Dream comic-book project: My own comic in which I could write and draw all the comics I want to.

✱ **Scott Garlin Shaw!** c/o Michael Naiman, 6684 Danville Avenue, San Diego, California 92120.

Agent: Michael Naiman.

Scott Garlin Shaw!

Born: September 4, 1951, in Queens, New York.

College or other education: California Western University (1968-1970); University of California at Fullerton (1970-1972).

Comics-related education: I'm essentially self-taught.

Biggest creative influences: Jack Kirby, Gilbert Shelton, Harvey Eisenberg, Ed "Big Daddy" Roth, Dr. Seuss, Carl Barks, Harvey Kurtzman, Mort Walker, animated cartoons by Hanna-Barbera and Jay Ward, writing by Hunter S. Thompson, music by Todd Rundgren, and comedy by Ernie Kovacs and Firesign Theatre.

1993 projects: Conceiving, designing, storyboarding, laying out, and art directing animated commercials and a Yogi Bear public service announcement about skin cancer, co-writing (with Floyd Norman) a *Flintstones* giveaway comic book for Post Pebbles Cereal (published by Harvey Comics), publicizing *Oddball Comics Set One* trading cards, assembling 36 more comics for Set Two, drawing a pin-up page for the *Conservation Corps* mini-series from Archie Comics, a two-part *Pointer Toxin* back-up for *Usagi Yojimbo*, inking the cover and doing a pin-up page for *Venturat* by Manuel Carrasco, developing a promotional comic book for Burger King's Kid's Club, designing and illustrating three Hanna-Barbera album covers for Kid Rhino, and producing, directing, writing, and designing a short animated film for Rhino Records (with Mike Kazaleh).

Past comics titles and related projects:

Comic Books: Renegade: *Amusing Stories (featuring Urban Gorilla)*. Archie: *Betty and Veronica, Little Archie, The Mighty Mutanimals, Sonic the Hedgehog*, and *Teenage Mutant Ninja Turtles Meet the Conservation Corps*. Bob Sidebottom: *California Comics*. DC: *Captain Carrot and His Amazing Zoo Crew* and *Who's Who*. Marvel: *Comix Book, The Flintstones, Hanna-Barbera Spotlight, Hanna-Barbera TV Superstars, Laugh-a-lympics, What If?*, and *Yogi Bear*. Go-Go: *Creepsville*. Fantagraphics: *Critters* and *Usagi Yojimbo*. Eclipse: *Destroyer Duck* and *DNAgents*. Disney: *Donald Duck* and *Uncle Scrooge*. Kitchen Sink Press: *Fear and Laughter*. Rip Off: *Fire Sale*. Harvey: *The Flintstones, Flintstones Big Book, Giant-Size Flintstones, Giant-Size Jetsons, Giant-Size Scooby-Doo, Giant-Size Yogi Bear, Hanna-Barbera's Comics and Stories, Hanna-Barbera Big Book, Hanna-Barbera Parade, The Jetsons, Jetsons Big Book, Scooby-Doo, Scooby-Doo Big Book, Yogi Bear*, and *Yogi Bear Big Book*. Ken Krueger: *Gory Stories Quarterly*. Star*Reach: *Quack!* Dark Horse: *San Diego Comic-Con Comics*. Print Mint: *Savage Humor*. Slave Labor: *Suburban High-Life*. Comic strips: *Bugs Bunny* and *Woodsy Owl*. Animated Series: *The Adventures of Sonic the Hedgehog, The All-New Popeye Hour, Alvin and the Chipmunks, Amigo and Friends, Camp Candy, Casper and the Angels, The Completely Mental Misadventures of Ed Grimley, Cro* (aka *The Way Things Work*), *Dennis the Menace, Fantastic Max, The Flintstone Kids, The Flintstones Comedy Show, Fonz and the Happy Days Gang, Fred and Barney Meet the Thing, Garfield and Friends, The Godzilla Show, Heathcliff and the Catillac Cats, Inspector Gadget Saves Christmas Special, Jim Henson's Muppet Babies, The Kwicky Koala Show, The Little Shop, Mother Goose and Grimm* (aka *Grimmy*), *Muppets, Babies, and Monsters* (aka *Little Muppet Monsters*), *The New Fred and Barney Show, Popeye and Son, The Real Ghostbusters, The Smurfs, The Snorks, Wake, Rattle, and Roll, Wish Kid*, and *Yogi's Treasure Hunt*. [Also covers for various Rhino Records albums, cereal boxes, ads, premium illustrations, restaurant giveaways, etc. Work on many animated commercials, including several for Post.]

Favorite comics not worked on: *Kona, Monarch of Monster Isle, Tales Calculated to Drive You Bats, Star-Spangled War Stories*, early '60s gems by Jack Kirby and Stan Lee, *Fighting American, Bucky Ruckus, Uncle Scrooge, The Adventures of Bob Hope, Little Lulu, Plastic Man* (Jack Cole), *Nick Fury, Agent of S.H.I.E.L.D.* (Steranko), *Herbie, Sugar and Spike,* [and many other classic comics]. Recent/current stuff: *Groo the Wanderer, Usagi Yojimbo, Zot!, Marshal Law, The American, Watchmen, The Rocketeer, Swamp Thing, Real Stuff, Ren & Stimpy Show, Bill & Ted's Excellent Comic Book, Sam and Max, Flaming Carrot, 1963* [and many others].

Dream comic-book project: Since "dream" is the operative word here, let's shoot the moon, shall we? *Scott Shaw!'s Comics and Stories,* a showcase for me to write and draw in collaboration with all my favorite cartoon creator-pals. Any insane trillionaires out there interested in investing . . . or am I still asleep?

Stan Shaw

✳ **Stan Shaw.** 3818 South 9th, Tacoma, Washington 98405.

Born: February 13, 1962, in Fort Eustes, Virginia.

College or other education: I can make a savage pot of coffee.

Biggest creative influences: Mr. Anrud, Al Parker, Vaughn Bodé, Al Hirschfeld, Helmut Newton, and many, many more.

1993 projects: *Moses Wine* for Byron Preiss. *The Tale of the Beauty and the Beast* for Dark Horse

Comics. *Alan Bland, the Winter of Our Discontent* for Hooze.

Past comics titles and related projects: *Billy Nouten, Gay Comix #14, The Amazing Eddie Van Halen, The Rise of Stevie Ray Vaughan, Deadline, Cheval Noir, Real Stuff, Alan Bland, 2-Live Crew* comic, *Cool World,* and *Creepy.*

Favorite comics not worked on: *Grendel, I Can't Tell You Anything, Nexus,* and *Hate.*

Dream comic-book project: A good book that gets to some truth about human nature or a super-hero slug-fest.

Will Shetterly

✳ **Will Shetterly.** P.O. Box 7253, Minneapolis, Minnesota 55407.

Agent: Valerie Smith.

Born: August 22, 1955, in Columbia, South Carolina.

College or other education: Beloit College, B.A., English Literature.

Biggest creative influences: Everything I read and see is an influence. I think I'm equally affected by things I love and things I hate.

1993 projects: *Gettysburg* for Epic's *Civil War* battle books.

Past comics titles and related projects: *Captain Confederacy* (first series), SteelDragon Press. *Captain Confederacy* (second series), Epic Comics. *Open Space,* Marvel Comics.

Favorite comics not worked on: *Sandman, Love and Rockets,* and *Yummy Fur.*

Dream comic-book project: *Will Shetterly's Comics and Stories.*

✳ **Lewis Shiner.** 206 Allensworth, San Antonio, Texas 78209-6304.

Born: December 30, 1950, in Eugene, Oregon.

College or other education: B.A. in English, SMU, 1973.

1993 projects: *Adventures of Luna Goodwin* (black-and-white which I'm writing, drawing, and lettering).

Past comics titles and related projects: *Time Masters* (with Bob Wayne), DC, January-August 1990. *Wild Cards* (with others), Epic, 1990. *The Hacker Files*, DC, August 1992-July 1993.

Favorite comics not worked on: *Sandman, Love and Rockets, Concrete, Tropo, Brotherman, Hepcats,* and *Exit.*

Dream comic-book project: *Adventures of Luna Goodwin.*

James C. Shooter

✳ **James C. Shooter.** Defiant, 232 Madison Avenue, New York, New York 10016.

Born: September 27, 1951, in Pittsburgh, Pennsylvania.

Comics-related education: Worked with Mort Weisinger for five years, Murray Boltinoff and Julie Schwartz for two years, Stan Lee for seven years, and many other comics greats throughout my career.

Biggest creative influences: Mark Twain, Stan Lee, Steve Ditko, Jack Kirby, and Mort Weisinger.

1993 projects: The Defiant Universe.

Past comics titles and related projects: Superman family titles, Marvel Comics, Valiant, and the *Spider-Man* syndicated strip.

Dream comic-book project: The Defiant Universe.

✳ **Galen Showman.** Caliber Press, 621-B South Main Street, Plymouth, Michigan 48170.

Born: July 25, 1972, in Youngstown, Ohio.

Biggest creative influences: Brian Bolland, Michael Golden, Dave Stevens, Jaime Hernandez, and the E.C. artists.

1993 projects: *Sinergy* (five-issue limited series), pencils and inks. *Deadworld* (new series), inks.

Past comics titles and related projects: *Thumbscrew* (horror anthology), # 1 and #2.

Favorite comics not worked on: *Sandman, Love and Rockets, Rocketeer, Animal Man, The Actress and the Bishop* (from *A1* anthology).

Dream comic-book project: To illustrate a *Sandman* story arc.

✳ **Marc Silvestri.** c/o Cynthia Sullivan, 9974 Scripps Ranch Boulevard, #354, San Diego, California 92131.

Agent: Cynthia Sullivan.

Born: March 29, in West Palm Beach, Florida.

College or other education: High-school art classes.

Biggest creative influences: Frank Frazetta, Bernie Wrightson, John Buscema, Walt Disney, Norman Rockwell, and Howard Pyle.

1993 projects: *CyberForce,* Image-Valiant crossover, *Stryke Force,* and *Ripclaw* mini-series.

Past comics titles and related projects: *Uncanny X-Men, Wolverine, Web of Spider-Man,* and *Conan the King.*

Favorite comics not worked on: *Spawn.*

Dream comic-book project: *CyberForce — The Movie.*

✳ **Mark Simon.** P.O. Box 1754, Dover, New Jersey 07802.

Mark Simon

Born: August 24, 1959, in Baltimore, Maryland.

College or other education: Graduate, Joe Kubert School of Cartoon and Graphic Art, class of 1992.

Comics-related education: Maryland Institute College of Art, one semester, 1977. Professional Institute of Commercial Art, Baltimore, Maryland, one year night course, 1980.

Biggest creative influences: John Romita Sr., Neal Adams, John Buscema, Jack Kirby, Joe Kubert, and Dave Stevens.

1993 projects: *Equinox Chronicles* published in June 1993 by Caliber Press. Inker. First professional comics work. Full-time employee at Backes Graphics Productions which publishes, under exclusive contract to the U.S. Army, *P.S.* magazine. Letterer, penciller, and inker. This magazine was previously contracted to Will Eisner from the 1950s to the 1970s, and Murphy Anderson in 1967-68 and 1973-83.

Favorite comics not worked on: *Amazing Spider-Man*.

Dream comic-book project: My own creations.

✳ **Louise Simonson.** c/o *CBG* Editorial Department, 700 East State Street, Iola, Wisconsin 54990.

Born: September 26, 1946, in Atlanta, Georgia.

Louise Simonson

College or other education: Georgia State.

Biggest creative influences: Edward Eager and Robert Heinlein.

1993 projects: *Superman: The Man of Steel* and *Superman: Doomsday and Beyond*, juvenile novelization of the "Death of Superman" story.

Past comics titles and related projects: Senior Editor, Warren Publications. Editor at Marvel: *X-Men, Conan, Star Wars, Indiana Jones, Star Trek,* and *New Mutants*. Writer: *New Mutants, Power Pack* (co-creator), *Web of Spider-Man, X-Factor, Superman: The Man of Steel, Batman, Teen Titans, Red Sonja,* and *Star Wars* (Dark Horse).

Favorite comics not worked on: *Groo the Wanderer* and *Sin City*.

Dream comic-book project: Romance comics.

✳ **Walter Simonson.** c/o *CBG* Editorial Department, 700 East State Street, Iola, Wisconsin 54990.

Born: September 2, 1946, in Knoxville, Tennessee.

College or other education: 1968, Amherst College, B.A. 1972, Rhode Island School of Design, B.F.A.

Biggest creative influences: J.R.R. Tolkien, Jim Holdaway (artist, *Modesty Blaise*), Jack Kirby, and Jean Giraud.

1993 projects: *Jurassic Park*, Topps; *CyberForce* #0 for Image, and *Star Slammers* limited series.

Past comics titles and related projects: *Manhunter, The Metal Men, Hercules Unbound, Batman, Rampaging Hulk, Battlestar Galactica, Star Wars, Alien, Thor, X-Factor, X-Men vs. the Teen Titans, The Fantastic Four, RoboCop vs. Terminator, The Star Slammers, CyberForce, Jurassic Park*, and *The Secret City*.

Favorite comics not worked on: *Groo the Wanderer*.

Dream comic-book project: Sardonic.

Don Simpson

✳ Don Simpson. P.O. Box 44326, Pittsburgh, Pennsylvania 15205.

Born: December 3, 1961, in Garden City, Michigan.

Biggest creative influences: American and European comics, TV, movies, painting, and pogs.

1993 projects: Pogs, *1963, Savage Dragon vs. Savage Megaton Man*, pogs, *Splitting Image* #1 and 2, and Savage Pogs.

Past comics titles and related projects: *Megaton Man* (Kitchen Sink), *Border Worlds* (Kitchen Sink), *King Kong* (Fantagraphics), and *Wendy Whitebread* (Eros).

Favorite comics not worked on: Pogs.

Dream comic-book project: Pogs.

✳ Howard Simpson. P.O. Box 717, Maplewood, New Jersey 07040-9996.

Born: June 10, 1959, in Newark, New Jersey.

College or other education: Tyler School of Art (B.F.A.).

Biggest creative influences: Ernie Colon and Bob Layton.

1993 projects: *Harbinger* for Valiant, adaptation of *Snow White* movie, *Ray Bradbury Comics* for Topps, and *Deathmate* — the Valiant/Image crossover.

Past comics titles and related projects: Wrote an article for *Comics Scene. Green Lantern, Secret Origins, Who's Who, Outsiders*, and *Young All-Stars* (DC). *Ninja, Wild Knights*, and *Shattered Earth* (Malibu/Eternity). *Unity* crossover, *Magnus, Solar, X-O Manowar*, and *Harbinger* (Valiant). *Flare, Champions, Icicle*, and *Captain Thunder and Blue Bolt* (Heroic). *Dark Horse Presents. Grimjack. Mr. Fixitt*.

Favorite comics not worked on: *Sandman, Shade, the Changing Man, John Byrne's Next Men*, the various Archie titles, and *The Mask*.

Dream comic-book project: Three projects: an adaptation of the original Zorro novel, illustrated stories from the Bible, and to work with Larry Niven on anything.

✳ Joe Sinnott. c/o *CBG* Editorial Department, 700 East State Street, Iola, Wisconsin 54990.

Born: October 16, 1926, in Saugerties, New York.

College or other education: Attended the Cartoonists and Illustrators School, 1949-1951.

Comics-related education: Assisted Tom Gill, a C and I instructor who also worked in the field for Timely, Dell, Fawcett, etc.

Biggest creative influences: Milton Caniff and Alex Raymond.

1993 projects: Having retired from Marvel last year, I work on a freelance basis for them now. Am doing *The Life of Mickey Mantle* (four issues) for Magnum Comics. Also ink Paul Ryan's pencils of the Sunday *Spider-Man* strip for Stan Lee and King Features.

Past comics titles and related projects: For many years (43) worked on: *The Fantastic Four, Mighty Thor, Captain America, Avengers, West Coast Avengers, Defenders, Incredible Hulk,* etc., for Marvel. Illustrated *The Life of the Beatles* for Dell Comics in 1964 plus their *Twelve O'Clock* series. For *Treasure Chest* I did the lives of many famous people: Pope John XXIII, Babe Ruth, John Kennedy, MacArthur, Eisenhower, Ty Cobb, etc. In the 1950s, I did countless titles on war, horror, westerns, science fiction, monsters, romance, etc., for Atlas.

Favorite comics not worked on: *Superman* — although I worked on the *Spider-Man/Superman* crossover book for Marvel/DC.

Dream comic-book project: Tell the life of my hero, my brother, Sgt. Jack Sinnott, killed in action in France in 1944 during World War II.

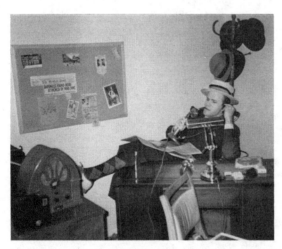

Ted Slampyak

✳ **Ted Slampyak.** 1232 Oriolo Drive, Bensalem, Pennsylvania 19020.

Born: December 15, 1965, in Abington, Pennsylvania.

College or other education: B.F.A. (cum laude), Tyler School of Art, Elkins Park, Pennsylvania.

Biggest creative influences: John Romita Sr., John Byrne, Will Eisner, Ian Gibson, Arthur Conan Doyle, Francis Ford Coppola, and Ayn Rand.

1993 projects: *Roadways* (which has yet to find a new publisher), pencilling. *Quantum Creep* (written by Nat Gertler, published by Parody Press), pencils, inks, and letters. *Suzi Romaine* (no publisher yet, probably released in 1994), everything. Still searching for a new publisher for *Jazz Age Chronicles.*

Past comics titles and related projects: *Jazz Age Chronicles* (everything) # 1-3 (E.F. Graphics, 1989), # 1-6 (Caliber Press, 1990-91). *Quantum Leap* #7 (writing), Innovation, August 1992. *Roadways* #1 (pencilling), Comic Zone, June 1992. *Pendulum* #1-4 (inking and lettering), Malibu, November 1992-present.

Favorite comics not worked on: *Tick, Concrete,* and *Spirit.*

Dream comic-book project: *Suzi Romaine* (and, as stated above, I *will* do it), an adventure tale of philosophy.

Photo: Bert Stern

Barbara Slate

✳ **Barbara Slate.** 61 West 68th Street, Apartment 8, New York, New York 10023.

Born: May 9, 1947, in Saint Louis, Missouri.

College or other education: Art Institute of Pittsburgh.

Biggest creative influences: Bert Stern (photographer), Jane Gennaro (stand-up comic), and Richard Minsky (artist).

1993 projects: *Barbie Fashion* for Marvel.

Past comics titles and related projects: Marvel: *Barbie.* Created, wrote, and drew: *Yuppies from Hell* and *Sweet XVI* for Marvel, *Angel Love* for DC, and *Ms. Liz* greeting cards, mugs, T-shirts, comic strip, etc. Writer of *New Kids on the Block* for Harvey and *Barbie Golden Books.* Also advertising illustrations.

Favorite comics not worked on: *Kid 'n' Play.*
Dream comic-book project: Girls, girls, girls!!!

Beau Smith

✴ **Beau Smith.** Eclipse Sales Ranch, P.O. Box 706, Ceredo, West Virginia 25507-0706.

Born: December 17, 1954, in Huntington, West Virginia.

College or other education: Marshall University, Journalism/Public Relations.

Biggest creative influences: Charles M. Russell, Louis L'Amour, John Beentien, John Ford, and Walter Hill.

1993 projects: *Parts Unknown, The Next Invasion, The Black Terror, Green Lantern Corps Quarterly, Buckaroo Betty,* and *Hard Nose.*

Past comics titles and related projects: *Scout, Beau LaDuke's Tips for Real Men, Dogs of Dansia, The Black Terror, Parts Unknown, The Bad One,* and *Total Eclipse.*

Favorite comics not worked on: The Sub-Mariner, *Punisher, Aquaman, Guy Gardner, Predator,* and *Space Ranger.*

Dream comic-book project: A *Wildcat* mini-series (DC Comics' Wildcat).

✴ **E. Silas Smith.** c/o David Scroggy, 2966½ Maple Court, San Diego, California 92104.

E. Silas Smith

Agent: David Scroggy.

Born: May 26, 1934, in Washington, D.C.

College or other education: Los Angeles Art Center College of Design. Thirty years aerospace and publishing fields.

Comics-related education: No formal education specifically related to comics. Did comic strip in junior high school and cartoons in the Marines.

Biggest creative influences: Illustrators such as N.C. Wyeth, Howard Pyle, Remington, Russell, Tom Lovell, etc.

1993 projects: UFO card project for Eclipse and *Dark Shadows* trade paperback (collects Innovation's *Dark Shadows Book One* #1-4).

Past comics titles and related projects: Innovation's *Dark Shadows Book One,* series of four comics, cover art and posters.

Favorite comics not worked on: Comics by Jean "Moebius" Giraud, graphic novels by Eclipse, Dark Horse, and others. The old classics.

Dream comic-book project: Uplifting stories having a positive influence on our time, especially on the young.

✴ **Jeff Smith.** Cartoon Books, P.O. Box 1583, Los Gatos, California 95031-1583.

Born: February 27, 1960, in McKees Rocks, Pennsylvania.

College or other education: Columbus College of Art and Design, The Ohio State University (no degrees).

Biggest creative influences: Walt Kelly and Neal Adams.

1993 projects: *Bone* and a compilation volume of the first six issues of *Bone*.

Favorite comics not worked on: *The Tick*.

Toren Smith

✳ **Toren Smith.** Studio Proteus, 105 Manchester Street, San Francisco, California 94110-5216.

Born: April 12, 1960, in Wetaskiwin, Alberta, Canada.

Biggest creative influences: Tom Clancy, Adam Warren, Shirow Masamune, and James P. Hogan.

1993 projects: *Version, Orion, Caravan Kidd, Ghost in the Shell, The Venus Wars II,* and *Hellhounds*.

Past comics titles and related projects: *Kamui, Nausicaä of the Valley of Wind, Cyber 7, The Dirty Pair, Epic, Alien Encounters, Voyages, Tales of Terror, Appleseed, Dominion, Black Magic, Outlanders, The Venus Wars, Terminator: Hunters and*

Killers, The True North II: Words and Thoughts, What's Michael?, etc.

Favorite comics not worked on: *Cerebus, Hate,* and *Sam and Max*.

Dream comic-book project: Comic based on the Bow Street runners of 1830 London, illustrated by David Lloyd.

✳ **Wayne R. Smith.** 48 West 4th Street, Apartment #5, Williamsport, Pennsylvania 17701.

Born: November 23, 1959, in Latrobe, Pennsylvania.

College or other education: Attended Lock Haven University, 1977-79.

Biggest creative influences: William Faulkner, Graham Greene, 1970s *Howard the Duck,* and underground comics.

1993 projects: *Blood of Beauty* with Dan Duncan and Alan Larsen. *Retrojet* with Duncan and Larsen. *The Truth Fairy* with E.J. Barnes and Myke Maldonado.

Past comics titles and related projects: Coplotted *Scarlet in Gaslight* with Martin Powell (Malibu, 1987-88). *Spacey* with Alan Larson (*Mangazine* #9 (1991)). *More Heat than Light* with E.J. Barnes (1992). Articles in *Amazing Heroes* (1985-1990).

Favorite comics not worked on: *Maus, Love and Rockets,* and *Journey*.

Dream comic-book project: A satire comic book I'm writing now.

✳ **Jack Snider.** 1441 Werner Northwest, Walker, Michigan 49504.

Born: August 24, 1964, in Hart, Michigan.

College or other education: A.S.A. in Illustration with a Graphics minor.

Biggest creative influences: Frazetta, Williamson, Eisner, Krigstein, Stout, Wrightson, Moebius, etc.

1993 projects: Inking *Robotech* over Tim Eldred, proposal for *Eric Warrior* © Scott Rosema.

Past comics titles and related projects: *New Humans* #3 pencils, Pied Piper Press; *Ex-Mutants* micro-series #1, featuring Vikki, pencils, Pied Piper Press; *Ex-Mutants* #8, inks, Pied Piper

Jack Snider

Press; *Shark the Killing Machine*, chapters 1-3, Big Shot Comics (back-ups done in *Bad Blood* # 2-4); *Bugs Be Gone* (*Looney Tunes*) for DC Comics, off-shore publication, pencils and inks; *Luck of the Draw*, pencils and inks, DC Comics, off-shore publication; *Do-Re-Mi Carrot*, pencils and inks, DC Comics, off-shore publication; *The Shaddup Strikes!,* inks only, DC Comics, off-shore publication.

Favorite comics not worked on: *Cages, Sandman, Animal Man,* and anything by Eddie Campbell.

Dream comic-book project: I have a couple self-generated projects I'd love to do eventually; also I would love to do *Hawkman* my way.

✳ **Tom Sniegoski.** 254 Park Street, Stoughton, Massachusetts 02072.

Born: February 4, 1962, in Massachusetts.

College or other education: Northeastern University, B.S. in English.

Biggest creative influences: Hemingway, F. Scott Fitzgerald, Stephen King, Frank Miller, Alan Moore, and Steve Bissette.

1993 projects: *Vampirella, Hyde 25, The Undead, The Rook, Gristle and Bone, Chains of Chaos,* and *Gutter Rat.*

Past comics titles and related projects:

*Swords of Shar-Pei, Guns of Shar-Pei, Vampirella #*2-4, 6, 7, 9, *Taboo #*1 (*Tooth Decay*).

Favorite comics not worked on: *Hellblazer, Sandman, Animal Man, Swamp Thing, Hulk,* and *Sin City.*

Dream comic-book project: A Vampirella/Batman crossover.

Wendy Snow-Lang

✳ **Wendy Snow-Lang.** Box 5010, Suite 115, Salem, Massachusetts 01970.

Born: August 27, 1957, in Lynn, Massachusetts.

College or other education: New England School of Art and Design, Boston, Massachusetts. Summa cum laude graduate.

Biggest creative influences: Barry Smith (before the Windsor) and Frank Thorne.

1993 projects: *Night's Children: Vampyr!* mini-series, *Night's Children: Exotic Fantasies* one-shot for FantaCo Enterprises.

Past comics titles and related projects: *Night's Children: Foreplay, Night's Children* mini-series, *Night's Children: Double Indemnity, Night's*

Children: Vampyr!, and a *Taboo Especial* short story, "Want," for Spiderbaby/Tundra.

Favorite comics not worked on: *Desert Peach, Sandman, Enigma, Death: High Cost of Living, From Hell,* and *Tank Girl.*

Dream comic-book project: I am *doing* my dream project.

✳ **Robert J. Sodaro.** Freelance Ink, P.O. Box 347, Norwalk, Connecticut 06856-0347.

Born: September 23, 1955, in Norwalk, Connecticut.

College or other education: Sacred Heart University, Fairfield, Connecticut.

Comics-related education: On the job.

Biggest creative influences: Stan Lee and Robert Heinlein.

1993 projects: Various writing assignments for several comics-related fan-press publications.

Past comics titles and related projects: *Agent Unknown,* Renegade Press; *Video Victor, Videogaming Illustrated*; articles for *Amazing Heroes, Marvel Age, Comics Buyer's Guide,* and others.

Favorite comics not worked on: *Concrete, Ms. Tree,* and *Uncanny X-Men.*

Dream comic-book project: Writing any of the Spider-Man titles.

Emilio Soltero

✳ **Emilio Soltero.** 8864 Sawtelle Way, Sacramento, California 95826.

Born: Stockton, California.

College or other education: A.A. from Fashion Institute of Design and Merchandising, 1985. B.A. from University of California-Davis, 1988. M.A., Sacramento State University, 1991.

Comics-related education: Art Instruction School certificate, 1983.

Biggest creative influences: Frazetta and Neal Adams.

1993 projects: Books on Gandhi, Cesar Chavez, Harriet Tubman, and *Janx* #3.

Past comics titles and related projects: I've worked with Sergio Aragonés, Moebius, and Frazetta on *Word Up* (1990), they contributed pages to my book. *Frida* (1991) sold at galleries, museums, and comics stores, story on the Mexican painter Frida Kahlo. *Janx* #1 and #2 (1985, 1986), science-fiction and adventure story. I've also created other books including educational ones like *Word* (1988), *Think* (1986), and *The Monkey House* (1991), 100,000 copies distributed throughout the United States and Mexico in two versions, Spanish and English. I also have strong positive letters from favorite authors like Dr. Seuss (letter from 1989). Video game covers for Atari, 1983-84. I've also done lettering and background for Morrie Turner's *Wee Pals* comic strip.

Favorite comics not worked on: Anything by Alan Moore.

✳ **Aaron Sowd.** c/o *CBG* Editorial Department, 700 East State Street, Iola, Wisconsin 54990.

Agent: Will Bercsa.

Born: November 3, 1970, in Canton, Ohio.

College or other education: Two years at Chico State University.

Comics-related education: None really, except studying and admiring just about everything done by the guys listed below.

Biggest creative influences: John Byrne, Frank Miller, Terry Austin, Scott Williams, Jim Lee, Bernie Wrightson, Neal Adams, and Jack Kirby.

1993 projects: *Strike Force America* (for Comico), *Darkstar* (for Rebel Studios).

Past comics titles and related projects: Artist on *The Elvis Presley Experience* #1-4, Mariah

Aaron Sowd

Carey in *Star Jam* #10, Aerosmith back cover for *Rock 'n' Roll Comics* #57 (all for Revolutionary Comics). Inker on *Strike Force America Special Edition* #2 (for Comico). Contributing artist in *Amazing Heroes* #199, 203, and 204.

Favorite comics not worked on: *John Byrne's Next Men, Cerebus, Groo, Sin City, Incredible Hulk, Static, 1963, Captain Sternn*, and *Cold Shock*.

Dream comic-book project: *Batman* or anything written by Peter David or John Byrne.

✳ **Bill Spangler.** c/o *CBG* Editorial Department, 700 East State Street, Iola, Wisconsin 54990.
Born: February 1, 1954, in DuBois, Pennsylvania.
College or other education: Penn State University, 1974.
Biggest creative influences: Archie Goodwin, Alan Moore, Gardner Fox, Philip José Farmer, and Poul Anderson.
1993 projects: *Robotech: Return to Macross* (writer), *Robotech: Invid War* (scripter and co-

Bill Spangler

plotter), *Argonauts: System Crash* (writer and creator).

Past comics titles and related projects: I've written: *Quantum Leap* #8 (original story, based on TV series), *Alien Nation: The Lost Episode* (adapted from unproduced TV script), *Alien Nation: The Spartans* (original story, based on TV show), *Tom Corbett, Space Cadet* (original story, based on TV show), *Bloodwing* and *Bloodbrothers* (a science-fiction-oriented super-hero I created), *Dollman* (original story, based on the Full Moon movie).

Favorite comics not worked on: All-time favorites: *Legion of Super-Heroes, Magnus Robot Fighter*. Current favorites: *Classic Star Wars, The Hacker Files*, and *Akira*.

Dream comic-book project: Basically, I want to do a sophisticated science-fiction comic with established characters, or ones that I create.

✳ **Bill Spicer.** 329 North Avenue 66, Los Angeles, California 90042.
Born: October 1, 1937, in Los Angeles, California.
1993 projects: Gladstone Disneys, *E.C. Library, Concrete, Squa Tront* (E.C.zine), and Basil Wolverton reprints.
Past comics titles and related projects: *Concrete* — Dark Horse. *Sinner, Young Witches*, and *Wolvertoons* — Fantagraphics. Various for Disney.

Photo: Steven P. Shumski

Bill Spicer

Dr. Giggles, Indiana Jones, and *Spacehawk* — Dark Horse. *E.C. Library* — Russ Cochran.

Favorite comics not worked on: *Xenozoic Tales, Blab!* (Monte Beauchamp), and the *Carl Barks Library.*

✳ **Dick Sprang.** c/o Ike Wilson, 2904 Rankin Terrace, Edmond, Oklahoma 73013.

Agent: Ike Wilson.

Born: July 28, 1915, in Fremont, Ohio.

Comics-related education: Excellent high school art classes. 1934-35, Art Department Scripps Howard *Toledo* (Ohio) *News-Bee:* best training for rapid production of deadline-imperative graphic art.

Biggest creative influences: N.C. Wyeth, Roy Crane, and Alex Raymond.

1993 projects: Two covers for DC Comics featuring my Golden Age Batman with Two-Face. Numerous licensed recreations of my Batman covers and conceptual Batman art for collectors.

Past comics titles and related projects: 1941-1962: *Batman:* 103 stories, 22 covers. *Detective Comics:* 77 Batman stories, 35 covers. *World's Finest Comics:* Batman teamed with Superman, 58 stories, three covers. Occasional *Superman, Jimmy Olsen, Lois Lane, Real Fact* stories. (Production figures in the 1941-1962 category are authenticated by Joe Desris.) After ending retirement in 1985, various *Batman Annuals* and *Detective Comics* Anniversary pin-ups, cover, and splash page recreations, Batman art for charity auctions: Literacy Volunteers of Chicago; Ronald McDonald Children's Charities of Northeastern Ohio (2); CFA-APA scholarship auction.

Favorite comics not worked on: Any books

by Joe Kubert, John Byrne, and Terry Beatty.

Dream comic-book project: Graphic novel of Major Powell's discovery expeditions of the Colorado River, 1869-1871.

✳ **Chris Sprouse.** c/o *CBG* Editorial Department, 700 East State Street, Iola, Wisconsin 54990.

Born: July 30, 1966, in Charlottesville, Virginia.

College or other education: B.F.A. in Graphic Design, James Madison University.

Biggest creative influences: Michael Golden, Frank Miller, Walter Simonson, and Hergé.

1993 projects: *Legionnaires* (penciller).

Past comics titles and related projects: *Hammerlocke* (1992), *Legends of the Dark Knight* #27 (1991), *Who's Who in the DC Universe* (1991-92), *Justice League America* (covers, 1991), *War of the Gods* (pin-ups, 1991), *Justice League International Quarterly* #1 (1990), *Batman Annual* #14 (1990).

Favorite comics not worked on: *Concrete, Love and Rockets,* and *Nexus.*

Dream comic-book project: I'd like to work on a science-fiction series that achieves popular and critical success.

✳ **Frank Stack.** c/o *CBG* Editorial Department, 700 East State Street, Iola, Wisconsin 54990.

Born: October 31, 1937, in Houston, Texas.

College or other education: B.F.A., University of Texas. M.A., University of Wyoming, one year at School of Art Institute of Chicago, and another at Academie Grande Chaumiere, Paris.

Comics-related education: Editor of *Texas Ranger* magazine 1957-59, University of Texas. No other comics-related education; I was an undergrounder and had no connection with overground comics.

Biggest creative influences: Varies all the time. For drawing comics early Gustave Doré, Roy Crane, and V.T. Hamlin. For writing: Poe, E.T.A. Hoffmann, Arthur Conan Doyle, Mark Twain, James Thurber, maybe Al Capp. Movie comedies like Laurel and Hardy, old cliffhanger

Frank Stack

radio and movie serials like *Superman, Phantom,* and *Lone Ranger.*

1993 projects: *The Bard Must Die* in *Blab!* #7 (due out any minute now), *American Splendor* #17 (three stories), *Our Cancer Year,* a 200-page non-fiction graphic novel with Harvey Pekar and Joyce Brabner. Editor of *Alley Oop* reprint Volume 3 *Oop's Moon Voyage* due, I guess, this year.

Past comics titles and related projects: *New Adventures of Jesus* sporadically since the early '60s, *Feel Good Funnies, Amazon Comics* 1971 and 1990 (Fantagraphics), *Frank Crankcase Stories, Dorman's Doggie* collected as a trade paperback by Kitchen Sink, *Alley Oop* reprint Volumes 1 and 2 (editor). Contributions to *Rip Off Review, Rip Off Comix, National Lampoon, Snarf, Drawn and Quarterly, Comics Journal, Blab!,* and others. *American Splendor* since issue #12. I'm on editorial board of Ohio State's new comics journal, *Inks,* though I haven't done anything yet.

Favorite comics not worked on: Robert

Crumb's work, Reid Fleming, all of Gilbert Shelton, Los Bros. Hernandez, *Calvin and Hobbes, Far Side, Popeye* (1930s), Hamlin's *Alley Oop,* Guido Crepax and Saudeli, Carl Barks, *Steven,* Marian Henley's *Maxine,* among others.

Dream comic-book project: Reprint my own comics as books. A graphic-story magazine devoted to cultural history as with my Van Gogh and Shakespeare stories. Have a publisher for whatever comic stories I want to write and draw. Edit a classic comic-strip reprint magazine like Dragon Lady Press tried to do. Maybe make some money on something some day. Or maybe quit messing with comics altogether and paint landscapes and nudes.

Rolf E. Stark

✳ **Rolf E. Stark.** P.O. Box 1634, Albany, New York 12201.

Born: October 28, 1939, in Ulm, West Germany.

College or other education: B.S. degree, Studio Art/Painting, September 1979, Empire State College, Albany, New York.

Biggest creative influences: Carl Barks, Floyd Gottfredson, José Muñoz, Carlos Sampayo, Alan Moore, Mike Baron, Steve Rude, Matt Wagner, Frank Miller, and William Messner-Loebs.

1993 projects: The collected version of *Rain.*

Past comics titles and related projects: Stories and/or art in: *Gore Shriek* #2-4, 6, and #6½, *Gore Shriek Delectus*, *Gore Shriek Annual*, *Shriek* #2, *Taboo* #1, 3, and #5, *Rain* #1-6. Articles in *CBG* #968, 969, and 972.

✳ **Rick Stasi.** c/o *CBG* Editorial Department, 700 East State Street, Iola, Wisconsin 54990.

Born: June 15, 1952, in Kansas City, Missouri.

College or other education: Associate Degrees in Advertising and Journalism from Columbia School of Broadcasting. Personnel Specialist and Counselor in the U.S. Army.

Biggest creative influences: Julius Schwartz, Curt Swan, Dick Giordano, Stan Lee, Jack Kirby, and Mike Gold.

1993 projects: *Twilight Zone* and *Green Hornet* (Now). *General Glory* (DC). Write/draw for Warners International Publishing, *Looney Tunes* and *Tiny Toons*.

Past comics titles and related projects: Pencils: *Warlord, Green Lantern, Legion of Super-Heroes, Secret Origins, Twisted Tales, Captain Marvel* (*Shazam*), *Captain Thunder and Blue Bolt*, lots of DC *Who's Who, Crimson Avenger, Zoom-Town, What The--?!* (Marvel), *Doom Patrol*, (unsuccessful *Creeper* mini-series that I wrote and wanted to pencil, oh well, life's been good to me).

Favorite comics not worked on: *Superman, Spider-Man, Thor, Fantastic Four*, and *Flash*.

Dream comic-book project: An Elseworlds Max Fleischeresque Superman special, a seminal Fantastic Four, Spider-Man, Thor, or Iron Man story.

✳ **John Robert Statema.** c/o *CBG* Editorial Department, 700 East State Street, Iola, Wisconsin 54990.

Born: July 25, 1961, in Kenosha, Wisconsin.

College or other education: American Academy of Art and the school of hard knocks (ouch).

Comics-related education: Purchased my education by weekly visits to the comic-book stores and then took my acquisitions home and studied them. ('Nuff said.)

Biggest creative influences: God and after that anybody who does this panel-to-panel continuity thing better than I do.

1993 projects: *Murcielaga She Bat* for Heroic Publishing.

Past comics titles and related projects: *Lunatic Fringe* (Innovation), *Rust* (Now), *Evangeline* (First), *Checkmate, Superman, Terminator, New Titans*, and finally, but in no way least, *G.I. Joe* for Marvel, a real guns and fun book.

Favorite comics not worked on: *Hawkworld, Lobo* (every artist should list *Lobo* as a favorite), and *Thor*.

Dream comic-book project: *Hawkworld, Lobo*, and *Thor* become an amalgamation for fan approval.

Bill Staton

✳ **Bill Staton.** Staton Graphics, P.O. Box 618, Winterville, Georgia 30683.

Born: April 13, 1959, in Providence, Rhode Island.

College or other education: Lee College.

Biggest creative influences: Sergio Aragonés.

1993 projects: Illustrate and co-writer of *Scratch*, co-created with science-fiction novelist Gino Dykstra.

Past comics titles and related projects: *Captain Armadillo*, illustrate, co-write, co-create. Current editorial cartoonist, published in several

Georgia newspapers. Writer of cartoon *Bernie* (gag panel) and *Flea Bags* (comic strip). Teach Cartooning and Comic Book Art and Production at the University of Georgia.

Favorite comics not worked on: *Groo* and *Spawn*.

Dream comic-book project: To have *Scratch* published by one of the big boys.

✴ **Joe Staton.** 130 Esopus Avenue, Kingston, New York 12401-1326.

Born: January 19, 1948, in Fort Bragg, North Carolina.

College or other education: B.F.A., Murray State University, Murray, Kentucky.

Comics-related education: Assistant to Gil Kane, 1972-73.

Biggest creative influences: Gil Kane, Steve Ditko, Jim Aparo, Chester Gould, and Wayne Boring.

1993 projects: *Guy Gardner: Year One*, Two-Face prestige format book, Joker story in *Batman: Legends of the Dark Knight*, *Ringworld* adaptation, and *E-Man* mini-series.

Past comics titles and related projects: *E-Man, Hulk, Avengers, Justice Society, Huntress, Legion of Super-Heroes, Elfquest, Superman, Batman, Green Lantern, Guy Gardner*, and *Classics Illustrated*. Art Director, First Comics, 1982-84.

Favorite comics not worked on: *Sandman*, Craig Russell's opera books.

Dream comic-book project: A *Dick Tracy* graphic novel by Max Collins. A girl's romance series by Joey Cavalieri.

✴ **Claude St. Aubin.** 58 Martin Ridge Crescent, Calgary, Alberta, Canada T3J 3M4.

Born: November 30, 1951, in Matheson, Ontario, Canada.

College or other education: C.E.G.E.P. Duvieux, Montreal, graduated as a graphic designer.

Biggest creative influences: George Freeman, Alex Toth, Jack Kirby, Joe Quesada, and Mike Mignola.

1993 projects: *Green Lantern* #40 and #43 (DC Comics).

Past comics titles and related projects: *Cap-tain Canuck, Chaos Corps, Beyond Captain Chinook*, McCain Cheese Nibbles mouse character development for an animated TV commercial, P.O.P. work using comic-book characters such as Spider-Man for UNICEF.

Favorite comics not worked on: *Justice Society of America* and *J'onn J'onzz*.

Dream comic-book project: *Challengers of the Unknown* (the originals).

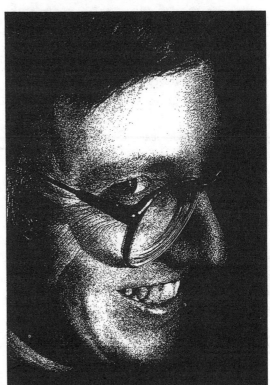

— ACTUAL UNRETOUCHED PHOTO OF KEN STEACY !!

✴ **Ken Steacy.** Sanctuary Woods Multimedia Corporation, 1006 Government Street, Victoria, British Columbia, Canada V8W 1X7.

Born: January 8, 1955, in Zweibrucken, Germany.

College or other education: A.O.C.A. (Associate, Ontario College of Art).

Comics-related education: Strictly on-the-job training since first professional work in 1974.

Biggest creative influences: Kirby, Steranko, Toth, Eisner, Manning, Hampson, Bellamy, Giraud, Mezieres, Tezuka, Miyazaki, Leialoha, Beauvais, etc.

1993 projects: Painted covers for various projects including *Ultraman* and *Ray Bradbury Comics*.

Past comics titles and related projects: *The Sacred and the Profane* (with Dean Motter), *Night and the Enemy* (with Harlan Ellison), *Tempus Fugitive* (all by myself), *Marvel Fanfare, Astro Boy, Jonny Quest, Doom Patrol*, etc., plus about a zillion painted covers for every publisher extant (and some that aren't).

Favorite comics not worked on: *Love and Rockets, Concrete*, and anything by Moebius, Eisner, P.C. Russell, etc.

Dream comic-book project: A CD-ROM interactive adventure, which is what I'm doing right now.

✳ **Brian Stelfreeze.** Gaijin Studios, 5581 Peachtree Road, Atlanta, Georgia 30341.

Born: In the '60s, in Myrtle Beach, South Carolina.

College or other education: Nothing to talk about.

Biggest creative influences: J.C. Leyendecker, Dean Cornwell, and Gil Kane.

1993 projects: *Batman: Shadow of the Bat* covers, *Punisher Summer Special, Maximum Velocity* for Dark Horse/Gaijin Studios *Ground Zero*.

Past comics titles and related projects: *Cycops, X-Men, Excalibur, Hulk, Namor, Fast Forward*, and covers too numerous to mention.

Favorite comics not worked on: *Batman: Sword of Azrael, Sin City, Deathblow, Ronin*, and Milo Manara's *Click!*

Dream comic-book project: *Barbie* covers, writing and drawing a *Bullseye* one-shot, or a *Domino* mini-series.

✳ **Roger Stern.** P.O. Box 701, Ithaca, New York 14851.

Born: September 17, 1950, in Noblesville, Indiana.

College or other education: B.A., Indiana University, 1972.

Comics-related education: Assistant Editor, Marvel Comics, 1975-78.

Biggest creative influences: Too many to list.

1993 projects: *Action Comics.*

Past comics titles and related projects: *The Incredible Hulk, Doctor Strange, Captain America, Spectacular Spider-Man, Amazing Spider-Man, Ghost Rider, The Avengers, West Coast Avengers, Fantastic Four, Thor, Power of the Atom, Starman, Superman*, Doctor Strange and Doctor Doom graphic novel, *Adventures of Superman, Action Comics, Magnus Robot Fighter*, and *Green Lantern Corps Quarterly*.

Favorite comics not worked on: *John Byrne's Next Men*, Neil Gaiman's *Sandman*, Jeff Smith's *Bone, Concrete*, Don Rosa's Donald Duck and Uncle Scrooge, *Elfquest*, and *Sam and Max.*

Dream comic-book project: A character of my own creation, still under my ownership, for a publisher who believed in my work and put his money where his mouth is.

✳ **st.EVE.** P.O. Box 1609, Madison Square Station, New York, New York 10159-1609.

College or other education: Two years at Cal Arts Disney Character Animation (awards: Disney Fellowship and Scholarship). One year each at New York University Advanced Animation and CinemaStudie.

Comics-related education: Courses at Cal Arts included character design, layout, composition, figure drawing. High School of Art and Design, New York City. Figure drawing at Society of Illustrators.

Biggest creative influences: Doré, James Montgomery Flagg, Milo Manara, Steve Ditko, Go Nagai, John Romita, Gene Colan, Buster Keaton, and Alex Raymond.

1993 projects: *Le Mage Blanc* trilogy (Rip Off Press), *Weird Smut* #5 (Jam Press), *Screw* magazine (story and art), inker for Grass Green's *Horny Comics and Stories* and *Up from the Ghetto* (Rip Off Press).

Past comics titles and related projects: (In)famous cover story for *Weird Smut* #1, as well as dozens of cartoons and comics, feature story illustrations and covers for *Screw* magazine, plus an illustration for a *Swank* letters digest.

Favorite comics not worked on: *Sandman, Cages, Dark Horse Presents, Flaming Carrot, Zone,* anything by Milo Manara, *Akira*, *The Spider* (Eclipse), and *Madman Adventures*.

Dream comic-book project: Ink *Doctor Strange*, draw in *Sandman*, do a graphic novel with a famous writer, draw people with clothes on for enough $$$.

✳ **Marlene Stevens.** P.O. Box 1634, Albany, New York 12201.

Born: December 6, 1946, in Schenectady, New York.

College or other education: Degree: B.A. Major: Sociology. Minor: Fine Arts. January 1969, State University of New York at Albany, Albany, New York. Degree: M.S.W. Concentration: Management. December 1977, Graduate School of Social Welfare, State University of New York at Albany, Albany, New York.

Biggest creative influences: Rolf Stark.

1993 projects: The collected version of *Rain*.

Past comics titles and related projects: Co-writer short stories in *Gore Shriek* #4, 1988, and *Taboo* #3, 1990. Co-writer limited series, *Rain* #1-6, 1991-93.

Steve Stiles

✳ **Steve Stiles.** c/o *CBG* Editorial Department, 700 East State Street, Iola, Wisconsin 54990.

Born: July 16, 1943, in New York City.

College or other education: School of Visual Arts.

Comics-related education: Night course with Vernon King (*Bringing up Father*).

Biggest creative influences: Eisner, Kurtzman, and Krigstein.

1993 projects: *Hideous Mutant Freekz* (Bruce Hamilton Publications). *Xenozoic Tales* (Kitchen Sink).

Past comics titles and related projects: *Hyper Comics* (All-Stiles U.G. anthology, Kitchen Sink), *Death Rattle* (Kitchen Sink), *Doc Savage* (Millennium), *Xenozoic Tales* (Kitchen Sink), *Royal Roy* (Star), *The Adventurers* (Malibu), *A.R.M.* (Adventure Comics), *The Adventures of Professor Thintwhistle* (Fantagraphics), *The Atom* (DC), cover for Al Capp's memoirs (*My Well Balanced Life on a Wooden Leg*), *Li'l Abner* (unpublished). Various humorous strips for *Heavy Metal, Stardate* magazine, *S.F. Eye, Snarf, Bizarre Sex*, and *Gothic Blimp Works*.

Favorite comics not worked on: *Sandman* and *Two-Fisted Tales*.

Dream comic-book project: Illustrating Michael Moorcock's *Dancers at the End of Time* trilogy.

✳ **Ernie Stiner.** c/o *CBG* Editorial Department, 700 East State Street, Iola, Wisconsin 54990.

Born: January 2, 1958, in Leisenring, Pennsylvania.

College or other education: Fayette Institute of Commerce and Technology (Associate degree: Drafting).

Comics-related education: Self-taught.

Biggest creative influences: Alex Toth, Michael Golden, Gil Kane, Gene Colan, Steranko, and Barry Windsor-Smith.

1993 projects: Various *Punisher* pin-ups and back-ups. Inking *Medal of Honor* stories for Dark Horse. Pencilling and inking some, as yet secret, creator-owned projects.

Past comics titles and related projects: Cartoons in *CBG* and *Marvel Age*. *X-Men Annual* #15 (four-page story, *Origin of the X-Men*, Marvel). *Desert Storm: Send Hussein to Hell* (six-page story, *Overkill*, Innovation). *Nick Fury, Agent of S.H.I.E.L.D.* #27-31, Marvel. *Freejack* #1-3, Now Comics.

Favorite comics not worked on: *Star Wars, Archer & Armstrong, Alien Legion*, and *Spider-Man 2099*.

Dream comic-book project: An ongoing parody-like title which lampoons comics in particular and anything in general. Tony Isabella should write it.

Chic Stone

✻ **Chic Stone.** 900 Thornfield Drive (F-1), Millbrook, Alabama 36054.

Born: January 4, 1923, in New York City.

Comics-related education: Eisner and Iger Studios, Chuck Thorndike, Bert Whitman, Loyd Jacquet Studios.

Biggest creative influences: C.C. Beck, Eisner, Caniff, Chic Young, and Kirby.

1993 projects: A new comic presentation directed towards young comic-book readers.

Past comics titles and related projects: *Batman, Superman, Fantastic Four, X-Men, Hulk, Amazing Spider-Man, Avengers, Sub-Mariner, Thor, Marvel Two-in-One, My Little Margie, Bobby Sox, Detective Comics, Kid Cowboy, War Comics, Georgie, Charlie Chan, Outer Space, Nemesis, Sheena, Human Torch, Archie, Romance Comics, Daredevil, Ghost Rider, Captain America, Iron Man, Not Brand Echh, Cracked, Nick Fury, Boy Comics, Defenders*, etc.

Favorite comics not worked on: I really don't have any. I enjoy good storylines and artwork that isn't overworked.

Dream comic-book project: Copyrighted.

✻ **Vince Stone.** 8409 Carlsbad Drive, Evansville, Indiana 47720.

Born: September 9, 1964, in Evansville, Indiana.

Comics-related education: One year completion of Joe Kubert School.

Biggest creative influences: John Byrne and Gil Kane.

Past comics titles and related projects: *Captain Confederacy* (SteelDragon Press), 1985-88. *Apex Project* (Stellar Grafix), 1990. *Captain Confederacy* (Epic), 1991.

Favorite comics not worked on: *Excalibur, She-Hulk, Fantastic Four*, and the Superman titles.

Dream comic-book project: *The Fantastic Four*.

✻ **Karl C. Story.** Gaijin Studios, 5581 Peachtree Road, Atlanta, Georgia 30341.

Born: October 28, 1967, in Laredo, Texas.

College or other education: Okaloosa Walton Community College, Art School, three semesters.

Comics-related education: Mentorship with Dave Dorman in senior year of high school.

Biggest creative influences: Michael Golden, Frank Miller, Mike Mignola, Kevin Nowlan, and Brian Stelfreeze.

1993 projects: Inking *Legionnaires* for DC; co-writing and inking *The Dude* for Dark Horse/Gaijin Studios project *Ground Zero*.

Past comics titles and related projects: Inker on following projects: *Legion of Super-Heroes, Aliens vs. Predator, Aliens: Genocide*, 17 *Cosmic Heroes II* trading cards for DC, *Cycops*, pin-up in *Homage Swimsuit Special*, inked part of *Namor Annual #3, Star Trek: Debt of Honor* graphic novel.

Favorite comics not worked on: *Appleseed, Akira, Orion, Sin City, Chain Gang War*, and *Version*.

Dream comic-book project: A project with one of my influences.

✻ **Len Strazewski.** 1321 West Birchwood, #106, Chicago, Illinois 60626.

Born: February 16, 1955, in Evergreen Park, Illinois.

College or other education: B.S. in Journalism, Northwestern University; M.A. in Creative Writing from University of Illinois; M.S. in Industrial Relations from Loyola University.

Biggest creative influences: Robert Heinlein, John D. MacDonald, Alan Moore, and Frederick Baley.

1993 projects: Malibu Comics — *Street Fighter*. Malibu Ultraverse — *Prime* and *Prototype*.

Past comics titles and related projects: *Trollords* — Tru Studios. *Flash* — DC Comics. *Phantom Lady* (*Action Comics Weekly*) — DC Comics. *Fly* — Impact Comics. *Web* — Impact Comics. *Starman* — DC Comics. *Justice Society of America* — DC Comics.

Favorite comics not worked on: *X-Men, Iron Man, Concrete*, and *Hellblazer*.

Dream comic-book project: *Hero Cycle*, graphic novel and screenplay.

Stephen D. Sullivan

✳ Stephen D. Sullivan. 2510 Lincoln Avenue, Kansasville, Wisconsin 53139.

Born: September 5, 1959, in Moline, Illinois.

College or other education: Southeastern Massachusetts University, Fine Arts program.

Comics-related education: Former staff editor and artist, TSR Inc., former Art Director, Pacesetter Ltd.

Biggest creative influences: Romita Sr., Stan Lee, Steve Ditko, Jack Kirby, Will Eisner, H.P. Lovecraft, J.R.R. Tolkien, Alan Moore, Robert Heinlein, Jim Starlin, Don MacGregor, Michelangelo, and Raphael.

1993 projects: *Teenage Mutant Ninja Turtles Adventures, The Twilight Empire, Lynx, Tall in the Saddle, Teenage Mutant Ninja Turtles Universe Handbook*, and others.

Past comics titles and related projects: *April O'Neil, Dinosaur Island, Newstralia, The Twilight Empire, Teenage Mutant Ninja Turtles Adventures Special, Racer X, Speed Racer, Astro Boy, Wabbit Wampage, Insane, Love Bites, Time Wankers, Erotic Fables and Faerie Tales*, and *Big Wanking Tales*.

Favorite comics not worked on: *Cerebus*, anything by Alan Moore, the Superman titles, *Nexus, Concrete, The Spirit, Groo, Crying Freeman, Omaha*, and *Usagi Yojimbo*.

Dream comic-book project: *Spider-Man, Batman, Superman, Spawn*, any of the heroic "big guns," or any of a half-dozen projects of my own including this superhero story I've been working on for three years or more.

✳ Alan Jude Summa. P.O. Box 585, Moscow, Pennsylvania 18444.

Agent: Stan Cohen: Creatif Licensing.

Born: December 27, 1960, in Scranton, Pennsylvania.

College or other education: A.A.: Keystone Junior College. B.F.A.: Kutztown State University.

Biggest creative influences: Howard Pyle, Frank Frazetta, and God.

1993 projects: *Interplanetary Lizards of the Texas Plains* comics and video games, to be released Christmas 1993.

Past comics titles and related projects: *Interplanetary Lizards of the Texas Plains, The Book of Lost Souls*, magazine covers and horror illustrations for dozens of magazines in the United States, Canada, and Europe, including the former U.S.S.R. Illustration and design for *Torg*, West End Games.

Favorite comics not worked on: *Batman*.

Dream comic-book project: I'm doing it. The Lizards.

✳ Brian Sutton. Antarctic Press, 7272 Wurzbach, Suite #204, San Antonio, Texas 78240.

Born: August 28, 1963, in Corpus Cristi, Texas.

College or other education: B.A., Trinity University.

Biggest creative influences: Walt Kelly's *Pogo*, Japanese manga, Jerry Collins, and Gary and Sylvia Anderson shows.

1993 projects: *Amy's Adventures* series for Genus.

Past comics titles and related projects: Colorist on several *Mangazine* covers and gaming supplements. Contributing editor on *Furrlough* and *Genus*, editor on *Wildlife*.

Favorite comics not worked on: *Bone, Deadworld* (when the plot isn't wandering), and *Usagi Yojimbo*.

Dream comic-book project: *Azhrika* or *Eurika*, a couple of projects that have been on the back burner.

✳ **Laurie S. Sutton.** 5600 North Dixie Highway, #2209, West Palm Beach, Florida 33407.

Born: March 19, 1953, in Wenonah, New Jersey.

College or other education: Sarah Lawrence College, B.A.

Biggest creative influences: Edgar Rice Burroughs' *Tarzan* books, Mike Grell's storytelling, and Will Eisner's storytelling.

Past comics titles and related projects: Editor: DC Comics, Marvel/Epic Comics, Donning/Starblaze (Thieves' World Graphics). Writer: *Adam Strange, Star Trek, Epic Illustrated*. Proofreader: DC Comics. Reviewer: Comics Code Authority.

Dream comic-book project: Anything sword-and-sorcery or fantasy.

✳ **Ronn Sutton.** #50-2845 Cedarwood Drive, Ottawa, Ontario, Canada K1V 0G6.

Born: December 17, 1952, in Toronto, Ontario, Canada.

Comics-related education: Ghost work for Howard Chaykin, Bernie Wrightson, and Gene Day. Occasional assist to Dan Day.

Biggest creative influences: Joseph Clement Coll, Roy G. Krenkel, Frank Frazetta, Al Williamson, and Jim Steranko.

Ronn Sutton

1993 projects: Adaptation of Gerard De Nerval's 1800s short story *Emilie* into graphic form. Also upcoming horror series.

Past comics titles and related projects: *Starbikers, T-Minus-1, Man from U.N.C.L.E., Ali Baba, Horror: The Illustrated Book of Fears, Cases of Sherlock Holmes, True North*, and others.

Favorite comics not worked on: *Xenozoic Tales*.

Tom Taggart

✳ **Tom Taggart.** 31 Huff Road, Wayne, New Jersey 07470.

Born: November 7, 1965, in Paterson, New Jersey.

Comics-related education: A few night classes at School of Visual Arts, New York.

Biggest creative influences: Frank Frazetta, Simon Bisley, Patrick Woodroffe, Dave DeVries, and movies.

1993 projects: *Doom Patrol* covers.

Past comics titles and related projects: Covers for: *Doom Patrol, Swamp Thing, Batman.* Pin-up pages for *Elfquest: New Blood.*

Favorite comics not worked on: *Sandman, Animal Man, Groo the Wanderer*, and *Usagi Yojimbo.*

Dream comic-book project: An entirely sculpted book.

✳ **Bryan Talbot.** c/o *CBG* Editorial Department, 700 East State Street, Iola, Wisconsin 54990.

Born: February 24, 1952, in Wigan, Lancashire, United Kingdom.

College or other education: Preston Polytechnic, L.S.I.A. in Graphic Design and Harris diploma.

Biggest creative influences: Book illustration, comic books (obviously), movies, and novels.

1993 projects: *Big Book of Conspiracies* (Piranha), *Sandman* # 51-56 framing sequences, *Raggedy Man* (Cult Press), covers. *The Tale of One Bad Rat* (Dark Horse) graphic novel.

Past comics titles and related projects: *Brainstorm Comix, Near Myths, Psst, The Adventures of Luther Arkwright, 2000 AD: Nemesis the Warlock* and *Judge Dredd, Hellblazer, The Nazz, Shade, the Changing Man, Sandman*, and *Legends of the Dark Knight.*

Dream comic-book project: I'm doing it, *The Tale of One Bad Rat.*

✳ **Trevor Tamlin.** R.R. #1, Woodville, Ontario, Canada K0M 2T0.

Born: January 11, 1968, in Lindsay, Ontario, Canada.

College or other education: Graphic Design graduate from Durham College in Oshawa,

Ontario. Currently studying Animation at Sheridan College in Oakville, Ontario.

Biggest creative influences: Will Eisner, Dave Sim, and Ty Templeton.

1993 projects: None at present, but am available.

Past comics titles and related projects: Lettering: *Retief: Diplomatic Immunity, Retief: Garbage Invasion, Retief: Giant Killer, Retief: Grime and Punishment, The Men in Black, Santa Claus Christmas Special*, and *Rocket Ranger.*

Richard G. Taylor

✳ **Richard G. Taylor.** c/o *CBG* Editorial Department, 700 East State Street, Iola, Wisconsin 54990.

Born: July 12, 1950, in Fergus, Ontario, Canada.

College or other education: B.F.A., York University.

Comics-related education: Honors painting certificate, Humber College.

Biggest creative influences: Al Williamson, Alex Toth, Ken Bald, Leonard Starr, and Stan Drake.

1993 projects: *The Cyclist*, a graphic novel, *Eroticom 2.*

Past comics titles and related projects: *Wordsmith* (Private Pages), *Silencers* (*Caliber Presents*), *Taboo* (Vortex), *Eroticom* (Quadrant), *A Kiss on the Lips* (Street Music), *Regarding Women*, and *American Splendor*.

Favorite comics not worked on: *Yummy Fur, Cages, Real Stuff*, and *Love and Rockets*.

Dream comic-book project: Sherlock Holmes adaptations.

✵ **Richard K. Taylor.** DC Comics, 1325 Avenue of the Americas, 27th Floor, New York, New York 10019.

Born: April 10, 1958, in Detroit, Michigan.

College or other education: Two years at the Joe Kubert School.

Biggest creative influences: C.C. Beck, Osamu Tezuka, Curt Swan, Kurt Schaffenberger, and Walt Disney.

1993 projects: Daily as Production Manager at DC. As a colorist: *Batman Adventures*.

Past comics titles and related projects: Production Manager at First Comics, colorist, *Dynamo Joe*. Art Director at Comico, colorist, *Jonny Quest, Robotech/Macross, Gumby, Sam and Max*, and *E-Man*.

Favorite comics not worked on: *Wonder Woman, Superman, Sam and Max, Freelance Police*, and *E-Man*.

Dream comic-book project: *Wonder Woman* collected edition, *Captain Action* revival, and *E-Man*.

✵ **Greg Theakston.** 88 Lexington, 2E, New York, New York 10016.

Born: November 21, 1953, in Detroit, Michigan.

Comics-related education: Assistant to Jim Steranko, 1971-72. Assistant to Neal Adams, 1975-79.

Biggest creative influences: Comics from 1956-1975, movies from 1930-1960, and illustrations from 1920-1960.

1993 projects: Publishing Jerry Bails' *Who's Who of American Comic Books, The Betty Pages Annual 1993*, numerous illustrations and writing.

Past comics titles and related projects: *Fan Informer* (fanzine), 1969-71. *Steranko's History of Comics Volume 2. Monster Times. National Lampoon* (numerous illustrations). *Rolling Stone.* Berkley Books, Ace Books, DAW Books, Dell Books, Tor Books, Zebra Books. *Invaders from Mars* (poster art). *Return of the Swamp Thing* (poster art). *Jungle Book* (video box). Various art for DC Comics, Eclipse, and Marvel Comics, 1973-93. Designed Cyclotron costume. Founded Pure Imagination in 1974. Developed Theakstonizing comics reconstruction system. Over 5000 pages of art have been reprinted using this system.

Dream comic-book project: A 500-page book, as large as an open newspaper, fully painted, yet still comics, magnum opus.

✵ **Brian Thomas.** 6438 North Hamilton Avenue, Chicago, Illinois 60645-5608.

Born: April 25, 1960, in Chicago, Illinois.

College or other education: Chicago Academy of Fine Arts (degree), Columbia College.

Comics-related education: Chicago artist-in-residence, 1979-81.

Biggest creative influences: Movies, comic books, TV shows, and life.

1993 projects: Various Teenage Mutant Ninja Turtles projects for Mirage Studios.

Past comics titles and related projects: *Astro Boy, Dinosaur Island, Speed Racer, Dynamo Joe, Insane, XXXenophile, Terminator*, and *Ghostbusters*.

Favorite comics not worked on: *Cerebus, Concrete, Hate, Madman, Groo, Sam and Max, Love and Rockets*, and *Herbie*.

Dream comic-book project: *Lawn Boy* (my own). Revival of Briefer's *Frankenstein* (with Don Glut). *Dinosaur Island* (with Steve Sullivan).

✵ **Dann Max Thomas.** c/o *CBG* Editorial Department, 700 East State Street, Iola, Wisconsin 54990.

Born: January 30, 1952, in Wisconsin.

College or other education: B.A., Economics, UCLA.

Biggest creative influences: Samuel Lover and Ray Bradbury.

1993 projects: *Avengers West Coast* and *Spider-Woman* mini-series.

Past comics titles and related projects: *Arak, Son of Thunder* (and *Valda* series therein), *Jonni Thunder, a.k.a. Thunderbolt, Wonder Woman, Captain Thunder and Blue Bolt, Infinity Inc., Crime-Smasher, All-Star Squadron, Shazam! A New Beginning, Young All-Stars, Captain Carrot and His Amazing Zoo Crew, Secret Origins, Wally Wood's T.H.U.N.D.E.R. Agents* (The Raven), *Conan* (various books), and *Red Sonja* (various stories).

Favorite comics not worked on: *Groo the Wanderer* and *Mad Raccoons* (by Cathy Hill).

Dream comic-book project: Adapting the works of P.G. Wodehouse and Harold Lamb into comics form.

✻ **Martin Thomas.** P.O. Box 321, Austin, Texas 78704.

Born: February 23, 1965, in Washington.

College or other education: Art Institute of Houston: Associate degree in Visual Communication.

Biggest creative influences: '60s super-hero cartoons.

1993 projects: *Comic Ball 5* trading cards. *Amerikkka* (new series, illustrating and writing) for Blackbird. *Just Friends* (compilation of back-ups).

Past comics titles and related projects: Coloring on: *Grimjack, Crying Freeman, Hepcats, Duncan and Malory*, Todd McFarlane's Spider-Man poster, *Jab* covers, wrote and illustrated back-up series.

Favorite comics not worked on: *Flash, Animal Man, Batman: Legends of the Dark Knight*, and *Legion of Super-Heroes*.

Dream comic-book project: To bring together Cage, The Black Panther, and The Falcon for a '90s version of *Three the Hard Way*.

✻ **Roy Thomas.** Marvel Comics, 387 Park Avenue South, New York, New York 10016.

Agent: Mike Friedrich, Star*Reach.

Born: November 22, 1940, in Jackson, Missouri.

College or other education: Southeast

Missouri State University (B.S. in Education and *some* graduate work).

Comics-related education: Assistant editor first to Mort Weisinger (DC, 1965), then to Stan Lee at Marvel (1965).

Biggest creative influences: The comics of the Golden Age and early Silver Age, especially Julius Schwartz's and Stan Lee's.

1993 projects: *Avengers West Coast, Conan the Barbarian, Savage Sword of Conan, The Invaders* (four issues), *Doctor Strange* (five issues), *The Secret Defenders, Fantastic Four Unlimited* (all Marvel). *Dracula: Vlad the Impaler* and *Secret City* (Topps).

Past comics titles and related projects: *Son of Vulcan, Blue Beetle, Modeling with Millie, Millie the Model, Patsy and Hedy, Doctor Strange, Iron Man, The X-Men, The Avengers, Sub-Mariner, The Hulk, Sgt. Fury, S.H.I.E.L.D., Captain America, Captain Marvel, Warlock, Iron Fist, Conan the Barbarian, Savage Tales, Savage Sword of Conan, Red Sonja, Kull, Worlds Unknown, Unknown Worlds of Science Fiction, All-Star Squadron, Arak, Son of Thunder, Young All-Stars, Infinity Inc., Shazam!, Secret Origins, Captain Thunder and Blue Bolt, Bram Stoker's Dracula*, etc.

Dream comic-book project: I prefer not to say.

✻ **Martha Thomases.** DC Comics, 1325 Avenue of the Americas, New York, New York 10019.

Agent: Jeanne Drewsen.

Born: April 19, 1953, in New York City.

College or other education: B.A. in History and Communications, Oberlin College.

1993 projects: Publicity, DC Comics.

Past comics titles and related projects: *Crazy* and *Dakota North*.

Favorite comics not worked on: *Sandman, Doom Patrol*, and *Superman*.

Dream comic-book project: Adapt *Ratner's Star*.

✻ **Don Thompson.** c/o *CBG* Editorial Department, 700 East State Street, Iola, Wisconsin 54990.

Don and Maggie Thompson

Born: October 30, 1935, in Warren, Pennsylvania.

College or other education: B.A. in Journalism, Pennsylvania State University.

Biggest creative influence: I read a lot. Also, while it is a negative influence, I became aware early on that a lot of writing courses and almost all college courses teach people to write in a pedantic, academic, boring style — something that teachers can get away with because they are in a position to *require* students to read it. I have worked ever since on developing a style that is easy to read, so that some, at least, will *choose* to read what I have written.

1993 comics projects: Am open to offers.

Past comics titles and related projects: Have written comic-book stories for Marvel, DC, and Eclipse and uncounted articles and features for Marvel and various other publishers, usually with Maggie. Co-edited (with Richard A. Lupoff) two nostalgia-oriented books on Golden Age comics — *All in Color for a Dime* and *The Comic-Book Book*. Have been co-editor of *Comics Buyer's Guide* since the start of 1983.

Favorite comics not worked on: *Sandman, Bone, Cerebus.*

Dream comic-book project: Something without a deadline. Failing that, something with a long deadline.

✳ **Maggie Thompson.** c/o *CBG* Editorial Department, 700 East State Street, Iola, Wisconsin 54990.

Born: November 29, 1942, in Ithaca, New York.

College or other education: B.A. from Oberlin College (English major).

Biggest creative influences: Will Eisner and Don Thompson.

1993 comics projects: *Dark Shadows* four-part mini-series (plot and script).

Past comics titles and related projects: Miscellany over the years, from some *Thor* plots for Roy Thomas to science-fiction stories and adaptations for Marvel's science-fiction publications. Have been co-editor of *Comics Buyer's Guide* since the start of 1983.

Favorite comics not worked on: There is so much, and the field is so rich — Earliest favorite creators (who taught me to read, by the way) included Carl Barks, C.C. Beck, Mo Gollub, Walt Kelly, Dan Noonan, and John Stanley. And my list of favorites has just expanded continually ever since.

Dream comic-book project: I've enjoyed every one I've done.

Frank Thorne

✳ **Frank Thorne.** 1967 Grenville Road, Scotch Plains, New Jersey 07076.

Born: June 16, 1930, in Rahway, New Jersey.

College or other education: Art Career School, New York City (three years).

Biggest creative influences: Alex Raymond, Hal Foster, and Rich Corben.

1993 projects: *The Iron Devil* series for Fantagraphics, which I write and draw.

Past comics titles and related projects: *Mighty Samson* (Gold Key), *Tomahawk, Korak* (DC), *Red Sonja* (Marvel), *Danger Rangerette* (Lampoon) . . . created, written, and drawn: *Moonshine McJuggs* (*Playboy*), *Lann* (*Heavy Metal*), *Ribit* (Comico), *Ghita of Alizarr* (editions in five languages), and *The Erotic Worlds of Frank Thorne* — seven books (Fantagraphics).

Dream comic-book project: I've been doing my dream comics since 1975.

✳ **Dave Thorpe.** c/o Sharon Cho, Star*- Reach, P.O. Box 2328, Berkeley, California 94702.

Agent: Sharon Cho (Star*Reach).

College or other education: Scriptwriting (London Academy of TV). Art and Creative Writing B.A. (Honors).

Comics-related education: Publishing Rights and Contract Law (London School of Publishing).

Biggest creative influences: A sense of wonder, a rabid curiosity, and a deep hunger for the startling.

1993 projects: *The Gene Police* (Eclipse), *After Life* (Taboo), and *Hothouse* (Greenpeace Comics).

Past comics titles and related projects: Writer: *Captain Britain* (Marvel UK) 1981-82. *Artman* (Pssst!) 1982-83. *Doc Chaos* # 1 and 2 (Escape) 1984-85. *Doc Chaos Word Photographs* (New Order) 1985. *Doc Chaos, the Chernobyl Effect* (Hooligan Press) 1988. *Doc Chaos* (Vortex) 1990. *Mutant Love* (in *Avalon Harrier*) 1986. *A.A.R.G.H.* (Mad Love) 1989. *Repossession Blues* (Heartbreak Hotel/Blaam) 1988. *Inkling* # 4-6, 1990-91. *Rise and Rall of the Soviet Union* trading cards (Eclipse) 1992. *Hothouse* (Greenpeace Comics) 1993. *After Life* (Taboo) 1992-93. *How the World Works* (Oxfam) 1992. Editor: Marvel UK (1981-82), *Pssst!* (1982-83), Titan Books (1987-91), MacDonald graphic novels (1990-91), Harper Collins' Eclipse Books graphic novels (1992-93).

Favorite comics not worked on: *Sandman, Doom Patrol, Moebius, Stray Toasters, Big Numbers,* and *Hate.*

Dream comic-book project: Writing a very popular, multi-leveled, large-scale fantasy based on the new science of complexity to be astonishingly drawn by Moebius.

✳ **Steven Tice.** 519 Valentine Hill Road, Bellefonte, Pennsylvania 16823.

Born: July 20, 1965, in Bellefonte, Pennsylvania.

College or other education: B.A. in English Literature, some significant graduate work.

Comics-related education: Otherwise self-taught.

Biggest creative influences: In literature: John Barth, Robert Coover, Thomas Pynchon, and Harlan Ellison. Comics writers: Moore, Morrison, Milligan, and Gaiman. Comics artists: Golden, Austin, Windsor-Smith, and Wrightson.

1993 projects: *Musings: A Journal of Comics Criticism and Commentary. The Tellurian* mini-series (examining the morally ambiguous life of the eco-terrorist — I'll be writing and doing some artwork, probably inking) and *The Rubaiyat of Omar Khayyam* (an illustrated critical edition — no artist determined at this time).

Favorite comics not worked on: *Doom Patrol, Shade, the Changing Man, Sandman, Hellblazer,* and *Legion of Super-Heroes.*

Dream comic-book project: Adapting the works of Barth, Coover, *et al.* to comics. Adapting Sandy Pearlman's *Imaginos* saga.

✳ **Mike Tiefenbacher.** W141 N5434 Van Buren Drive, Menomonee Falls, Wisconsin 53051.

Born: July 17, 1952, in Milwaukee, Wisconsin.

College or other education: University of Wisconsin-Milwaukee (four years).

Biggest creative influences: Murphy Anderson, Carmine Infantino, Gil Kane, John Broome, Gardner Fox, John Stanley, Alex Toth, and Mike Maltese.

1993 projects: Still looking.

Past comics titles and related projects: *DC Comics Presents* (*Whatever Happened to . . . ?*

Mike Tiefenbacher

Johnny Thunder, Prince Ra-Man, Rex the Wonder Dog/Detective Chimp, Star Hawkins, Rip Hunter). *Funny Stuff Stocking Stuffer* (Nutsy Squirrel, Doodles Duck). *Mighty Mouse, Underdog, Screwy Squirrel* (Spotlight), ICG Official Index series, *ComicKeeper* computer software, *Menomonee Falls Gazette and Guardian*, and *The Comic Reader*.

Favorite comics not worked on: Don Rosa's Uncle Scrooge and Jerry Ordway's Superman.

Dream comic-book project: Warner Bros.-type funny-animal comics for children. New *Little Lulu and Tubby*. My own early-1960s-set superhero team book.

✳ **John Tighe.** Homage Studios, 10606-8 Camino Ruiz, Suite #209, San Diego, California 92131.

Born: October 22, 1962, in Los Angeles, California.

College or other education: East Los Angeles College, A.A.

Comics-related education: Scott Williams assistant.

Biggest creative influences: Scott Williams and Jim Lee.

1993 projects: *WildC.A.T.S, CyberForce, Wetworks, Pitt*, and *Champions Classics*.

Past comics titles and related projects: *The Maze Agency, Flare, Lady Arcane, Power Factor, Vindicators* + (roleplaying game book).

Favorite comics not worked on: *Superman, The Spirit, Archer & Armstrong, Wildstar*, and *H.A.R.D. Corps*.

Dream comic-book project: To be the regular artist on *Captain America* or working on my own creator-owned book.

✳ **Matt Tolbert.** 2778 Deerwood Avenue, Simi Valley, California 93065.

Born: December 10, 1954, in Minneapolis, Minnesota.

College or other education: University of California, Santa Barbara, B.S., Business.

Biggest creative influences: Stan Lee.

Past comics titles and related projects: *Read My Lips*, cartoon biography of George Bush. *World Class Wrestling #8*.

Favorite comics not worked on: *X-Men, Thunderstrike, Avengers*, and *Batman*.

Dream comic-book project: *Avengers*.

Noel John Tominack

✳ **Noel John Tominack.** 149-E Jenkins Lane, Indian Head, Maryland, 20640.

Born: December 23, 1967, in LaPlata, Maryland.

College or other education: A.A., Computer Programming, Charles County Community College. B.S., Information Systems Management, University of Maryland.

Biggest creative influences: Disney animation and early-mid 1980s funny-animal titles.

1993 projects: *Furrlough* and *Wild Life Tales* for Antarctic Press.

Past comics titles and related projects: *Furrlough* #1 (untitled story). *Wild Life Tales* #1 (*Junkyard Dogs*).

Favorite comics not worked on: *Punisher, Ninja High School, Albedo, Justice League, XXXenophile,* and *What The--?!*

Dream comic-book project: Writing my own scenario with funny animals for Dark Horse.

✱ **John Totleben.** 315 Lighthouse Street, Erie, Pennsylvania 16507.

Born: February 16, 1958, in Erie, Pennsylvania.

College or other education: Joe Kubert School (one year).

Biggest creative influences: F. Booth, V. Finlay, Rembrandt, A. Dürer, J.M.W. Turner, among many others.

1993 projects: *Hellhead* with Rick Veitch (Tundra), *Unbelievable N-Man* with Alan Moore and Steve Bissette, *Horus* with Alan Moore and Rick Veitch.

Past comics titles and related projects: *Swamp Thing, Miracleman,* and *Taboo.*

Favorite comics not worked on: *Sandman, Eightball,* and *Cages.*

Dream comic-book project: I hate questions like this.

✱ **Sal Trapani.** 5 Jupiter Drive, Seymour, Connecticut 06483.

Agent: Neal Rubinstein, NSR Productions Inc.

Born: April 30, 1927, in Brooklyn, New York.

College or other education: After discharge from USAF in 1947, entered Cartoonists and

Sal Trapani

Illustrators School (School of Visual Art) for a four-year course.

Comics-related education: Started working in 1943 for various artists, doing backgrounds and occasional pencils and inks, until tour of duty in 1945.

Biggest creative influences: Hal Foster, Burne Hogarth, and Alex Raymond.

1993 projects: None, semi-retired.

Past comics titles and related projects: American Comics Group, Archie Comics, *Batman,* Charlton Press, Comico, Classics Illustrated, Dell Publishing, DC Comics, Eclipse, Gold Key, Grosset and Dunlap, S.M. Iger Services, King Features, Marvel Comics, Warren Publishing, Whitman Publishing Co., and Cambria Productions in 1961 in Hollywood, working on *Space Angel.* In 1980, was hired to ink the syndicated *Superman* comic strip, until its demise in 1985. Presently creating and writing new material for future projects for comics, TV, and film.

Favorite comics not worked on: None; I'm not at all happy with the quality of features and artists in current titles.

Dream comic-book project: My own, *Adam.*

✱ **Chas Truog.** 5108 Minnetonka Boulevard, #1, St. Louis Park, Minnesota 55416.

Born: December 10, 1959, in central Minnesota.

College or other education: B.A. degree, Southwest State University, Marshall, Minnesota (1982).

Biggest creative influences: Frank Thorne,

Chas Truog

Frank Frazetta, John Buscema, Milo Manara, and José Garcia-Lopez.

1993 projects: *Chiaroscuro*, a 10-issue miniseries for Vertigo. It's historical fiction set in the Renaissance and its central character is Leonardo da Vinci.

Past comics titles and related projects: *Coyote, Animal Man, Forgotten Realms, Dr. Fate, Starman, Justice League Quarterly*, and *Green Lantern Corps Quarterly*.

Favorite comics not worked on: *Sandman, Conan, The Warlord, Hawkman, Nexus*, and *Sub-Mariner*.

Dream comic-book project: I'm hoping to do an adaptation of the *Gilgamesh* epic (someday).

✯ **Timothy Truman.** Timothy Truman Studio, P.O. Box 5208, Lancaster, Pennsylvania 17606-5208.

Born: February 9, 1956, in Gauley Bridge, West Virginia.

College or other education: Columbus College of Art and Design, West Virginia University.

Comics-related education: Joe Kubert School of Cartoon and Graphic Art (Dean's List graduate).

Biggest creative influences: The E.C. artists (particularly John Severin), Sam Glanzman, Roger Dean, Frank Frazetta, Joe Kubert, Barry Smith, Russ Heath, Brian Froud, Greg Irons, and Spain.

1993 projects: *Jonah Hex: Two-Gun Mojo;*

Turok Dinosaur Hunter #4-9; *Machine Gun* for authorized Jimi Hendrix comic (Tom Yeates, editor); *World of Lore: Wormworld*, comics/roleplaying game project for Palladium Books.

Past comics titles and related projects: *Grimjack* (co-creator with John Ostrander), *Scout, Hawkworld* (three-issue Prestige Format series), *Wilderness: The True Story of Simon Girty, The Spider* (Series 1 and 2), *Grateful Dead Comix, The Prowler.* Editor/co-creator: The new *Airboy* and *Skywolf*.

Favorite comics not worked on: *The Complete Crumb Comics, Propeller Man*, and *The Heckler*.

Dream comic-book project: *Mighty Samson, Elric of Melnibone*, Fritz Lang's *Metropolis*, historical comic based on the life of frontiersman James Smith, Baron Strucker, and *Kona*.

✯ **Wayne Truman.** 103 North Ellis, Lancaster, Texas 75146.

Born: March 28, 1936, in Akron, Ohio.

College or other education: Memphis Academy of Art (two years).

Comics-related education: Practice, practice, practice.

Biggest creative influences: Frank Engli and Milton Caniff.

1993 projects: *Miracleman* (Eclipse), have lettered every new issue of *Miracleman* published by Eclipse.

Past comics titles and related projects: Many Eclipse titles including: *Miracleman*, Clive Barker titles, others. Many, many Viz books from their beginning. Bet I hold the record for the number of manga pages retouched/lettered . . . about 13,000. (May not be a *record*, but it's a darn good *average*! Yuk yuk!) Worked as a package designer for thirty years before becoming full-time comics letterer in 1987.

Dream comic-book project: *True Man Adventures* written and drawn by Wayne Truman, autobiographical.

Todd S. Tuttle

✳ **Todd S. Tuttle.** 2107 South 4th Street, Rockford, Illinois 61104-7101.

Born: September 14, 1964, in Rockford, Illinois.

College or other education: 1½ years at Rock Valley College.

Comics-related education: Two years at Joe Kubert School of Cartoon and Graphic Art Inc.

Biggest creative influences: Jaime Hernandez, George Pérez, Paul M. Smith, Glenn Whitmore, and John Workman.

1993 projects: *Married with Children: Quantum Quartet, Green Hornet*, and *Twilight Zone.*

Past comics titles and related projects: *Universal Soldier* and *Twilight Zone.*

Favorite comics not worked on: *Excalibur, Legion of Super-Heroes*, the Superman books, and *Avengers.*

Dream comic-book project: Writing and drawing or coloring my own characters in the Todd Universe.

Dan Tyree (left) with Sheldon Moldoff

✳ **Dan Tyree.** 1801 Snake Creek Road, Belfast, Tennessee 37019.

Born: April 18, 1960, in Lewisburg, Tennessee.

College or other education: B.S. in Mass Communications (Broadcast Journalism sequence) from Middle Tennessee State University (Murfreesboro, Tennessee).

Biggest creative influences: Al Capp, Chester Gould, Lee and Kirby, Denny O'Neil, Steve Englehart, Steve Gerber, Cat Yronwode, Monty Python, and Don and Maggie Thompson.

1993 projects: *Dan T's Inferno* and an interview with *Doom Patrol* co-creator Arnold Drake, both for *CBG*.

Past comics titles and related projects: *Dan T's Inferno* for *CBG* since 1983. Henry Boltinoff article in *Revolver Annual* #1 (Renegade Press). Former staff writer for *Comics Review* (now called *Comics Revue*). Co-wrote *Scaramouch* mini-series and two *Blatherskite* stories, both for Innovation.

Favorite comics not worked on: *Sandman, Groo, Incredible Hulk, Cerebus, Walt Disney's Comics and Stories,* and *Superman.*

Dream comic-book project: To write a *Mandrake* comic book; to develop my own creator-owned universe; and to find a publisher for the final issue of *Scaramouch* storyline.

✱ **Dave Ulanski.** 875 Buffalo Avenue, Calumet City, Illinois 60409.

Born: December 29, 1970, in Calumet City, Illinois.

College or other education: Attended American Academy of Art in Chicago, miscellaneous classes.

Biggest creative influences: John Romita Jr., Art Adams, Ron Frenz, John Byrne, and Al Williamson.

1993 projects: Pencilling *Cambion* for Northstar.

Past comics titles and related projects: *Screem in the Dark* (fanzine, writing, pencils, and inks). *Fantastic Fanzine* (Arrow Comics, pencils and inks).

Favorite comics not worked on: *Daredevil, Animal Man,* and *Hulk.*

Dream comic-book project: Co-plotting and pencilling a *Star Wars* mini-series.

✱ **Chris Ulm.** Malibu Comics, 5321 Sterling Center Drive, Westlake Village, California 91362.

Born: May 3, 1963, in Los Angeles.

College or other education: B.A., History, California State University.

Comics-related education: Internship at Marvel Productions. I've also managed specialty game distributorships (Last Grenadier, Sunrise Distribution).

Biggest creative influences: For comics, the

work of Alan Moore, Frank Miller, Barry Windsor-Smith, and Steve Englehart.

1993 projects: Editing the Ultraverse titles for Malibu Comics. Freelancing a three-issue mini-series based on a horror/humor character named Dead Clown.

Past comics titles and related projects: *Robotech II: The Sentinels* (co-scripter), *Prime, Hardcase, The Strangers,* and *Ninja High School* (all editor).

Favorite comics not worked on: *The Savage Dragon.*

Dream comic-book project: I'm working on it now for Malibu's Ultraverse. Stay tuned. (I can't reveal the project yet).

Rod Underhill

✱ **Rod Underhill.** 4468 Bermuda Avenue, San Diego, California 92107.

Born: October 7, 1953, in Los Angeles, California.

College or other education: B.S., Philosophy, 1976, Northern Arizona University. Juris Doctorate, Western State University.

Biggest creative influences: Andy Warhol and Robert Heinlein.

1993 projects: *Airlock,* including the continuing serials *Caligula* and *Malice Defeated. Wonderwall, The Forbidden Airlock,* and various lithoprints by myself and other artists.

Past comics titles and related projects: *Airlock, The Forbidden Airlock, Wonderwall*, various fine art works, and various lithoprints.

Favorite comics not worked on: *Cerebus*.

Dream comic-book project: Cover art for DC and others. Write a limited series featuring The Martian Manhunter.

✳ **Donna Karen (D.K.) Upshaw.** 4228 Magoun Avenue, East Chicago, Indiana 46312.

Born: October 4, 1959, in East Chicago, Indiana.

College or other education: B.A. degree in Spanish.

Comics-related education: College minor: Art. Two courses at American Academy of Art, Chicago: Life Drawing and Fundamentals of Art.

Biggest creative influences: Fred Hembeck and Bobby London.

1993 projects: Comic panels *Lizanne* and *La pandilla de 3* in The East Chicago News.

Past comics titles and related projects: *Celluloid Dreams* in *CBG*. Bart Simpson parody strip in *Simpsons Illustrated*.

Favorite comics not worked on: DC's *Angel Love* mini-series and Bobby London's daily *Popeye* strip.

Dream comic-book project: A revival of *Angel Love*.

✳ **Michael E. Uslan.** c/o *CBG* Editorial Department, 700 East State Street, Iola, Wisconsin 54990.

Born: June 2, 1951, in Jersey City, New Jersey.

College or other education: A.B., 1973, Indiana University. M.S., 1975, Indiana University. J.D., 1976, Indiana University School of Law.

Comics-related education: Worked for DC Comics circa 1971 to 1976.

Biggest creative influences: Bob Kane, Dennis O'Neil, Neal Adams, Marshall Rogers, Dick Sprang, Jerry Robinson, Bill Finger, and Julie Schwartz.

1993 projects: *Batman III, Terry and the Pirates* weekly hour TV series, *The Black Cat* feature film, *Adam Link* feature film, *Hellblazer* fea-

ture film, *Swamp Thing* live action TV series.

Past comics titles and related projects: DC: Batman (co-writer) in *Detective Comics, The Shadow*, assorted mystery comics, war comics, *Amazing World of DC Comics* (writer/editor), *Edugraphics, The Comicmobile*, many others for DC. *Charlton Bullseye, The Question, The Phantom*. Taught the world's first accredited course on comic books at college (Indiana University, 1971). Wrote books: *The Pow! Zap! Wham! Comic Book Trivia Quiz* (William Morrow). *The Best of Archie* (E.P. Putnam's Sons). *America at War* (Simon and Schuster). *Mysteries in Space* (Simon and Schuster). *The Comic Book in America* (Indiana University). Executive Producer: *Batman, Batman Returns, Fish Police, Swamp Thing* (both animated and live action series). Producer: *Swamp Thing* and *Return of Swamp Thing*.

Favorite comics not worked on: *Justice Society, Spectre*, and *Spirit*.

Dream comic-book project: Produce the definitive *Spirit* movie.

Andrew Vachss

✳ **Andrew Vachss.** 299 Broadway, Suite 1803, New York, New York 10007-1901.

Agent: The Martha Kaplan Agency.

Born: October 19, 1942, in New York City.

College or other education: B.A., J.D. For details see *Who's Who in American Law*, 1990-91.

Biggest creative influences: I would not stigmatize anyone with such a designation.

1993 projects: *Hard Looks* (series), *Predator: Race War* (mini-series), *Underground* (special): Dark Horse. *Blue Belle* (graphic novel), with Neal Barrett.

Favorite comics not worked on: *Crow* (O'Barr), anything by Geof Darrow, *Grendel*, *Dead in the West* (Lansdale/Barrett).

Dream comic-book project: *Shella*.

Jim Valentino

✳ **Jim Valentino.** c/o *CBG* Editorial Department, 700 East State Street, Iola, Wisconsin 54990.

Agent: Randy Chalenor.

Born: October 28, 1952, in Bronx, New York.

College or other education: Some college, no degree.

Biggest creative influences: Too many to adequately list.

1993 projects: *Shadowhawk II, Images of Shadowhawk, 1963,* and *Shadowhawk III*.

Past comics titles and related projects: *normalman, Valentino, Myth Adventures, What If? Guardians of the Galaxy,* and *Shadowhawk*.

Favorite comics not worked on: *Bone.*

Dream comic-book project: *The Justice Society of America.*

✳ **James Vance.** c/o *CBG* Editorial Department, 700 East State Street, Iola, Wisconsin 54990.

Agent: Paul McSpadden.

Born: April 2, 1953, in Tulsa, Oklahoma.

College or other education: Goodman School of Drama (Chicago), various other colleges.

Biggest creative influences: Will Eisner, Harvey Kurtzman, Eugene O'Neill, and Edward Albee.

1993 projects: Three-part story for *Batman: Legends of the Dark Knight* (DC Comics).

Past comics titles and related projects: *Kings in Disguise, Owlhoots, Images of Omaha*, introduction to *The Collected Omaha #4, Republicans Attack!* trading cards (writer on all of the above for Kitchen Sink Press).

Favorite comics not worked on: *Omaha* and *Xenozoic Tales.*

Dream comic-book project: I'm working on it, but it's too soon to announce.

Michael Vance (Michael Lail)

✳ **Michael Vance (Michael Lail).** 1427 South Delaware Avenue, Tulsa, Oklahoma 74104.

Born: July 18, 1950, in Oklahoma City, Oklahoma.

College or other education: East Central University, B.A., English, minors: Art and Music.

Biggest creative influences: Harvey Kurtzman, William Faulkner, H.G. Wells, V.T. Hamlin, William Gaines, Wally Wood, etc.

1993 projects: New super-hero series (created in conjunction with R.A. Jones) called *Blood Tide. Suspended Animation* into fourth year and ten newspapers. Comics reviews.

Past comics titles and related projects: Ghosted *Alley Oop* briefly, created/wrote *Holiday Out* comic strip since 1982, *Holiday Out* comic book (Renegade) with appearances in Now, Comico, *CBG*, and Ocean Publications. *Straw Men* series (Innovation), *Angel of Death* series (Innovation), *The Adventures of Captain Nemo* (one issue released, Rip Off Press), dozens of comics-related features and articles in national magazines and newspapers. *Suspended Animation* weekly review column.

Favorite comics not worked on: *Flaming Carrot, The Spirit*, and *Sandman*.

Dream comic-book project: Another series like *Straw Men*. I'd love to write *Herbie* or horror comics.

✳ **James Van Hise.** 57754 Onaga Trail, Yucca Valley, California 92284.

Born: December 20, 1949, in Buffalo, New York.

Biggest creative influences: Ray Bradbury, Edgar Rice Burroughs, Harlan Ellison, Robert E. Howard, Stan Lee and Jack Kirby, and Gardner Fox.

Past comics titles and related projects: *The Real Ghostbusters* #1-3, 5-20, 22-28. *Tales of the Green Hornet. The Green Hornet: Solitary Sentinel. Twilight Zone* #8. *Tyrannosaurus Tex. Wap!* #1, *Fright Night* #3-7.

Favorite comics not worked on: *Magnus, Solar, Adam Strange, Concrete, Batman: Legends of the Dark Knight, Spawn*, and *Sandman*.

Dream comic-book project: John Carter of Mars.

✳ **Wayne Vansant.** 61 Park Road, Mableton, Georgia 30059.

Born: July 13, 1949, in Atlanta, Georgia.

College or other education: B.F.A., Atlanta College of Art.

Biggest creative influences: John Severin and Sam Glanzman.

1993 projects: *The 'Nam, Days of Wrath* (Apple), *Two-Fisted Tales*, and *King David* (Marvel/Nelson).

Past comics titles and related projects: *Savage Tales, Semper Fi, Battron, Red Badge of Courage* for First Comics, and *Real War Stories* (Eclipse).

Favorite comics not worked on: *Cadillacs and Dinosaurs*.

Dream comic-book project: To work with a knowledgeable Russian writer on a World War II Russian Front series, much like I'm doing with *Days of Darkness*, and sell it to a Russian market.

Here's my most recent publicity photo. I've had a rough time since falling into that volcano, so please don't tease me.   *Dan Vebber*

✳ **Dan Vebber.** 5732 North Shoreland Avenue, Whitefish Bay, Wisconsin 53217.

Born: August 7, 1970, in Columbia Hospital in beautiful downtown Milwaukee, Wisconsin.

College or other education: B.S.A. in Art, University of Wisconsin-Madison. M.F.A., School of Hard Knocks.

Comics-related education: Graphics Editor, *Daily Cardinal* (1991-92). Current Editor of *The Onion* (humor weekly).

Biggest creative influences: Chuck Jones, Mark Beyer, Peter Bagge, Devo, *Raw*, and *Drawn and Quarterly*.

1993 projects: Developing a new strip and trying to sell *Adventure!* to a nationwide publisher/distributor.

Past comics titles and related projects: *Adventure!* (currently running in *CBG*). *Cute Widdle Bunnies*.

Favorite comics not worked on: *Raw, Drawn and Quarterly*, and other such underground comics compendiums.

Dream comic-book project: Like everyone else, I'd love to illustrate a *Sandman* story. Or to work with Mark Beyer on something.

Tom Veitch

❋ **Tom Veitch.** Sky River Studios Ltd., P.O. Box 192, Bennington, Vermont 05201.

Born: September 26, 1951.

Biggest creative influences: Rimbaud, Henry Miller, William Burroughs, Carl Jung, and Jack Kirby.

1993 projects: *Kamandi: At Earth's End, Star Wars: Dark Empire II*, and *Tales of the Jedi*.

Past comics titles and related projects: *The Legion of Charlies, Sgt. Rock, Animal Man, Skull Comics, Death Rattle, Star Wars: Dark Empire, Slow Death, The Light and Darkness War, Light Tragicomics, The Nazz, Deviant Slice, My Name Is Chaos, Grunt Comics, Clash*, and *Two-Fisted Zombies*.

Favorite comics not worked on: *1963*.

Dream comic-book project: A 350-page hardbound comic-book novel, deep, philosophical, with dozens of characters, for an audience of people over thirty.

Sal Velluto

❋ **Sal Velluto.** 97 South Coolidge Street, Midvale, Utah 84047-3807.

Born: May 25, 1956, in Taranto, Italy.

College or other education: Academy of Fine Arts (Italy), B.F.A. degree.

1993 projects: I'm pencilling *Justice League Task Force* (DC Comics).

Past comics titles and related projects: Continuity: *Armor* and *Megalith*. DC: *Flash* and *Justice League America*. Marvel: *Captain America Special Edition, Double Dragon, Marvel Age, Moon Knight, Power Man* (for *Marvel Comics Presents*), *Power Pack and Cloak and Dagger* graphic novel, and *Power Pack*. Now: *Black Beauty Special, Green*

Hornet, and *Tales of the Green Hornet*. Valiant: *Rai* and *X-O Manowar*. Star Comics (Italy): *Lazarus Ledd*.

Favorite comics not worked on: Any black-and-white mystery/suspense comic.

Dream comic-book project: A progressive approach to visual storytelling.

✴ **Mark Verheiden.** c/o *CBG* Editorial Department, 700 East State Street, Iola, Wisconsin 54990.

Born: March 26, 1956, in Portland, Oregon.

College or other education: B.S., Portland State University.

Biggest creative influences: Alan Moore, Martin Scorsese, and Francis Ford Coppolla.

1993 projects: *Predator* and *Batman: Legends of the Dark Knight*.

Past comics titles and related projects: Comics: *American, Aliens, Predator*, and *Time Cop* (all for Dark Horse). *Stalkers* (Epic). *The Phantom* (DC). Movie screenplays: *Doomsday Conspiracy* (Warner Bros.), *Time Cop* (Largo), *American* (Warner Bros.), *The Mask* (New Line), *The Face* (Warner Bros.), and *Mr. Popper's Penguins* (New Line).

Favorite comics not worked on: Golden Age "all-star" comics.

Dream comic-book project: *Bizarro World* for DC.

✴ **Charles Vess.** c/o *CBG* Editorial Department, 700 East State Street, Iola, Wisconsin 54990.

Agent: Merille Heifetz, Writer's House.

Born: June 10, 1951, in Virginia.

College or other education: B.F.A., Virginia Commonwealth University.

Comics-related education: Instructor, William King Regional Art Center, Abingdon, Virginia: Drawing with Imagination (1992). Instructor, Parson School of Design, New York City: The Art of Science Fiction and Fantasy Illustration (1980-1982).

Biggest creative influences: Hal Foster and Arthur Rackham.

1993 projects: DC *Swamp Thing* covers, Marvel *Prince Valiant* mini-series, Dark Horse *Aliens*

Charles Vess

illustrated novel, and *StarDust*, a fairy tale for adults with Neil Gaiman (120 pages, full color).

Past comics titles and related projects: *Amazing Spider-Man, Web of Spider-Man, Marvel Fanfare, Thor, Rocketeer, Sandman, Concrete, Tales from the Heart, Books of Magic, Raven Banner, The Book of Night, Epic Illustrated, Spider-Man: Spirits of the Earth.* (Writing, inking, painting, covers, etc.) Also posters, magazine covers, and illustrations, game covers, prints, and books.

Favorite comics not worked on: Gladstone, *Bone*, and *Tintin*.

Dream comic-book project: The dream is ever-changing, but it certainly involves trees, fairies, ravens, adventure, and romance — and magic and mystery and fun.

✴ **Edd Vick.** 5014-D Roosevelt Way NE, Seattle, Washington 98105.

Born: November 14, 1958, in Houston, Texas.

College or other education: B.S. in Computer Science, 1983.

Edd Vick

1993 projects: *Wild Kingdom, Furkindred*, and *Heroes*.

Past comics titles and related projects: *Wild Kingdom, Furkindred*, and *A Death in the Cards*.

Dream comic-book project: Too late — I'm doing it!

Joe Vigil

✳ **Joe Vigil.** 5935 Auburn Boulevard, #96, Citrus Heights, California 95621.

Born: June 30, 1955, in Dayton, Ohio.

College or other education: Four years college (American River College).

Biggest creative influences: Frank Frazetta, Jack Kirby, Russ Heath, Wally Wood, and Bernie Wrightson.

1993 projects: *Gunfighters in Hell*, to be published in August.

Past comics titles and related projects: *Fritz Whistle, Chain Gang*, (Northstar), *Raw Media, Faust Saga, Bloodlines, Dog* (Rebel).

Favorite comics not worked on: *Xenozoic Tales, Spring Heel Jack, Darkstar, E.O.*

Dream comic-book project: I would like to adapt classics, *Moby Dick, Macbeth*, etc.

✳ **Timothy B. Vigil.** Rebel Studios, 4716 Judy Court, Sacramento, California 95841.

Born: September 29, 1958, in Sacramento, California.

Biggest creative influences: Frank Frazetta, Bernie Wrightson, Gil Kane, Hal Foster, Wally Wood, Klimt, Barry Smith, and Kaluta.

1993 projects: *Faust, Raw Media* magazines, and *E.O.*

Favorite comics not worked on: *Akira, Grendel*, and *Sin City*.

✳ **Tom Vincent.** 146-148 Barrett Street, Suite 303, Schenectady, New York 12305.

Born: January 27, 1956, in Schenectady, New York.

College or other education: Studied Fine Arts at Junior College of Albany, Russell Sage College (no degree).

Comics-related education: TBF (trial by fire), self-taught airbrush by studying work of nationally and internationally known illustrators, specifically the work of medical and technical illustrators.

Biggest creative influences: Flemish painters of the Renaissance, Impressionist and post-Impressionist painters, Maxfield Parrish, Peter Ledger, and '60s Marvel Comics.

1993 projects: Marvel/Epic: *Thor, Midnight Men, Lawdog*, and *Dragon Lines*.

Past comics titles and related projects:

Tom Vincent

Marvel (1988-present): *Silver Surfer, Speedball, What If?, Marvel Comics Presents, Marvel Super-Heroes, X-Factor, Fish Police, Nick Fury, Defenders of Dynatron City*, miscellaneous fill-ins. Full color: *Thanos Quest*, miscellaneous trade paperback covers and promotional material, *Infinity War* poster, *Conan* (graphic novels *Horn of Azoth* and *Ravagers in Time*). *Kull* (graphic novel *The Vale of the Shadow*). *Hellraiser.* Comico (1985-88): *Grendel, Fish Police, Justice Machine, Robotech* (*Macross, Masters* graphic novel), miscellaneous promotional material. First (1988): *Crossroads*, miscellaneous fill-ins. Warner Books (1987): Cover, *Fish Police* trade paperback. First Team Press: *Silver Surfer* print (Ron Lim).

Favorite comics not worked on: *The Spirit*, books drawn by Barry Windsor-Smith, Bernie Wrightson, Jack Kirby, P. Craig Russell, Mike Kaluta, Charles Vess, Val Seimeiks. *Taboo.*

Dream comic-book project: *At Play among the Stars*, a fully painted graphic novel by Bill Townsend and Tom Vincent, a story inspired by the genius of Stephen Hawking.

✱ **Neil Donald Vokes.** Iris Studios, P.O. Box 379, Lumberton, New Jersey 08048.

Agent: Mike Friedrich (Star*Reach).

Neil Donald Vokes

Born: May 12, 1954, in Fort Lauderdale, Florida.

Biggest creative influences: Steve Ditko, Jack Kirby, and lots more.

1993 projects: *Judah the Hammer, Elvira*, and *Teen Agents*.

Past comics titles and related projects: *Robotech Masters, Eagle, Blood of Dracula, Fright Night, Tarzan the Warrior, Congorilla, Speed Racer, Love Bites, Classex Illustrated, Black Hood, Fox*, and *Shuriken.*

Favorite comics not worked on: *Batman Adventures* (not yet, but soon!), *Doctor Strange, Nexus, Badger*, and *The Creeper.*

Dream comic-book project: If I tell, someone may steal my dream (seriously it would be something personal, something that said: Neil Vokes!).

✱ **Daniel Vozzo.** c/o *CBG* Editorial Department, 700 East State Street, Iola, Wisconsin 54990.

Born: November 22, 1962, in Brooklyn, New York.

Comics-related education: DC Comics, Assistant to Production Director (1987).

Biggest creative influences: Steve Oliff's work (old and new).

1993 projects: Coloring DC's Vertigo titles: *Sandman, Shade, the Changing Man, Doom Patrol, Kid Eternity, Ghostdancing*, and also *Scarlett.*

Past comics titles and related projects: DC

Daniel Vozzo

Comics: *Dragonlance, Gammarauders, Hellblazer* #27 and 58, *The Greatest Batman Stories Ever Told, The Greatest Joker Stories Ever Told, The Greatest Team-Up Stories Ever Told, Superman Archives Volume 1, Secret Origins* #50, *The Art of Walt Simonson* (Batman story), *Doom Force,* and *Lobo's Back.* Posters: *Sandman, Death,* and *Doom Patrol.* Statues: *Sandman.* Marvel Comics: *What If?, What The--?!.*

Favorite comics not worked on: *Animal Man, Batman, Star Trek: The Next Generation,* and *Swamp Thing.*

Dream comic-book project: Anything, as long as I can get the chance to use a computer again.

✳ Mark Waid. c/o *CBG* Editorial Department, 700 East State Street, Iola, Wisconsin 54990.

Born: March 21, 1962, in Hueytown, Alabama.

College or other education: Virginia Commonwealth University.

Biggest creative influences: Harlan Ellison, Bill Loebs, Robert Loren Fleming, Larry David (*not* Peter David — *Larry* David).

1993 projects: *Flash, L.E.G.I.O.N. '93, Metamorpho, Justice League Quarterly,* and *Valor.*

Past comics titles and related projects: Fantagraphics editor: *Amazing Heroes.* DC editor: *Secret Origins, Christmas with the Superheroes, Legion of Super-Heroes, Batman: Gotham by Gaslight, Daily*

Planet, and *Doom Patrol.* Archie writer: *Archie's Pals and Gals.* DC writer: *Flash Annuals* 1991-93, *Detective Comics Annual* 1989, *Flash TV Special, Superboy* #7, and pretty much the entire Impact line.

Favorite comics not worked on: *Green Lantern, Sam and Max, Concrete, Hate,* and *Eye of Mongambo.*

Dream comic-book project: I'd write *Jerry Seinfeld Comics and Stories* for free.

✳ Alex Wald. 1217 West School Street, Chicago, Illinois 60657.

Born: July 25, 1949, in Chicago, Illinois.

College or other education: B.F.A., School of the Art Institute of Chicago, 1972.

Biggest creative influences: Chas. Addams, Ernie Bushmiller, R. Crumb, Harvey Kurtzman, and Will Elder.

1993 projects: *American Splendor* (Dark Horse), *Urban Legends* (Dark Horse), also assorted logos for DC Comics.

Past comics titles and related projects: First Comics, Art Director, 1983-90. *Lone Wolf and Cub,* English adaptation. Curated exhibitions: *Robo Kaiju,* S.A.I.C. Gallery, 1979; *Thank You, Godzilla,* Japan Society, New York, 1979. Miscellaneous design or coloring, 1985-present, DC Comics, Dark Horse, First, and Kitchen Sink.

Favorite comics not worked on: *Eightball, Hate,* and *Love and Rockets.*

Dream comic-book project: I'm still dreaming.

✳ Reed Waller. P.O. Box 7439, Powderhorn Station, Minneapolis, Minnesota 55407.

Born: August 3, 1949, in Albert Lea, Minnesota.

College or other education: Three years studying Psychology (no degree).

Biggest creative influences: Crumb, Ward Kimball, and Preston Blair (animators), Frank King, Mucha, and Dan DeCarlo.

1993 projects: *Omaha* continues, *Speakingstone* to continue, and *Girlie* strip for LEP.

Past comics titles and related projects: *Munden's Bar Annual* #2, First. *Strip AIDS USA, Choices,* and *True North* benefits. Omaha appear-

Reed Waller

ance in *Gauntlet* and *Reflex*. *Critters*, Fantagraphics. *Grateful Dead Comix*, Kitchen Sink Press.

Favorite comics not worked on: *Beanworld, Zot!, Flaming Carrot,* and *Naughty Bits.*

Dream comic-book project: If I could, I wouldn't reveal it now.

✳ Andrew T. Walls. 410 2nd Avenue Southwest, Dyersville, Iowa 52040.

Born: June 27, 1966, in Oskaloosa, Iowa.

College or other education: B.F.A., Graphic Design, minor in Drawing.

Comics-related education: Part-time assistant to Phil Hestor.

Biggest creative influences: Alan Davis, Brian Bolland, Jim Lee, and Rick Leonardi.

1993 projects: *Metaphysical Man and Miracle Woman* (writing, pencilling, and inking) for The Association of Unity Churches. *The Revenge of the Andromeda Men*, a four-issue mini-series (no publisher yet).

Past comics titles and related projects:

Adventure Comics: *Interactive Comics #3 — Dudley Serious and the Space Patrol* (pencils). *Roger Wilco #2* and *3* (pencils). Eternity: *Kid Cannibal*, four-issue mini-series (pencils). Caliber: Back cover to *Steel Angel #1* (pencil and ink).

Favorite comics not worked on: *Archer & Armstrong* and *Sandman.*

Dream comic-book project: I'd like to write and pencil the *X-Men* and I'd like to do an adaptation of the *Bhagavad Gita.*

Bradley Walton

✳ Bradley Walton. 818 Oakland Street, Harrisonburg, Virginia 22801.

Born: July 31, 1972, in Harrisonburg, Virginia.

College or other education: As of summer 1993, I am a rising senior in college aiming for a B.A., with a double major in English and Philosophy and Religion.

Biggest creative influences: Karl Story, Neil Gaiman, and Frank Miller.

1993 projects: Inking *Lazaretto VI* for Caliber's anthology *Negative Burn*. For London Night Studios I'm inking the cover of *Savage Blood #1* and inking the cover and lead story as well as writing, inking, and lettering the backup story for a book which is untitled as of this writing.

Favorite comics not worked on: *Sandman, The American, Watchmen, Batman: Legends of the Dark Knight*, and *Books of Magic*.

Dream comic-book project: Inking anything written by Neil Gaiman, Frank Miller, or Alan Moore. Writing a super-hero book with heavy philosophical and religious (but not necessarily Christian) overtones. Inking a *Star Wars* comic.

Alonzo L. Washington

✳ **Alonzo L. Washington.** 2313 North Early, Kansas City, Kansas 66101.

Agent: Dan Washington.

Born: June 1, 1967, in Kansas City, Kansas.

College or other education: Kansas City Community College.

Comics-related education: Kansas City media project.

Biggest creative influences: The whole comic-book industry and Malcolm X.

1993 projects: A new company called X. Comics. *The Mighty Ace* and *Omega 7* (these two titles will be published by Omega 7).

Past comics titles and related projects: *Original Man* and *Dark Force*.

Favorite comics not worked on: Image, *Batman, Spawn, Rai and the Future Force, Brotherman*, and *Spider-Man*.

Dream comic-book project: I'd like to do something with Image and Big City Comics.

✳ **Vinson Watson.** Trinity Visuals c/o Vinson Watson, P.O. Box 16582, Chicago, Illinois 60616-0582.

Born: March 26, 1973, in Chicago, Illinois.

College or other education: Basic Art certificate from AIS (Art Instruction Schools). Studying Film/Video.

Comics-related education: Agent, AIS student, publisher, executive writer, editor, and art director/editor for Dark Universe (a division of Trinity Visuals).

Biggest creative influences: Jesus, Freazie White, DC Comics, Image, Whitney Barber, Wes Craven, Everette Hartsoe, Lorraine Reyes, and Bruce and Brandon Lee.

1993 projects: *Re-Action: The Ultimate Man, Sweet Childe*, and *Street Rat* for New Moon Studios. *The Nightmen*, the premiere black superhero group; *Trinity Visuals Con Keeper Pack*; and my line of prints.

Past comics titles and related projects: *The Re-Action Specials, Empire Rose* (1989). The special comics have just gotten distribution by Capital City Comics Distribution, and so has *Sweet Childe* #0 and *Re-Action* #0, which Capital has gained exclusive distribution rights to, strangely enough. We're glad to have them on our list of distributors, as well as Diamond, Heroes World, Friendly Franks, and Raw, but Capital has really been most helpful to us and we hope to be able to do more business with them in the future.

Favorite comics not worked on: *Superman, Humants, Razor, Youngblood, Robin, WildC.A.T.S, Spawn, Project Newman, Doctor Strange*, and *Ebony Warrior* #1.

Dream comic-book project: A Spawn/Drac/ Maxx team-up, a Re-Action/Ebony Warrior team-up, or Spawn versus Jeremiah Thrash, Demon Hunter.

✳ **Lawrence Watt-Evans.** c/o Russell Galen, Scott Meredith Literary Agency, 845 Third Avenue, New York, New York 10022.

Agent: Russell Galen, Scott Meredith Literary Agency.

Born: Midnight between July 25 and July 26, 1954 (legally, the 26th), in Arlington, Massachusetts.

Lawrence Watt-Evans

College or other education: Dropped out of Princeton University after junior year.

Biggest creative influences: Al Feldstein, Will Eisner, Marv Wolfman, Doug Moench, Steve Gerber, Alan Moore, and Neil Gaiman.

1993 projects: Nothing definite; a couple are under consideration at Dark Horse.

Past comics titles and related projects: *Open Space* #1 and #2 (and #5 and #7 which never appeared). Had a story adapted in *Orbit* #2. 112 installments of *CBG* column *Rayguns, Elves and Skin-Tight Suits*.

Favorite comics not worked on: *Sandman*.

Dream comic-book project: The New Blackhawks.

✳ **Bill Webb.** 396 21st Avenue Court, Milton, Washington 98354.

Born: June 14, 1957, at Hamilton Field Air Force Base, California.

College or other education: Merced College (A.A.).

Biggest creative influences: Alex Toth, Gus Arriola, and Don Bluth.

Past comics titles and related projects: *Josie*

and the Pussycats/Archie Comics. *Aida-Zee*/Nate Butler Studios.

Favorite comics not worked on: *Batman: The Animated Series*.

Dream comic-book project: Science-fiction graphic novels based on my characters.

✳ **Kathleen A. Webb.** 396 21st Avenue Court, Milton, Washington 98354.

Born: October 6, 1956, in Puyallup, Washington.

College or other education: College course in Fashion Illustration and writing classes.

Biggest creative influences: Dan DeCarlo of Archie Comics and Charles Schulz of *Peanuts* fame.

1993 projects: Pencils for *Barbie Fashion*, Marvel Comics; one-page comic *Holly and the Ivy Halls* for *Brio* magazine, Focus on the Family Publishers.

Past comics titles and related projects: From 1985-1991 worked at Archie Comics as a freelance writer/artist. Titles included: *Betty's Diary, Veronica, Betty and Veronica, Archie, Jughead, Archie 2000, Betty and Me, Little Archie,* and *Josie*. 1990 — one page pencil art for Nate Butler Studios' *Aida-Zee*. 1991 — pencilled and wrote tract entitled *The Monster* for Nate Butler Studios; also pencilled and co-wrote story titled *The Truest Kind of Love* for *Parodee* comic from Nate Butler Studios (to be released this year, 1993).

Favorite comics not worked on: DC's *Batman: The Animated Series* comic book.

Dream comic-book project: A teen-age girl comic like Archie's *Betty and Veronica* or a graphic fantasy/romance book.

✳ **Len Wein.** 6300 Jumilla Avenue, Woodland Hills, California 91367.

Agent: Scott Schwartz (animation and live-action only), Dytman and Schwartz.

Born: June 12, 1948, in New York City, New York.

College or other education: Associate in Advertising Art, State University of New York at Farmingdale.

Biggest creative influences: Rod Serling,

Len Wein

Ray Bradbury, Paddy Chayefsky, and Robert Kanigher.

1993 projects: *Danger Trail #1-4, Twilight Zone Volume 3 #1, Deathstroke, the Terminator Annual #2, Batman: Legends of the Dark Knight:* "Premiere," *Green Lantern Corps Quarterly:* "Nobler in the Mind . . . "

Past comics titles and related projects: *Superman, Batman, Wonder Woman, Flash, Green Lantern, Swamp Thing, Justice League, Phantom Stranger, Human Target, Star Trek, Blue Beetle, Amazing Spider-Man, Hulk, Thor, Fantastic Four, Defenders, Marvel Team-Up, Wolverine, New X-Men, Man-Thing, Werewolf by Night, Mister Miracle, Danger Trail, DC Who's Who, Legends,* and numerous others.

Favorite comics not worked on: *Sandman.*

✱ **Joan Weis.** Now Comics, 60 Revere Drive, Northbrook, Illinois 60062.

Born: February 15, in Evanston, Illinois.

College or other education: Oakton College, A.A. Roosevelt University, B.A. (English).

Biggest creative influences: Neal Adams, Harlan Ellison, Jeff Butler, Chuck Dixon, and Mike Baron.

1993 projects: All Now titles.

Past comics titles and related projects: All Now titles.

Favorite comics not worked on: *Star Trek.*

Dream comic-book project: *Star Trek.*

✱ **Greg Weisman.** c/o *CBG* Editorial Department, 700 East State Street, Iola, Wisconsin 54990.

Born: September 28, 1963, in Los Angeles, California.

College or other education: Stanford, B.A. University of Southern California, M.P.W. (Masters of Professional Writing).

Biggest creative influences: Faulkner, Hemingway, Shakespeare, and *Hill Street Blues.*

1993 projects: Currently working as head of series development for Disney TV Animation. For Fall 1993, we have two new shows: *Bonkers!* and *Marsupilami.*

Past comics titles and related projects: Writer: *Captain Atom, Secret Origins, Who's Who in the DC Universe.* Associate Editor DC Comics: *Teen Titans, Shazam!, Young All-Stars, All-Star Squadron, Justice League of America, Justice League, Infinity Inc., Justice League International, Teen Titans Spotlight,* and *New Teen Titans.*

Favorite comics not worked on: *Cerebus, Sandman, Bone,* and *Love and Rockets.*

Dream comic-book project: Too many to count.

Werner Wejp-Olsen

✱ **Werner Wejp-Olsen.** 35 New South Street, Northampton, Massachusetts 01060.

Agent: Judi Schuler.

Born: January 7, 1938, in Copenhagen, Denmark.

College or other education: College/Journalism.

Biggest creative influences: Sam Cobean, Ronald Searle, Mort Walker, Dik Browne, Carl Barks, and Wilson McCoy.

1993 projects: *Albert the Troll*, a comic book with humor, satire, and adventure.

Past comics titles and related projects: *Aesop's Fables* (Fantagraphics), *Professor Yuk-Yuk's Cartooning Class* (United Feature Syndicate newspaper feature), *Tales of Hans Christian Andersen* (Asterisk newspaper feature), *Maestro and Amalita* (Field Newspaper Syndicate newspaper feature), and *Granny and Slowpoke* (Field Newspaper Syndicate newspaper feature).

Favorite comics not worked on: *Wizard of Id, Calvin and Hobbes, Doonesbury*, and reprints of Carl Barks' Disney material.

Dream comic-book project: A combination of humor and adventure.

✳ **Larry Welz.** P.O. Box 4662, Santa Rosa, California 95402.

Agent: Denis Kitchen.

Born: November 21, 1948, in Bakersfield, California.

College or other education: One semester at California College of Arts and Crafts in Oakland.

Biggest creative influences: Wally Wood.

1993 projects: Cherry Look-Alike Contest, *Cherry* #15 and #16, and *Cherry's Jubilee* #3 and #4.

Past comics titles and related projects: *Yellow Dog, Captain Guts, American Flyer, Monolith, Tuff Shit, Slow Death, San Francisco Comics, Earth* magazine, *Organ* magazine, *Aquarian Age* magazine (really), *Kid's Liberation Coloring Book, Ramparts* magazine, *Bakersfield Kountry Komics*, and *Weird Smut*.

Dream comic-book project: Doing the Ellie Dee book with computer enhancements.

✳ **David Wenzel.** 95-R Maple Avenue, Box 294, Durham, Connecticut 06422.

Born: November 22, 1950, in Utica, New York.

College or other education: M.F.A., Hartford Art School.

Biggest creative influences: Howard Pyle, N.C. Wyeth, Arthur Rackham, and Hal Foster.

1993 projects: *Wizards of Evernight* for Eclipse, a three-part graphic novel written by Kurt Busiek.

Past comics titles and related projects: *Marvel Team-Up, Avengers, Savage Sword of Conan*, and *Iron Fist* (Marvel). *Kong the Untamed* and *Warlords* graphic novel (DC). *The Hobbit*, a three-part graphic novel (Eclipse).

Dream comic-book project: To finish the Tolkien project for *Lord of the Rings*.

✳ **Mark Wheatley.** Insight Studios, 7844 St. Thomas Drive, Baltimore, Maryland 21236.

Agent: Mike Friedrich (Star*Reach).

Born: May 27, 1954, in Portsmouth, Virginia.

College or other education: B.F.A. from Virginia Commonwealth University in Communication Arts and Design.

Comics-related education: Published a fanzine, *Nucleus*, from 1969-1974.

Biggest creative influences: Ditko, McCay, Williamson, Crane, N.C. Wyeth, Eisner, Kurtzman, and Degas.

1993 projects: TBA/Two issues of *Batman: Legends of the Dark Knight*: "Suicide." Write/art/color.

Past comics titles and related projects: Short stories for *Heavy Metal, Epic, Gasm, Tales of Terror*. Series: *Mars, Jonny Quest, Blood of the Innocent, Baron Munchausen, The Black Hood, Breathtaker*, and *Tarzan the Warrior*.

Favorite comics not worked on: *Cages, Yummy Fur*, and there must be more, but my mind is a blank.

Dream comic-book project: *Cat in Control*, a fantastic story set in the 'burbs.

✳ **Doug Wheeler.** c/o *CBG* Editorial Department, 700 East State Street, Iola, Wisconsin 54990.

Born: December 21, 1960, in Palo Alto, California.

Doug Wheeler

College or other education: Penn State, B.S., Computer Science.

Biggest creative influences: Clark Ashton Smith, Woody Allen, George Orwell, Alan Dean Foster, Aleksandr Solzhenitsyn, Monty Python, Arthur C. Clarke, Olaf Stapledon, *Star Trek* (original), Sergei Eisenstein, Fritz Lang, Norman Lear, *Laugh-In*, and *Saturday Night Live* (original cast).

1993 projects: *Doctor Strange*, Alan Dean Foster's *Midworld, Taboo, Twilight Zone, Aesop's Desecrated Morals/Classics Desecrated*, and *Cheval Noir*.

Past comics titles and related projects: *Swamp Thing* (1989-91), *Classics Desecrated* (1991-present), *Alien Encounters* (Eclipse), *Comico Christmas Special* (1988), *Dark Horse Presents, Cheval Noir*, and *April Horrors*.

Favorite comics not worked on: *Bone, Cerebus, Comic Relief, Dirty Plotte, Maximortal, Nausicaä, Nexus, Sandman*, and *Tales from the Heart*.

Dream comic-book project: To launch a horror/supernatural universe I've developed and my own monthly anthology.

✳ **Shannon Wheeler.** Adhesive Comics, P.O. Box 5372, Austin, Texas 78763-5372.

Born: August 13, 1966, in San Francisco, California.

College or other education: Architecture degree from Berkeley.

Biggest creative influences: Charles Schulz.

1993 projects: *Too Much Coffee Man, Too Much Coffee Man* cartoon, and Too Much Coffee Man Brand Coffee (?).

Past comics titles and related projects: College newspaper strip, *Tooth and Justice*.

Favorite comics not worked on: *Yummy Fur, Tropo, Hate, Eightball*, and *A1*.

Dream comic-book project: Exactly what I'm doing, *Too Much Coffee Man*.

✳ **Geoffrey White.** Now Comics, 60 Revere Drive, Suite 200, Northbrook, Illinois 60062.

Born: May 28, 1971, in Maywood, Illinois.

College or other education: College of Lake County, A.A. University of Illinois at Chicago, B.A., English.

Comics-related education: One semester's internship at Now.

Biggest creative influences: Neil Gaiman, Frank Miller, Bob Kane, John Byrne, and Marc Silvestri.

1993 projects: *The Green Hornet, The Twilight Zone, Married with Children: 2099, Married with Children: Off Broadway, Married with Children: Quantum Quartet, Ralph Snart Adventures, Green Hornet: Dark Tomorrow, Ghostbusters, Speed Racer*, and *Black Beauty Special*.

Past comics titles and related projects: Every Now title of 1993.

Favorite comics not worked on: *X-Men, Sandman, CyberForce, Shade, the Changing Man, The Crow*, and *Batman*.

Dream comic-book project: A Green Hornet mini-series co-written and drawn by Frank Miller (but I don't think Miller co-writes anything). Writing the X-Men.

✳ **Richard C. White.** 406 Newman Drive, Clarksville, Tennessee 37042.

Born: July 12, 1959, in Fayette, Missouri.

College or other education: B.S., History, Criminal Justice minor, Central Missouri State University.

Biggest creative influences: John Byrne, David Drake, Chris Claremont, Mike Grell, and Glenn Cook.

1993 projects: *Troubleshooters* and *Hellspoint*

for Starwarp Concepts. Editing for *5th Panel Comics* (a fanzine).

Favorite comics not worked on: *Harbinger, Grendel, Solar, Dark Horse Presents, Justice Society of America*, and *Femforce*.

Dream comic-book project: An X-Men story with John Byrne pencils and Terry Austin inks.

✻ **Jeff Whiting.** 875 Derbyshire Road, Apartment 183, Daytona Beach, Florida 32117.

Born: December 23, 1964, in Daytona Beach, Florida.

College or other education: Daytona Beach Community College, Commercial Art.

Comics-related education: I did background work for John Beatty for several years (inking).

Biggest creative influences: John Beatty, Mark Farmer, and Scott Williams.

1993 projects: *Street Fighter* — inking the monthly series for Malibu (first issue comes out in May). *The Tick* — published occasionally, issue #12 out soon (inking).

Past comics titles and related projects: I inked *The Tick* #11 and #12 for NEC. Also inked *Paul the Samurai* #1 and #2 and *Man Eating Cow* #1 and #2 for NEC.

Favorite comics not worked on: *Spawn, WildC.A.T.S, Amazing Spider-Man*, and *X-Men*.

Dream comic-book project: Working with some of my favorite pencillers and writers.

✻ **Al Wiesner.** c/o *CBG* Editorial Department, 700 East State Street, Iola, Wisconsin 54990.

Born: July 2, 1930, in Philadelphia, Pennsylvania.

College or other education: Post-graduate Commercial Art Course, one semester Beginner Oil, one semester Advanced Oil Painting.

Biggest creative influences: Caniff, Raymond, and Eisner.

1993 projects: *New Adventures of Shaloman* comic.

Past comics titles and related projects: *Mark I* comic series (three issues), *Primer* (Comico, one story), *Shaloman* comic (nine issues), *New Adventures of Shaloman* (two issues), *Superfan 1999*

Al Wiesner

— Baseball comic (one issue), and illustrations for Senior Publications, Melville, New York.

Favorite comics not worked on: *Phantom* comic strip, Flor Dery *Spider-Man* strips.

Dream comic-book project: Shaloman and Superman fight world's evil.

✻ **Joe Wight.** P.O. Box 224, Elk, Washington 99009.

College or other education: Bachelor's Degree, English Writing.

Biggest creative influences: Johji Manabe (Outlanders) and Joe Kubert.

1993 projects: *Twilight-X* (monthly series).

Past comics titles and related projects: *Twilight-X* (self-published, Pork Chop Press), *Twilight-X: Interlude* (six-issue Antarctic mini-series), and *Mangazine* #8 and #9 (short Twilight-X story).

Favorite comics not worked on: *Dirty Pair.*

Dream comic-book project: Working on what I want right now. *Star Wars, Star Trek*, also.

✻ **Doug Wildey.** c/o *CBG* Editorial Department, 700 East State Street, Iola, Wisconsin 54990.

Doug Wildey

Born: May 2, 1922, in Yonkers, New York.
Biggest creative influences: Caniff, Sickles, Raymond, and Foster.
1993 projects: *Rio #4, Rio Outgunned*.
Past comics titles and related projects: *Buffalo Bill, Top Secret, Underworld Crime*, war, romance, sci-fi, horror, *Outlaw Kid, Wyatt Earp, Frontier Western, Lash LaRue, Hopalong Cassidy, Dr. Kildare, Gomer Pyle, Tarzan, Sgt. Rock, Psycho, Nightmare, Buster Crabbe*, etc. Newspaper syndicated strips: *The Saint, Ambler*, ghost art on *Steve Canyon*. TV animation — designer, director, producer: Creator *Jonny Quest, Return to the Planet of the Apes, Godzilla, Jana of the Jungle*. Models: *Mr. T, Turbo Teen*, etc. Graphic novels: *Rio #1-3*.
Dream comic-book project: *Rio #5*.

✳ **Patrick J. Williams.** 7824 South Kilpatrick, Chicago, Illinois 60652-1133.
Born: October 11, 1958, in Chicago, Illinois.
College or other education: B.A., University of Illinois at Chicago.
Comics-related education: Staff internship at Now Comics.
Biggest creative influences: Jim Aparo, Walt Simonson, Steve Oliff, and Curt Swan.
1993 projects: *Mr. T and the T-Force, Green Hornet*, and *The New Adventures of Speed Racer*.

Patrick J. Williams

Past comics titles and related projects: *Green Hornet* (monthly), *Sting of the Green Hornet, Real Ghostbusters, Speed Racer, Ralph Snart Adventures, Elementals*, and *Planet of the Apes*.
Favorite comics not worked on: *Superman, James Bond*, and *Tiny Toons*.
Dream comic-book project: A *Twin Peaks* book, but based on the characters as they were in the late 1960s-early '70s, when the older characters were young and just getting started.

✳ **Skip Williamson.** P.O. Box 5496, Riverforest, Illinois 60305-5496.
Born: August 19, 1944, in San Antonio, Texas.
College or other education: Four years attendance at Culver-Stockton College, a creatively vapid little liberal arts diploma mill (no diploma).
Comics-related education: Nothing formal. I've found that jumping feet first into an impossible project is the best way to learn. Better to learn from your own mistakes than those of others.
Biggest creative influences: Harvey Kurtzman and the indisputable contemptibility of the human animal.
1993 projects: Self-publishing a variety of comix projects. Just released: *Class War Comix: A Brief History of the Revolution* (a collection of wild-

Photo: Harriett Hiland

Skip Williamson

eyed, seditious comix from the '60s and '70s).
Soon to be released: *Pighead* #1 (all new comix
from Skip Williamson).

Past comics titles and related projects: Co-
creator with Jay Lynch: *The Chicago Mirror* #1-3
(1967-68), *Bijou Funnies* # 1-8 (1968-73). Editor: *Conspiracy Capers* (1969), *Skip Williamson's
Comix and Stories featuring Snappy Sammy Smoot*
(1979). Contributor: *Yellowdog* (1969), *Tasty
Comix* (1969), *Hungry Chuck Biscuits Comics and
Stories* (1971), *Don Dohler's Pro Junior* (1971),
Mom's Homemade Comix (1971), *Comix Book*
(1974-76), *National Lampoon* (1975-76), *Playboy*
magazine (1976-85), *Blab!* (1987-93). Anthology of Skip Williamson Comix: *The Scum Also
Rises* (Fantagraphics, 1988), *Halsted Street: Tor-
ment and Drama from the Hog Butcher*, a collection
of comic strips originally published in the *Chicago
Daily News* (Kitchen Sink Press, 1991), *Skip
Williamson's Naked Hostility*, a sketchbook collection (self-published, 1992), *Class War Comix: A
Brief History of the Revolution*, a collection of
crazed, revolutionary comix from the '60s and

'70s (self-published in association with Mike
Johnson, 1993).

Favorite comics not worked on: Anything
by Art Spiegelman, R. Crumb, Jay Lynch, S. Clay
Wilson, Kim Deitch, Peter Bagge, Justin Green,
Harvey Pekar, Frank Stack, Shel Silverstein,
Robert Williams, Spain, Julie Doucet, Aline
Kominsky-Crumb, and Gilbert Shelton.

Dream comic-book project: Edit and publish a coffee-table book featuring the best work
from all of the above and have it lodge firmly for
a long period of time on *The New York Times Best-
seller List* so that everyone makes a mint and so
that the "legit art" book market becomes a venue
for the best in comic art.

✱ **Damon Willis.** c/o Insight Studios, 7844
St. Thomas Drive, Baltimore, Maryland 21236.

Born: May 4, 1963, in Schenectady, New
York.

College or other education: B.F.A. from the
University of Maryland.

Biggest creative influences: Jack Kirby.

1993 projects: *The Catalyst* from Dark Horse.

Past comics titles and related projects:
Aliens: Genocide (pencils), Dark Horse. *The Black
Hood* #6 (inks), # 9 (pencils), DC. *Tarzan the
Warrior* (colors), Malibu. *Blood of Dracula*
(pencils), Apple Comics. *Tarzan Forbandelsen* # 3
(script and art), Semic.

Favorite comics not worked on: *Gregory*,
Piranha Press.

Dream comic-book project: An illustrated
version of *The Caves of Steel* by Isaac Asimov.

Daniel Wilson
(for picture, see Darren Goodhart)

✱ **Daniel Wilson.** c/o *CBG* Editorial Department, 700 East State Street, Iola, Wisconsin
54990.

Born: January 9, 1957, in Saint Louis,
Missouri.

College or other education: A.A.S. in Advertising and A.A. in Broadcasting.

Biggest creative influences: Alan Moore,
Frank Miller, Jack Kirby, and Gene Colan.

1993 projects: Writer, . . . *absolute power* . . .
(Alpha Productions), a four-issue mini-series.

Past comics titles and related projects: Writer: *Shattered Earth #3: Doc Apocalypse, Shattered Earth #6: Prophet and Laws, Erotique #1: Straight on 'Til Morning, Scum of the Earth #1-3,* and *Flesh Gordon #1-4.*

Favorite comics not worked on: *Shade, the Changing Man, Animal Man, Batman: Legends of the Dark Knight, Death: The High Cost of Living,* and *Hellblazer.*

Dream comic-book project: Anything with Frank Miller, Brian Bolland, or Arthur Adams.

Gavin Wilson

✳ **Gavin Wilson.** c/o *CBG* Editorial Department, 700 East State Street, Iola, Wisconsin 54990.

Born: June 3, 1965, in New York City.

College or other education: B.F.A. in Fine Art Painting from The Art Center College of Design (Los Angeles, California).

Biggest creative influences: Visually oriented culture, too many to mention.

1993 projects: *Sandman Mystery Theatre* covers and *Skin Graft* covers.

Past comics titles and related projects: *Doom Patrol #54* and *Shade, the Changing Man #23* covers.

✳ **Keith S. Wilson.** Misc. Mayhem Studio, 1101 FM 1825, Pflugerville, Texas 78660.

Born: February 24, 1958, in Anchorage, Alaska.

College or other education: Associate of Applied Arts, TSTC, Waco, Texas.

Biggest creative influences: Chuck Jones.

1993 projects: DC: *Scarlett* (co-creator/co-plotter), *Bloodlines* (inker). Marvel: *King Arthur and the Knights of Justice* (pencils). Upper Deck: *Comic Ball 5* cards.

Past comics titles and related projects: DC: *Hammerlocke* (co-plotter/co-creator/inker), *Power of the Atom* (inker), *Angel and the Ape* (inker). Comico: *Elementals* first series (inker). Marvel: *What The--?!* (pencils and inks). Upper Deck: *Comic Ball Trading Cards Series 3 and 4* (character illustration).

Favorite comics not worked on: *Bone* and *Madman.*

Dream comic-book project: What, tell you and ruin the surprise?

✳ **Marilee Woch.** c/o *CBG* Editorial Department, 700 East State Street, Iola, Wisconsin 54990.

Born: November 8, 1964, in San Rafael, California.

College or other education: San Francisco State University, Political Science major, four years.

Comics-related education: Warehouse manager, Eclipse. Assistant editor, Majestic.

Biggest creative influences: Tom Waits and Lou Reed.

1993 projects: *Comics Futurestars 1993 —* trading card set and other Majestic titles.

Favorite comics not worked on: *Love and Rockets* and *Sandman.*

✳ **Stan Woch.** c/o *CBG* Editorial Department, 700 East State Street, Iola, Wisconsin 54990.

Agent: Sharon Cho (Star*Reach).

science-fiction and monster stories of Jack Kirby and Steve Ditko.

1993 projects: *Widow: Kill Me Again* and *War Monsters — King Boltrax vs. Grinzon*; both are three-issue mini-series from Ground Zero Comics.

Past comics titles and related projects: *Daikazu, Daikazu vs. Gugoron, Dark Horse Presents, Monsters!* role-playing game, and *Widow: Flesh and Blood*.

Favorite comics not worked on: *Wonder Man* (Marvel), *John Byrne's Next Men* (Dark Horse), and *anything* Richard Corben has to do with.

Dream comic-book project: To illustrate a story featuring Godzilla or other Toho monsters.

Stan Woch

Born: July 8, 1959, in Niagara Falls, New York.

College or other education: Pratt Institute, School of Art and Design, two years. Kubert School, 1½ years.

Comics-related education: Assistant to Gray Morrow, 1½ years.

Biggest creative influences: Neal Adams, Bernie Wrightson, Jeff Jones, Stan Drake, Gray Morrow, and Al Williamson.

1993 projects: *Doom Patrol* and *Black Orchid*.

Past comics titles and related projects: *World's Finest, Teen Titans, Swamp Thing, Airboy, Tapping the Vein, Sandman,* and *Hellblazer*.

✱ **Mike Wolfer.** Ground Zero Comics, P.O. Box 1832, Dover, Delaware 19903-1832.

Born: March 9, 1963, in Cape Cod, Massachusetts.

College or other education: Joe Kubert School of Cartoon and Graphic Arts Inc.

Comics-related education: Joe Kubert School of Cartoon and Graphic Arts Inc.

Biggest creative influences: The 1950s

Marv Wolfman

✱ **Marv Wolfman.** c/o *CBG* Editorial Department, 700 East State Street, Iola, Wisconsin 54990.

Born: May 13, 1946, in Brooklyn, New York.

College or other education: Queens College, B.F.A. degree.

Comics-related education: High School of

Art and Design (Cartooning major). College, Art Major. Interned two summers at DC Comics. Assistant editor to Joe Kubert.

Biggest creative influences: Outside writers: Ray Bradbury and Alfred Bester. In comics: H. Kurtzman, Al Capp, John Broome, Stan Lee, and Charles Biro.

1993 projects: Writer: *New Titans, Deathstroke, the Terminator, Team Titans,* and others. Editor/writer: *Disney Adventures* magazine.

Past comics titles and related projects: *Superman, Batman, Mickey Mouse, DuckTales, Spider-Man, Fantastic Four, Tomb of Dracula, Daredevil, John Carter of Mars, Tarzan, Nova, Spider-Woman, Night Force, Green Lantern, Vigilante, Omega Men, Luke Cage, Doctor Strange, Crazy* magazine, *Crisis on Infinite Earths, Wolverine, Sable, Star Trek, House of Mystery, House of Secrets, Captain Marvel, Marvel Two-in-One, Wonder Woman, Who's Who, Werewolf by Night, Frankenstein,* etc.

Favorite comics not worked on: *Spirit, Mad* #1-23, *Goodman Beaver, Sandman, Watchmen, Superman, Spawn, Bone,* etc.

Dream comic-book project: To be able to write, draw, letter, color, edit, and publish my own title.

✳ **Jim Woodring.** 5736 17th Avenue Northeast, Seattle, Washington 98105.

Born: October 11, 1952, in Los Angeles, California.

Biggest creative influences: R. Crumb, Justin Green, Geo. Herriman, T.S. Sullivant, and Harry McNaught.

1993 projects: *Aliens, Tantalizing Stories, Blue Block, Collected Frank Comics,* and *Heavy Metal* (various small contributions).

Past comics titles and related projects: *Jim, Frank in the River, Real Stuff, Tantalizing Stories, Freaks,* miscellaneous covers and illustrations.

Favorite comics not worked on: *Hate, Love and Rockets, Eightball, Steven,* etc.

Dream comic-book project: *Book of Revelations.*

✳ **Chad Woody.** Route 1, Box 172-B1, Willard, Missouri 65781.

Born: July 16, 1973, in Woodstock, Illinois.

College or other education: Two years of college toward a B.F.A. in Fine Art and a B.A. in Writing.

Biggest creative influences: Frank Miller, Ray Bradbury, Charles Vess, Ted Bolman, and Jeff Nicholson.

1993 projects: *¡El Toasterhead! Tales, Cranial Stomp Comix,* and *Inland.*

Past comics titles and related projects: Letterer on *Through the Habitrails* and *Ultra Klutz Dreams,* creator of *Cranial Stomp Comix,* and co-creator of *Red Rogue.*

Favorite comics not worked on: *Sandman, Hellblazer, Flaming Carrot,* and *Groo.*

Dream comic-book project: To continue what I'm doing but make a living at it.

✳ **John E. Workman Jr.** c/o *CBG* Editorial Department, 700 East State Street, Iola, Wisconsin 54990.

Born: June 20, 1950, in Beckley, West Virginia.

College or other education: Grays Harbor College, 1970, A.A. degree/Art major, Journalism minor.

Biggest creative influences: Edgar Pangborn, William Goldman, Noel Sickles, Alex Toth, Johnny Craig, Harvey Kurtzman, Carl Barks, Jim Steranko, Moebius, and Bernard Krigstein.

1993 projects: Lettering what seems like a million different books for different companies, working on a novel, and working up two miniseries that I will write, draw, letter, and color.

Past comics titles and related projects: Over the years, I've lettered for almost every comics company. I've also written and drawn for quite a few of them. My most satisfying time spent in comics was the seven years spent at *Heavy Metal,* where I had the opportunity to do everything involved in the creation of comics. I edited, wrote, penciled, inked, lettered, colored, did color separations, designed, and had the great pleasure of working with some of the very best people involved in the comics medium on an international level.

Favorite comics not worked on: I'd love to write and do the complete art job on a Batman story. I have never worked on an Archie comic, and it'd be fun to draw Betty and Veronica.

Dream comic-book project: To edit and art-direct a comics-related magazine aimed primarily at the general newsstand audience that has turned away from comics over the past 15 or 20 years.

Kate Worley

✳ **Kate Worley.** P.O. Box 7439, Powderhorn Station, Minneapolis, Minnesota 55407.

Born: March 16, 1958, in Belleville, Illinois.

College or other education: Psychology major, no degree taken.

Biggest creative influences: Will Eisner, Milton Caniff, and Frank King.

1993 projects: Short comics stories with a variety of artists, for collection, and several graphic novel projects, as well as continuing *Omaha*.

Past comics titles and related projects: *Omaha, the Cat Dancer*, issue #2-on, Kitchen Sink Press. *Roger Rabbit Adventures*, Disney. *Critters*, Fantagraphics. *Strip AIDS USA, Choices, Wimmin's Comix, Fire Sale, Gay Comix*, and *Grateful Dead Comix. Omaha Trading Cards.* Edited *Images of Omaha* benefit books.

Favorite comics not worked on: *American*

Splendor, Naughty Bits, Jab, Xenozoic Tales, and *Cud*.

Dream comic-book project: Adaptation of a particular science-fiction classic novel . . . which, I'm not telling.

✳ **Chuck Wojtkiewicz.** c/o *CBG* Editorial Department, 700 East State Street, Iola, Wisconsin 54990.

Born: January 25, 1959, in Trenton, New Jersey. (Motto: Trenton makes, the world takes.)

College or other education: B.A., Duke University.

Biggest creative influences: Jack Kirby, Mike Golden, and Juan Giménez.

1993 projects: *The Crucible*, Impact (DC); *Mecha*, Dark Horse; and *Speed Racer* video sleeves, Now Comics.

Past comics titles and related projects: *The Jaguar* and *The Crusaders*, Impact. 1992 *Iron Man Annual*, Marvel. *Buck Rogers Warhawks*, TSR. *Dinosaurs for Hire*, Malibu. *Dreadstar*, First. *Southern Knights*, Comics Interview.

Favorite comics not worked on: *Archer & Armstrong, Appleseed*, and anything by Juan Gimenez.

Dream comic-book project: *The Fantastic Four* or *The New Gods*.

✳ **Link Yaco.** 526 North Main, Ann Arbor, Michigan 48104-1027.

Born: January 30, 1965, in Sittwe, Myanar.

College or other education: Masters in Telecommunications, U of M, 1989. MIT Management Seminars 1981-85.

Comics-related education: Independent film producer with shows in Frankfurt, Germany, Institute of Contemporary Art (Boston, Massachusetts), and DeCordova Museum (Massachusetts).

Biggest creative influences: Al Williamson, Archie Goodwin, and Arnold Toynbee.

1993 projects: *Aliens*, Dark Horse. *MetaCops*, Caliber.

Past comics titles and related projects: *Quantum Leap*, Innovation. Horror books, Gladstone/Hamilton. *Erewhon*, Caliber. *MetaCops, Candide*, and *Cosmic K*, Fantagraphics.

Link Yaco

Favorite comics not worked on: *Mad, Uncle Scrooge,* and *X-Men.*

Dream comic-book project: *Caesar's War against the Gauls* with Al Williamson.

Phil Yeh (left) with Moebius

✳ **Phil Yeh.** Cartoonists across America, c/o Phil Yeh, P.O. Box 670, Lompoc, California 93438-0670.

Born: October 7, 1954, in Chicago, Illinois.

College or other education: Attended California State University Long Beach 1972-1976, studied Art, Journalism, Film in the Honors Program, no degree.

Comics-related education: Began self-publishing career in high school at the age of 16 in 1970. We continue to self-publish to this date. Published *Uncle Jam* (a free newspaper) from 1973-1990 on a regular basis, published infrequently now. Comic-book work is largely self-taught.

Biggest creative influences: (In terms of how to draw and write): Vincent Van Gogh, John Lennon, Paul Klee, Sheldon Mayer, Hergé, Stan Lynde, Dick Moores, Jack Cole, Alex Niño, Rick Griffin, Hal Robinson, Sergio Aragonés, Winsor McCay, Jack Kerouac, Ray Bradbury, Mark Twain, and Lao Tzu. Personal influences (in terms of being an artist): Alfredo Alcala, Herbert Huncke, Jean Giraud (Moebius), Wally "Famous" Amos, and Dave Thorne.

1993 projects: *The Winged Tiger* (with illustrated introductions by Wendy Pini and Moebius). *Frank the Unicorn — Island Adventures or Voyage to Veggie Isle. Patrick Rabbit* #7 (with introduction by former First Lady Barbara Bush; features back-up story: *Patrick Rabbit Meets Panda Khan* by Monica Sharp and Dave Garcia.). *Patrick and Hives.*

Past comics titles and related projects: (All books are graphic novels except where noted). *Cazco* comic book (1976), *Jam* with Roberta Gregory and friends, comic book (1977), *Even Cazco Gets the Blues* (1977) — the first graphic novel for the direct-sales market, *Ajaneh* (1978), *Godiva* (1979), *Cazco in China* (1980), *The Adventures of a Modern Day Unicorn* (1981), *The Magic Gumball Machine and Company* (1982), *Frank on the Farm* (1982), *Mr. Frank Goes to Washington, D.C.* (1984), *Frank and Syd on the Brooklyn Bridge* with Dennis Niedbala (1986), *Frank in England* (1987), *The Penguin is Mightier than the Swordfish* with Leigh Rubin (1987), the *Frank the Unicorn* comic books since 1986, the *Penguin and the Pencilguin* comic books since 1987, the *Patrick Rabbit* comic books since 1988,

Theo the Dinosaur — full-color book of oil paintings (1991).

Favorite comics not worked on: *Zot!* by Scott McCloud, *Omaha the Cat Dancer* by Reed Waller and Kate Worley, *The Flaming Carrot* by Bob Burden, *Rick O'Shay* by Stan Lynde, *Concrete* by Paul Chadwick, *Groo* by Sergio Aragonés, *Usagi Yojimbo* by Stan Sakai, the work of Moebius, and lots of independent titles usually in black and white where the artist is actually trying to tell a story.

Dream comic-book project: A series of 48-page graphic novels in full color that take my characters around the entire planet *à la Tintin* only updated for today's audience.

Catherine Yronwode

✳ **Catherine Yronwode.** Eclipse Enterprises, P.O. Box 1099, Forestville, California 95436.

Agent: I don't gotta show you no stinkin' agents!

Born: May 12, 1947, in San Francisco, California.

Biggest creative influences: Will Rogers, Herb Caen, Will Eisner, Alex Toth, and Milton Caniff.

1993 projects: The entire output of Eclipse Enterprises, *True Crime Comics*, Clive Barker graphic novels, etc.

Past comics titles and related projects: Virtually every Eclipse title from *Destroyer Duck* #1 (1981) to the present, with the exception of the parody and manga lines — and even those I oversaw as editor-in-chief.

Favorite comics not worked on: *Terry and the Pirates* . . . oh, you mean ongoing as of this date? . . . well, Carl Barks reprints, I guess.

Dream comic-book project: The story of a woman (with a 5-year-old daughter) who tracks down and kills rapists for hire, her clients being women whose rape and child-abuse charges were ignored or not prosecuted. But I don't write fiction, so maybe I'll wait until someone like Louise Simonson or Ann Nocenti does it, and then I'll read it. Oh yeah, she doesn't just shoot 'em, she works with her clients to devise appropriate confrontations, tortures, exposures in the media, or whatever will most thoroughly help the clients triumph over their "enemies." Lots of variation in emotion-tone each issue, and lots of violence, too. (And it would have a really *great* artist, like Barry Smith, John Bolton, or Alex Toth . . .)

Michael J. Zeck

✳ **Michael J. Zeck.** c/o *CBG* Editorial Department, 700 East State Street, Iola, Wisconsin 54990.

Born: September 6, 1949, in Greenville, Pennsylvania.

College or other education: Ringling School of Art, Sarasota, Florida.

1993 projects: Two-part *Batman: Legends of the Dark Knight* story. *Deathstroke, the Terminator* covers.

Past comics titles and related projects: *Master of Kung Fu, Captain America, Secret Wars* (first series), *Punisher* (five-issue limited series), *Punisher: Return to Big Nothing* graphic novel, and *Spider-Man: The Death of Kraven* storyline.

✳ **Howard Zimmerman.** 241 Central Park West, New York, New York 10024.

Born: September 30, 1946, in Brooklyn, New York.

College or other education: B.A., Hunter College, part of the City University of New York (CUNY).

Biggest creative influences: Kurtzman, Kirby, Eisner, A.E. Van Vogt, Asimov, Harrison, and Douglas Adams.

1993 projects: *Ray Bradbury Comics, New Two-Fisted Tales, Hitchhiker's Guide to the Galaxy, Bill, the Galactic Hero, Slaughterhouse Five, Amber, Neuromancer,* and *I, Robot.*

Past comics titles and related projects: *Harvey Kurtzman's Visual History of the Comics: From Aargh! to Zap! The Ray Bradbury Chronicles. My Life as a Cartoonist* by Harvey Kurtzman. *Robin 3000* #1 and #2. *The Bank Street Collections* (digest black-and-white comics from Pocket).

Favorite comics not worked on: *Cadillacs and Dinosaurs.*

Dream comic-book project: Adapting A.E. Van Vogt's *Slan* into graphic novels.

✳ **Mark S. Zimmerman.** 100 West 6th, #11, South Hutchinson, Kansas 67505.

Born: July 14, 1961, in Beloit, Kansas.

College or other education: Attended classes for two years at Hutchinson Community College (did not graduate).

Biggest creative influences: '50s E.C. horror books.

1993 projects: I am a regular writer for Allied Comics' *Tales from the Balcony.* I am currently

Mark S. Zimmerman

writing a mini-series entitled *Dark Reign*, which will (hopefully) be published in 1994.

Favorite comics not worked on: I enjoy the Valiant titles.

Dream comic-book project: To write *The Death of Spider-Man* trade paperback.

Randy Zimmerman

✳ **Randy Zimmerman.** 3116 Delaware Street, Flint, Michigan 48506-3027.

Born: October 2, 1959, in Saginaw, Michigan.

College or other education: Two years in Commercial Art at Genesee Area Skill Center.

Biggest creative influences: Will Eisner, Jack Cole, Carl Barks, and C.C. Beck.

1993 projects: *The New Breed* for Gauntlet (writing, lettering, and inking), *The Unforgiven* (writing, lettering, and inking), and *The Fool* (writing and lettering).

Past comics titles and related projects: *The Aniverse* for Arrow, WeeBee, Caliber, and Massive. *The Realm* for Arrow, WeeBee, and Caliber. *Shuriken: Cold Steel* (inks) for Eternity. Plus short stories for *Just Imagine Comics and Stories, Journey, Fantastic Fanzine, Caliber Presents, Quest for Dreams Lost,* and the *Caliber Christmas Special.*

Favorite comics not worked on: *Avengers, Teen Titans, Tick, Elfquest, Cerebus, 1963, Yummy Fur* (lots more) . . .

Dream comic-book project: Any Marvel or DC book for a year with a liberal editor or to adapt to comics a selection of Harry Chapin songs using "name" talent and donating all profits to hunger relief.

✶ **Ray Zone.** 3-D Zone, 1872 Hillhurst Avenue, Los Angeles, California 90027.

Born: May 16, 1947, in Cleveland, Ohio.

Comics-related education: Fandom.

Biggest creative influences: Joe Kubert, L.B. Cole, Steve Ditko, Arch Oboler, and Fredric Wertham.

1993 projects: *Zori J's 3-D Bubble Bath, 3-D Space Zombies, Mr. Monster's Triple-Threat 3-D, 3-D Heavy Metal Monsters, Forbidden 3-D, Kite Safety* giveaway comic for Southern California Edison Company.

Past comics titles and related projects: *Batman 3-D* (graphic novel), *Disney Comics in 3-D, Roger Rabbit in 3-D, Rocketeer 3-D, Simpsons 1993 3-D Annual, Disney Adventures 3-D,* (writer) *Ray*

Ray Zone

Bradbury Chronicles #1 and 3, *Zombie 3-D, Dracula 3-D, Brain-Bat 3-D, Dr. Frankenstein's House of 3-D, 3-D True Crime, Wolvertunes* (Basil Wolverton record), *Blab!* #5: *4-Color Frenzy* (article), *3-D Substance, Rat Fink 3-D, Flash Gordon 3-D, Krazy Kat 3-D, Sheena 3-D, Three-Dimensional Alien Worlds,* and *normalman 3-D annual.*

Favorite comics not worked on: *Shade, the Changing Man, Hate, Eightball, Trailer Trash,* and any comic with a foil-embossed or hologram cover.

Dream comic-book project: *Little Nemo 3-D* in large format or *M.C. Escher in 3-D.*

Born in January

Jan. 1, 1950: Jack Enyart
Jan. 1, 1951: Kay Reynolds
Jan. 1, 1971: Walter Antonio McDaniel
Jan. 2: Don Heck
Jan. 2, 1958: John Heebink
Jan. 2, 1958: Ernie Stiner
Jan. 2, 1965: Kevin Bricklin
Jan. 2, 1968: Timothy T. Markin
Jan. 3: Cheryl L. Ferraro
Jan. 3, 1956: Tom Artis
Jan. 4, 1923: Chic Stone
Jan. 4, 1954: Denis McFarling
Jan. 4, 1955: Dennis Yee
Jan. 4, 1967: Bob Almond
Jan. 5, 1959: Sandy Hausler
Jan. 6, 1951: Kay Reynolds
Jan. 6, 1953: Bruce Douglas Patterson
Jan. 7, 1938: Werner Wejp-Olsen
Jan. 7, 1945: Jay Lynch
Jan. 7, 1953: Bob Wiacek
Jan. 7, 1953: Kevin J. Dooley
Jan. 7, 1959: Karl Kesel
Jan. 7, 1964: Aaron A. Lopresti
Jan. 8, 1941: Boris Vallejo
Jan. 8: John Wellington
Jan. 8, 1955: Ken Steacy
Jan. 8, 1966: Joe Pruett
Jan. 8, 1966: James Pruett
Jan. 9: M.J. Cullumber
Jan. 9, 1957: Daniel Wilson

Jan. 9, 1965: Fred Burke
Jan. 11: Brad Joyce
Jan. 11, 1958: Terry Beatty
Jan. 11, 1959: Bob Harras
Jan. 11, 1960: Miyako Matsuda Graham
Jan. 11, 1963: Sam Kieth
Jan. 11, 1968: Trevor Tamlin
Jan. 12, 1962: Joe Quesada
Jan. 12, 1965: "Franchesco"
Jan. 13, 1933: Ron Goulart
Jan. 13, 1961: Jerry Acerno
Jan. 13, 1965: Anina Bennett
Jan. 14, 1921: John Tartaglione
Jan. 14: Rudy D. Nebres
Jan. 14, 1958: Steven J. Woron
Jan. 15: Stan Kay
Jan. 15, 1964: Norman Felchle
Jan. 16, 1932: Jim Berry
Jan. 16, 1953: Randy H. Crawford
Jan. 16, 1960: Steve Erwin
Jan. 16, 1963: Christopher Richard Schenck
Jan. 16, 1966: David M. DeVries
Jan. 17, 1957: Ann Nocenti
Jan. 17, 1959: Peggy May
Jan. 18, 1964: Fred Bauman
Jan. 18, 1965: Bill Fountain
Jan. 19, 1922: Milton Schiffman
Jan. 19, 1932: Jack Caprio
Jan. 19, 1948: Joe Staton
Jan. 19, 1955: Tom Yeates

Jan. 20: Keith Pollard
Jan. 21, 1954: Rich Rankin
Jan. 21, 1956: Mark Martin
Jan. 21, 1958: Bill Riling
Jan. 22, 1946: Steve Perrin
Jan. 22, 1950: Marshall Rogers
Jan. 22, 1955: Dennis Mallonee
Jan. 22, 1958: Howard Mackie
Jan. 22, 1959: Mark Miraglia
Jan. 22, 1959: Lisa Trusiani Parker
Jan. 22, 1966: Richard D. Irving
Jan. 23, 1934: Don Wright
Jan. 23, 1949: Tom Condon
Jan. 23, 1952: Klaus Janson
Jan. 23, 1952: Cara Sherman-Tereno
Jan. 23, 1960: Franz Henkel
Jan. 24, 1930: John Romita
Jan. 25, 1926: Robert J. Clarke
Jan. 25, 1945: Bill Crouch, Jr.
Jan. 25, 1952: Gary Cohn
Jan. 25, 1952: Turtel Onli
Jan. 25, 1953: John Lustig
Jan. 25, 1959: Chuck Wojtkiewicz
Jan. 26, 1929: Jules Feiffer
Jan. 26, 1936: Sal Buscema
Jan. 26, 1951: Gary L. Colabuono
Jan. 26, 1952: Dwight R. Decker
Jan. 26, 1960: Daniel A. Reed
Jan. 26, 1965: Jacob Pander
Jan. 27, 1948: Dan DeCarlo Jr.
Jan. 27, 1948: James DeCarlo
Jan. 27, 1952: Steve Leialoha
Jan. 27, 1954: Peter Laird
Jan. 27, 1956: Tom Vincent
Jan. 27, 1957: Frank Miller
Jan. 27, 1959: Stefan Petrucha
Jan. 28, 1947: Daerick Gröss Sr.
Jan. 28, 1951: Todd Klein
Jan. 28, 1959: Andrea Beam
Jan. 29, 1958: Jeph Loeb
Jan. 29, 1960: David W. Olbrich
Jan. 30, 1952: Dann Maxx Thomas
Jan. 30, 1953: Fred Hembeck
Jan. 30, 1957: Guy Gilchrist
Jan. 30, 1961: Denys Cowan
Jan. 30, 1965: Link Yaco
Jan. 30, 1968: Todd Michael Wright
Jan. 31: Paty Cockrum
Jan. 31, 1949: Wendy Fiore

Born in February

Feb. 1, 1954: Nate Butler
Feb. 1, 1954: Bill Mumy
Feb. 1, 1954: Bill Spangler
Feb. 1, 1955: Diana Schutz
Feb. 1, 1957: Gilbert Hernandez
Feb. 1, 1960: Ron Frenz
Feb. 1: Suzanne Gaffney
Feb. 2, 1912: Creig Flessel
Feb. 2, 1940: Larry Wright
Feb. 2, 1955: Bob Schreck
Feb. 3: Byron Erickson
Feb. 3, 1949: Richard Marschall
Feb. 3, 1951: Tim A. Conrad
Feb. 3, 1953: Randy Lofficier
Feb. 4, 1951: Dez Skinn
Feb. 4, 1960: Scott Saavedra
Feb. 4, 1962: Tom Sniegoski
Feb. 4, 1966: Francis J. Mao
Feb. 5, 1920: George Evans
Feb. 5, 1925: Jess M. Jodloman
Feb. 5, 1941: Marty Pahis
Feb. 5, 1955: Val Semeiks
Feb. 5, 1963: Mark Bloodworth
Feb. 5, 1967: Kelly McQuain
Feb. 5, 1972: D. Alexander Gregory
Feb. 6, 1949: Richard Buckler
Feb. 7, 1953: Richard Bruning
Feb. 7, 1955: Miguel Ferrer
Feb. 7, 1956: Bob Camp
Feb. 7, 1966: Paul Castiglia
Feb. 8: Terry Stewart
Feb. 9, 1928: Frank Frazetta
Feb. 9, 1946: Danny Bulanadi
Feb. 9, 1954: Jo Duffy
Feb. 9, 1956: Timothy Truman
Feb. 9, 1962: Sarah E. Byam
Feb. 9, 1964: T.C. Ford
Feb. 9, 1975: Whitney Barber
Feb. 11: Rich DuFour
Feb. 11, 1938: Maily Holmes Wilkinson
Feb. 11, 1946: Jim Bradrick
Feb. 11, 1962: Shon Howell
Feb. 12: Joe Albelo
Feb. 12, 1957: Ken Meyer Jr.
Feb. 12, 1966: Lou Bank
Feb. 13: Barb Kaalberg
Feb. 13, 1962: John A. Peck
Feb. 13, 1962: Stan Shaw
Feb. 14: Suzanne Dechnik
Feb. 14, 1912: Oliver Harrington

Feb. 14, 1959: Gordon Purcell
Feb. 15: Albert DeGuzman
Feb. 15: Joan Weis
Feb. 15, 1933: Bud Gordinier
Feb. 15, 1948: Art Spiegelman
Feb. 15, 1954: Matt Groening
Feb. 15, 1959: Les Dorscheid
Feb. 15, 1963: Marc Hansen
Feb. 16: J.A. Fludd
Feb. 16: Ron Wilson
Feb. 16, 1955: Len Strazewski
Feb. 16, 1958: John Totleben
Feb. 16, 1967: Timothy Bradstreet
Feb. 17: David Fox
Feb. 17, 1920: Curt Swan
Feb. 17, 1944: Bernd Metz
Feb. 17, 1969: Nelson
Feb. 18, 1930: Gahan Wilson
Feb. 18, 1931: Johnny Hart
Feb. 18, 1950: Terry Echterling
Feb. 18, 1959: Aaron McClellan
Feb 18, 1960: Jay Allen Sanford
Feb. 18, 1963: Mark Bodé
Feb. 19, 1914: Henry Boltinoff
Feb. 19, 1949: William Messner-Loebs
Feb. 19, 1953: Bob Palin
Feb. 19, 1957: Gerry Shamray
Feb. 19, 1960: Jim Lawson
Feb. 19, 1965: Mark Winfrey
Feb. 20, 1952: Anthony Tollin
Feb. 20, 1960: Dave Roberts
Feb. 21: Barry Kaplan

Feb. 21, 1949: Frank Brunner
Feb. 21, 1967: Brian Douglas Ahern
Feb. 21, 1968: Joseph M. Monks
Feb. 22, 1956: Doug Allen
Feb. 23: Ken Selig
Feb. 23, 1948: Doug Moench
Feb. 23, 1955: Jim Main
Feb. 23, 1957: Eric Lurio
Feb. 23, 1958: Janet Jackson
Feb. 23, 1965: Martin Thomas
Feb. 24, 1952: Bryan Talbot
Feb. 24, 1954: Jim Borgman
Feb. 24, 1954: Greg LaRocque
Feb. 24: Mindy Fisch
Feb. 24, 1958: Keith S. Kez Wilson
Feb. 25, 1929: Arnold Roth
Feb. 25, 1946: Rick Geary
Feb. 25, 1960: Phil Lasorda
Feb. 26: Ron Aiken
Feb. 26, 1928: Ric Estrada
Feb. 26, 1953: David Boswell
Feb. 26, 1958: Karen Berger
Feb. 26, 1958: Jeffrey Butler
Feb. 27, 1953: Jeff Smith
Feb. 27, 1960: Norm Breyfogle
Feb. 27, 1960: Jeff Smith
Feb. 27, 1962: Andy Kubert
Feb. 27, 1969: Eiwin Mark
Feb. 27: Lisa Patrick
Feb. 28: Joe Brozowski (J.J. Birch)
Feb. 29: Nelson Yomtov
Feb. 29, 1956: Wendi Lee

Born in March

March 1955: Chuck Rozanski
March 1: Tom Orzechoswki
March 1, 1922: William M. Gaines
March 1, 1952: Joyce Brabner
March 1, 1956: Ralph Ellis Miley
March 1, 1957: George Kochell
March 2, 1904: Theodor Seuss Geisel
March 2, 1952: Mark Evanier
March 2, 1956: Kevin Farrell
March 3, 1948: Max Allan Collins
March 3, 1953: Dan Mishkin
March 4, 1956: Randy Stradley
March 4, 1963: Bill Fitts
March 4, 1969: Glenn Hauman
March 5: Nathan Massengill
March 6: Allen Milgrom
March 6, 1917: Will Eisner
March 6, 1954: Carl Knappe
March 6, 1967: Kieron Dwyer
March 6, 1971: Robert Lewis
March 7: Alan Weiss
March 7, 1934: Gray Morrow
March 7, 1958: Peter Gross
March 7, 1969: Cully Hamner
March 8, 1955: Joellyn Dorkin

March 9, 1952: Rick Burchett
March 9, 1962: Mike Kazaleh
March 9, 1963: Mike Wolfer
March 9, 1966: Richie Prosch
March 11: Steve Novak
March 12: Carol Jazwynski
March 12, 1928: Sy Barry
March 12, 1953: R.A. Jones
March 12, 1962: Graham Nolan
March 13, 1921: Al Jaffee
March 14: Helen Hamilton
March 14: Stephen R. Bissette
March 14, 1920: Hank Ketcham
March 14, 1947: Tom Batiuk
March 14, 1952: Brian Walker
March 14, 1957: Mike DeCarlo
March 14, 1959: Felipe Echevarria
March 14, 1966: Steve Brooks
March 15: Bob Budiansky
March 15: Dave Marchman
March 15, 1937: Dan Adkins
March 15, 1943: John R. Cochran
March 15, 1962: Steve Kimball
March 15, 1972: Robert S. Elinskas
March 16, 1957: Steve Lafler

March 16, 1958: Kate Worley
March 16, 1961: Todd McFarlane
March 17: Flo Steinberg
March 17: Veronica Carlin
March 17, 1960: Rich Powers
March 18, 1935: Frank McLaughlin
March 18, 1955: Kent Marshall Burles
March 18, 1955: Bill Reinhold
March 18, 1968: Shea Anton Pensa
March 19: Michael Jantze
March 19, 1953: Laurie S. Sutton
March 19, 1952: Willie Schubert
March 20: Diana Albers
March 20, 1960: Steven Philip Jones
March 20, 1960: Vince Argondezzi
March 20, 1968: David Gross
March 21, 1931: Al Williamson
March 21, 1947: Don Markstein
March 21, 1956: Pasguale "Pat" Gabriele
March 21, 1962: Mark Waid
March 22: Diane Valentino
March 22, 1914: John Stanley
March 22, 1919: Bernard Krigstein
March 22, 1967: Lisa Moore
March 23, 1946: Jim Friel
March 23, 1968: Chuck Bordell
March 25: Neil Grahame
March 25, 1964: Angel Medina
March 26, 1948: José Luis Garcia-Lopez
March 26, 1951: Brian Bolland
March 26, 1956: Mark Verheiden
March 26, 1959: Robert Kraus
March 26, 1961: Mitch O'Connell
March 26, 1973: Vinson Watson
March 27: Steve Calrow
March 27, 1901: Carl Barks
March 27, 1927: Hy Eisman
March 27, 1949: Mike Friedrich
March 27, 1955: Mike Chen
March 28, 1936: Wayne Truman
March 28, 1952: Adam Philips
March 28, 1953: Peter Hsu
March 29, 1924: Jack Elrod
March 29, 1929: Mort Drucker
March 29, 1950: Val Mayerik
March 29, 1957: Elizabeth Hand
March 29, 1959: Marc Silvestri
March 29, 1960: G. Raymond Eddy
March 31, 1965: Steven T. Seagle

Born in April

April 1948: Freddy Milton
April 1, 1917: Sheldon Mayer
April 1, 1951: Bob Lappan
April 1, 1963: Mark Shainblum
April 1, 1963: James Robinson
April 1, 1964: Bill Oakley
April 2, 1953: James Vance
April 2, 1955: Mike Barreiro
April 3, 1952: Butch Burcham (F. Newton Burcham)
April 3, 1957: Mark Nevelow
April 4, 1927: Joe Orlando
April 4, 1949: John Wooley
April 4, 1951: Bob Rozakis
April 4, 1966: Dave Johnson
April 5, 1926: Gil Kane
April 5, 1957: Roger A. Brown
April 5, 1960: Ray Murtaugh
April 5, 1963: Arthur Adams
April 6, 1956: Mark Askwith
April 7, 1952: Jacques Boivin
April 7, 1957: Larry Nadolsky
April 8: Michele Wolfman
April 8, 1959: Martin Powell
April 9, 1967: John Drury
April 10, 1957: James D. Hudnall
April 10, 1958: Richard K. Taylor
April 10, 1959: Scott Hampton
April 10, 1962: Bill Marks
April 10, 1963: Robert Durham
April 10, 1964: Michael Anthony Delepine
April 11: Harry Eisenstein
April 11, 1906: Dale Messick
April 11, 1960: Mindy Eisman
April 12, 1943: Bruce H. Bolinger
April 12, 1956: Gary Martin
April 12, 1960: Toren Smith
April 12, 1972: Troy Nixey
April 13, 1950: Dennis Janke
April 13, 1955: Topper Helmers
April 13, 1959: Bill Staton
April 14, 1920: Sheldon "Shelly" Moldoff
April 14, 1949: Dave Gibbons
April 14, 1954: Chuck Dixon
April 14, 1959: Gerhard
April 15: Geoff Blum
April 15, 1937: Tom Sutton
April 15, 1961: Mike Kanterovich
April 15, 1970: Daniel Presedo
April 16, 1951: Leonard Rifas
April 16, 1955: Kim DeMulder

April 16, 1959: Paul Rivoche
April 16, 1964: Steve Haynie
April 17: Earl Norem
April 17, 1964: Ben Dunn
April 18, 1952: Roger Salick
April 18, 1960: Dan Tyree
April 19, 1925: Jim Ivey
April 19, 1949: Sandra I.H. Wehner
April 19, 1953: Martha Thomases
April 19, 1954: Steve Schanes
April 19, 1957: Mark McKenna
April 20, 1949: John Ostrander
April 20, 1956: Steve Keeter
April 20, 1960: Dale W. Berry
April 20, 1965: Evan Dorkin
April 20, 1965: Mark A. Lester
April 22, 1947: Steve Englehart
April 22, 1956: Larry Mahlstedt
April 22, 1965: Timothy Dzon
April 23: L. Lois Buhalis
April 23, 1953: Cynthy J. Wood
April 24, 1930: Howie Schneider
April 24, 1955: Al Vey

April 24, 1957: John MacLeod
April 24, 1960: Ralph Griffith
April 24, 1965: Randy Carpenter
April 25, 1925: Jerry Grandinetti
April 25, 1926: Johnny Craig
April 25, 1952: Peter Sanderson Jr.
April 25, 1960: Brian Thomas
April 25, 1965: Thomas A. Tenney
April 26, 1916: George Tuska
April 26, 1954: Kerry Gammill
April 26, 1955: Brad Foster
April 27, 1947: Barry Shapiro
April 27, 1952: Larry Nibert
April 27, 1953: Jan Mullaney
April 27, 1963: Faye Perozich
April 28, 1924: Dick Ayers
April 28, 1953: Will Murray
April 28, 1969: Greg Hyland
April 29, 1958: Michael Davis
April 30, 1926: William Overgard
April 30, 1927: Sal Trapani
April 30, 1954: Laura Ward
April 30, 1965: Nat Gertler

Born in May

May 1, 1940: Alex Nino
May 1, 1956: Phil Foglio
May 1, 1956: Tim Sale
May 1, 1971: Mike Anderson
May 2: Glenn Herdling
May 2, 1922: Doug Wildey
May 2, 1944: Howard Cruse
May 2, 1955: Jerry Scott
May 2, 1959: Debbie David
May 2, 1962: Ryan Brown
May 3, 1919: John Cullen Murphy
May 3, 1927: Mell Lazarus
May 3, 1939: Denny O'Neil
May 3, 1958: Bill Sienkiewicz
May 3, 1963: Chris Ulm
May 3, 1964: Harrison Fong
May 3, 1967: Adam Hughes
May 4, 1928: Nestor Redondo
May 4, 1937: Wayne R. Reid
May 4, 1940: John Ridgway
May 4, 1953: Doug Cushman
May 4, 1963: Damon Willis
May 4, 1966: Tom Richmond
May 5, 1932: Stan Goldberg
May 5, 1938: Moebius (Jean Giraud)
May 6, 1948: David Michelinie
May 6, 1951: Rob Carosella
May 6, 1952: Dennis Jensen
May 7, 1942: Tony Auth
May 7, 1951: Michael T. Gilbert
May 7, 1952: Vince Musacchia
May 8, 1970: Erich Mees
May 9, 1931: Richard H. Hodgins Jr.
May 9, 1947: Barbara Slate
May 9, 1958: David Campiti
May 9, 1963: Ty Templeton
May 10, 1901: Vincent T. Hamlin
May 10, 1905: Alex Schomburg
May 10, 1951: Murray R. Ward

May 11, 1910: Ed Furness
May 11, 1953: Mike Curtis
May 11, 1955: Matt Feazell
May 11, 1957: Nick Burns
May 11, 1962: Sandy Carruthers
May 12, 1915: Tony Strobl
May 12, 1947: Catherine Yronwode
May 12, 1950: Tom Armstrong
May 12, 1954: Neil D. Vokes
May 12, 1957: Scott Deschaine
May 13, 1946: Marv Wolfman
May 13, 1969: Andrew Pepoy
May 14, 1924: Brad Anderson
May 14, 1952: Eric Dinehart
May 14, 1954: Bob Wayne
May 15, 1938: John G. Fantucchio
May 15, 1949: Victor Ramon Mojica
May 15, 1957: Gary Leach
May 15, 1958: Paul Curtis
May 15, 1961: Jeff Dee
May 16, 1947: Ray Zone
May 16, 1952: Christopher K. Browne
May 16, 1957: Henry Vogel
May 16, 1960: Chester Brown
May 17: Steve Geiger
May 17: Gary Leach
May 17, 1956: Dave Sim
May 17, 1958: Chris Ecker
May 17, 1962: (Dr.) Malcolm Bourne
May 17, 1968: Pete Fitzgerald
May 18: Alan Kupperberg
May 18, 1939: Don Martin
May 18, 1953: Arthur Suydam
May 18, 1960: James W. Fry
May 18, 1963: James L. Sanders III
May 19, 1954: Neil A. Robertson
May 19, 1955: Frank Albanese
May 19, 1963: Reggie Byers

May 19, 1967: Anthony Monzo III
May 19, 1968: Robert Bostick
May 20, 1942: Gail Beckett
May 20, 1963: Alan D. Oldman
May 20, 1965: Al Bigley
May 21, 1915: Don Trachte
May 21, 1920: Lee Elias
May 21: Nansi Hoolahan
May 21, 1956: Gary Reed
May 22, 1945: Carlos Garzón
May 22, 1958: Jim Rohn
May 23, 1919: Win Mortimer
May 23, 1951: John Bolton
May 24: Evan Skolnick
May 24, 1925: Carmine Infantino
May 24, 1967: Everette Hartsoe
May 25, 1934: Clay Geerdes
May 25, 1949: Barry Windsor-Smith
May 25, 1953: Stan Sakai
May 25, 1956: Sal Velluto
May 25, 1957: Marc Hempel
May 25, 1957: Terry Nantier
May 25, 1963: Bud Rogers
May 25, 1970: Kyle J. Bertelsen
May 26, 1934: E. Silas Smith
May 26, 1939: Herb Trimpe
May 26, 1950: Marcus David
May 26, 1961: Verzell Keith James
May 26, 1961: Rachelle A. Menashe
May 27: Carrie Spiegle
May 27: Vince Westerband
May 27, 1934: Harlan Ellison
May 27, 1951: George Freeman
May 27, 1953: Louis Scarborough Jr.
May 27: 1954: Mark Wheatley
May 27, 1955: Charles Santino
May 28, 1947: Lynn Johnston
May 28, 1963: Charles Marshall
May 28, 1965: Chad Hunt
May 28, 1971: Geoffrey White
May 29: Jim Salicrup
May 29, 1951: Larry Marder
May 30, 1916: Mort Meskin
May 30, 1952: Mike W. Barr
May 30, 1957: Peter Quinones
May 30, 1962: Kevin Eastman
May 31, 1944: Andy Yanchus
May 31, 1952: David Anthony Kraft
May 31, 1960: Glenn Boyd
May 31, 1967: Dean E. Haspiel

Born in June

June 1, 1967: Alonzo L. Washington
June 2: Julia Schick
June 2, 1948: Barry Grossman
June 2, 1951: Michael E. Uslan
June 2, 1953: Dwight Jon Zimmerman
June 2, 1958: Scott Rosema
June 2, 1963: Joe Gentile
June 3: Bob le Rose
June 3, 1913: Tom Gill
June 3, 1965: Gavin Wilson
June 3, 1972: Ken Mennell Jr.
June 4, 1951: Wendy Pini
June 4, 1957: Michal Jacot
June 4, 1958: Josef Rubinstein
June 6, 1926: Tom K. Ryan
June 6, 1958: Greg Adams
June 6, 1958: Arlen Schumer
(Dynamic Duo Inc.)
June 7, 1915: Graham Ingels
June 7, 1941: Barb Rausch
June 7, 1949: Larry Hama
June 7, 1952: Rick Hoberg
June 7, 1955: Mark Schultz
June 8: Michael Higgins
June 8, 1910: C.C. Beck
June 8, 1958: David Seidman
June 8, 1971: Jeff Meyer
June 9: Pamela Rutt
June 9: Helen Ramirez
June 9, 1928: Bob Bolling
June 9, 1953: Chris Kalnick
June 9, 1954: George Pérez
June 9, 1965: Tim Eldred
June 10, 1951: Charles Vess
June 10, 1959: Howard Simpson
June 10, 1960: Scott McCloud
June 10, 1963: Bill Anderson
June 10, 1970: Matt Holey
June 11, 1949: Rich Margopoulos
June 11, 1959: Susan van Camp
June 11, 1967: Kevin Paul Shaw
Broden
June 11, 1967: Terry Collins
June 12, 1920: Dave Berg
June 12, 1946: George Olshevsky
June 12, 1948: Len Wein
June 13, 1929: Jon D'Agostino
June 13, 1956: Frank Cirocco
June 14: Sam Grainger (deceased)
June 14, 1955: Paul Kupperberg

June 14, 1957: Bill Webb
June 14, 1958: Mark Heike
June 14, 1962: Den Beauvais
June 14, 1963: Mike Bannon
June 14, 1965: Zolastraya
June 15, 1925: Ross Andru
June 15, 1941: Neal Adams
June 15, 1945: Don McGregor
June 15, 1952: Rick Stasi
June 15, 1955: Brent Anderson
June 16, 1930: Frank Thorne
June 16, 1963: Gary Thomas
Washington
June 16, 1964: Myke Maldonado
June 16, 1967: Arnold Pander
June 17, 1948: Bob "Chance"
Browne
June 17, 1950: Dana J. Summers
June 17, 1957: Hilary Barta
June 17, 1961: Jim Somerville
June 17, 1962: Richard Maurizio
June 18, 1948: Linda Lessmann
June 18: Brian C. Boerner
June 18, 1953: Mark Gruenwald
June 18, 1954: Dean Mullaney
June 18: Brian C. Boerner
June 19, 1915: Julius Schwartz
June 20, 1950: John E. Workman
Jr.
June 20, 1965: Stephan K. Lau
June 21: Leonard (John) Clark
June 21, 1903: Al Hirschfeld
June 21, 1957: Gary Carlson
June 21, 1961: Barry D. Petersen
June 21, 1969: Laughland Pelle
June 22, 1953: Alan Gordon
June 22, 1956: Susan Barrows
June 22, 1956: Kevin Fagan
June 22, 1956: Paul Simione
June 22, 1959: Armando Gil

June 22, 1961: Bill Jaaska
June 23, 1924: Frank Bolle
June 24: Doreen Frederick
June 24, 1948: Alan N. Zelenetz
June 24, 1954: Russ Maheras
June 24, 1963: Denis Rodier
June 24, 1965: Kevin VanHook
June 25, 1917: William Woolfolk
June 25, 1928: Alex Toth
June 25, 1953: Jerry Bingham
June 26, 1921: Warren Kremer
June 26, 1933: Jerry Bails
June 26, 1934: Bob Weber
June 26, 1950: Tom DeFalco
June 26, 1954: Terry Tidwell
June 26, 1960: Gerry Giovinco
June 27, 1924: Paul Conrad
June 27, 1959: Willie Peppers
June 27, 1959: Dan Jurgens
June 27, 1961: Jackson "Butch"
Guice
June 27, 1961: Bernie Mireault
June 27, 1964: Barry Kraus
June 27, 1966: Andrew T. Walls
June 28, 1944: Philippe Druillet
June 28: Mike Royer
June 28, 1951: Tom Floyd
June 28, 1953: Adrienne Roy
June 29, 1950: Bobby London
June 29, 1950: Mike Richardson
June 29, 1951: Keno Don Rosa
June 29, 1954: Bo Hampton
June 30: Tim Allen
June 30, 1955: Joe Vigil
June 30, 1958: Shawn McManus
June 30, 1958: Phil Lord
June 30, 1961: Jim Owsley
June 30, 1966: Steve Firchow
June 30, 1970: Tonne Forquer
June 30, 1972: Dave Galvan

Born in July

July 1, 1935: Billy Graham
July 1, 1935: Draper Hill
July 1, 1949: Mike Baron
July 1, 1958: Ray Lago
July 1, 1961: Julianna Ferriter
July 1, 1964: Tom Poston
July 2, 1930: Al Wiesner
July 2, 1954: Dana Lewis
July 3: Russ Cochran
July 3, 1925: Jerry DeFuccio
July 3, 1949: Pat Mills
July 3, 1954: Arne Starr
July 3, 1955: Nanette Injeski
July 3, 1962: Tom Heintjes
July 4, 1952: Rick J. Bryant
July 4, 1963: Dan Nakrosis
July 5, 1921: Floyd "Bill" Yates
July 5, 1933: Shel Dorf
July 6: Eric Fein
July 6, 1947: Arn Saba
July 6, 1949: Tony Franco
July 6, 1950: John Lindley Byrne
July 6, 1951: Christy Marx
July 6, 1953: Joe Zabel
July 6, 1955: Chuck Fiala
July 6, 1956: Stan Timmons
July 6, 1959: Louis Paradis
July 7, 1947: Lon Roberts
July 7, 1949: Rich Markow
July 7, 1950: E. Larry Dobias
July 8, 1918: Irwin Hasen
July 8, 1946: Mort Castle
July 8, 1955: Mickey Allen Clausen
July 8, 1959: Stan Woch
July 8, 1963: Whilce Portacio
July 8, 1971: Brian LeBlanc
July 9: Virginia Romita
July 9: Craig Anderson
July 9: Terry Kavanagh

July 9, 1921: Tony DiPreta
July 9, 1926: Murphy Anderson
July 9, 1956: Joe Delbeato
July 9, 1957: Kurt Mausert
July 10: Tom Mason
July 10, 1914: Joe Shuster
July 10, 1949: Bob Larkin
July 10, 1957: Gerard Jones
July 10, 1964: Sandra Chang
July 11, 1923: Dan Barry
July 11: Ron Zalme
July 12, 1950: Richard G. Taylor
July 12, 1959: John Holland
July 12, 1959: Richard C. White
July 12, 1965: George Booker
July 12, 1970: Phil Jimenez
July 13: Ernie Colon
July 13, 1940: Mike Ploog
July 13, 1942: Tom Palmer
July 13, 1949: Wayne Vansant
July 13, 1958: Scott Rockwell
July 14, 1910: William Hanna
July 14, 1927: Mike Esposito
July 14, 1939: Ron Foss
July 14, 1948: Jerry Sinkovec
July 14, 1961: John K. Snyder III
July 14, 1961: Mark Zimmerman
July 15, 1925: Henry Martin
July 15, 1927: Jack Abel
July 15, 1969: Pat Duke
July 16, 1943: Steve Stiles
July 16, 1973: Chad Woody
July 17, 1952: Mike Tiefenbacher
July 17, 1959: Brad Johnson
July 17, 1962: Steven S. Crompton
July 18, 1950: Michael Vance
 (Michael Lail)
July 18, 1959: S.A. Bennett
July 19: Mike Maier

July 19: Pete McDonnell
July 19, 1950: Richard Pini
July 19, 1952: Bob Burden
July 19, 1959: Luke McDonnell
July 19, 1961: Terry LaBan
July 20: Laurie Rozakis
July 20, 1932: Dick Giordano
July 20, 1952: Mark Hamlin
July 20, 1965: Steven Tice
July 20, 1969: Drew Hayes
July 21, 1962: Bill Knapp
July 22: Mike Rockwitz
July 22, 1963: Paula Sohn
July 23: Mike Vosburg
July 23, 1962: Kelley Jones
July 23, 1956: Frank Fosco
July 24, 1935: Pat Oliphant
July 24: Helen Vesik
July 24: Trevor Von Eeden
July 24: Ricardo Villamonte
July 24, 1958: Bob Greenberger
July 24, 1963: Colleen Doran
July 25: Gen Mitchell
July 25, 1949: Alex Wald
July 25, 1953: Chuck Melville
July 25, 1961: John Robert Statema
July 25, 1963: George Roberts, Jr.
July 25, 1972: Galen Showman
July 26, 1942: Jeremy Kay
July 26, 1953: Bob Pinaha
July 26, 1954: Lawrence Watt-
 Evans
July 26, 1962: Harry Candelario
July 27, 1938: Bill Pearson
July 27, 1940: Ernie Chan
July 27, 1954: H.P. McElwee
July 27, 1972: Mark Pate
July 28, 1915: Dick Sprang
July 28, 1945: Jim Davis
July 28, 1951: Mike Smith
July 28, 1959: Ian Akin
July 28, 1960: Jon J. Muth
July 29, 1949: Kurt Goldzung
July 29, 1953: Randy Maxson
July 29, 1954: D. Larry Hancock
July 29, 1954: Lovern Kindzierski
July 29, 1955: Dave Stevens
July 29, 1958: John Nordland II
July 30, 1955: Tom Ziuko
July 30, 1966: Chris Sprouse
July 31, 1927: George Wildman
July 31, 1957: Gary Barker
July 31, 1970: N. Blake Seals
July 31, 1972: Bradley Walton

Born in August

Aug. 1, 1931: Tom Wilson
Aug. 1, 1955: Ray Fehrenbach
Aug. 2, 1944: Bruce Bristow
Aug. 2, 1955: Dave Hunt
Aug. 2, 1955: Robert E. McTyre
Aug. 3: E.R. Cruz
Aug. 3, 1924: John Belfi
Aug. 3, 1930: Rowland B. Wilson
Aug. 3, 1949: Reed Waller
Aug. 3, 1962: Julie Ann Sczesny
Aug. 4: Muffy Greenough
Aug. 4, 1942: Rick Norwood
Aug. 4, 1950: Mike Gold
Aug. 4, 1954: Steve Hauk
Aug. 4, 1954: Martin Pasko
Aug. 4, 1959: Cindy Goff
Aug. 4, 1966: Charlie Adlard
Aug. 5, 1953: Steve Mitchell
Aug. 5, 1960: Bob Orzechowski
Aug. 5, 1963: Avido Khahaifa
Aug. 6: Ed Hannigan
Aug. 6, 1958: Susan Dorne
Aug. 6, 1966: Terry Pallot
Aug. 7, 1959: Kathy Kotsivas
Aug. 7, 1970: Dan Vebber
Aug. 8, 1952: Janice Cohen
Aug. 8, 1965: Sheldon Inkol
Aug. 9: Rick Leonardi
Aug. 9: Bob McLeod
Aug. 9, 1929: Fred Fredericks
Aug. 9, 1954: Mark Braun
Aug. 9, 1954: Lou Manna
Aug. 9, 1955: Steve Gallacci
Aug. 9, 1957: Steve Moncuse
Aug. 10, 1955: Clint McElroy
Aug. 10, 1957: Christie "Max" Scheele
Aug. 10, 1972: Mike Leonard
Aug. 11, 1961: Letitia Glozer
Aug. 11, 1964: Pat Brosseau
Aug. 11, 1964: Jim Lee
Aug. 11, 1969: Shelley Braga
Aug. 12, 1958: Eleanor J. Barnes
Aug. 12, 1964: Rusty Haller
Aug. 13, 1917: Selby Kelly
Aug. 13, 1919: Jim Mooney
Aug. 13, 1952: Donna Barr
Aug. 13, 1954: Rob Davis
Aug. 13, 1954: Robin Ator
Aug. 13, 1960: Bret Blevins
Aug. 13, 1966: Shannon Wheeler
Aug. 14, 1943: John Costanza
Aug. 14, 1959: Ken Holewczynski
Aug. 14, 1960: Lawrence D. Hubbard

Aug. 14, 1961: Tracy Hampton
Aug. 14, 1961: Bill Nichols
Aug. 14, 1965: Nabile P. Hage
Aug. 15, 1950: Jim Korkis
Aug. 15, 1953: Paul Gulacy
Aug. 15, 1954: Lamar Waldron
Aug. 15, 1955: Dale Kanzler
Aug. 15, 1960: Terry Shoemaker
Aug. 15, 1962: Tammy Brown
Aug. 16, 1952: Dick Foreman
Aug. 16, 1970: Chancellor R. Knight
Aug. 17: Trina Robbins
Aug. 17, 1945: Rachel Pollack
Aug. 17, 1956: John S. Romita Jr.
Aug. 17, 1958: Andy Helfer
Aug. 18, 1960: Jeffrey Lang
Aug. 18, 1961: David Barbour
Aug. 18, 1965: Skip Dietz
Aug. 18, 1967: Brian Michael Bendis
Aug. 19, 1925: George Roussos
Aug. 19, 1944: Skip Williamson
Aug. 19, 1966: Stefano Gaudiano
Aug. 20, 1930: Bill Rechin
Aug. 20, 1964: Kirk Chritton
Aug. 21: Marie Severin
Aug. 21: Bobbie Chase
Aug. 21, 1955: Darrell Goza
Aug. 22, 1951: Ken L. Jones
Aug. 22, 1955: Will Shetterly
Aug. 22, 1956: Anna-Maria B. Cool
Aug. 22, 1964: D.G. Chichester
Aug. 23, 1925: Alfredo P. Alcala
Aug. 23, 1952: Terry Austin
Aug. 23, 1965: Chris Bachalo

Aug. 24, 1932: Jim Aparo
Aug. 24, 1941: Jim Scancarelli
Aug. 24, 1959: Mark Simon
Aug. 24, 1960: Jack F. Harris
Aug. 24, 1964: Jack Snider
Aug. 24, 1966: Mark Lucas
Aug. 25, 1920: Fred Schwab
Aug. 25, 1947: Michael W. Kaluta
Aug. 26, 1920: Brant Parker
Aug. 26, 1967: Charles Moore
Aug. 27: Rick Parker
Aug. 28, 1917: Jack Kirby
Aug. 27, 1922: Frank Kelly Freas
Aug. 27, 1929: Don Perlin
Aug. 27, 1946: Denis Kitchen
Aug. 27, 1957: Wendy Snow-Lang
Aug. 27, 1958: Bob Garcia
Aug. 27, 1966: Phillip Hester
Aug. 28: Dell Barras
Aug. 28, 1963: Mike Leeke
Aug. 28, 1963: Brian Sutton
Aug. 28, 1966: Keith Quinn
Aug. 29, 1970: Jason Pearson
Aug. 30, 1935: Sheldon Oppenberg
Aug. 30, 1943: Robert Crumb
Aug. 30, 1947: Jack C. Harris
Aug. 30, 1952: Ken Bruzenak
Aug. 30, 1952: Rickey Shanklin
Aug. 30, 1955: Craig Boldman
Aug. 31: Hector Collazo
Aug. 31: Clara Noto
Aug. 31, 1946: Rick Parker
Aug. 31, 1948: Cyril Jordan
Aug. 31, 1954: Michael Cohen

Born in September

Sept. 1: Gaspar Saladino
Sept. 1, 1926: Gene Colan
Sept. 1, 1954: Patricia Jeres
Sept. 1, 1975: Chris Chandler
Sept. 2, 1946: Walt Simonson
Sept. 2, 1948: Rick Obadiah
Sept. 2, 1961: Sherri Wolfgang
    (Dynamic Duo Inc.)
Sept. 3, 1923: Mort Walker
Sept. 3, 1957: Paul Chadwick
Sept. 3, 1959: Flint Henry
Sept. 3, 1961: Pat Redding
Sept. 3, 1962: Sholly Fisch
Sept. 4: Jean Simek
Sept. 4: Ken Lopez
Sept. 4: Rosemary McCormick-
    Lowy
Sept. 4, 1951: Scott Shaw!
Sept. 4, 1953: Cathy Palin
Sept. 4, 1954: Paul Smith
Sept. 5: Arvell Jones
Sept. 5: Lee Marrs
Sept. 5, 1950: Cathy Lee Guisewite
Sept. 5, 1952: Bob Chapman
Sept. 5, 1959: Stephen D. Sullivan
Sept. 6, 1937: Sergio Aragonés
Sept. 6, 1947: Roger May
Sept. 6, 1949: Mike Zeck
Sept. 6, 1967: Brian Clopper
Sept. 7, 1934: Warren Sattler
Sept. 7, 1954: Barry Lawrence Blair
Sept. 8, 1937: Archie Goodwin
Sept. 8, 1954: David Schwartz
Sept. 8, 1954: Sam Kujava
Sept. 9, 1917: Frank Robbins
Sept. 9, 1953: Leslie Zahler
Sept. 9, 1959: Dan Vado

Sept. 9, 1960: Kevin Maguire
Sept. 9, 1963: Jerry Prosser
Sept. 9, 1964: Vince Stone
Sept. 10, 1922: Roy Doty
Sept. 10, 1929: Frank Hill
Sept. 10, 1946: Jackie Estrada
Sept. 10, 1952: Gerry Conway
Sept. 10, 1959: Nancy A. Collins
Sept. 11, 1954: Rod Whigham
Sept. 11, 1964: Jon Macy
Sept. 12, 1930: Don Sherwood
Sept. 13, 1947: Mike Grell
Sept. 13, 1955: Lynn Cohen
Sept. 13, 1961: Gary Kwapisz
Sept. 14: Jim Novak
Sept. 14, 1943: Bill Black
Sept. 14, 1951: Mary Fleener
Sept. 14, 1958: S. Clarke Hawbaker
Sept. 14, 1964: Todd S. Tuttle
Sept. 15, 1951: Peter Poplaski
Sept. 15, 1952: Carol Lay
Sept. 15, 1953: Alan L. Light
Sept. 15, 1953: Kim Metzger
Sept. 15, 1955: Lawrence Schick
Sept. 15, 1968: Milton Pagan
Sept. 16: "Seth"
Sept. 16, 1953: Joel Thingvall
Sept. 16, 1956: Brenda Mings
Sept. 16, 1957: Keith Williams
Sept. 16, 1960: Mike Mignola
Sept. 16, 1960: Kurt Busiek
Sept. 17: Danny Fingeroth
Sept. 17, 1947: Jeff MacNelly
Sept. 17, 1950: Roger Stern
Sept. 17, 1958: Don Martinec
Sept. 18: Irene Vartanoff
Sept. 18, 1926: Joe Kubert

Sept. 18, 1949: William Stout
Sept. 18, 1957: Dan Davis
Sept. 19, 1948: Matthew Costello
Sept. 19, 1954: Garry Leach
Sept. 19, 1960: Brad Moore
Sept. 19, 1961: Cynthia Martin
Sept. 19, 1961: Brian Garvey
Sept. 20, 1947: Steve Gerber
Sept. 20, 1954: Doug Hazlewood
Sept. 20, 1957: Steve Ringgenberg
Sept. 20, 1962: Gary Dunaier
Sept. 22, 1922: Will Elder
Sept. 22, 1958: Peter Kuper
Sept. 22, 1962: Steve Lavigne
Sept. 22, 1965: Richard A. Martel
    Jr.
Sept. 23, 1931: Stan Lynde
Sept. 23, 1955: Robert J. Sodaro
Sept. 23, 1956: Peter David
Sept. 23, 1956: Dan Day
Sept. 23, 1963: Dan Raga
Sept. 24: Al Aiola
Sept. 24, 1949: David Rawson
Sept. 24, 1952: Bill Vallely
Sept. 24, 1962: Darren Goodhart
Sept. 24, 1962: Mark Mazz
Sept. 24, 1969: Eric Pavlat
Sept. 25: Bob Layton
Sept. 25, 1951: Howard Bender
Sept. 25, 1956: Kim Thompson
Sept. 26: Dawn Geiger
Sept. 26, 1946: Louise Simonson
Sept. 26, 1959: Gabriel Morrissette
Sept. 26, 1961: Tom Veitch
Sept. 27: Jim Sinclair
Sept. 27: Bob Sharen
Sept. 27, 1927: Jack Katz
Sept. 27, 1951: Jim Shooter
Sept. 27, 1955: Randy Emberlin
Sept. 28, 1957: Michael Eury
Sept. 28, 1958: Ken Penders
Sept. 28, 1963: Greg Weisman
Sept. 29, 1926: Russ Heath
Sept. 29, 1958: Timothy B. Vigil
Sept. 29, 1959: Mark Pennington
Sept. 29, 1959: Sylvie Rancourt
Sept. 29, 1964: Vince Stone
Sept. 30: Daryl Edelman
Sept. 30, 1946: Howard Zimmer-
    man
Sept. 30, 1951: Ken Feduniewicz
Sept. 30, 1951: Deni Loubert
Sept. 30, 1966: Dan Danko

Born in October

Oct. 1, 1937: Bill Spicer
Oct. 1, 1940: Richard Corben
Oct. 1, 1958: David Dorman
Oct. 1, 1958: Don Daley
Oct. 1, 1962: William Byrne
Oct. 1, 1964: Ande Parks
Oct. 2, 1954: Mark Borax
Oct. 2, 1959: Randy Zimmerman
Oct. 2, 1960: Barbara Randall Kesel
Oct. 2, 1964: John Talbot Marshall
Oct. 3, 1924: Harvey Kurtzman
Oct. 4, 1952: Tod Smith
Oct. 4, 1955: Chris Warner
Oct. 4, 1959: Donna Karen (D.K.)
    Upshaw
Oct. 4, 1964: Marc McLaurin
Oct. 5, 1957: Tim Burgard
Oct. 5, 1962: Jeff Nicholson
Oct. 6: Joanne Spaldo
Oct. 6, 1913: Alfred Harvey
Oct. 6, 1955: John Nyberg
Oct. 6, 1956: Kathleen A. Webb
Oct. 6, 1958: Michael Carlin
Oct. 6, 1962: Jim Nelson
Oct. 6, 1966: Darwin McPherson
Oct. 7, 1950: Howard Chaykin
Oct. 7, 1953: Marvin Perry Mann
Oct. 7, 1953: Rod Underhill
Oct. 7, 1954: Phil Yeh
Oct. 8, 1939: Harvey Pekar
Oct. 9: Adam Blaustein
Oct. 9, 1938: Russell Myers
Oct. 9, 1943: Mike Peters
Oct. 9, 1954: Michael Catron
Oct. 9, 1955: Michael Netzer
Oct. 9, 1961: Matt Wagner
Oct. 9, 1970: Andrew C. Robinson
Oct. 10: Linda Grant
Oct. 10, 1959: Paul Nagy
Oct. 10, 1967: Douglas W. Dlin
Oct. 11, 1915: Joe Simon
Oct. 11: Bruce Hamilton
Oct. 11: Kathryn Mayer
Oct. 11, 1949: Todd R. Reis
Oct. 11, 1952: Jim Woodring
Oct. 11, 1958: Patrick J. Williams
Oct. 12: Barbara Johnston
Oct. 12, 1917: Roger Armstrong
Oct. 12, 1947: Pat Brady
Oct. 12, 1965: Dan Abnett
Oct. 13: Margaret Clark
Oct. 13: Ed Magalong
Oct. 13, 1952: Robert M. Ingersoll

Oct. 14, 1952: Charlie Williams
Oct. 14, 1965: Michael R. Hawkins
Oct. 14, 1969: Brandon Peterson
Oct. 15: Vince Colletta
Oct. 15, 1944: Cam Kennedy
Oct. 16, 1926: Joe Sinnott
Oct. 16, 1944: Bob Hall
Oct. 16, 1958: Mark Badger
Oct. 17, 1914: Jerry Siegel
Oct. 17, 1958: Bill Holbrook
Oct. 18, 1952: Larry Blake
Oct. 18, 1955: Sandy Plunkett
Oct. 18, 1959: Jim Massara
Oct. 19: Jim Starlin
Oct. 19, 1923: Jack Tippit
Oct. 19, 1940: Nadine Messner-Loebs
Oct. 19, 1961: Michael Manley
Oct. 19, 1963: Don Chin
Oct. 20: Sid Jacobson
Oct. 20, 1956: Jim Engel
Oct. 20, 1962: Len Kaminski
Oct. 20, 1963: Paul Fricke
Oct. 21: Pat Bastienne
Oct. 21: Tom Morgan
Oct. 21, 1950: John Dennis
Oct. 21, 1956: Paul Levitz
Oct. 21, 1957: Jeff Albrecht
Oct. 21, 1959: Michael Dooney
Oct. 21, 1960: Stuart Kerr
Oct. 22, 1953: Steven Grant
Oct. 22, 1962: John Tighe
Oct. 23: Russell Harvey

Oct. 23, 1963: Eric Shanower
Oct. 24: Paul Laikin
Oct. 24, 1916: Bob Kane
Oct. 24, 1925: Al Feldstein
Oct. 24, 1953: Mindy Newell
Oct. 24, 1953: Laurel Fitch
Oct. 24, 1962: Mark H. Campos
Oct. 24, 1966: Scott Alexander Frantz
Oct. 25, 1945: Peter Ledger
Oct. 25, 1941: Michelle Wrightson
Oct. 25, 1960: June Brigman
Oct. 26, 1931: Larry Lieber
Oct. 26, 1954: Steve Collins
Oct. 26, 1957: Pierangelo Boog
Oct. 26, 1962: John Morelli
Oct. 26, 1949: Glynis Oliver
Oct. 27, 1948: Bernie Wrightson
Oct. 28, 1925: Leonard Starr
Oct. 28, 1939: Rolf E. Stark
Oct. 28, 1952: Jim Valentino
Oct. 28, 1959: Stephen Donnelly
Oct. 28, 1959: Jim Gillespie
Oct. 28, 1967: Ian Shires
Oct. 28, 1967: Karl C. Story
Oct. 29, 1921: Bill Mauldin
Oct. 29, 1938: Ralph Bakshi
Oct. 29, 1944: Nicola Cuti
Oct. 29, 1953: Batton Lash
Oct. 30, 1935: Don Thompson
Oct. 30, 1951: P. Craig Russell
Oct. 30, 1968: Michael O'Connell
Oct. 31, 1957: Frank Stack

Born in November

Nov. 1: Michael Fleisher
Nov. 1, 1924: James E. Galton
Nov. 1, 1947: Ken Leach
Nov. 1, 1954: David Darrigo
Nov. 1, 1960: Tony Akins
Nov. 1, 1964: Roland Mann
Nov. 2, 1926: Howard Post
Nov. 2, 1927: Steve Ditko
Nov. 2, 1953: Tom Lyle
Nov. 2, 1954: Brian Augustyn
Nov. 2, 1959: Sharon Wright
Nov. 3: Susan Ehrenreich
Nov. 3, 1953: Holly M. Sanfelippo
Nov. 3, 1961: Tom Grindberg
Nov. 3, 1963: Mik Pascal
Nov. 3, 1966: Carlos Kastro
Nov. 3, 1970: Aaron Sowd
Nov. 4, 1959: Anthony Burcher
Nov. 5, 1938: Jim Steranko
Nov. 5, 1946: Ron Fortier
Nov. 5, 1954: Paul S. Power
Nov. 5, 1956: Robert Loren Fleming
Nov. 6, 1954: Mike Reynolds
Nov. 7, 1965: Tom Taggart

Nov. 7, 1966: Vincent Locke
Nov. 8: Roger McKenzie
Nov. 8, 1964: Marilee Woch
Nov. 9: Bill Mantlo
Nov. 9, 1945: Phil Normand
Nov. 9, 1950: Ken Landgraf
Nov. 9, 1961: Mort Todd
Nov. 9, 1961: Jack Herman
Nov. 9, 1967: Patrick Hayes
Nov. 10, 1954: Bruce Chrislip
Nov. 10, 1960: Neil Gaiman
Nov. 11: Roger Slifer
Nov. 11, 1943: Dave Cockrum
Nov. 11, 1950: Jim Stenstrum
Nov. 11, 1960: Susan F. Daigle-Leach
Nov. 11, 1969: James A. Owen
Nov. 12, 1952: Carl Potts
Nov. 12, 1966: Kelley Jarvis
Nov. 13, 1947: Doug Murray
Nov. 13, 1958: Larry Doyle
Nov. 13, 1963: Randy Clark
Nov. 14, 1923: Alberto Giolitti
Nov. 14, 1958: Edd Vick
Nov. 15: Heidi D. MacDonald

Nov. 15: Stu Schwartzberg
Nov. 15, 1915: Martin Nodell
Nov. 15, 1951: Michael Gallagher
Nov. 15, 1953: Mike Gustovich
Nov. 15, 1957: George Broderick Jr.
Nov. 16: Richard Howell
Nov. 16: Joe Judt
Nov. 17: Sue Flaxman
Nov. 17, 1960: Vincent Giarrano
Nov. 17, 1969: Steve Remen
Nov. 18, 1952: Alan Moore
Nov. 19, 1954: Rick McCollum
Nov. 19, 1959: Steve Lightle
Nov. 20, 1946: Dave Schreiner
Nov. 20, 1963: Rian Hughes
Nov. 20, 1966: Guy Davis
Nov. 20, 1966: David Gatzmer
Nov. 20, 1966: Jill Thompson
Nov. 21, 1948: Larry Welz
Nov. 21, 1953: Greg Theakston
Nov. 21, 1955: Dennis LaSorda
Nov. 22, 1940: Roy Thomas
Nov. 22, 1950: David Wenzel
Nov. 22, 1953: Kim Yale
Nov. 22, 1956: Ron Randall
Nov. 22, 1962: Daniel Vozzo
Nov. 23, 1953: Carl Gafford
Nov. 23, 1959: Wayne R. Smith
Nov. 25: Chris Claremont
Nov. 25, 1911: Paul Murry
Nov. 25, 1963: Sean Deming
Nov. 25, 1963: Ken Lester
Nov. 26: Dan Green
Nov. 26, 1922: Charles M. Schulz
Nov. 26, 1949: Barbara Marker
Nov. 26, 1950: Doug Rice
Nov. 26, 1953: Pat Broderick
Nov. 26, 1957: Darrell McNeil
Nov. 27, 1962: Paul Guinan
Nov. 28: Shelley Eiber
Nov. 28: Dale Crain
Nov. 28, 1953: Mark A. Nelson
Nov. 28, 1955: Brian Apthorp
Nov. 28, 1957: Jerry Ordway
Nov. 29: James Reddington
Nov. 29, 1915: Gill Fox
Nov. 29, 1942: Maggie Thompson
Nov. 29, 1967: Andrea Albert
Nov. 30, 1951: Claude St. Aubin
Nov. 30, 1952: Keith Giffen
Nov. 30, 1961: Brian Pulido
Nov. 30, 1973: Matthew Kelleigh

Born in December

Dec. 2, 1924: Jack Davis
Dec. 2, 1950: Tim Corrigan
Dec. 2, 1966: Andy Mangels
Dec. 3, 1921: Leonard Dworkins
  (Leon Gordon)
Dec. 3, 1952: John Warner
Dec. 3, 1959: Mike Saenz
Dec. 3, 1961: Donald Simpson
Dec. 4, 1960: Geoff Isherwood
Dec. 4, 1965: Jill (Beth) Miller
Dec. 4, 1968: Ashley Holt
Dec. 5, 1924: Sam Glanzman
Dec. 5, 1965: Daniel Howard Fogel
Dec. 6, 1929: Frank Springer
Dec. 6, 1946: Marlene Stevens
Dec. 6, 1954: Ken Macklin
Dec. 6, 1961: Valarie Jones
Dec. 6, 1962: Scott Beaderstadt
Dec. 6, 1966: Leonard Kirk
Dec. 8, 1936: Michael Hobson
Dec. 8, 1960: Jonathan Peterson
Dec. 8, 1962: Erik Larsen
Dec. 8, 1962: Mike Mulvihill
Dec. 8, 1965: John Mundt
Dec. 9, 1933: Jose Delbo
Dec. 9, 1949: Gary T. Kato
Dec. 9, 1953: David C*J Bunn
Dec. 10, 1917: Bill Crooks
Dec. 10, 1920: Dan Spiegle
Dec. 10, 1954: Matt Tolbert
Dec. 10, 1959: Chas Truog
Dec. 11, 1920: Richard Rockwell
Dec. 11, 1923: Morrie Turner
Dec. 11, 1927: John Buscema
Dec. 11, 1940: Frederick Patten
Dec. 12, 1919: Dan DeCarlo
Dec. 12, 1920: Fred Kida
Dec. 12, 1949: Doug Marlette
Dec. 12, 1953: Mark Landman
Dec. 12, 1953: Paul McCusker
Dec. 12, 1963: Bill Kieffer
Dec. 13, 1961: Greg Shoemaker
Dec. 13, 1965: Kyle Baker
Dec. 14, 1952: Deborah Purcell
Dec. 14, 1959: David Quinn
Dec. 15, 1920: Kurt Schaffenberger
Dec. 15, 1952: Ed Quinby
Dec. 15, 1953: J. Marc DeMatteis
Dec. 15, 1957: Steven Bove
Dec. 15, 1965: Ted Slampyak
Dec. 16: Clem Robins
Dec. 16, 1959: Steve Mattsson

Dec. 16, 1959: Dean Clarrain
Dec. 16, 1968: Jose Collado
Dec. 16, 1971: John Nadeau
Dec. 17, 1948: Andy Mushynsky
Dec. 17, 1949: Greg Walker
Dec. 17, 1952: Ronn Sutton
Dec. 17, 1954: Michael Cherkas
Dec. 17, 1954: Beau Smith
Dec. 17, 1968: Matthew Hollingsworth
Dec. 18, 1952: Bill Neville
Dec. 18, 1956: Ted Boonthanakit
Dec. 18, 1961: Gary Fields
Dec. 19, 1951: David Scroggy
Dec. 19, 1952: Peter Gillis
Dec. 19, 1954: Eliot Brown
Dec. 19, 1958: Lurene Haines
Dec. 19, 1962: Eric Hess
Dec. 20: Dave Simons
Dec. 20, 1949: James Van Hise
Dec. 21: Chris Marrinan
Dec. 21, 1920: Bob Bindig
Dec. 21, 1921: John Severin
Dec. 21, 1959: Glen Johnson
Dec. 21, 1960: Doug Wheeler
Dec. 21, 1965: Mark Engblom
Dec. 22: Gregory Wright
Dec. 22, 1928: Ed McGeean
Dec. 22, 1951: Tony Isabella
Dec. 22, 1956: Bill Willingham
Dec. 22, 1967: Richard Klaw
Dec. 23: Rick Magyar

Dec. 23, 1954: Phil Felix
Dec. 23, 1957: Tony Caputo
Dec. 23, 1963: Edward K. Keller
Dec. 23, 1964: Jeff Whiting
Dec. 23, 1967: Noel John Tominack
Dec. 24, 1958: Tim Harkins
Dec. 24, 1966: Wade Winningham
Dec. 25, 1920: Joe Rosen
Dec. 26, 1956: Steve Saffel
Dec. 27: Jack Bradbury
Dec. 27, 1918: John Celardo
Dec. 27, 1955: Mark Bright
Dec. 27, 1960: Bruce McCorkindale
Dec. 27, 1960: Alan Jude Summa
Dec. 27, 1966: Joan Hilty
Dec. 28, 1922: Stan Lee
Dec. 28: Tauby Calrow
Dec. 28, 1955: Janice Chiang
Dec. 28: Ralph Macchio
Dec. 29, 1952: Paul Becton
Dec. 29, 1960: Jay Geldhof
Dec. 29, 1964: Barry Dutter
Dec. 29, 1968: Joe Doughrity
Dec. 29, 1970: Dave Ulanski
Dec. 30, 1960: Lewis Shiner
Dec. 31: Fabian Nicieza
Dec. 31, 1952: Bunny Hampton-Mack
Dec. 31, 1956: Lela Dowling
Dec. 31, 1956: Steve Rude
Dec. 31, 1967: Robert de Jesus